AF674181

ENCYCLOPAEDIA OF EDUCATIONAL TERMS

(In 5 Vol.)

Edited & Compiled by:

Ekta Thani, Rohit Sharma, Anoop Jain, Mohit Sharma, Kanika K., C.H. Judd, & L.B. Earhart

Vol. I

SPORTS PUBLICATION

4264/3, Ansari Road, Darya Ganj, Delhi-2
Ph.: 23290142, 27241050, 27562163 (R)

Published by:

Lokesh Thani

SPORTS PUBLICATIONS

II.O. 4264/3, Ansari Road, Darya Ganj, New Delhi-110002
B.O. WP-474, Ist Floor, Shiv Market, Ashok Vihar, Delhi-52
Phones: 23290142, 27241050,
(R) 27562163, (M) 9868028838
E-mail: sportspublication1@rediffmail.com
Website: *www.sportsbookshouse.com*

© 2004 Publishers

I.S.B.N. – 81-87818-68-9

PRINTED IN INDIA 2004

All Rights Reserved

No part of this publication may be stored in a retrieval system, transmitted, or reproduced in any way, including but not limited to photocopy, photograph, magnetic or other record, without the prior agreement and written permission of the publisher.

Laser Typeset by:

JAIN MEDIA GRAPHICS

B-4/40-A, Lawrence Road, (Keshav Puram),
New Delhi-110035 Ph.: 27183573, (M) 9811430646

Printed by:

BANDEMATRAM PRESS

Maujpur, Delhi

Price: Rs. 4,200/- (In 5 Vol.)

PART 1

PHYSICS

a

a symbol used for angstrom. (1 $A^{o} = 10^{-8 \text{ cm.}}$)

a⁰

an abbreviation for Angstrom unit.

a⁺

is the symbol used for A-Positive.

a-bomb

atomic Bomb

ab

a prefix, which when attached to names of practical electric units indicates the corestponding units in the electromagnetic system.

abampere

unit of electric current in the electromagnetic centimetre-gram-second system of units.

abampere per square centimetre

it is the unit of current density in the electromagnetic centimetre-gram-second system of units.

abbe condenser

the optical condenser used in microscopes, consisting of two or three lenses having a wide aperture. Named after Earnest Abbe.

abbe number

the term is used in optics and expresses the deviating effect of an optical glass on light comprising of different wavelengths.

abbe prism

a combination of two right-angled prisms which involves four reflections of light wave. Used in optics for the erection of images of various types of objects.

abbe refractometer

an optical instrument for the measurement of the refractive index of liquids.

abberation

it refers to a disturbance of the rays of pencil of light because of which they can no longer be brought to a sharp focus. This disturbance arises because the refractive index of glass is different for different wave lengths and so they are focused at different points. Due to this the image formed is surrounded by coloured fringes.

abbe's sine condition

a relationship which must hold

to prevent aberration of a mirror or lens from producing a coma.

abbe's theory

according to this theory, a lens must be quite large so that it enables the transmission of the entire diffraction pattern of the object, otherwise the lens will not produce the true image of the object.

abcoulomb

the unit of electric charge in the electromagnetic centimetre gram second system, equal to 10 coulombs, abbreviated aC.

abcoulomb centimetre

in the electro-magnetic centimetre gram second system of units, the unit of electric dipole moment. Abbreviated aCcm.

aberration

the term used for a defect of optical image which is attributable to the fact than no lens system is able to form an absolutely perfect image. The chief varieties of such defects have been : astigmatism, coma, chromatic aberration curvature of field, lens distortion, and spherical aberration.

aberration, chromatic

a defect in the image formed by a lens. The refractive index of glass being different for different wavelengths of light, the different colours are focused at different points. The image is thus surrounded by coloured fringes.

aberration, spherical

it is a defect of an image that is formed by a lens or a mirror. It is due to the fact that focal length of the lens is different for rays of light incident on different portions of the lens. The focal length of paraxial rays is more than the focal length of the marginal rays. Hence, one does not obtain a sharp image of an object.

abiabatic flow

the motion of an fluid which does not involve any transference of heat is called an adiabatic flow.

ablation

to remove material from surface by decomposition or vaporisation.

abmho

it is the unit of conductance in the electro-magnetic centimetre-gram-second system of units.

1 abmho = 109^{mhos} (in the M.K.S. system)

abney effect

a shift in the apparent hue of the light which occurs as coloured light is desaturated by the addition of white light.

abnormal reflections

sharply defined reflections of substantial in tensity of frequencies greater than the critical frequency of the ionized layer of the ionosphere.

abohm centimetre

the centimetre gram second unit of resistivity.

ab power pack

assembly in a single unit of a battery and b battery for a battery operated vacuum-tube circuit.

abrasion

the term used for the wearing away of the surface of an object by the cutting action of solides.

abrasive

refers to a substance which is used to smooth, wear down and polish solids. Abrasive may be natural.

abrasive hardness

refers to the resistance of a material to surface scratching or wear by rubbing or grinding.

absolute altimeter

an electronic instrument which indicates altitude above the surface of the earth, in contradistinction to the readings of aneroid altimeters which indicate altitude above sea-level.

absolute electrometer

a very precise type of attracted disk electrometer in which the attraction between two disks is balanced against the force of gravity.

absolute expansion

if refers to the true expansion of a liquid.

absolute expansion of liquid

the coefficient of absolute expansion of a liquid is equal to the sum of the coefficient of apparent expansion of the liquid and coefficient of volume of the containing vessel.

absolute gain of an antenna

gain in a given direction when the reference antenna is an isotropic antenna isolated in space.

absolute humidity

the mass of water vapour per unit volume of air, usually measured in kilograms per cubic metre.

absolute luminosity

the luminosity of an object expressed in units of fundamental quantities.

absolute motion

when the motion of an object is described by measuring its coordinates or parameters with respect to some definite frame of reference, provided this frame of reference is preferred over all other frames, the motion of the object is regarded as absolute motion.

absolute pitch

the pitch of a musical tone expressed as the frequency of the sound wave of that tone.

absolute potential

the absolute electric potential at a point may be defined as the work per unit charge which is required so as to bring a positive charge of electricity from an infinite distance to that point.

absolute pressure

the pressure above the absolute zero value of pressure that theoretically obtains in empty space or at the absolute zero of temperature, as distinguished from gauge pressure.

absolute scale

the zero of this scale of temperature corresponds to absolute zero. It is a fundamental scale which is based on Charle's law according to which the volume V of a gas at any temperature θ is related to its volume V_0 at 0^0 by the relation

$V = V_0 \ (1 + \alpha\theta)$, where α is the coefficient of expansion of the gas. Its value is $\frac{1}{273.15}$

absolute specific gravity

the ratio of the weight of a given volume of a substance in a vacuum at a given temperature to the weight of an equal volume of water in a vacuum at a given temperature.

absolute standard

a particle or object designated as a standard by assigning to it a mass of one unit; used in defining quantities in newton's second law of motion.

absolute system of units

a set of units for measuring physical quantities, defined by inter-related equations in terms of arbitrary fundamental quantities of length, mass, time and charge or current.

absolute temperature scale

a scale with which temperatures are measured relative to absolute zero. Also known as absolute scale.

absolute vacuum

it is also referred to as perfect vacuum. Absolute vacuum is the space which has no matter in it.

absolute value (modulus)

the square root of the sum of the squares of the real numbers in a * complex number, i.e. the absolute value of the complex number $z = x + iy$ is $[z] = \sqrt{(x^2 + y^2)}$.

absolute viscosity

the tangential force per unit area of two parallel planes at unit distance apart when the space between them is filled with a fluid and one plane moves with unit velocity in its own plane relative to the other.

absolute wave meter

a type of wavemeter in which the frequency of an injected radio frequency voltage is determined by measuring the length of a resonant line.

absolute zero

zero of thermodynamic * temperature (0 kelvin) and the lowest temperature theoretically attainable. It is the temperature at which the kinetic energy of atoms and molecules is minimal. It is equivalent to –273.15°C or –459.67°F. See also zero-point energy; cryogenics.

absorb

to take up energy from radiation. To take up matter or radiation.

absorbed dose

the amount of energy imparted by ionizing particles to a unit-mass of irradiated material at a place of interest. Also known as dosage; dose.

absorber

a material that absorbs neutrons or other ionizing radiation.

absorptance

symbol a. The ratio of the radiant or luminous flux absorbed to the flux falling on it also called absorptivity, the absorbency of a black body is taken as 1.

absorption

in nuclear physics, this phenomenon refers to the taking up of energy from the incident radiation as they pass through the medium.

absorption band

a range of wavelengths or frequencies in the electromagnetic spectrum within which radiant energy is absorbed by a substance.

absorption coefficient

symbol : a. The ratio of the absorbed sound energy at a boundary to the incident- sound energy. Its value depends on the material as well as on the frequency of the sound.

absorption control

control of a nuclear reactor by a material that absorb neutrons, such as cadmium or boron steel. Also known as absorber control.

absorption cross section

in radar, the ratio of the amount of power removed from a beam by absorption of radio energy by a target to the power in the beam incident upon the target.

absorption curve

a graph showing the curvilinear relationship of the variation in absorbed radiation as a function of wavelength.

absorption edge

the x-ray wavelength at which a dis-continuity is observed in the intensity of an x-ray absorption spectrum.

absorption hygrometer

it is a device that is used for measuring the humidity of air. For measuring the humidity, the air is allowed to pass through a weighed quantity of drying agent and then the increase in its weight is determined.

absorption lens

it is a special type of lens which prevents selected wavelengths from passing through it. It is used in preparing eyeglasses.

absorption line

a minute range of wavelength or frequency in the electromagnetic spectrum within which radiant energy is absorbed by the medium through which it is passing.

absorption of light

the process by which a substance or object "soaks up" all the component colours of a beam of white light except certain specific colours which it reflects or transmits.

absorption of radiation

loss of energy during transmission of radiation by a medium. The energy is converted to some other form within the medium.

absorption peak

a wavelength of maximum electromagnetic absorption by a chemical sample; used to identify specific elements, radicals or compounds.

absorption spectrophoto-meter

an instrument used to measure the relative intensity of absorption spectral lines and bands. Also known as difference spectrophoto-meter.

absorption spectroscopy

the study of spectra obtained by the passage of radiant energy from a continuous source through a cooler, selectively absorbing medium.

absorption spectrum

is the group of absorption lines or bands which results from the passage or radiant source energy through a cooler body.

absorption wavemeter

a device for measuring wavelength by tuning a resonant circuit so that it absorbs the maximum energy from the source to be measured.

abtesia

gauss.

abundance

of an isotope is the ratio of the number of atoms of a particular isotope to the total number of atoms of the substance present. Mostly expressed as a percentage.

abundance ratio

the ratio of the number of atoms of an isotope to the total number of atoms in a mixture of isotopes. It is also known as abundance.

abvolt per centimetre

in the electromagnetic centimetre gram second system of units, the unit of electric field strength. Abbreviated av/cm.

abwatt

the unit of electrical power in the centimetre gram second system; 1 abwatt equals 1 watt in the absolute metre kilogram second system.

ac

it stands fr. alternating current. In such a current the direction of current reverses at regular intervals. Such a current has a magnitude that changes continuously in a sinusoidal manner.

accelerate

means to bring about an increase in velocity of the body.

accelerated test

when an electric cable is in use for some time we test its serviceability by applying twice the voltage which is normally carried by the cable. This testing is common called an accelerated test.

acceleration

may be defined as the rate of change in velocity per unit time, customarily expressed in metre per second per second.

acceleration due to gravity (g)

it is the uniform acceleration produced in a freely falling body due to the gravitational pull of the earth.

value of 'g' = 9.81 m/sec^2

For a body of mass m, its force of attraction towards earth of mass, M, and radius, R, is given by

F = m.g.

$$\therefore \quad m.g. = \frac{G.M.m}{R^2}$$

$$\text{or } g = \frac{G.M.}{R^2}$$

Thus we find that 'g' is independent of the mass of body. It depends upon the mass and radius of earth.

Acceleration due to gravity is also known as acceleration of free fall.

Variation in value of 'g' :

(i) variation with altitude height):

$$gh = g\left(1 - \frac{2h}{g}\right)$$

Where gh = acceleration due to gravity at a height h

Thus we find that the value of acceleration due to gravity decreases with increase in height.

(ii) Variation with depth:

$$g' = g\left(1 - \frac{d}{R}\right)$$

Where g' is the acceleration due to gravity, at a depth d.

Thus we find that the value of acceleration due to gravity decreases as depth increases. At the centre of earth d = R and so g' = o. i.e. at the centre of earth acceleration due to gravity becomes zero.

(iii) Variation due to shape of the earth:

$$\text{We have } g = \left(\frac{G.M.}{R^2}\right)$$

$$\text{or } g \ \alpha \left(\frac{1}{R^2}\right) (\because \text{ G, M are constant})$$

Since the polar radius of earth is smaller as compared to its equatorialradius. Thus the value of 'g' at poles will be more than its value at equator.

(iv) Variation of 'g' with rotation of earth:

$$g' = g\left(1 - \frac{R\omega^2 \cos^2\phi}{2}\right)$$

where

ϕ = the latitude on the surface of earth where the body under consideration is present.

ω = angular velocit of rotation of earth.

At poles $\phi = 90^0$, hence g' =g

Thus apparent weight of a body at poles is the same as that of the body if earth were at rest.

At equator $\phi = 0$

$$\text{Hence } g' = g\left(1 - \frac{R\omega^2}{2}\right)$$

Thus apparent weight of body is minimum at equator.

acceleration in a string connected to two unequal masses

T = Tension in string

M = Heavier mass

m = Lighter mass

From figure we can find:

downward force on M is

M. a = Mg – T ....(i)

upward force on m is

m.a. = T – mg ....(ii)

$$\therefore a = \left[\frac{M-m}{M+m}\right].g$$

$$\text{and } T = \left[\frac{2Mm}{M+m}\right].g$$

acceleration potential

the sum of the potential of the force field acting on a fluid and the ratio of the pressure to the fluid density; the negative of its gradient gives the acceleration of a point in the fluid.

acceleration of free fall

is same as acceleration due to gravity.

accelerator

an apparantus for increasing the kinetic energies of charged particles, used for research in nuclear and particle physics.

accelerometer

an instrument for measuring acceleration, especially the acceleration of an aircraft or rocket.

acceptor

materials used for doping semiconductors whose atoms accept electrons from neighbouring atoms for completion of atomic bonds leaving behind positive holes. See also semiconductors.

acceptor impurity

is the impurity which accepts the electron from parent atom.

acceptor levels

energy levels of an acceptor atom in a * semiconductor, such as aluminium, in silicon. These energy levels are very near the top of the valence band, and therefore cause p-type conduction. See also energy bands.

accessory plate

thin plate of quartz, gypsum or mica used with a petrological microscope to modify the effects of polarized light and intensify qualities in translucent minerals.

accommodation

the process by which the focal length of the * lens of the eye is changed so that clear images of objects at a range of distances are displayed on the retina. In man and some other mammals accommodation is achieved by reflex adjustments in the shape of the lens brought about by relaxation and contraction of muscles within the ciliary body.

accordion cable

it is a flat, zig zag shaped cable which is employed to make connections to any movable equipment.

accretion disc

a disc-shaped rotating mass formed by gravitational attraction. See black hole; neutron star; white dwarf.

accumulator (secondary cell; storage battery)

a type of voltaic cell or battery that can be recharged by passing a current through it from an external d.c. supply. The charging current, which is passed in the opposite direction to that in which the cell supplies current, recverses the chemical reactions in the cell. The common types are the read acid accumulator and nickel-iron accumulator.

A.C. Circuits:
(1) A.C. Circuit containing only resistance:
It is shown in fig.
For such a circuit we have
$V = V_0 \sin\omega . t$.
and $I = I_0 \sin\omega . t$.
$\phi = o$ (i.e. current in phase with applied voltage) in this case:
(i) Voltage is maximum when current is maximum.
(ii) Voltage is zero when current becomes zero.
Power of such circuit is given by
$P + P^2 .R$
(2) A.C. Circuit containing only inductance:
$V = V_0 \sin w. t$.

in this case $X_1W_1 = \frac{2\pi}{L}$
Where X_1 = Inductive resistance in ohms. voltage and current in such a system are given by:
$V = V_0 \sin(\omega t + 90)$ or $V = V_0 \sin \omega.t.$
$I = I_0 \sin \omega.t.$ or $I = I_0 \sin(\omega.t. - 90)$
in such circuit phase difference,

$\phi = \frac{\pi}{2}$ The voltage leads the current by $\frac{\pi}{2}$

power in such circuit is zero.
(3) A. C. Circuit containing only capacitance :
$V = V_0 \sin \omega t$
The voltage and current in such a circuit is given by $V = V_0 \sin(\omega t - 90)$
$I = I_0 \sin(\omega t + 90)$ or $I = I_0 \sin \omega.t.$
In this case phase difference, $\phi = \frac{\pi}{2}$
i.e. current leads the voltage by $\frac{\pi}{2}$

The ratio $\frac{V}{I}$ or $\frac{V_0}{I_0}$ called capacitive reactance (X_c).
power in such circuit is zero.
(4) A.C. circuit containing resistance and inductance:
in this case
$V = V_0 \sin \omega.t.$
$I = I_0 \sin \omega.t.$
Impenitence is the effective resistance offered to flow of current in circuit containing an inductance (L) and resistance (R). Impenitence (Z) of the circuit is given by

$$Z = \sqrt{R^2 + \omega^2.L^2}$$

$V = V_0 \sin \omega t$
$I = I_0$ sine ωt
$V_L = I, X_L$
$V_R = I, R$
In such a circuit the phase difference ϕ is given by

$$\tan \phi = \frac{V_L}{V_R} + \frac{X_L}{R} = \frac{\omega.L}{R}$$

Where $\omega.L \geq R$, then R is negligible as compared to $\omega.L$ and in such a case the circuit behaves as pure inductive curcuit. When $\omega.L. \leq R$, i.e. ωL is negligible as compared to R, their Z = R and in such a case the circuit behaves as pure resistance circuit.
(5) A.C. circuit containing resistance and capacitance :
the voltage and current in such a circuit is given by $V = V_0 \sin \omega t$, $I = I_0 (\sin \omega.t. + \phi)$. The total impedance (z) is given by

$$Z = \sqrt{R^2 + X_c^2}$$

$$\text{but } X_c = \frac{1}{\omega.C}$$

$$\therefore Z = \sqrt{R^2 + \left(\frac{1}{\omega C}\right)^2}$$

in such a case I leads the voltage (V) by an angle ϕ (phase difference), ϕ is given by

$$\tan\phi = \frac{V_v}{V_R} = \frac{X_c}{R} = \frac{1}{\omega CR}$$

condition of resonance in a circuit containing inductance and capacitance is

$$X_L = X_c \text{ i.e. } \omega L = \frac{1}{\omega C} \text{ or}$$

$$f = \frac{1}{2\pi\sqrt{LC}}$$

where f = resonance frequency of the circuit.

(6) A.C. circuit containing capacitance and inductance:

In this circuit induced potential difference (V_L) leads the current (I) by 90^0 in phase. So phase difference between both is 180^0. The resultant potential in such a circuit is given by

$V = V_L - V_c$

$V = V_0 \sin \omega.t.$

impendence of circuit is, $Z = X_L - X_c$, when $X_L = X_c$, $Z = 0$, and amplitude of current will be infinite in this case. The condition is known as electrical resonance.

Frequency (f) of resonance circuit in this case is called resonant frequency of circuit.

(7) A.C. circuit containing resistance, inductance and capacitance:

The voltage and current in such a circuit is given by

$V = V_0 \sin \omega t$, $I = I_0 \sin (\omega t + \phi)$

$$\text{where, } I_0 = \frac{V_0}{\sqrt{R^1 + \left(\omega L - \frac{1}{\omega c}\right)^2}}$$

the phase angle (ϕ) between I and V is given by

$$\tan\phi = \frac{X_L - X_c}{R} = \frac{\omega L - \frac{1}{\omega c}}{R}$$

The impendance of LCR circuit is given by

$$Z = \sqrt{R^2 + (X_L - X_c)^2}$$

For resonant circuit

$$\omega L = \frac{1}{\omega c} \text{ or } \omega = \frac{1}{\sqrt{LC}}$$

so $\tan\phi = 0$ or $f = 0$

$$\text{and } f = \frac{1}{2\pi}\sqrt{\frac{1}{LC}}$$

where f is neutral or reaonance frequency

$$\text{Power} = \frac{1}{2} I_0 E_0 \cos\phi$$

achromat

an achromatic lens.

achromatic

a term applied to lenses signifying their more or less complete correction for chromatic aberration.

achromatic colour

known as host a colour that has

no colour; i.e., black, white or grey.

achromatic combination

refers to a combination of (two) lenses of different refractive indices, such that it does not produce any chromatic aberration, i.e., it focuses different colours at the same point. Such a combination must satisfy the condition $\omega_1 P + \omega_2 P_2 = 0$, where, ω is the dispersive power and P is the power of the lens.

achromatic condenser

a condenser designed to eliminate chromatic and spherical spherical aberrations, usually through the use of four elements, two of which are achromatic lenses; used in microscopes having high magnification.

achromatic fringe

an interference fringe of light whose position is independent of the wavelength of the light used; forest fringe of a Lloyd's mirror system and the central fringe of a fresnel by prism system are examples.

achromatic lens

refers to an optical lens which has been corrected partly or chromatic aberration, so that the focal length does not depend on the colour of light being used. Also termed as achromat. The condition for achromatism is:

$$w_1 P_1 + w_2 P_2 = 0$$

where w_1 and w_2 are the dispersive powers of the glasses of the lenses, and P_1 and P_2 are the powers of the lenses. Achromatic lenses could be corrected for chromatic aberration at two different wavelengths See Apochromatic lens.

acid accumulator

it is also called lead storage battery or lead accumulator. In this the following reaction occur during discharging of accumulator and its recharging.

discharging of acid-accumulator:
Reactions at Anode:
$PbO_2 + 2H^+ H_2SO_4 + 2e^- \rightarrow PbSO_4 + 2H_2O$
reactions at Cathode:
$Pb + SO_4^{-2} \rightarrow PbSO_2 + 2e^-$
Recharging of the acid-accumulator:
For recharging current is passed through the accumulator, various reactions are
At cathode
$PbSO_4 + SO^{-2}_4 + 2H_2O \rightarrow PbO_2 + 2H_2SO_4 + 2e^-$

aclastic

the property of a substance of

not refracting light is called aclastic.

aclinic line

(magnetic equator). Isoclinic line.

acoustic approximation

the approximation that leads from the non linear hydrodynamic equations of a gas to the linear wave equation for sound wave propagation.

acoustic branch

one of the parts of the dispersion relation, frequency as a function of wave number, for crystal lattice vibrations, representing vibration at low frequencies.

acoustic compliance

the reciprocal of acoustic stiffness or acoustic reactance is called acoustic compliance or acoustic capacitance.

acoustic dispersion

a complex sound wave's separation into its frequency components as it passes through a medium; usually measured by the rate of change of velocity with frequency.

acoustic domain

a concentration of crystal lattice vibrations travelling at the speed of sound, used to generate light from an array of pn junctions.

acoustic emission

the phenomenon of transient elastic-wave generation due to a rapid release of strain energy caused by a structural alteration in a solid material. Also known as stress-wave emission.

acoustic fatigue

the tendency of a material to lose its strength after acoustic stress.

acoustic grating

a series of rods or other suitable objects of equal size placed in a row a fixed distance apart; causes sounds with different wavelengths to be diffracted in different directions.

acoustic image

the geometric space figure that is made up of the acoustic foci of an acoustic lens, mirror, or other acoustic optical system and is the acoustic counterpart of an extended source of sound. Also known as image.

acoustic impedance

the complex ratio of the sound pressure on a given surface to the sound flux through that surface, expressed in acoustic ohms.

acoustic interferometer

this is the device for measuring the velocity and attenuation of sound waves in a gas of liquid.

acoustic intensity

the limit approached by the ratio of the acoustic power in a given area to the magnitude of this area as the magnitude approaches zero.

acoustic interferometer

a device for measuring the velocity and attention of sound waves in a gas or liquid by an interference method.

acoustic levitation

the process of using a highly intense acoustic or sound wave to enable a body to remain suspended above the source producing the sound wave is called acoustic levitation.

acoustic mass reactance

the part of the acoustic reactance associated with the kinetic energy of a medium. Also known as mass reactance.

acoustic mass

the quantity which after multiplication by 2 times the frequency results in the acoustic reactance associated with the kinetic energy of the sound medium. Also known as acoustic interance.

acoustic measurement

the process of finding one or more properties of sound quantitatively is called acoustic measurement.

coustic microscope

an instrument which employs acoustic radiation at microwave frequencies to allow visualization of the microscopic detail exhibitedin elastic properties of an object.

acoustic noise

noise in the acoustic spectrum, usually measured in decibels.

acoustic ohm

it is the unit of acoustic reactance or acoustic impedance. It is also known as acoustic resistance unit.

acoustic phonon

quantum of excitation of an acoustic mode of vibration is called an acoustic phonon.

acoustic radiation pressure

when a surface is exposed to a sound wave, a steady-state, unidirectional pressure exerted upon the surface is called acoustic radiation pressure.

acoustic radiation

infrasonic, sonic or ultrasonic waves propagating through a solid, liquid or gaseous medium.

acoustic reactance

the imaginary component of the acoustic impedance.

acoustic reflectivity

ratio of the rate of flow of sound energy reflected from a surface, on the side of incidence, to the incident rate of flow. Also known as acoustic reflection coefficient.

acoustic refraction

variation of the direction of sound transmission due to spatial variatial of the wave velocity in the medium.

acoustic resistance

the real component of the acoustic impedance.

acoustic resonator

an enclosure that produces resonance due to sound-wave of a particular frequency is called an acoustic resonator.

acoustic scattering

the process of irregular reflection, refraction and diffraction of a sound in many directions is called acoustic scattering.

acoustic shadow

the effect which is produced by an obstacle placed in the path of a sound wave, analogous in many respect to an optical shadow.

acoustic shielding

the prevention of transmission of sound energy using a barrier.

acoustic spectrum

the range of acoustic frequencies extending from subsonic to ultrasonic frequencies, that is approximately from zero to at least 1 megahertz.

acoustic stiffness

the product of the angular frequency and the acoustic stiffness reactance.

acoustic velocity

acoustic velocity is nothing but speed of sound.

acoustical doppler effect

the apparent change in the frequency of sound due to relative motion between source and observe is called acoustical doppler effect or commonly known as doppler effect.

acoustical stiffness

the acoustic reactance associated with the potential energy of a medium multiplied by times the sound frequency.

acoustical stoffness

the potential energy of a medium multiplied by 2 times the sound frequency measures the acoustical stiffness of the medium or the acoustical reactance of the medium.

acoustical

having a characteristic concerning sound, of an object or quantity that in and of itself does not have properties associated with sound, such as a device, measurement or symbol.

acoustics

the study of the production and properties of sound.

acoustoelectronic devices (electroacoustic devices)

which electronic singles are converted into acoustic waves. Such devices d\are used in constructing delay lines and also in converting digital data from computers for transmission by telephone lines.

acoustooptical cell

a device in which an acoustic or ultrasonic electric input signal acts on a beam of light.

acoustooptics

the branch of science which deals with interactions between sound waves and light.

acromatic prism

a prism consisting of two or more prisms with different refractive indices combined so that light passing through the device is deviated but not dispersed.

acting force

the force exerted by one body on another, and which, according to Newton's third law of motion, makes the second body to exert an equal force on the first one.

actinic focus

the point in an optical system at which the chemically most effective rays (usually those in the ultraviolet) coverage.

actinic glass

a special type of glass which transmits more of the visible components of incident radiation as compared to that of ultraviolet and infrared components.

actinic radiation

radiation which can cause a chemical reaction; e.g. ultraviolet radiation is actinic.

actinic rays

the portion of the sun's radiation rich in ultraviolet radiation, having a strong effect on a photographic plate.

actinic

pertaining to electromagnetic radiation capable of initiating photochemical reactions, as in photography or the fading ot pigments.

actinism decay series

a series of radioactive disitengration products derived from uranium-235.

actinium

symbol ac. A silvery radioactive metallic element belonging to group 3 (formerly IIIA) of the periodic table; a.n. 89; mass number of most stable isotope 227 (half-life 21.7 years); m.p. 1050 ± 50°C; b.p. 3200°C.

actinoid contraction

a smooth decrease in atomic or ionic radius with increasing proton number found in the actinoids.

actinology

a branch of science which deals with the chemical effects of electromagnetic radiation.

actinometer

the general name for any instrument used to measure the intensity of radiant energy, particularly that of the sun, e.g., bolometer, dosimeter, photometer, radiometer etc.

actinon

a radioactive isotope of radon belonging to the actinium series, symbol an, atomic number 86, atomic weight 219.

action

refers to the product of work and time.

action at a distance theory

a theory of the interaction of two bodies separated in space.

actionelectricity

the phenomenon of production of electromotive force in a material by allowing electromagnetic radiation to be incident upon it is called actionelectricity.

action potential

the change in electrical potential that occurs across a cell membrane during the passage of a nerve impulse. As an impulse travels in a wavelike manner along the axon of a nerve, it causes a localized and transient switch in electrical potential across the cell membranes from -60 m^V. Nervous stimulation of a muscle fibre has a similar effect.

action-reaction law

when one body exerts force on another, the second body exerts a collinear force on the first equal in magnitude but oppositely directed.

action spectrum

a graphical plot of the efficiency of electromagnetic radiation in producing a photochemical reaction against the wavelength of the radiation used. For example the action spectrum for photosynthesis using light shows a peak in the region 670-700 mm. This corresponds to a maximum absorption in the absorption spectrum of chlorophylls in this region.

activate

to make a cell or battery operative by addition of a liquid. To induce radioacitivity through bombardment by neutrons or other types of radiation. To start activity or motion in a device or material.

activation

the process of inducing radioactivity in a substance.

activation analysis

a method of chemical analysis based on the detection of characteristic radion uclides following a nuclear bombardment.

active current

in an alternating-current circuit, the component of electric current which is in phase with the applied voltage. Active current is also known as watt-current.

active device

1. an electronic component such as a transistor, that is capable of amplification. 2. An artificial satellite that receives information and retrasmits it after amplification. 3. A radar device that emits microwave radiation and provides information about a distant body by receiving a reflection of this radiation.

active electric network

electric network containing one or more sources of energy.

active element

an element having one or more radioactive isotopes is called an active element.

active material

a fluorescent material used in screens for cathedral tubes. An energy-storing martial such as lead oxide used in plates of a storage battery. A material capable of releasing substantial quantities of nuclear energy during fission.

active power

the product of the voltage across a branch of an alternating-current and the component of the electric current that is in phase with the voltage.

active substrata

a semiconductor on ferrite material in which active elements are formed.

active voltage

in an alternating current circuit the component of voltage which is in phase with the current.

activity

the average number of radioactive disintegration of a substance per unit time.

actual height

highest altitude at which refraction of radio waves actually occurs.

acyclic

continually varying without a regularly repeated pattern.

adaptation luminance

the average luminance or brightness of objects and surface in the immediate vicinity of an observer estimating the visual range.

adapter

an additional component added to a camera which permits its use in a manner for which it was not designed.

adaptive optics

the theory and design of optical systems that measure and correct any wave front aberration in real time, that is simultaneous with the operation of the system.

additive primary colours

the three primary colours usually green, blue and red which are mixed together in a additive process are referred as additive primary colours.

additive process

a process of colour mixing by addition.

adhesion

holding of two surfaces together by interfacial forces. The effect is produced by forces between molecules.

adhesive bond

the force such as dipole bonds which attract adhesives and bare materials to each other.

adhesives

substances used for sticking surfaces together like glues, cements etc.

adiabatic

thermally insulated or self-contained. The term finds us in thermodynamics referring to change in volume without loss or gain of heat.

adiabatic calorimeter

refers to a calorimeter which theoretically remains unaffected by its surroundings and neither gains nor loses heat.

adiabatic change

a change during which no energy erters enters or leaves the system. For an ideal gas undergoing a reversible adiabatic change it can be shown that

$pV^g = K_1$,
$T^g P^{1-g} = K_2$
and $TV^{g-1} = K_3$
where K_1, K_2 and K_3 are constants and g is the ratio of the principal specific heat capacities.

adiabatic compression

a reduction in volume of a substance without heat flow, in or out.

adiabatic cooling

a process in which the temperature of a system is lowered without any exchange of heat between the system and its surroundings.

adiabitic curve

a curve or graph which shows the relation between pressure and volume in substances having or assumed to have the property of adiabatic expansion and contraction.

adiabatic demagnetisation

a method of producing temperatures which is close to absolute zero. A sample of paramagnetic salt is cooled in liquid helium in a strong magnetising field. The field is removed, demagnetizing the sample and cooling it further.

adiabatic ellipse

a plot of the speed of sound as a function of the speed.

adiabatic envelope

a surface enclosing a thermodynamic system in an equilibrium such that no heat can flow through the surface.

adiabatic expansion

increase in volume without heat flow, in or out.

adiabatic flow

movement of a fluid without heat transfer.

adiabatic process

any thermodynamic procedure which takes place in a system without the exchange of heat with the surroundings.

adiabatic vaporization

the phenomenon of vapourization of a liquid, which does not involve any exchange of heat between the substance and its surroundings.

adiathermanous

the term is referred to a system or body which is unable to transmit any radiant heat.

adjustable resistor

a resistor having one or more sliding contacts whose position may be changed.

admittance

it is the reciprocal impedance of an electrical circuit.

adsorbate

a substance that is adsorbed on a surface.

adsorption

it is the phenomenon of higher concentration of molecular species (gases or liquids) at the surface of a solid than in the bulk. The molecules so held on he surface are said to be adsorbed and the adsorbed layer may be held together by weak vender waals forces (physiosorption) or by strong chemical bonds (chemisorption).

advanced gas-cooled reactor

a power-generating nuclear reactor which has steel-clad uranium dioxide fuel elements and is cooled by carbon dioxide gas.

advanced potential

any electromagnetic potential arising as a solution of the classical maxwell field equations.

aerial

the part of a radio system that, transmits energy into or receives energy from, the atmosphere or space.

aerial array

an assembly of simple aerials arranged in space so that transmitted or received energy is concentrated in one or more directions.

aerial camera

a camera designed for use in aircraft and containing a mechanism to depose the film in continuous sequence at a steady state.

aerial perspective

the effect produced by diffusion of light in the atmosphere whereby more distant objects have less clarity of outline and are lighter in tone.

aeriform

having the form or nature of air.

aerodynamic

pertaining to forces acting upon any solid or liquid body moving relative to a gas.

aerodynamic drag

a retarding force that acts upon a body moving through a gaseous fluid and that is parallel to the direction of motion of the body; it is a component of the total fluid forces acting on the body.

aerodynamic heating

the heating of a body produced by passage of air or other gases over its surface curved by friction and by compression process significant at high speeds.

aerodynamic lift

that component of the total aerodynamic force acting on a body perpendicular to the undisturbed airflow relative to the body.

aerodynamic noise

an acoustic noise caused by turbulent airflow over the surface of a body.

aerodynamic phenomena

acoustic, thermal, electrical and mechanical effect resulting from the flow of air over a body.

aerodynamics

the study of the motion and control of solid bodies in air. The study of air or other gases in motion.

aerodynamic smooth surface

a surface whose irregularities are sufficiently small to be entirely embedded in the laminar sublayer.

aerodynamic trail

a condensation trail formed by adiabatic cooling to saturation of air passing over the surface of high-speed aircraft.

aerodynamic trajectory

a trajectory in which the missile encounters sufficient air resistance to stabilize its flight or to modify its course significantly.

aerodynamic turbulence

a state of fluid flow in which the instantaneous velocities exhibit irregular fluctuations.

aerodynamically rough surface

a surface whose irregularities are sufficiently high that the turbulent boundary layer reaches right down to the surface.

aerogenerator

a device which is driven by wind and generates electricity.

aerometer

an instrument which is used for measuring the weight and density of air and gases.

aeronautics

a branch of science which deals with flight through air.

aeropause

an upper region of the atmosphere in which the atmosphere ceases to function for manned or unmanned flight.

aerosol

a dispersion of small particles of solid or droplets of liquid in a gas.

aerospace

the earth's atmosphere and the space beyond.

aes

see auger electron spectroscopy.

aether

an imaginary fluid which was thought to permeate all space through which light waves were assumed to propagate. It was shown by Michelson-Morley experiment that the existence of such a medium is unfounded.

afm

see atomic force microscope.

afocal lens

a lens whose convergence power is zero is called an afocal lens. The focal points for such a lens are infinitely distant apart.

afocal system

an optical system of zero convergent power. The most common example is a telescope.

aftercooling

the phenomenon of cooling of a nuclear reactor after it has been shut down.

afterglow

the term is closely related to phosphorescence.

afterheat

heat derived from residual radioactivity, after a nuclear reactor has been completely shut down.

afterwind

a wind produced by the up-draft accompanying the rise of the fireball of a nuclear explosion and directed toward the burst centre.

agate

a very hard natural form of silica, used for knife-edges of balances, for mortars for grinding hard materials.

ageing

refers to the changes that occurs in the properties of a substance with the passage of time.

age of the earth

the time since the earth emerged as a planet of the sun, estimated by dating techniques to be about 4.6×10^9 years.

agglomerate

small particles bonded together into an integrated mass.

agonic line

this is the line of zero declination.

agr

advanced gas-cooled reactor.

ai

see artificial intelligence.

air

gaseous mixture that surrounds the earth. It contains Nitrogen, Oxygen, Carbon dioxide, Argon etc. In addition to these atmospheric gases it also contains water vapour, hydrocarbons, hydrogen peroxide, sulphur compounds, dirt partic!es etc.

air brake

a system of brakes that is operated by compressed air.

air compression

the decrease of volume of a quantity of air as a result of an increase in pressure, e.g. piston moving in a cylinder.

air conditioner

a device that is used for reducing the temperature and humidity of air in an enclosed space.

air current

any moving stream of air.

air density

the mass per unit volume of air.

air depolarized battery

a primary battery which is kept depolarized by atmospheric oxygen rather than chemical compounds.

air gap

a thin film of air, in a magnetic circuit.

air plane

a plane or air-craft that is kept aloft due to the upward thrust produced b the passing air on the fixed wings of the air craft. Such air-craft is driven by propellers etc.

air pressure

the force per unit area that the air exerts on any surface in contact with it, arising from the collisions of the air molecules with the surface.

air resistance

wind-drag which gives rise to wearing and tearing of buildings and other structures is called air resistance.

air switch

it is an air-break switch where breaking off the electric circuit takes place in air.

air-pressure drop

the pressure lost in overcoming friction along an airway.

air-velocity measurement

the measurement of the rate of displacement of air or gas at a specific location, as when ascertaining wind speed or airspeed of aircraft.

air-water vapour mixture

a mixture of dry air and water vapour, such as the

atmosphere.

air wedge

it is a wedge shaed film of air formed between two plates which are inclined at an angle to each other. Such an arrangement is generally used for producing localised interference fringes by reflection at the two sides of the wedge shaped film of air. In case of monochromatic light the fringes produces consist of the wedge.

aircraft decibel rating

the ratio of the radar reflectivity of a specific type of aircraft to that of a selected reference aircraft measured in decibels.

aircraft noise

effective sound output of the various sources of noise associated with aircraft operation, such as propeller and engine exhaust, jet noise and sonic boom.

albedo

the ratio of the amount of electromagnetic radiation reflected by a body to the amount incident upon it often expressed as percentage, the albedo of the earth is 34%.

alcohol thermometer

a thermometer that is based on the expansion of ethanol in glass as a function of temperature. A red dye is commonly added to ethanol to make it clearly visible.

alfven number

the ratio of the speed of the alfven wave to the speed of the fluid at a point in the fluid.

alfven wave

a transverse wave in a magneto-hydrodynamic field in which the driving force is the magnetic field which acts along the lines of force. It is also called mangeto-hydrodynamic wave.

algebraic sum

the total of a set of quantities paying due regard to sign, e.g. the algebraic sum of 3 and –4 is –1.

alidade

an instrument which is used to measure vertical elevations and distaces.

alkaline cell

a primary cell that uses an alkaline electrolyte, usually potassium hydroxide, and delivers about 1.5 volts at much higher current rates than the common carbon-zinc cell. Also known as alkaline manganese cell.

alkaline storage battery

a storage battery in which the electrolyte consists of an alkaline solution, usually potassium hydroxide.

allobar

a form of an element differing in isotopic composition from the naturally occurring from.

allochromy

emission of electromagnetic radiation that results from incident radiation at a different wavelength as occurs in fluorescence or the Raman effect.

allog nuclear fuel

an alloy of a fissionable substance and a non-fissionable metal or metals. Used as fuel in nuclear reactors.

all-sky camera

a special type of camera which enables us to photograph the entire sky simultaneously.

allotropes

different physical structures of a solid substance. Diamond and graphite are, for example allotropes of carbon.

allotropy

the existence of a solid substance in different physically forms. Tin, for example, has metallic and non-metallic crystalline forms. Carbon has two crystalline allotropes-diamond and graphite.

alloy

a mixture of two or more metals or a metal with small amounts of non-metals. Alloys may be completely homogenous mixtures or may contain small particles of one phase in the other phase.

alnico

a tradename for a series of alloys, containing iron, aluminium, nickel, cobalt, and copper, used to make permanent magnets.

alnico magnet

a permanent magnet made up of alnico and is commonly used in electromagnetism.

alnico

trade name for an alloy of nickel, aluminium, cobalt, and copper which provides a high energy permanent magnet material.

alpha cross-section

the cross-section of a substance for its interaction with alpha particles.

alpha decay

any radioactive decay with the emission of alpha particles.

alpha inrradiation

when a substance or target is subjected to beam of alpha particles, it is called alpha irradiation.

alpha particle (α)

an α-particle consists of two neutrons and two protons which are bonded together and so it carries two units of positive charge. It may be considered as helium nuclei. Many radioactive nuclei give off alpha particles when they decay. e.g.

$$\frac{238}{92}U \rightarrow \frac{234}{90}Th + \frac{4}{2}\alpha + \text{enegry}$$

(α – particle)

alpha particle scattering

deviation at various angles of a stream of alpha particles passing through a foil of material.

alpha ray

a stream of alpha particles.

alternating current (A.C.)

a current which flows alternately in one direction, then in the opposite direction around a circuit. This cycle of variation of currents repeats continuously. The simplest type of A.C. can be represented by $I = I_0 \sin \omega t$.

alternating current circuit

a circuit having a.c. source. A general a.c. circuit has the circuit elements as resistance, inductances and capacitors. These circuit elements are connected in series and/or in parallel

alternating current generator

a machine usually rotary, which converts mechanical power into alternating current electric power.

alternating current motor

a machine that converts alternating current electrical energy into mechanical energy by utilizing forces exerted by magnetic fields produced by the current flow through conductors.

alternating current power supply

a power supply that provides one or more alternating current output voltages, such as an ac generator, dynamotor, inverter or transformer.

alternating stress

a type of stress developed in a material by forces such that each force alternately acts in opposite directions.

alternating voltage

the voltage whose magnitude and direction change with time and after a certain time the voltage recur with the same magnitude and in the same direction is called alternating voltage. Alternating voltage at any time may be represented by $V = V_0 \sin \omega t$
where V_0 = max. value of voltage.

alternator

a device to produce alternating electric current.

altimeter

a device used to measure high above sea level. It usually consists of an aneroid *barometer measuring atmospheric pressure.

altimeter capacitance

an altimeter which measures the height of an aircraft in terms of its capacitance to earth.

altitude

height. Altitude of the sun, or any heaven body, is its angle of elevation.

alu

the part of the central processor of a *computer in which simple arithmetic and logical operations are performed electronically. For example, the ALU can add, subtract, multiply, compare two numbers, or negate a number.

aluminimum conductor

any of several aluminium alloys employed for conducting electric current because its weight is one-half of that of copper for the same conductance. It is used in high voltage transmission lines.

alvarez, luis walter

US physicist most of whose working life was spent at the university of California, Berkeley.

amagat diagram

a figure which contains a series of isothermal curves for gas pressure plotted against the gas pressure-volume product for a given gas.

amalgam

an alloy containing mercury.

amasthenic lens

a special type of lens which is used to refract light rays into one focus.

ambient light

the surrounding light such as that reaching a television picture tube screen from light sources in a room.

ambient noise

the pervasive noise associated with a given environment being usually a composite of sounds from sources both near and distant.

ambient pressure

the pressure of the surrounding medium, such as a gas or liquid which comes into contact with an apparatus or with a reaction.

ambient temperature

temperature of the surrounding medium, which is in contact with the equipment.

americium

symbol Am. A radioactive metallic transuranic element belonging to the actinioids; a.n. 95f; mass number of most stable isotope 243 (half-life 7.95×10^3 years); r.d. 13.67 (20°C); m.p. 994 ± 4°C; b.p. 2607°C.

ammeter

an istrument which is used for measuring electric current, with a scale calibrated in amperes.

ammonia colck

a form of atomic clock in which the frequency of a quartz oscillator is controlled by the vibrations of excited ammonia molecules. The ammonia molecules (NH_3) consists of a pyramid with a nitrogen atom at the apex and one hydrogen atom at each corner oa the triangular base. When the molecule is excited, once every 20.9 microseconds the nitrogen atom passes through the base and forms a pyramid the other side: 20.9 microseconds later it returns to its original position. This vibration back and forth has a frequency of 23870 hertz and ammonia gas will only absorb excitation energy at exactly this frequency. By using a crystal oscillator to feed energy to the gas and a suitable feedback mechanism, the oscillator can be locked to exactly this frequency.

amonton's law

in any gas whose volume and mass are kept constant, the same rise in temperature produces the same increase of pressure.

amorphous

describing a solid that is not crystalline; i.e., one that has no long-range order in its lattice.

Many pwders that are described as 'amorphous' in fact are composed of microscopic crystals, as can be demonstrated by X-ray diffraction. Glasses are examples of true amorphous solids.

amount

it is a measure of the no. of particles present in a substance. It is symbolized by n.

amount of substance

symbol: n. A measure of the numbers of particles present in a substance.

amp/hr

an abbreviation of ampere-hour.

ampacity

the current-crying capacity of a cable is called its ampacity, it is a standard used in electricity as a rating for power cables.

amperage

the amount of electric current in amperes is called amperage.

ampere

symbol: A. The SI base unit of electric current, which is defined as the constant current which is maintained in two straight parallel infinite conductors of negligible circular cross-section kept one metre apart in vacuum, would produce a force between the conductors of 2×10^{-7} newton per metre.

ampere, andre marie

french physicst who from 1809 taught at the Ecle polytechnique in Paris. He is best known for putting electromagnetism on a mathematical basis. In 1825 the formulated Ampere's law. The ampere is named after him.

ampere circuit law

it stales that the line integral of magnetic field B around any closed circuit it equal to μ_0 times the total current passing through the closed circuit.

In case of straight long conductor carrying a current I, the magnetic field produced at point P at a distance r from the conductor.

$$B = \frac{\mu 0}{4\pi} \cdot \frac{21}{r}$$

$$= \frac{\mu 0.1}{2\pi r}$$

The line $\int \vec{B} d\vec{l}$ is given by

$$\int B \int \vec{B} d\vec{l} = \int B dl = \int \frac{\mu o I}{2\pi r} dl$$

$$= \frac{\mu o.I}{2\pi r} \times 2\pi r$$
$$= \mu o.I.$$

ampere-hour

the practical unit of quantity of electricity : the amount of electricity flowing per hour through a conductor when the current in it is one ampere. 1 ampere-hour = 3600 coulombs.

ampere-hour meter

an electricity meter that registers the quantity of electricity in ampere-hours. Ampere-hour meters have been sometimes adapted to register in kilowatt hours at the rated voltage of the cirtuit.

ampere per meter

the si unit of magnetic field strength and magnetization. Abbreviated a/m.

ampere rule

the rule which states that the direction of the magnetic field surrounding a conductor will be clockwise when viewed from the conductor if the direction of current flow is away from the observer.

ampere-minute

unit of electrical charge. Equal to the amount of charge transporting in one minute by a current of one ampere.

ampere, thermal

the si unit of thermal current. 1 thermal ampere corresponds to an entropy flow of 1 watt per kelvin. Formerly, the thermal ampere corresponded to a heat flow rate of 1 watt.

ampere's law

the magnetic intensity at any point near a currentcarrying conductor can be computed on the assumption that each infinitesimal length of the conductor produces at the point an infinitesimal magnetic density. The resulting magnetic intensity at the point has been the vector sum of the contributions of all the elements of the conductor.

ampere's rule

it is a rule to find the polarity of magnetism in a coil carrying a curent. To apply the rule, imagine a man swimming in the circuit in the direction of the curent, with his face towards the bar, then his left hand will point towards north pole of the magnet.

ampere-turn

the ampere-turn is the practical, mks, and si unit of

magnetomotive force. 1 ampereturn is the magnetomotive force resulting from the passage of a current of 1 ampere through one turn of a coil.

amorphous

any non-crystalline solid substance e.g. glass.

amplification

refers to any increase in the strength of current, voltage or power.

amplification factor

refers to the ratio of the change in plate voltage that can produce a change in the plate current to the change in grid voltage that produces the same change in plate current for a tripod valve.

amplifier

a device that increases the strength of an electrical signal by drawing energy from a separate source to that of the signal.

amplitude

the maximum displacement of an oscillating quantity from its mean position. In the case of a simple pendulum for example, the amplitude is equal to the distance between the mean and extreme position of the bob.

amplitude level

the natural logarithm of the ratio of two amplitudes, each measured in the same units.

amplitude modulation

a method of transmitting information by radiowaves. In this method, the amplitude of the carrier waves is varied in accordance with the frequency of the signal to be transmitted.

amplitude modulator

the device or electronic circuit which carries out the amplitude modulation is called amplitude modulator.

amplitude of accommodation

refers to the eye's rane of accommodation in terms of power. It is given by $(1/u_1 - 1/u_2)$, where u_1 is the distance from the near point to the lens and u_2 is the distance from the far point to the lens.

a.m.u.

stands for atomic mass unit.

analogous pole

it is that pole of a crystal which acquires a positive charge when the crystal. Is heated.

analyser

it refers to the second Nicol prism in a polarimeter. It is rotated to 90^0 E relative to polariser it does not allow any polarised light to pass. In case the plane of polarised light is parallel to the analyser's direction, the intensity of transmitted light is maximum.

analytical geometry

a form of geometry in which points are located in a two-dimensional or three-dimensional space by means of a system of coordinates.

analyzer

in a polariscope or polarimeter, the second Nicol prism which can be said to analyze the light arriving to it from the first Nicol and the intervention crystal section.

anamorphic

one that produces unequal magnification along two axes which are perpendicular to each other.

anastigmatic lens

a compound lens corrected for astigmatism and curvature of field. Also known as anastigmatic.

anchor

refers to any device that is used for dropping by a chain, cable or rope to avoid or to restrict the motion of a vessel or any other floating object.

Anderson, Carl David

US physicist who became a professor at the California Institute of Technology, where he worked mainly in particle physics. In 1932 he discovered the positron in cosmic radiation, and four years later was awarded the Nobel Prize. In 1939 he discovered the mumeson (muon).

Andrew's experiment

by this experiment, Andrew, showed that it is no possible to liquify gases by the application of pressure alone if the gas is maintained at a temperature above the critical point of the gas. Howerver the gas can be liquified by the application of pressure alone if it is at a temperature below its critical temperature.

anechoic

having a low degree of reverberation with little or no reflection of sound. An anechoic chamber is one designed for experiments in acoustics. The walls are covered with small pyramids to avoid the formation of stationary waves between facing surfaces and the whole of the interior surface is covered with an absorbent material to avoid reflections.

anechoic chamber

a room designed so that thee is little or no reflection or sound from its internal walls.

anelasticity

the phenomenon of deviation from Hooke's law, i.e. stress is directly proportional to strain within elastic limits, is called anelasticity.

anelectric

the process by virtue of which a body does not get charged by friction is referred to as anelectric.

anemometer

an instrument used for measuring the speed of the wind or any other flowing fluid. The simple vane anemometer is made up of a number of cups or blades.

aneroid

it means without liquid.

aneroid barometer

an instrument which is used for measuring atmospheric pressure. It consists basically of a flat box which is partially exhausted off air, so that a partial vacuum is created in it; an external spring is used to keep it from collapsing, although there are models which require no such spring. The changes in atmospheric pressure cause the box to expand or to contract, and these expansions and contractions are indicated, through mechanical devices, on a graduated dial.

aneroidograph

an aneroid barometer equipped with a mjechanism for the continuous automatic recording of atmospheric pressure.

angle of contact

it is the angle which the tangent plane to the liquid surface makes with the tangent plane to the solid surface drawn into the liquid at any point on the line of contact between the liquid and the solid.

angle of deviation

it is equal to the difference between the angle of incidence and the angle of refraction of a ray of light that passes through the surface between one medium another having different refractive index.

angle of dip

inclination.

angle of fall

the term is frequently used in projectile motion. It is the vertical angle at the level point between the base of the trajectory and the line of fall.

angle of friction

the angle between surfaces at which slipping first (just) occurs. It depends on the nature of the surfaces in contact.

angle of incidence

the angle between a ray which is reflected from surface and the normal to the surface at the point of reflection.

angle of radiation

angle between the surface of the earth and the centre of the beam of energy radiated upward into the sky from a transmitting antenna.

angle of reflection

1. the angle between a ray leaving a reflecting surface and the perpendicular to the surface at the point at which the ray leaves the surface. 2. The angle between a wavefront and a surface that it leaves.

angle of refraction

the angle between a refracted ray and the normal to the surface at the point of refraction.

angle of repose

the angle, α, which the inclined plane makes with horizontal when body placed in it just begins to slide down, is known as angle or repose. It is equal to angle of friction.

Thus $\tan \alpha = \tan \theta = \mu$

angle of twist

also called angle of tension, is the angle through which a part of an object, such as a shaft or wire, is rotated from its normal position when some torque is applied.

angle of view

the angle subtended by an image at the second nodal point of a lens.

angstrom

symbol A. A unit of length equal to 10^{-10} metre. It was formerly used to measure wavelengths and intermolecular distances but has now been replaced by the nanometre. 1 A = 0.1 nanometre. The unit is named after A.J. Angstrom.

angstrom coefficient

the multiplying amplitude parameter inserted in angstrom's formula for the scattering of electromagnetic radiation by atmospheric dust.

angular acceleration

the rate of change of the angular velocity of an object.

angular displacement (q)

the angular or rotational displacement of an object from a given position about an axis.

angular distribution

the distribution in angle, relative to an experimental specified direction, of the intensity of photons or particles resulting from a nuclear or extra nuclear process.

angular frequency (ω)

the number of complete rotations made per unit time.

angular harmonic motion

angular harmonic motion or harmonic motion of rotation-periodic oscillatory angular motion in which the restoring torque is proportional to the angular displacement.

angular magnification

symbol: M. Refers to the ratio of the angle substandard at the eye by an image to that substended by the object: $M = q_1/q_0$.

angular momentum

symbol L. The product of the angular velocity of a body and its moment of inertia about the axis of rotation, i.e. $L = I\omega$.

angular resolution

a measure of the ability of a radar to distinguish between two targets solely by the measurement of angles.

angular speed

change of direction per unit time as of a target on a radar screen, without regard to the direction of the rotation axis; in other words the magnitude of the angular velocity vector. Also known as angular rate.

angular velocity

symbol: w. Refers to the rate of change of angular displacement w = dq/dt. See rotational motion.

angustrom unit

unit of measurement of the wavelength of light and other radiations, so named in honour of the Swedis physicist Jonas Angstrom (1814-1874). 1

angstrom unit equals one-tenth of a millimicron (.1 mm), i.e., one hundred millionth of a centimetre.

angus-smith process

when iron is heated to about 370 degree c and then immersed in a solution of coal-tar in oil and paranaphthalene, an anti-corrosive layer is formed.

anharmonic oscillator

an oscillating system in which the restoring force opposing a displacement from the position of equilibrium is a non linear function of the displacement.

anion

negatively charged ion. In electrolysis, such ions are attracted towards the positive electrode called anode.

anisometric

not isometric. Applicable to crystals which have axes of different lengths.

anisotropic

denoting a medium in which certain physical properties are different in different directions.

anisotropic crystal

a crystal which has unequal axes and exhibits different properties when tested along axes extending in different directions.

anisotropy

property of possessing different physical properties in different directions. Substances which show such behaviour, are called anisotropic substances.

anisotropy constant

in a feromagnetic material, temperature dependent parameters relating the masgnetization in various directions to the anisotropy energy.

anisotropy energy

energy stored in a ferromagnetic crystal by virtue of the work done in retaining the magnetisation of a domain away from the direction of easy magnetization.

annealing

very slow regulated cooling of metals to relieve strains set up during heating or other treatment.

annealing point

is a temperature at which the viscosity of glass is 10^{13} poise.

annihilation

refers to a reaction between a particle and its antiparticle; for example, between an electron and a positron. The energy produced has been equivalent to the sum of the rest masses of the annihilating particles and their kinetic energies. Annihilation also can take place between a nucleon and its antiparticle. In this case mesons are produced.

annular eclipse

an eclipse of the sun in which a ring of its surface is visible surrounding the darkened moon.

annular space

the space between two rings.

annulus

the plane figure that is formed between two concentric circles of different radii, R and r. Its area is p.

anode

a positive electrode. In electrolysis anions are attracted to the anbode. In an electronic vacuum tube it attracts electros flow out of the device.

anode ray

stream of positively charged particles, originating from the anode of vacuum tube.

anode dark-space

a narrow dark zone observed near the surface of the anode in a glow discharge tube.

anode glow

a narrow bright zone on the anode side of the positive column in a gas tube.

anodize

placing protective film on metal surface by electrolytic or chemical action.

anodizing

producing an oxide overcoating on a metallic surface by making it the anode in an electrolytic bath.

anomaloscope

it is an optical device used for the detection and classification of defective colour vision.

anomalous dispersion

refers to a discontinuity in the curve of refractive constant against wavelength caused by high absorptivity of the medium at certain wavelengths.

anomalous expansion

expansion of certain substances with a decrease in temperature. Such a behaviour is shown, for example, by water when it is cooled below 4 degree c. Water expands on cooling between 4 degree c and 0 degree c.

anomalous zeeman effect

is the splitting of light spectrum under strong magnetic fields which occurs for any line arising from a combination of terms of multiplicity greater than one.

anomaly

an angle used to fix the position of a body, such as a planet, in an elliptical orbit. The true anomaly of a planet is the angle between the perihelion, the sun, and the planet in the direction of the planet's motion.

ansi

American National Standards Institute: a US body that accredits organizations to write industrial standards – publicly available definitions, requirements, criteria, etc. Following the rules established by ANSI.

antenna

a conductor with the help of which electromagnetic waves are sent out or received.

antenna gain

is comparable study of the effectiveness of directional and non-directional antennas.

antiatom

an atom made up of antiprostate, antineutrons and positrons in the same way that an ordinary atom is made up of protons, neutrons and electrons.

antibaryon

one of a class of antiparticles, including the antinucleons and the antiperons, with strong interactions, baryon number -1, and hypercharge and charge opposite to those for the particles.

antibonding orbital

an atomic or molecular orbital whose energy increases as atoms are brought closer together, indicating a net repulsion rather than a net attraction and chemical bonding.

anti-coincidence

the phonemenon of occurrence of an event at a given place without any simultaneous event at another place is called anticoincidence.

antideutron

is the antiparticle to Deutron. It is composed of antineutron and antiproton.

antiferromagnetic substance

a substance composed of antiferromagnetic domains.

antiferromagnetic sesceptibility

the magnetic response to an applied magnetic field of a substance whose atomic magnetic moments are aligned in anti parallel fashion.

antiferromagnetism

the anti parallel alignment of successive magnetic moments in a substance. The susceptibility of such substances with rise in temperature upto a certain point, known as Neel temperature, above which the substance becomes paramagnetic.

antifriction

the process of minimising friction by various methods is called antifriction.

antigravity

the repulsion of one body by another by means of a gravitational type of force. This has been observed.

antimatter

matter composed of anti particles e.g. anti oxygen consists of eight anti protons and positrons that move around these in orbits.

antinodal line

a line which joins the antinodes in an interference pattern.

antinodal region

the term used for the area where two waves of the same wavelength and amplitude and travelling through a medium at identical speeds in directly opposite directions cancel out the effects of each other; these areas are separated from each other b half a wavelength.

antinodes

these are the points of maximum displacement in a stationary wave pattern. The distance between successive antinodes in a stationary wave is equal to one half of the wavelength.

antiparallel

having parallel lines of action that are directed in opposite directions.

antiparallel vectors

vectors that are directed along the same line but in opposite directions.

antiparticle

a generic term which is used for a sub-atomic particle which is identical with another sub-atomic particle in every characteristic and property, except that its electric charge and spin or magnetic moment, while being equal in magnitude to those of the latter, are opposite in sign, respectively direction

antiproton

is the antiparticle to the proton. It carries unti –ve charge, spin, half-life and mass equal to proton.

aperture

the size of the opening that admit light in an optical instrument. The effective diameter of mirror or lens.

aperture ratio

it is the ratio of the effective diameter of a lens to its focal length.

aphelion

the time, or point, in a planet's orbit when it is farthest from the sun. Aphelion is the opposite of perihelion.

aplanatic

refers to a reflecting or refracting surface which is aplantic with respect to two points a and b, if it produces a point image at b of an object placed at a, irrespective of the angle at which the rays fall on the surface from the object.

aplanatic lens

a lens that minimize both its astimatic and coma aberration.

apochromat

a technical term applied to photographic and microscope objectives indicating the highest degree of colour correction.

apogee

it is the greatest distance of a satellite from the earth during its orbit around the earth.

apparent change in weight of a body in lift

1. lift at rest or moving with uniform velocity: in such a case the apparent weight is the same as actual weight (w = mg).

2. Lift is moving upwards with an acceleration, a: the apparent weight is more than the actual weight.
actual weight = mg
apparent weight = m (g+a)
3. Lift is moving down wards wit an acceleration, a: in such a

case the apparent weight is less than the actual weight.
Apparent weight = m (g-a)
4. Lift is falling freely with an acceleration a = g: Man in lift will feel weight less.
Apparent weight = m (g-g) =0

apparent depth

the depth of a liquid in a vessel, for example, water in a pond, appears to be less than the actual depth due to the refraction of light. This visible or observed depth is called the apparent depth. The refractive index of the medium is given by,

$$\mu = \frac{\text{Real Depth}}{\text{Apparent Depth}}$$

apparent expansion

it is the directly observed expansion of a liquid being the difference between the actual expansion of a liquid and the expansion of the vessel containing it.

apparent force

the force introduced in a relative coordinate system in order that newton's laws be satisfied in the system. examples are the coriolis force and the centrifugal force incorporated in gravity.

apparent power

In any A.C. circuit, it is the product of root mean square (r.m.s) voltage and r.m.s. corrent.

apparent volume

the difference between the volume of a binary solution and the volume of the pure solvent at the same temperature.

apparent weight

it is equal to the true weight minus the weight of displaced fluid, in case of a body immersed in a fluid.

applications software

computer programs, or collections of programs, designed to meet the needs of the users of computer systems by directly contributing to the performance of specific roles.

approximation technique

a method used to solve a problem in mathematics, or its physical applications, that does not give an exact solution but that enables an approximate solution to be found.

aprochromatic

corrected for both, spherical and chromatic abberation.

aprochromatic lens

a lens designed to correct for chromatic aberration at three different wavelengths.

apocynthion

the point in the orbit around the moon of a satellite launched from the earth that is furthest from the moon. For a satellite launched from the moon the equivalent point is the a polune. Compare pericynthion.

apogee

the greatest distance of a satellite from the earth during its orbit around the earth.

apsides

the two points in an astronomical orbit that lie closest to and farthest from the centre of gravitational attraction. The line of apsides is the major axis of the ellipse.

aqueous

describing a solution in water.

aqueous humour

the liquid between the cornea and the lens in the eye.

arc

it refers to the luminous bridge that is formed in a gap between two conductors or terminals when they are separated.

archimedes'number

one of a dimensions group of numbers denoting the ration of gravitational force to viscouse force.

archimedes'principle

the apparent loss in the weight of a body when it is immersed in a fluid is equal to the weight of the fluid displaced by it.

argon laser

it is a highly monochromatic, coherent and collimated beam of a gas laser which comprises of ionized argon. The collimated beam has a wavelength of 4880 a and also contains infrared radiation.

argument

1. a sequence of logical propositions based on a set of premises and leading to a conclusion. 2. See complex number.

arithematic unit

the section of a computer in which arithematic and logical operations are performed.

armature

refers to the coils of a dynamo or an electric motor. A part of an electric machine wherein an e.m.f. is induced by a changing magnetic field, e.g. electromagnetic relay.

armature resistance

the ohmic resistance in the main current carrying windings of an electric generator of motor.

armor

metal sheath enclosing a cable, primarily for mechanical protection.

armored cable

an electrical cable provided with a sheath of metal primarily for mechanical protection.

armstrong oscillator

an oscillator circuit, invented by E.H. Armstrong in which both anode and grid circuits are tuned.

arrhenius theory of electrolytic dissociation

the theory states that the molecules of an electrolyte can give rise to two or more electrically charged atoms or ions.

artificial intelligence

a field of computing concerned with the production of programs that perform tasks requiring intelligence when draughts, forming plans, understanding speech and natural languages, interpreting images, reasoning, and learning.

artificial radioactivity

radioactivity produced by nuclear reactions. Various methods are available.

artificial satellite in geostationary orbit

$$r^3 = G.\frac{M.T^2}{4\pi^2}$$

or

$$r = \left[\frac{T^2 g R^2}{4\pi^2}\right]^{\frac{1}{3}}$$

where M = Mass of earth (5.98×10^{24} Kg)

T = Period of rotation of earth and evolution of satellite (6400 sec).

aspect ratio

in television, the ratio of the frame width to the frame height of the picture.

aspirator

a device used to produce a partial vacuum for high vacuum pumps. It is based on Bernoulli's principle and reduces the pressure in a vessel in a very short duration to about 2 cm of mercury.

astable circuit

refers to a multivibrator circuit that switches continuously ad regularly from one state to another.

astatic

is the factor or quality without orientation or directional characterisic.

astatic coils

two identical magnetic needles suspended on the same vertical axis with their N-ans S-poles pointinj in opposite directions.

astatic galvanometer

a sensitive form of moving-mangent galvanometer in which any effects of the earth's magnetic field are can called out. Two smalloppositely directed magnets are suspended at the centres of two oppositely wound coils. As its resultant moment on the magnets is zero, the earth's field has no effect and the only restoring torque on the magnets is that provided by the suspending fiber. This makes a sensitive but delicate instrument.

astatic pairs

it consists of two identical magnetic needles suspended on the same vertical axis with their N-and S-poles pointing in opposite directions. The rotating forces on the needles are equal and opposite. Astatic pairs are used in very sensitive galvanometers in which the current-carrying coils are wound round each needle in opposite directions. The current therefore rotates them both in the same direction so that external magnetic effects are cancelled out.

astatic pendulum

a pendulum which never attains the position of equilibrium.

asteroids

a number of small bodies that revolve around the sun between the orbits of Mars and Jupiter in a zone between 1.7 and 4.0 astronomical units from the sun.

asthenosphere

a layer of earth's mantle that underlies the lithosphere at a depth of about 70 km. The velocity of seismic waves is considerably reduced in the asthenosphere and it is though to be a zone of partial melting.

astigmatic lens

a planocylindrical, spherocylindrical or spherotoric lens used in eyeglasses to correct astigmatism. Also known as astigmat.

astigmatism

defect of an optical image where in the horizontal and vertical objects at the same distance from the lens do not get focused simultaneously as seen by an observer.

astigmatized

a device as attached to a range finder, for drawing out a point of light into a line or band.

astigmometer

an optical instrument which is used to measure the amount of astigmatism in an optical system.

Aston, Francis Willian

British chemist and physicist, who until 1910 worked at Mason College and then with J.J. Thomson at Cambridge University.

aston dark space

in a gas discharge the dark space in the immediate vicinity of the cathode, in which the emitted electrons have a velocity insufficient to excite the gas.

aston rule

the atomic weights of isotopes are approximately integers , and deviations of the atomic weights of the elements from integers are due to the presence of several isotopes with differing weights.

astroballistics

the study of phenomena arising out of the motion of a solid through a gas at speeds high enough to cause ablation for example, the interaction of a meteoroid with the atmosphere.

astrography

refers to that branch of astronomy which deals with the positions, composition and other characteristic of the stars.

astrolable

an ancient instrument used to determine the position and altitude of heavenly bodies.

astrology

it is the branch of science that is concerned with the study of influence of heavenly bodies on human affairs.

astrometry

the branch of astronomy

concerned with the measurement of the positions of the celestial bodies on the celestial sphere.

astron

a proposed thermonuclear device in which a deuterine plasma is confined by an axial magnetic field produced by a shell of relativistic electrons.

astronaut

any person who is engaged in or trained for space flight.

astronautics

the scientific study of travel outside the earth's atmosphere.

ustronomical

pertaining to astronomy.

astronomical camera

a camera designed to record either point sources extended sources or the spectra of celestial bodies.

astronomical photography

the use of the photographic process to record surface features of celestial objects, their positions and motions as their radiation and spectra.

astronomical spectroscopy

the use of spectrographs in conjunction with telescopes to obtain observational data on the velocities and physical conditions of astronomical objects.

astronomical telescope

a telescope designed for viewing astronomical objects.

astronomical unit

a unit of distance in astronomy in the solar system. It is equal to approximately 1.496×10^{11} metres that is the mean distance of the sun from the earth.

astronomy

the study of the universe beyond the earth's atmosphere. The main branches are astrometry, celestial mechanics, and astrophysics.

astrophysics

the study of the physical and chemical processes involving astronomical phenomena. Astrophysics deals with stellar sructure and evolution the properties of the interstellar medium and its interactions with stellar systems, and the structure and dynamics of systems of stars , and of systems of galaxies.

asymmetric

not identical on both sides of a central line.

asymptote

a line that a curve approaches but only touches at infinity.

asymptotic series

a series formed by the expansion of a function in the form $a_0 + a_1/x + a_2/x^2 + ... + a_n/x^n + ...$, such that the error resulting from terminating the series at the term a_n/x^n tends to zero more rapidly than $1/x^n$ as x tends to infinity. An asymptotic series expansion is not necessarily a convergent series.

athermanous bodies

bodies that absorb the heat radiation falling on them are known as athermanous bodies.

athermanous bodies

bodies which absorb the heat radiation falling on them are called athermanous bodies.

atmolysis

the separation of mixture of gases by using the difference in their rates of diffusion.

atmometer

an instrument used for the measurement of rate of evaporation of water.

atmosphere

refers to the body of air which surrounds the earth, defined at its outer limits by the actual presence of air particles but in such few numbers that collisions between them have been so rare as to make the force of gravity the only means of keeping them associated with air particles at lower altitude.

atmospheric drag

a major perturbation of close artificial satellite orbits caused by the resistance of the atmosphere; the peculiar effects are decreasing eccentricity, semidiameter and period.

atmospheric pressure

the pressure at any point in an atmospheres due solely to the weight of the atmospheric gases above the point concerned. Also known as barometric pressure.

atmospheric radio wave

radio wave that is propagated by reflection in the atmosphere; may include either the ionospheric wave or the tropospheric wave or both.

atmospherics

electrical discharges which take place in the atmosphere, causing crackling noise in radio receivers.

atom

the smallest particle of an element capable of taking part in a chemical reaction.

atom bomb

a nuclear weapon in which an explosion, caused by a fast uncontrolled nuclear fission reaction, is capable of causing widespread destruction. Its explosive power is comparable to that of tens of kilotons of t.n.t.

atom smasher

a popular name for an accelerator.

atomic bomb

a military weapon which utilizes the induced nuclear fission chain reaction of radioactive substance as its source of energy.

atomic charge

the electric charge of an ion equal to the number of electrons the atom has gained or lost in its ionization multiplied by he charge on one electron.

atomic clock

an apparatus used for measuring time by the frequency of radiation emitted or absorbed in transitions of atoms.

atomic cloud

the cloud of hot gases, smoke, dust, and other matter that is carried aloft after the explosion of a nuclear weapon in the air or near the surface, frequently has a mushroom shape.

atomic constants

the physical constants which play a fundamental role in atomic physics, including the electronic charge, electronic mass, speed of light, Avogadro number and Planck's constant.

atomic distance

the average distance between the centres of two atoms.

atomic energy

the constitutive internal energy of the atom which was absorbed when it was formed. Energy derived from the mass converted into energy in nuclear transformations.

atomic ground state

the state of lowest energy in which an atom can exist. Also known as atomic unexcited state.

atomic heat

refers to the thermal capacity of 1 gram-atom of an element, or the quality of heat required to raise the temperature of 1 gram atom of the element by 1°C.

atomic hydrogen maser

a maser in which dissociated hydrogen atoms from an electric discharge source are formed into a beam that undergoes selective magnetic processing; can be used as an atomic clock.

atomic magnetic movement

it is a megnetic moment (permanent or temporary) associated with an atom.

atomic mass

it is the mass of an atom of an element as compared to the mass of an atom of C - 12 taken as 12.

atomic mass unit

a mass equal to 1/12 of the mass of an atom of carbon-12, used as a unit of mass for expressing the masses of individual elements.

atomic magnet

the name is given to an atom which has a magnetic moment either in the ground state or in an excited state.

atomic number

it is equal to the number of protons present in the nucleus of an atom.

atomic orbitals

the volume containing all the points within a free atom at which the wave function of an electron has an appreciable magnitude.

atomic pile

a type of a nuclear reactor constructed by piling up graphite blocks and uranium rods.

atomic power plant

a means for converting stored nuclear energy into work, such as a nuclear electric power generating station.

atomic second

as defined in 1967, the duration of 9, 192, 631.770 periods of the radiation corresponding to the two hyper fine levels of the fundamental state of the atom of cesium-133.

atomic spectroscopy

the branch of physics concerned with the production, measurement and interpretation of spectra arising from either emission or absorption of electro-magnetic radiation by atoms.

atomic spectrum

the spectrum of radiations due to transitions between energy levels in an atom, either absorption or emission.

atomic standard

any supposedly immutable property of an atom, such as the wavelength or frequency of a characteristic spectral line in terms of which a unit of a physical quantity is defined.

atomic strecture

the arrangement of the parts of an atom, which consists or a massive positively charged nucleus surrounded by a cloud of electrons arranged in objects describable in terms of quantum mechanics.

atomic unit of energy

1. the potential energy of an electron in the first orbit in Bohr's theory of the hydrogen atom. It is given by e^2/a_0, where e is the electron's charge and a_0 the atomic unit of length. It is equal to 27.190 electron volts or 4.850×10^{-18} joule. 2. Rydberg. The tomic unit of energy is sometimes defined as one half of this value. This is the ionization potential of the hydrogen atom.

atomic unit of length

symbol: a_0. The radius of the first orbit in Bohr's theory of the hydrogen atom. It is equal to 5.29×10^{-9} metre.

atomic unit of mass

a unit of mass equal to rest mass of the electron, $9.1084 \pm 0.003 \times 10^{-31}$ kg.

atomic vibration

periodic, nearly harmonic changes in position of the atoms in a molecule giving rise to many properties of matter, including molecular spectra, heat capacity and heat condition.

atomic volume

the volume in the solid state of one mole of an element.

atomic weight

means the mean weight of the atoms of a given element expressed in terms of an atomic mass unit.

atomicity

the number of atoms per molecule of a compound. Methane, for instance has an atomicity of five.

atomiser

a device that is used for reducing liquids to a fine spray.

attenuate

means to reduce in force, intel sity etc.

attenuation

the reduction in power or intensity of radiation as it passes through matter. The reduction may be due to absorption or scattering of radiation.

attenuation equalizer

an electrical network used to provide compensation for attenuation distortion in a specific band frequencies.

attenuator

a network or transducer designed to reduce the amplitude of a wave without distorting it. It may be fixed or variable; a fixed attenuator is sometimes called a pad. Usually calibrated indecibels.

atto

symbol a. A prefix used in the metric system to denote 10^{-18}. For example, 10^{-18} second = 1 attosecond (as) a circuit.

audibility

the limits of audibility of the human ear are between about 20 hertz and 20 000 hertz. With increased age the upper limit falls quite considerably.

audibility curve

the limits of hearing represented graphically as an area by plotting the minimum audible density of a sine wave sound versus frequency.

audibility threshold

the sound intensity of a given frequency which is the minimum perceptible by a normal human ear under specified standard conditions.

audibility, limits of

the limits of frequencies that can be heard by the human ear. The lowest audible frequency is about 20 hz, and the highest frequency is 20,000 hz.

audible

loud enough to be heart.

audible tone

sound of a frequency which the average human can hear, ranging from 30 to 16000 hertz. Also known as audible frequency.

audio

of or pertaining to sound in the range of frequencies considered audible at reasonable listening intensifies to the a average young adult Westerner, approximately 15,000 to 20,000 hertz.

audio frequency

a frequency that lies in the range 20-20,000 hz and is audible to the human ear.

audio frequency transformer

is an iron core transformer used for coupling audio frequency circuits.

audio metry

the study of hearing ability by means of audiometers.

audio signal

an electric signal having the frequency of a mechanical wave that can be detected as a sound by the human ear.

audiogram

a graph depicting the percent hearing loss as a function of frequency.

audiology

the science of hearing.

audiometer

instrument for measuring human hearing.

audio-visual

involving both sight and sound.

audition

1. it refers to the sense or power of hearing. 2. It refers to a trial hearing given to an actor, musician, speaker etc.

auger effect

when a k electron is ejected from an atom, an outer electron can fall into the k shell and give up its energy in two ways.

auger electron

an electron that is expelled from an atom in the auger effect.

auger electron spectroscopy

the energy analysis of auger electrons produced when an excited atom relaxes by radiationless process after ionization by a high energy electron, ion or x-ray beam.

auger recombination

recombination of an electron and a hole in which no electromagnetic radiation is emitted and the excess energy and momentum of the recombining electron and hole are given up to another electron or hole.

aural signal

a signal that can be heard. The sound portion of a television signal.

auronal line

a prominent green line in the spectrum of the aurora at the wavelength of 5577 angstroms resulting from a certain forbidden transition of oxygen.

aurora

an intermittent electrical discharge that takes place in the rarefiedlupper atmosphere. Charged particles in the solar wind become rapped in the earth' magnetic field and move in helical paths allong the lines of force between the two magnetic poles. So on entering the upper atmospere the charged particles excite the air molecules and cause and emission of light. The intensity of the aurora is greatest in polar regions although it is seen in temperate zones.

aurora borealis

a display of coloured light glows mainly red and green, visible in the regions of the north and south poles. The aurora borealis provides an impressive plasma display in earth's upper atmosphere.

auto starter

automatic starting and switch over penerating system consisting of a stand by generator coupled to the station load through an automatic power transfer control unit.

auto transformer

a transformer in which part of the winding is common to both primary and secondary circuits.

autoelectric effect

the emission of electrons from a cold cathode subjected to a strong electric field.

autoemission

autoelectronic emission.

autoionization

it is a form of ionization. It involves two steps, the excitation of an atom (or molecule) into a state with an energy above its ionization potential and de-excitation from this state to give a positive ion wit a lower energy and an ejected electron. Autoionization results in a singly charged positive ion A : A $\rightarrow$ A + e, where A is an excited atom. The electron ejected has a characteristic energy equal to the difference between the energy of the excited atom and that of the ion.

autoluminescence

luminescence of a material

resulting from energy originating within the material itself.

automatic cutout

a device usually operated by centrifugal force or by an electromagnet, that automatically shorts part of a circuit at a particular time.

automatic data processing

refers to the processing of information by electronic computers.

automatic focus

a device in a camera or enlarger which automatically keeps the objective lens in focus through a range of magnification.

automatic frequency control

refers to a method that automatically maintains the frequency of any source of alternating voltage within specified limit.

automatic gain control

a method that automatically holds the output volume constant in a radio receiver, despite changes in the input signal.

automatic short circuiter

device designed to automatically short circuit the commutator bars in some form of single phase commutator motors.

autoradiograph

if a thin specilen of metal, biological tissue, etc., is labelled with a radioisotope and placed in contact with a photographic plate for a suitable exposure time an image is produced by the action of the radiation emitted. On developing the film, known as an autoradiograph, the distribution of the radioisotope in the specimen can be seen.

autotransductor

a transductor wherein the same windings are used for the main and control currents.

autotransformer

a transformer having a single winding tapped at intervals, instead of two or more independent windings tapped at intervals, instead of two or more independent windings. The voltage drop across each tapped section is related to the total applied voltage in the same proportion as the number of turns of the section is related to the total number of turns of the winding.

auxillary switch

a switch actuated by the main

device for signalling interlocking or other purposes.

avalanche

a stream of formed by collision of a high energy ionising particle with matter. The electrons and the ions formed in the first collision ionize more atoms and the process continues.

avalanche breakdown

of a semiconductor diode, a break down caused by the cumulative multiplication of carriers resulting from field induced impact ionization. See zanier breakdown.

average

1. the arithmetic average of a set of n numbers is the sum of the numbers divided by n. 2. The geometric average of a set of n numbers is the nth root of their product. See also root-mean-square value.

average file

it is equal to the sum of the life times of all atoms divided by the total number of atoms.

average life or lifetime

mean life.

average velocity

a ratio of distance to time.

avogadro constant

symbol N_A or L. The number of atoms or molecules in one mole of substance. It has the value 6.022 1367(36) $\times 10^{23}$. Formerly it was called avogadro's number.

avogadro's hypothesis

equal volumes of all gases contain the same number of molecules at the same temperature and pressure.

avogadro's law

equal volumes of all gases contain the same number of molecules at the same temperature and pressure.

avogadro's number, n

it refers to a constant. Its value is 6.023 $\times 10^{23}$.

axial flow

flow of fluid through an axially symmetric device such that the direction of flow is along the axis symmetry flow.

axial jet

a flowing turbulent stream which mixes with standing water in three dimensions.

axial lead

a wire lead extending from the end along the axis of a resistor, capacitor, or other component.

axial ratio

the relative lengths of the three edges of the unit cell of a crystal lattice, taking that of the b axis as unity.

axis

a line around which a given body or system rotates.

axis of rotation

a straight line passing through the points of a rotating rigid body that remain stationary, while the other points of the body move in circles about the axis.

axis of symmetry

a line about which a given figure is symmetrical.

ayrton shunt

a small resistance which is connected across a galvanometer to increase its range without changing the damping.

azeotrope (azeotropic mixture; constant-boiling mixture)

a mixture of two liquids that boils at constant composition; i.e. the composition of the vapour is the same as that of the liquid. Azeotropes occur because of deviations in Raoult"s law leading to a maximum or minimum in the boiling-point-composition diagram. When the mixture is boiled, the vapour initially has a higher proportion of one component than is present in the liquid, so the proportion of this in the liquid falls wit time. Eventually, the maximum and minimum point is reached, at which the two liquids distil together without change in composition. The composition of an azeotrope depends on the pressure.

azeotropic mixture

a mixture of two liquids that boils without any change in composition. The properties of components in vapour are the same as in the liquid. Azeotropic mixtures cannot be separated by distillation.

azimuth

refers to position as measured by an angle round some fixed point or pole.

azimuth marker

a bright radial line on the cathode-ray oscilloscope of a radar set.

azimuth resolution

angle or distance by which two

targets must be separated in azimuth to be distinguished by a radar set, when the targets are at the same range.

azimuthal quantum number

it is one of the series of Quantum Numbers accompanied by Principal quantam number, Magnetic and spin quantam Numbers.

B

it is used as a symbol for flux density in a magnetic circuit.

b

it is used as a symbol for susceptance in a.c. circuit.

babbit metal

any of a group of related alloys used for making bearings. They consist of tin containing antimony (about 10%) and copper (1-2%), and often lead. The original alloy was invented in 1839 by the US inventor Isaac Babbit (1799-1862).

babcock coefficient of friction

it is an approximation to the coefficient of friction for steam flowing in a circular pipe of diameter d inches, given by 0.0027 (1+3.6/d).

babinet compensator

two narrow angle wedges of quartz having parallel refracting edges and hypotenuse faces adjacent, cut in such a manner that their poetic axes perpendicular and parallel to the refracting edges. At one prism opposes the effect of the other with respect to ordinary and extraordinary components, although outwardly a parallel slab, the effect across the plate will be one of different thickness. If the prisms slide over one another maintaining parallel thickness. If the prisms slide over one another maintaining parallel edges, the effect of a different thickness at one point may be obtained. Linearly or elliptically polarized light of different path differences can be produced as desired.

babinet point

it is a neutral point and is located about 20 degree directly above the sun.

babinet's principle

the diffraction patterns obtained from a complementary pair of diffraction screen, that is two screens in which the opaque parts of one are replaced by transparent parts in the other, are the same.

babo's law

the lowering of the vapour pressure of a solvent by the addition of a non-volatile solute is proportional to the concentration of the solute.

back bond

a chemical bond between an atom in the surface layer of a solid and another atom in the second layer.

back e.m.f.

the e.m.f. set up in an electrolytic cell, when its poles become polarized. It opposes the natural e.m.f. of the cell.

back echo

an echo signal which is produced on a radar screen by one of its minor back lobes from the main radar beam.

back electromotive force

an e.m.f. which opposes the normal flow of current in an electric circuit.

back flow

the term is commonly used in fluid mechanics and refers to the flow of a fluid in a direction opposite to its natural direction of flow.

back focal length

the distance between the last surface of a system and the second principal focus.

back ground

it refers to the totality of effects that tend to obscure a phenomenon under investigation and above which the phenomenon must be detected.

back lash

refers to any sudden or forceful or reaction.

back pressure

pressure due to a force that is operating in a direction opposite to that being considered, such as that of a fluid flow.

back scatter

the scattering process in which radiation emerges from the same surfaces of a material as that through which it enters.

back scattering

the scattering into the sensitive part of a measuring instrument of radioactive radiations which originally has no component of motion towards that part.

background luminance

the brightness of the background against which a target is viewed.

background noise

the term is used for unwanted residual sound, which is present whether or not the sound source being studied is in operation.

background radiation

low intensity ionizing radiation present on the surface of the earth and in the atmosphere as a result of consmic radiation and the presence of radioisotopes in the earth's rocks, soli, and atmosphere. The radioisotopes are either natural or the result of nuclear fallout or waste gas from power stations. Background counts must be taken into account when measuring the radiation produced by a specified source.

backup

a resource that can be used as a substitute in the event of, say, a fault in a component or system or loss of data from a computer file. A backup file is a copy of a file taken in case the original is destroyed or unintentionally altered and the data lost.

backup relay

it is a relay designed to protect a power system in case a primary relay fails to operate as desired.

backward scatter

refers to the scattering wherein the radiation emerges out from the same surface of a material as that through which it enters.

badger rule

an empirical relationship between the force constants and the vibrational frequencies of electron orbits in diatomic molecules.

baffle

a device used to deflect oil or gas in a circuit-breaker.

baily's beads

just before a solar eclipse becomes total, the advancing dark limb of the moon appears to break up into a series of bright points.

bairstow number

a term which was previously used for Mach number.

balance

a device used to find the mass of an object. It consists of a lever, two equal arms with a pan suspended at the end of each arm.

balance, physical

it is used to weigh the mass of an object. It consists of a lever having two equal arms with a pan suspended at the end of each arm. The weights should be placed in the left pan and the masses in the right pan. A Rider could be used for weighing small masses.

balanced currents

currents flowing in the two conductors of a balanced line which at every point along the line are equal in magnitude and opposite in direction.

balanced network

hybrid network in which the impedances of the opposite branches are equal.

balanced transmission line

transmission line having equal conductor resistance per unit length and equal impedances from each conductor to earth and to other electrical circuits.

balanced voltages

voltages that are equal in magnitude and opposite in polarity with respect to ground.

balancer

a mechanism for equalizing the loads on the outer lines of a three-wire system for electric power distribution.

ballast

a circuit element that serves to limit an electric current or to provide a starting voltage, as in certain types of lamps.

ballast lamp

a light-producing electrical resistance device which maintains nearly constant current by increasing in resistance as the current increases.

ballast resistor

a specially designed resistor whose resistance increases as current passing through it increases and decreases as current passing through it decreases.

ballistic camera

a ground-based camera which is used to record the trajectory of a rocket on the same plate using multiple exposures.

ballistic curve

the curve described by the path of a bullet, a bomb, or other projectile.

ballistic entry

movement of a ballistic body without to within a planetary atmosphere.

ballistic galvanometer

the term used for an instrument which is able to measure the total electric charge passing through it in a sudden pulse of current. It has been a moving-coil instrument which is constructed and calibrated so that the maximum deflection of the pointer has been proportional to the total charge that has passed.

ballistic missile

a ground-to-ground missile with a parabolic flight path. A missile which is propelled and guided only during the starting phase of its flight.

ballistic pendulum

it is a heavy pendulum and is used to measure the velocity of a projectile. The pendulum is struck by the projectile whose velocit can be calculated by measuring the resultant displacement of the pendulum using the law of conservation of momentum.

ballistic trajectory

the path followed by a body being acted upon only by gravitational forces and resistance of the medium through which it passes.

ballistic wave

an audible disturbance caused by compression of air ahead of a missile in flight.

ballistic wind

wind which produces the same effect upon the trajectory of a projectile as the actual wind encountered in light.

ballistics

the study of path of projectiles.

ball lightning

a white or reddish luminous sphere, about 50 cm in diameter, that sometimes appears at ground level in a thunderstorm. Ball lightning is slow moving and usually disappears without detonation.

balmer

a term sometimes used for the unit of wave-number, i.e., it is the number of waves in a centimetre and has units of cm. See also Redbridge and KaYser.

balmer series

a series of spectral lines of the hydrogen atom corresponding to electrons jumping from higher allowed orbits to second allowed energy level (n = 2). The wave lengths of radiations in this series are given by

$$\frac{1}{\lambda} = \bar{v} = R\left[\frac{1}{2^2} - \frac{1}{2_2^2}\right], n_2 = 3, 4, 5$$

· R is the Raydberg's constant and is equal to

$\frac{2\pi^2 me^4}{ch^3}$. The value or R is $1.0967758 \times 10^7 m^{-1}$.

band

a restricted range in which the energies of electrons in solids lie.

band gap

sometimes called as forbidden gap, it is an energy difference between two allowed bands of electron energy in a metal.

band spectrum

in such a spectrum there appears a number of bands of emitted or absorbed radiations. This type of spectrum are characteristic of molecules. Generally a band can be resolved into a number of closely spaced lines.

band theory

explains the quantum mechanical treatment of the crystalline state.

bandwidth

the frequency range over which a radio signal of specified frequency spreads

bar

unit of pressure in the c.g.s. system of units. It is equal to the pressure exerted by a mercury column 76 cm long and its value is 10 dyne/cm.

barium fuel cell

a cell which comprises barium with either chlorine or oxygen to transform chemical energy into electrical energy.

barium meal

a white crystalline insoluble powder m.p. 1580 degree c, used as a pigment and since it is opaque to x-rays form the basis of barium meal in x-ray diagnosis.

bark contact

normally closed stationary contact on a relay that is opened when the rely is energized.

barkhausen effect

refers to a discontinuous variation inmagnetization in ferromagnetic substances because the magnetizing force has been continuously increased or decreased.

barlow lens

a planococoncave lens placed between the objective and eyepiece in a telescope. It increase magnification.

barmagnet

a straight permanent magnet with north and south pole at two ends.

barn

it is a unit of area. It is generally used for measuring nuclear cross section.

1 barm = 10^{-24} cm^2.

barnett effect

it is a phenomena of development of a slight magnetization in an initially unmagnetized iron rod when it is rotated at a high speed about its axis.

baroclinic

of, pertaining to, or characterized by baroclinity.

baroclinity

the state of stratification in a fluid in which surfaces of constant pressure intersect surfaces of constant density.

barodynamics

the mechanics of heavy structures which may collapse under their own weight.

barograph

a recording barometer. It consists of an aneroid barometer operating a pen which traces a line on a sheet of graph paper mounted on a slowly revolving drum.

barometer

an instrument which is used for measuring atmospheric pressure. Commonly used barometer is the fortin's barometer. It consists of a long tube closed at the upper end and filled with mercury and inverted in a vessel containing mercury.

barometric

is a term used loosely pertaining to the atmospheric pressure.

barometric height

the height of liquid column in a barometer, because the commonly used liquid is mercury and the barometric height is thus generally expressed in terms of mm of mercury. The standard value of atmospheric pressure is 760 mm of hg.

barometric pressure

atomospheric pressure.

barometric surface

a surface which has the same

barometric pressure at all points.

baromil

unit of length which is used in graduating a mercury barometer in the c.g.s. system of units.

barostat

a constant pressure device that compensates for changes of atmospheric pressure.

baron counter tube

a counter tube filled with baron floride or having electrodes coated with baron or boron compounds; used for detecting slow neutrons.

barotropy

the state of a fluid in which surfaces of constant density are coincident with surfaces of constant pressure.

barretter

an instrument used for stabilizing voltage, consisting of a sensitive metallic resistor whose resistance increases with temperature. The resistor is usually enclosed in a glass bulb.

barrier

this term is used for potential barrier.

barrow

it is a flat, rectangular frame that is used for carrying a load.

bartlett force

an exchange force between nucleons in which spin is exchanged.

barycentre

the centre of mass of a system.

barye

a former c.g.s. unit of pressure. 1 barye = 0.1 pascal.

baryon

the nucleons and other fermions that decay into nucleons by the emission of mesons. All baryons have a mass equal to or strong interactions. A quantum number, knowns as the baryon number (B), may be defined in such a way that baryons have baryon number B = 1, antibaryons B = -1, and all other particles B = 0. The total baryon number is conserved in all particle ineractions. Baryons are thought to be composed of three tightly bound quarks, anti-baryons of three anti-quarks.

baryon number

a conserved quantum number equal to the number of baryons minus the number of antibaryons in a system; neutrons and protons have baryon number one; mesons and leptons have baryon number zero.

baryon spectroscopy

the science of the energy levels and changes of state occurring among baryon particles.

baryons

a group of heavy elementary particles, which includes protons and neutrons. The baryons form a subclass of the hadrons. They are further subdivided into nucleons and hyperons.

base

the region in a juction transistor that separate the emitter and collector, to which the base electrode is attached.

base magnification

the ratio of the distance between the centres of the objectives of a pair of binoculars to the distance between the centres of the eyepieces.

base pressure

the pressure exerted on the base end of a body.

base unit

a unit that is defined arbitrarily rather than being defined by simple combinations of other units. For example, the ampere is a base unit in the SI system defined in terms of the force produced between two current-carrying conductors, whereas the coulomb is a derived unit, defined as the quantity of charge transferred by one ampere in one second.

basic frequency

frequency in any wave which is considered the most important.

bass

the low frequency part of the audio-frequency spectrum, below about 250 hz.

bathymetry

measurement of depth, especially of the sea.

battery

refers to a combination of two or more galvanic cells which are electrically connected to work together to produce electrical energy.

battery charger

it is a rectifier used for changing A.C. into D.C. for charging a storage battery.

baud

a unit for measuring single speed in a computer or

communications system. When the signal is a sequence of bits, the baud rate is given in bits per second. The unit is named after J.M.E. Baudot (1845-1903).

baume scale

refers to a hydrometric scale which is used for measuring the density of liquids. There have been two separate scales. Fine of which is used with liquids. There have been two separate scales, one of which is used with liquids heavier than water, sinks to 0 degrees in pure water, and 15 degrees in a 15% salt solution; the other, for liquids lighter than water, sinks to 0 degrees in a 1% salt solution, and to ten degrees in pure water.

bcs theory

it is the most successful theory for superconductivity. This was developed by Bardeen, Cooper and Schrieffer in 1975, known as bcs theory.

bead

it is a glass, ceramic or plastic insulator through which if a bare wire passes, it protects other bodies from electrification.

beam

the locus of all series of wavefronts projected from the source and directed toward given objects or positions in space.

beam hole

a hole through the shield, and usually the reflector of a nuclear reactor which allows a beam of radiation, especially fast neutrons, to escape for experimental purposes.

beam splitter

a mirror that reflects part of a beam of light falling on it and transmits part.

bearing capacity

load per unit area which can be safely supported by the ground.

bearing pressure

load on a bearing surface divided by its area. Also known as bearing stress.

bearing strain

the deformation of parts subjected to a load.

beat

refers to the periodic variation of the amplitude of a wave phenomenon because of the interference of two waves of the same nature but of different frequencies. In sound, this term refers to the regular alteration of strengthening and fading of the auditory sensation as the sound waves given out by two acoustic sources differing slightly in frequency alternately reinforce and cancel out each other.

beat frequencies

the different frequency produced by the intermodulation of two frequencies. It refers to number of beats per second.

beating

the combination of two or more frequencies to produce beats.

beaufort scale

a scale used in meteorology in which successive values of wind velocities are assigned numbers ranging from o (calm) to 12 (hurricane) to indicate wind forces. Numbers 13-17 are often added to indicate specific hurricane speeds.

beck hydrometer

a type of hydrometer generally used to measure the relative density of liquids lessdense than water. Such a hydrometer is graduated in degrees Beck, where Beck = 20 (l-relative density).

beckmann thermimeter

it is a mercury thermometer. It is used to measure small changes in temperature with great precision.

becquerel

symbol Bq. The SI unit of activity (see radiation units). The unit is named after the discoverer of radioactivity A.H. Becquerel.

becquerel effect

if two similar electrodes are immersed in an electrolyte, a current flows when one of the electrodes is illuminated.

becquerel rays

the radiation discovered by H. Becquerel to be emitted by uranium. Although uranium emits alpha, beta and gamma rays, they were beta rays which Becquerel detected using a photographic plate.

beer-lambert law

the proportion of light absorbed by a dilute liquid medium changes exponentially with the product of the path length of the light in the medium, the molar concentration, and the molecular extinction coefficient.

beilby layer

a microcrystalline or amorphous layer formed on the surface of metals by polishing.

bel

the fundamental division of logarithmic scale for expressing the ratio of two amounts of power, the number of bels denoting such a ratio being the logarithm to the base 10 of this ratio.

bell metal

a type of bronze used in casting bells. It consists of 60-85% copper alloyed with tin, often with some zinc and lead included.

bellows

an accordion like component of a camera which forms a passage between the lens and the film and allows one to vary the distance between them.

bending moment

the bending moment about any point in a loaded beam is the algebriac sum of the moments of all the vertical forces to one side of that point.

bending stress

it stands for internal tensile or compressive longitudinal stress developed in a beam in response to curvature induced by an external load.

benedick' effect

an e.m.f. produced in a closed circuit, made up of one metal only, under asymmetrical temperature sistribution. The effect is not present if the metal is spectroscopically pure and free from internal strain.

berkelium

symbol Bk. A radioactive metallic transuranic element belonging to the actinoids; a.n. 97; mass number of the most stable isotope 247 r.d. 14. There are eight known isotopes. It was first produced by G.T. Seeaborg and associates in 1949 by bombarding americium–241 with alpha particles.

bernoullei's theorem

if a small amount of an incompressible liquid flows from one point to another without any friction, its total energy remains the same through out the displacement.

Mathematically

$$p + p.\ h.\ g. + \frac{1}{2} p\ v^2 = \text{constant.}$$

Bernoulli, Daniel

(1700-82) Swiss mathematician. In 1724 he published a work on differential equations, which earned him a professorship at St Petersburg. He returned to Basel, Switzerland, in 1733 and began researches on hydrodynamics, the work for which he is best known.

bernoulli's effect

there occurs a decrease in the pressure of the liquid as the velocity of the fluid increases. Thus in the region where the pressure in less, the liquid will flow through with large velocity and vice-versa.

bernoulli theorem

at any point in a pipe through which a fluid is flowing the sum of the pressure energy, the kinetic energy, and the potential energy of a given mass of the fluid is constant.

berthelot's equation of state

the equation.

$$\left(p+\frac{a}{Tv^2}\right)(v-b)=RT$$

berthelot principle

it states that a chemical reaction can only occur spontaneously if accompanied by an evolution of heat. It has numerous exdceptions.

Berzelius, Jons Jacob

(1779-1848) Swedish chemist. After moving to Stockholm he worked with mining chemists and, with them, discovered several elements, including cerium (1803), selenium (1817), lithium (1818), thorium (1828), and vanadium (1830). He also worked on atomic weights and electrochemistry.

bessel functions

a power series in x which are solution of a linear differential equation of the form

$$x^2\frac{d^2y}{dx^2}+x\frac{dy}{dx}+(x^2-n^2)y=0$$

They are put to many applications in physics, for example in problems of heat conduction, etc.

beta current gain factors

symbol : β. The short-circuit current amplification factor of a transistor with common-emitter connection given by :

$$\beta=\left(\frac{\partial iC}{\partial iB}\right)_{VCEconstant}$$

Where iC is the collector current and iB is the base current. β is always greater than unity and can takes values up to 500.

beta decay

radioactive decay involving the emission of an electron. The atomic number of the nucleus changes by one whereas its mass number remains beta decay.

beta factor

the term is used in plasma physics. It is defined as the ratio of the plasma kinetic pressure to the magnetic pressure.

beta interactions

this term is used for weak interactions.

beta-iron

a nonmagnetic allotrope of iron that exists between 768^{0}C and 900^{0}C.

beta-ironta

a nonmagnetic allotrope of iron that exists between 768^{0}C and 900^{0}C.

beta particles

fast moving negatively charged electrons. They are emitted with a range the velocities from the atomic nuclei; the maximum velocity may be quite close to the velocity of light.

beta rays

stream of beta particles possessing large penetrating powers.

beta tramsformation

beta process, beta decay. The transformation effected by the emission of a beta particle. A beta transformation produces a unit change of atomic number but no change of mass number.

betatron

a particle accelerator used to accelerate a beam of electrons using an electrical field arising due to a changing magnetic field.

bev

a billion electron volts, a unit in the U.S., international unit, which has the same value.

bevatron

refers to the designate of a high-energy proto accelerator which is able to impart energies of several billions of electrons volts to positively charged sub-atomic particles.

bhabha scattering

scattering of positrons by electrons.

bias

it refers to the steady voltage inserted in series with an element of an electronic device as of a vacuum tube or transistor.

bias, bias voltage

voltage applied permanently to the control grid of a vacuum tube so as to make it permanently negative.

bias grid

refers to the potential applied to the grid of a themionic valve with respect to the cathode.

bias, resistor

a resistor across which a bias voltage is developed.

biaxial

having two axis.

biaxial crystal

a type of birefringent crystal having two axes parallel to which the ordinary ray and the extraordinary ray travel at the same speed.

biconcave (biconvex) lens

a lens having two concave (convex) surfaces.

bidirectional antenna

an antenna that radiates or receives most of its energy in only two directions.

bifilar resistor

a specially disigned resistor wound with a wire doubled back on itself to minimise the effect of inductance.

bifilar winding

a method of winding a resistance wire to form non-inductive resistors, the wire is doubled back on itself and wound double from the looped end.

bifocal lens

a lens with two parts having different focal lengths. An eyeglass lens having one part that corrects for distant vision and one part for near vision.

big-bang

the cosmological theory that all the matter and energy in the universe originated from a state of enormous density and temperature that exploded at a finite moment in the past. See Feature (pp 38-39).

big-bang theory

states that about 10 billion years ago, all the matter of the universe was packed into superdense small agglomeration, subsequently being hurled in all directions at enormous speeds by a cataclysmic explosion.

bilateral

located on opposite sides of an axis.

bilateral slit

a slit used in spectrometer. It consists of two metal strips whose separations can be accurately adjusted.

billet split lens

a lens cut in two, in such a way that the optical centres of the semi-lenses are slightly displaced laterally; As a result two real images of a slit are formed and in the overlapping region in front of these (coherent) images interference occurs.

billion

formerly in the UK, one million, 10^{12}, but the US meaning of one thousand million, 10^9, has now been adopted worldwide.

bimetallic

made up of two metals.

bimetallic strip

a strip made of two metals joined together so that an increase of temperature causes it to bend towards one side. It is based on the unequal coefficient of expansion of the metals.

bimorph cell

two plates of piezo-electric material joined together so that they bend in proportion to an applied voltage.

binary notation

it is a change of decimal (0 — 9) system to Binary (0 and 1) system such as :

Decimal	Binary
0	000
1	001
2	010
3	011
4	100
5	101
6	110
7	111
8	1000
9	1001
10	1011
12	1100
13	1101
14	1110
15	1111

binary star

a system of two stars which revolve around a common centre of gravity.

binding energy

the binding energy of the nucleus may be defined as the quantity of energy released when nucleons combine to from an atomic nucleus, or conversely, as the energy required to distrupt a given nucleus. It has been the energy which has been equivalent of the mass defect, on the basis of I a.m.u. = 931 MeV.

binding energy of nucleus

it refers to the energy, equivalent to the difference between the mass of a nucleus and the sum of the masses of its constituent protons and neutrons. Binding energy for $_ZX^A$ equals $[Zm_p + (A - Z) m_n - M]$, where m_p, m_n and M are the masses for proton, neutron and nucleus respectively.

bingham fliud

a substance which remains rigid under a shear stress until the magnitude of the stress exceeds the yield stress, whereupon the substance flows like a newtonian liquid.

binocular

any optical instrument designed for the simultaneous use of both eyes, e.g., binocular field-glasses.

binocular vision

the ability, found only in animals with forward-facing eyes, to produce a focued image of the same object simultaneously on the retinas of both eyes. This permits three-dimensional vision and contributes to distance judgement.

binomial theorem

a rule for the expansion of a binomial expression. The general binomial expression $(x+y)^n$ expands to:

$x^n+nx^{n-1}y+[n(n-1)/2!]x^{n-2}y^2+...y^n$.

bioconcave (convex) lens

it is a double concave (convex) lens.

bioenergetics

the study of the flow and the transformations of energy that occur in living organisms. Tpically, the amount of energy that an organism takes in (from food or sunlight) is measured and divided in the amount used for growth of new tissues;

biological shield

a radiation absorbing shield used to protect personnel from the effects of radiation in the vicinity of a nuclear reactor.

bioluminescence

the emission of light without heat by living organisms. The phenomenon occurs in glow-worms and fireflies, bacteria and fungi, and in many deep-sea fish (among others); in animals it may serve as a means of protection (e.g. by disguising the shape of a fish) or species recognition or it may provide mating signals. The light is produced during the oxidation of a compound called luciferin (the composition of which varies according to their species), the reaction being catalysed by an enzyme, liciferase. Bioluminescence may be continuous (e.g. in bacteria) or intermittent (e.g. in fireflies).

bionics

the application of electronics to the study of biology.

biophysics

the application of physics to the study of biology.

biot-fourier equation

it explains the equaton of conduction of heat through a solid:

$$\frac{\partial Q}{\partial t} = \frac{\lambda}{cp} \nabla^2 T.$$

$\frac{\partial Q}{\partial t}$ is the rate of heat flow, λ is therm conduct. c is sp. heat, p is av. density and ∇^2 T is temp gradient.

biot-savart law

according to this law, the elemental field strength dB at a point disant r from a current element Id/ infree space may be given by:

$$dH = \frac{i.\,dl.\,\sin\theta}{r^2} \text{oersteds}$$

$$\text{or } H = \int \frac{i.\,dl.\,\sin\theta}{r^2} \text{oersteds}$$

$$B = \int \frac{\mu.\,i.\,d.\,\sin\theta}{r^2} \text{gauss.}$$

This field is perpendicular to both the current and the radius vector.

biot's law

the degree of rotation of the plane of polarization of light propagated through an optically active medium is inversely proportional (approximately) to the square of the wave-length of the light and directly proportional to the path length in the medium and to the concentration if the medium is a loquid.

bipod

a two legged support.

bipolar

having two poles or containing charges of opposite polarity.

bipolar electrode

electrode, without metrical connection with the current supply, one face of which acts as anode surface and the opposite face as a cathode surface when an electric current is passed through a cell.

bipolar transistor

a transistor having both

electrons and holes play an essential part, e.g. a junction transistor.

biparous interference

light interference fringes seen on screen near a baprism.

biprism

a glass prism with an obtuse angle that functions as two acuteangle prisms placed base-to-base. A double image of a single object is thus formed; the device was used by fresnel to produce two coherent beams for interference experiments.

biprism fresnel's

fresnel's biprism.

biprism interference

stands for interference fringes of light seen on a screen placed near a biprism.

biquartz

a device consisting of two adjoining pieces of quartz of equal thickness that rotate the plane of polarization of light in opposite directions.

birefringence

this term is used for splitting of a light beam into two components, which travel at different velocities, b a material. It happens when light passes through a calcite crystal.

birefringent crystal

refers to a crystal that is able to split incident transmitted light into two beams each polarized perpendicularly to the other.

birefringent filter

a filter consisting of alternate layers of polarizing films and plates cut from a birefingent crystal; transmits light in a series of sharp, widely spaced wavelength bands.

birefringent plate

a piece of birefringent optic material with parallel plane surfaces.

biscope

it was an early form of motion picture projector.

bistable

bistable multivibrator. A type of circuit having two stable states.

bit

either of the digits 0 or 1 as used in the binary notation. Bits are therefore that basic unit of information in a computer system.

bitter pattern

refers to a microscopic pattern of domain boundaries on a ferromagnetic surface, which is made visible by painting the surface with colloidal suspension of very small iron particles.

black

quality of an object which uniformly absorbs large percentages of light of all visible wavelengths.

black body

a substance that asborbs all the radiation falling on it. Its absorptance and emissivity are both equal to 1.

black body radiation

refers to the radiation emitted by a black body. It generally covers the entire wavelength range, the exact distribution of power depends on the temperature of the body.

blackbody radiations

the emission of radiant energy which would take place from a blackbody at a fixed temperature.

blackbody temperature

the temperature of a black body that emits the same amount of heat radiation per unit area as a given object.

black-coated mirror

glass with a reflective coating applied against the rear surface.

black hole

a region of space-time from which nothing can escape, according to classical physics.

black, joseph

(1728-99) British chemist and physician, born in France. He studied at Glasgow and Edinburgh, where his thesis (1754) contained the first acurate description of the chemistry of carbon dioxide. In 1757 he disco ered loatent heat, and was the first to distinguish between hear and temperature.

black light

the term is referred to an invisible light which when incident-upon fluorescent materials enables them to emit visible light.

blackout

the shutting off of power in an electrical power transmission system.

blanket

a layer of fertile material that surrounds the core of a nuclear reactor either for that purpose of breeding new fuel or to reflect some of the neutrons back into the core.

blanzed grating

a diffraction grating so calibrated that the reflected light is concentrated into a few, or even a single order of the spectrum.

blast

the brief and rapid movements of air or other fluid away from a centre of outward pressure, as in explosion.

blast effect

violent air movements and pressure changes and the destruction resulting the reform generally caused by an explosion.

blast pressure

the impact pressure of the air set in motion by an explosion.

blast wave

is a kind of air wave set in motion by an explosion.

bleeder resistor

a resistor permanently connected across the output of a power supply.

blind spot

the region of the retina in the eye where the optic nerve leaves the eye.

blink

a unit of time equal to 0.864 second.

blister

a protuberance that sometimes develops on the surface of a nuclear-reactor fuel element during use generally because of entrapped gases.

bloch's law

all flashes of light shorter than some critical duration cause equal effects on the eye. However, many quanta are contained within a flash. The critical duration is approximately thirty milliseconds.

bloch's theorem of supercnductivity

Bloch proved that the lowest state of a quantum mechanical system in the absence of a magnetic field can carry no current.

bloch wall

the boundary of region inside a ferromagnetic material where in the magnetic moments point in nearly the same direction.

block diagram

a diagram in which the vital units of any system are drawn in the form of blocks, usually rectangular.

block wall

the boundary of regions inside a ferromagnetic material in which the magnetic moments point in nearly the same direction.

blocking layer photocell

rectifier photocell.

blocking oscillator

a type of oscillator in which, after completion of one cycle of oscillation, blocking takes place for a period of time determined by the circuit constants.

bloom

colour of oil in reflected light.

blooming

a method of coating lenses to reduce back reflection from their surfaces. It involves destructive interference in the thin layer.

blooming of lenses

depositing of a transparent film of lower refractive index on the surface of a lens of higher index, so that surface reflection is eliminated.

blown-fuse indicator

a neon warning light connected across a fuse so that it lights when the fuse is blown.

blowout

the melting of an electric fuse because of excessive current.

blue

the hue evoked in an average observer by monochromatic radiation having a wavelength in the range from 455 to 492 manometers.

board of trade unit

a unit of energy equivalent to the kilowatt hour. It was formerly used in the U.K. for the sale of electricity.

body burden

the amount of radioactive material present in the body of an individual is called body burden.

body capacitance

is that which is formed between the human hand or body and a circuit.

body-centred

crystal structure in which the atoms occupy the centre of the lattice as well as the vertices.

bohr atom

an atomic model having the structure postulated in the bohr theory.

bohr orbit

one of the electron paths about the nucleus in bohr's model of the hydrogen atom.

bohar radius

is the radius of the ground state orbit of the hydrogen atom.

bohr's correspondence principle

the behaviour of the electrons in an atomic system must approach more and more that predicted by classical physics the higher the quantum number of the orbit.

bohr's radius

According to Bohr's model for hydrogen atom, the electron in its lowest energy state, moves round the nucleus in a circular orbit or radius.

$$a_0 = \frac{4\pi\varepsilon_0 h^2}{m_e . e^2} = 0.5292 \times 10^{-10} \text{ m.}$$

bohr sommerfeld atom

refers to atoms obeying modifications of Bohr's laws as suggested by sommerfeld. It allows for the possibility of elliptical electron orbits.

bohr-sommerfeld theory

a modification of the bohr theory in which elliptical as well as circular orbits are allowed.

bohr's stomic concept

according to it the electrons are considered as moving in limited number of circular orbits about the nucleus of an atom. These are known as stationary states. Emission or absorption of electro magnetic radistions occur only when an electron jumps from one orbit to another orbit. Only those orbits are allowed for which angular momentum of the electron about the nucleus is an integral multiple of $\frac{h}{2\pi}$.

bohar theory

a theory introduced by Niels Bohr (1911) to explain the spectrum of atomic hydrogen.

bohr-wheeler theory of fission

a theory of fission based on a liquid-drop model of the nucelus in which there are coulombic and surface tension forces.

boil-off

the vapourization of a liquid,

such as liquid oxygen or liquid hydrogen, as its temperature reaches it boiling point under conditions of exposure.

boiler

a closed vessel used for generating steam.

boiling point

the constant temperature at which a liquid changes into gaseous form. At this temperature the saturated vapour pressure is equal to the external pressure.

boiling water reactor

a nuclear reactor in which the coolant used is water which is maintained at such a pressure as to allow it to boil and form steam ultimately. It is abbreviated as bwr.

bolometer

refers to a metallic resistance thermometer of very high sensitivity which is used for the measurement of thermal radiation.

boltzamann constant

symbol: k. The constant 1.380 54 J K^{-1}. It is equal to the gas constant (R) divided by the Avogadro constant (N_A).

boltzmann equation

the entropy of a system of particles is proportional to the logarithm of the probability of its macroscopic state. The constant of proportionality is known as boltzaman's constant.

bomb

a prodjectile exploded by means of a fuse, by impact or otherwise.

bomb ballistics

the special branch of ballistics concerned with bombs dropped from aircraft.

bomb calorimeter

a type of calorimeter measuring the heat evolved by the combustion of a fuel

bombard

to direct a stream of particles or photons against a target.

bombardment

by neutrons, particularly using a nuclear reactor, can give very many artificial radioactive substances, most of which are beta active, emitting electrons.

bond

valency bond, linkage. A representation of a valency link by which one atom is attracted to another in a chemical compound.

bond energy

the energy characterizing a chemical bond between two atoms. It is measured by the energy required to separate the two atoms.

bond length

the distance between the nuclei of two atoms joined by a chemical bond.

bonding electron

an electron which holds together two atoms in a molecule.

bonding pad

metal pads arranged around the edge of a semiconductor chip on to which wires may be bonded to make electrical connection to the component or circuit on the chip.

bonding wire

wire used to connect metal objects so that they have the same potential.

bone seeker

a radio isotope that tends to accumulate in the bones when it is introduced into the body, e.g. strontium.

booster

a device connected in series with a current for increasing or decreasing the normal circuit voltage.

boot

a protective covering over any part of a wire.

born approximation

a method of obtaining the asymptotic form for a scattered wave depending on performing a sequence of iterative integrations.

Born, Max

(1882-1970) German-born British physicist who was awarded the 1954 Nobel Prize for physics (with W. Bothe, 1891-1957) for his work on statistical mechanics. With Heisenberg he also developed matrix mechanics.

boron chambers

a device for detecting low energy neutrons in which a compound of boron fills an ionization chamber.

boron counter

A counter tube containing a boron chamber, used for counting slow neutrons. The boron chamber is lined with boron or a boron compound or is filled with the gas boron trifluoride (BF_3). As natural boron contains about 18% of the isotope boron–10, and as this isotope absorbs neutrons with the emission of an alpha particle, the chamber can be coupled with a Geiger counter to count the alpha particles emitted when neutrons enter the chamber.

borrman effect

when a crystal of high perfection is placed in the path of monochromatic x-ray beam, it results in an irregular transmission of x-rays. This effect is called borrman effect.

bose gas

an assembly of non-interacting or weakly interacting bosons.

bose-einstein distribution

for an assembly of independent bosons, such as photons or helium atoms of mass number 4, a function that specifies the number of particles in each of the allowed energy states.

bose-einstein statistics

it is the statistical mechanism of a system of indistinguishable particles for which there is no restriction on the number of particles that may exist in the same state simultaneously.

bose gas

it is an assemblage of non-interacting or weakly interacting bosons.

bosons

particles which obey bose-einstein statistic, such as photons and mesons, whose number are not conserved in particle interaction. Bosons have integral spin.

bound charge

electric charge which is confined to atoms or molecules.

bound electron

an electron whose wave function is negligible except in the vicinity of an atom.

bound level

an energy level in a nucleus so close to the ground state that it can only decay by gamma emission.

bound particle

a particle which is confined to some finite region.

bound state

a system in which two (or more)

parts are bound together in such a way that energy is required to splid them. An example of a bound state is a molecule formed from two (or more) atoms.

boundary layer

The thin layer of fluid formed around a solid body or surface relative to which the fluid is flowing. Adhesion between the molecules of the fluid and that of the body or surface causes the molecules of the fluid closest to the solid to be stationary relative to it.

bourdon gauge

it is a direct reading pressure gauge and is commonly used in industry. It is made up of a thin walled flattened brass phosphor – bronze tube T which is bent into an arc of a circle. Its closed end C is connected to a ratchet end a cog wheel which moves a pointer over a scale. Pressure is applied at the open end A and pressure in excess of atmospheric pressure is indicated on the scale.

bow wave

it is a highly compressed shock wave occurring in front of a body or apparently with forward tip of the body.

bow's notation

a method of notation of forces acting at a point, wherein the spaces between forces are lettered or numbered, any force being defined by the letters or numbers on each side of it.

boy's experiment

a method of determining the gravitational constant.

boys' camera

a specially designed camera used to observe lighting flashes.

boy's radiomicrometer

a thermocouple and moving coil galvanometer combined to make a sensitive detector of radiant energy.

boyle's law

it states. At constant temperature, the pressure of a fixed mass of a gas is inversely proportional to its volume i.e.

$$p \propto \frac{1}{V}$$

or PV = constant
The law holds goods for ideal gases.

brackett series

it is a series of specitral lines in hydrogen spectrum. The series of wavelengths are given by $\frac{1}{\lambda} = R\left(\frac{1}{4^2} - \frac{1}{n^2}\right)$, where $R = 1.0974 \times 10^7\ m^{-1}$, n = 5,6,7.........

bragg scattering

scattering of x-rays or neutrons by the regularly spaced atoms in a crystal for which constructive interference occurs only at definite angles called bragg angles.

bargg's angle

the angle incident and diffracted X-rays make with a crystal plane when the Bragg equation is satisfied for the maximum diffracted intensity.

bragg's law

when a beam of X-ray strikes a crystal surface in which the layers of atoms or ions are separated by a distance, the maximum intensity of the reflected rays occurs when sin θ = l/2d' where θ (Bragg angle) is the complement of the angle of incidence and n is an integer.

brake

a device used for slowing down or stopping a vehicle or other moving mechanism.

branch circuit

a portion of a wiring system in the interior of a structure that extends from a final overload protective device to a plug receptacle or a load such as a lighting fuxture or heater.

branch

a portion of a network consisting of one of more two-terminal elements in series. Also known as arm.

brass

a group of alloys consisting of copper and zinc. A typical yellow brass might contain about 67% copper and 33% zinc.

bravais lattice

these are 14 distinct lattices which can be formed by and array of representative points in the study of crystal structures.

bravas' law

those crystal forms which tend to occur most frequently are those with faces parallel to planes of smallest recticular area.

brazing

joining metals above 800 degree F, but below the melting point of the joined metals.

break

the term is commonly used in electricity to denote some fault in the circuit.

break contact

it is the contact of a switching device which opens a circuit upon the operation of the device.

breakdown

a large usually abrupt rise in electric current in the presence of a small increase in voltage.

breakdown voltage

it is the volage measured at a specified current in the electric breakdown region of a semiconductor diode.

breaking load

the stress which when steadily applied to a structure is just sufficient to break or rupture it.

breaking strength

the ability of a material to resist breaking or rupture from a tension force.

breaking stress

the stress required to fracture a material whether by compression, tension or shear.

breeder

it is a fusion mchine where in further fuel (tritium) is bred from lithium.

breeding

the production of nuclear fuel by absorption of neutrons in a nuclear reactor, at a rate exceeding that at which fuel is being consumed.

breeding gain

the term is used in nuclear reactors and denotes the excess of fissionable atoms produced per fissionable atom in the breeder reactor.

breeding ratio

the ratio of the number of fissionable atoms produced in a breeder reactor to the number of fissionable atoms consumed in the reactor.

breedor reactor

a nuclear reactor which produces the same type of fissile materials it burns. Usually the amount of fuel produced is greater than the fuel consumed.

brewster window

a reflecting surface which is used in some gas lasers in order to reduce reflection losses that arise from using external mirrors.

brewster's law

(i) the tangent of an angle of polarisation is numerically equal to the refractive index of the medium.

(ii) The reflected andrefracted rays are perpendicular to each other.

$$\mu = \tan i = \frac{\sin i}{\cos i}$$

brewster window

a reflecting surface that is used in some gas lasers so as to reduce reflection losses that arise from using external mirrors.

bridge

an electrical instrument having four or more branches by means of which one or more of electric constants of an unknown component may be measured.

bridge circuit

an arrangement of four electrical elements arranged in a square, the input is connected across two opposite corners and detector across the remaining opposite corners.

bridge rectifier

a full-wave rectifier made up of a bridge with a rectifier in each arm.

bridgman effect

this effect is the absorption or liberation of heat when an electric current passes through an anisotropic crystal. It arises from non-uniformity in the current distribution and is additional to the peltier and thomson effects.

bright fingers

$$\frac{x.d}{D} = n.\lambda, \text{ where } n = 0, 1, 2, 3...$$

Difference between two consective fringes

$$x_2 - x_1 = \frac{\lambda.D}{2}$$

where D = Distance between screen and coherent sources.
d = distance between two virtual coherent sources.

brightness

brightness of a surface is that property by which the surface appears to emit more or less light in the direction of view. This is only a subjective quantity.

brillouin scattering

the scattering of electro-magnetic waves at optical frequencies by sound waves at microwave frequencies and analogous to raman scattering.

brillouin zone

on solving schrodinger's equatons for electronic energies with a periodic function u(k) to give the energies of an electron in a solid, these solutions fall into permitted bands: If these solutions are plotted in the reciprocal lattice of the cystal under consideration the zones enclosing the solutions for k = 1, 2...n, are called Brillouin zones.

brinell machine

It is an instrument that is used for determining the hardness of metals by forcing a hard ball into the material being tested.

brinell number

a numberical expression for expressing the Brinell hardness.

brinell test

a way of measuring the hardness of a material. A standard steel ball of known hardness is pressed into the materials surface with a known force. The size of the indentation indicates the hardness.

britannia metal

a silvery alloy consisting of 80–90% tin, 5–15% antimony, and sometimes small percentages of copper, lead, and zinc. It is used in bearings and some domestic articles.

british thermal unit

the quantity of heat required to raise the temperature of 1 lb of water by 1 degree F. btu - 1055.06 j or 251.997 calories.

brittleness

refers to the property of a material which permits little bending or deformation without fracture. Brittleness and hardness have been closely associated.

brittle temperature

the temperature point below which a material, especially metal, is brittle.

broad-band antenna

an antenna that functions satisfactorily over wide range of frequencies.

broca galvanometer

an instrument with an astatic system formed by two magnets capable of movement, each with a consequent pole in the middle. The arrangement combines a large magnetic moment with a small moment of inertia, and gives a high sensitivity with a reasonable small period.

bronson resistance

an ionization chamber that encloses a constant source of ionization, generally a layer of uranium oxide. If the potential difference between the electrodes is small compared with that required for saturation, the ionization current is approximately proportional to the applied p.d., and the system acts as a high resistance.

brownian movement

radom movement of small particles in a fluid. It is caused by the continuous bombardment of the particles by the molecules of the medium.

brush

an electrical contact, in an electrical motor or generator, with a moving part.

brush discharge

a stream of charged gas particles near sharp points at a high potential. Characterised by luminous streamers.

BSR

stands for Builk shielding reactor.

BTU

is the prefix used for British thermal unit.

bubble

a small approximately, spherical body of fluid within another fluid or solid.

bubble chamber

a device in which the tracks of an ionizing particle are made visible as a row of tiny bubbles the distance of the liquid inside a large chamber.

bubble raft

a visual demonstration for the structure of dislocation in metal lattices; it consists of many identical bubbles floating on a liquid surface in something like a crystalline array.

bubbles

for curved surfaces which separate a liquid from a gas or from its own vapours, the following formula apply

$$p - po = \frac{4\tau}{R}$$

where p = Pressure inside the bubble (a nearly spherical body of gas contained in a liquid).
po = Pressure outside the bubble
R = Radius of the bubble
$\tau = Nm^{-1}$.

bucking transformer

a transformer whose voltage

opposes some other transformer in its neighbourhood.

bucking voltage

a voltage having a polarity opposite to that of another voltage against which it acts.

buckling

a constant that measures the curvature of the neutron flux distribution inside a nuclear reactor.

buckling stress

force exerted by the crippling stress.

budde effect

the expansion observed on exposing halogen vapours to light caused by the rise in temperature resulting from heat evolved in the recombination of atoms.

buffer

an electric circuit or component that prevents undesirable electrical interaction between two circuits or components.

buffer element

it is a low impedance inverting driver circuit.

built-in antenna

an antenna located inside the cabinet of a radio or television receiver.

bulk density

mass divided by bulk volume.

bulk lifetime

the average time lapse between the generation and recombination of minority carriers in the bulk material of a semiconductor.

bulk modulus

the ratio of the volume stress to the volume strain for fluid. Its reciprocal is called the comprehensibility of the fluid. It is measured in n/m.

bulk strength

the magnitude or strength per unit volume of any solid is called its bulk strength.

bullet drop

the vertical drop of a bullet.

bulygen number

a dimensionless number which is used to study the transference of heat during evaporation.

bumping

violent boiling of a liquid caused

by superheating so that bubbles form at a pressure above atmospheric pressure. It can be prevented by putting pieces of porous pot in the liquid to enable bubbles of vapour to form at the normal boiling point.

bunched pair

group of pairs tied together or otherwise associated for identification.

bunsen burner

a gas burner in which a regulated amount of air is allowed to mix with the gas stream at the bottom of the tube of the burner.

bunsen cell

a pr:mary cell, the negative pole is amalgamated dipped in dilute sulphuric acid in a porous pot. The positive pole is a plate of hard gas carbon dipped in strong nitric acid. The e.m.f. is about 1.9 volt.

bunsen ice calorimeter

a calorimeter to measure the specific heat capacity of a solid or liquid when only a small quantity is available

buoyancy

when a body is wholly or partly immersed in a fluid, it experiences an upward force equal to the weight of the fluid.

buoyant density

a technique that uses the sedimentation equilibrium in a density gradient to characterize a solute.

buoyant force

the force exerted vertically upward by a fluid on a body wholly or partly immersed in it; its magnitude is equal to the weight of the fluid displaced by the body.

burble

1. it exhibits a separation or breakdown of the laminar flow past a body. 2. A turbulent flow resulting from this occurrence.

burden

the load across the secondary terminals of an instrument transformer under specified conditions, generally expressed in volt-amperes.

burger's vector

the vector necessary to close burger's circuit. It is at right angles to the dislocation for a pure dege dislocation and parallel to the dislocation for a screw dislocation.

burial ground

a place for burying unwanted radioactive objects to prevent escape of their radiations, the earth acting as a shield. Also known as graveyard.

burn-up

refers to the significant reduction in the quantity of one or more nuclides due to neutron absorption in a nuclear reactor.

burning glass

a converging lens used to produce intense heat by converging the rays of the sun on a small area.

burnount

failure of a device due to excessive heat produced by excessive current.

burst pressure

is the maximum internal pressure that a process vessel can safely withstand.

burst-wave

wave of compressed air caused by a bursting projectile or bomb; a detonation wave it may produce extensive local damage.

bursting strength

a measure of the ability of a material to withstand pressure without pture; it is the hydraulic pressure required to burst a vessel of given thickness

bus

a set of conducting paths — wires or optical fibres – connecting several components of a computer system and allowing the components to sent signals to each other. The colponents take it in turns to transmit.

busbar

bus, baseline. Refers to conductor of low impedance or high current-carrying capability relative to other connections in a system.

bush

it is a lining of metal let into an orifice to guard against wearing by friction.

buzzer

a device similar in working principle to the electric bell, but without a hammer or gong. The superfast vibration of the arm produces a definite buzzing note when the current flows.

bypass

the term is commonly used in electricity and denotes a shunt path around some circuit element or elements.

bypass capaciter

refers to a capacitor that is allowing alternating currents to pass through it rather than through another component which is connected in parallel.

byte

a subdivision of a word in a computer, it usually consists of eight bits. A kilobyte is 1024 bytes (not 1000 bytes). A gigabyte is 2^{30} = 1 073 741 824 bytes.

c

the symbol for centigrade.

c

the symbole for the velocity of light in a vacuum = 2.99796 $\times 10^{10}$ cm per second.

c battery

the battery that supplies the steady lines voltage acquired by the control grid electrodes of electron tubes in battery operated equipment. Also known as grid battery.

c.g.s.system

a system of physical units derived from centimetre, gram, second as the fundamental units.

ca

symbol for calcium – 45.

cable

refers to an insulated electrical conductor, generally in strands or a combination of electrical conductors insulated from one another.

cable complement

group of wire pairs in a cable having some common distinguishing characteristic.

cable messaenger

standard group of wires supported above ground at intervals by poles or other structures and employed to furnish within these intervals, frequent points of support for conductors or cables.

cable run

path occupied by a cable on cable racks or other support from one termination to another.

cadence

refers to the rhythmic flow of a sequence of sounds.

cadmium cell

it is a standard cell whose e.m.f. is 1.0186 volts at 20^{0}C.

cadmium lamp

a lamp containing cadmium vapour; wavelength of light emitted is a standard of length.

cadmium ratio

symbol : Rcd. It is the ratio of the neutron-induced radioactivity in a sample to the radioactivity induced under indentical conditions when the sample to the radioactivity induced under identical conditions when the sample is covered with cadmium, a high capture cross section for thermal neutrons.

cadmium red line

spectrum line formerly chosen as a reproducible standard of length.

Weve length = 643.8496 m.

cadmium silver oxide cell

it is an alkaline electrolyte cell that may be used without recharging or may be recharged for a secondary battery.

cadmium sulphide cell

a compact photoconductive cell consisting of a layer of cadmium sulphide sandwiches between two electrodes. A battery provide the current. It is used in exposure meters and cameras. It has a higher sensitivity than the selenium cell.

caesium clock

an apparatus which is used to produce the steady frequency used in defining the second. It depends on the fact that, in a magnetic field, caesium-133 atoms can be having two different energy levels between which transitions take place by absorption of radio-frequency 9 192631 770 hertz. In a acaesium clock, the number f atoms in the higher state has been detected, and the signal used to stabilize the oscillator producing the radiation.

cahn–hilliard mode

a model describing critical dynamics in which the dynamics is dissipative and the order parameter is conserved. The Cahn–hilliard model was introduced by J.W. Cahn and J.E. Hilliard in 1958.

calcite

a naturally occurring crystalline substance which exhibits the phenomenon of double refraction or fire fringence. It is calcium carbonate chemically.

calibration

refers to determination of the absolute values of the arbitrary indications of an instrument.

calipers

an instrument used for measuring internal and external diameters. It is a graduated rule with one fixed and one sliding jaw.

call circuit

it is a communication circuit between switching points used by traffic forces for transmitting switching instructions.

callendar and barnes' apparatus

an apparatus which is used for measuring the specific thermal capacity of a fluid under steady-state conditions.

calorescence

the term used for the absorption of heat radiations, their concession into heat, and the emission of this heat by the absorbing surface.

caloric theory

an obsolete theory that heat was a weightless fluid,. The theory was abandoned in the nineteenth century.

calorie

amount of heat which is requited to raise the temperature of 1 gm of water through 1 degree c. 1 kilocalorie is equal to 1000 calories. 1 cal = 4.2 j.

calorific value

the amount of heat liberated on complete combustion of unit mass of a fuel. The determination is carried out in a bomb calorimeter and the value is usually expressed in j kg.

calorimeter

any vessel used to carry out thermal measurements quantitatively.

calorimetry

it is the study of the measurement of quantities of heat.

calutron

an electromagnetic separator of isotopes, used to separate the fissile radioisotope uranium-235 from uranium-238.

calx

a metal oxide formed by heating an ore in air.

calzecchi-onesti effect

the conductivity of loosely aggregated metallic powders changes under the action of applied electromotive forces.

camera

an optical instrument with which it is possible to produce a permanent representation of a scene. Light from scene is focused on, and absorbed by, emulsion on a film. It causes chemical changes at each spot on the emulsion. The nature of thechanges depend upon the colour and brightness of light. Processing the film makes the picture permanent.

camera cable

cable of group of wires that carries the picture from the television camera to the control room.

camera lucida

a microscope part for attachment at the eyepiece end, that an image is projected in the plane of drawing paper. It permits the simultaneous view of a hand-manipulated pencil to draw the outline.

camera obscura

a primitive camera in which the real image of an object can be observed or traced on the wall of the enclosure opposite the aperture, rather than being recorded photographically,

camera, photographic

it is a box, in which light can enter through a small aperture, containing a lens at one end and a light-sensitive film at the other. Light falls on the film through a shutter, over the lens, for a short duration which forms the image of the external object on the film.

campbell bridge

a bridge designed for comparison of mutual inductances. A circuit for measuring frequencies by adjusting a mutual inductance, until a current across a detector is zero

canada balsam

a yellowish liquid derived from fir tree with a refractive index similar to that of glass. Used for mounting microscopic slides and as an adhesive for optical instrument.

canal rays

positively charged ions formed during the discharge of electricity in gases, driven to the catnode by the applied potential difference and allowed to pass through canals toned in the cathode.

candela

symbol Cd. The SI unit of luminous intensity equal to the luminous intensity in a given direction of a source that emits monochromatic radiation of frequency 540×10^{12} Hz and has a radiant intensity in that direction of 1/683 watt per seradian.

candle meter

refers to a unit of illumination which is synonymous with the meter-candle, and equal to one lux.

candle power

it is the luminous intensity of a light source expressed in terms of the candela.

canning

the process involves the covering of a slug of uranium with a jacket before it is inserted is the nuclear reactor.

cannon

a mounted gun for firing heavy projectiles.

cantilever vibration

transverse oscillatory motion of a body fixed at one end.

cantilever

a beam of rectangular or circular cross-section clamped at one end and loaded at the other free end is called a cantilever.

capacitance

the capacitance of a conductor is defined as the ratio of charge on either of a part of conductors.

$C = \frac{Q}{V}$, where Q is the change on the conductor and V is the potential to which the conductor is raised by this charge.

capacitive coupling

use of a capacitor to transfer energy from one circuit to another.

capacitive load

a load in which the capacitive reactance exceeds the inductive residence; the load draws a leading current.

capacitive reactance

mathematically expressed as the product of reciprocals of capacitance and angular frequency i.e., $\left(\frac{1}{C\omega} = X_c\right)$. It is the equivalent resistance of a part of circuit. It is expressed in ohms.

capacitor

an electric conductor or a system made up of electrical conductors that can store a charge. The most widely used condenser is a parallel plate condenser.

capacitor antenna

antenna consisting of two conductor or system of conductors, the essential characteristic of which is its capacitance. Also known as condenser antenna.

capacitor colour code

a method of marking the value on a capacitor by mean of dots or bands of colours as specified in the electronic industry association colour code.

capacitor in parallel

when a number of capacitors C_1, C_2 C_3 ...capacities are joined in parallels, their combined capacity is equal to $C_1 + C_2 + C_3$ .....

capacitor in series

When a number of capacitors having capacities C_1 ,C_2, C_3.....are joined in series, their combined capacity is given by

$$\frac{1}{C}=\frac{1}{C_1}+\frac{1}{C_2}+\frac{1}{C_3}+......$$

capacitor microphone

a microphone consisting of a capacitor with a steady voltage applied across its parallel plates. One plate is fixed, The other is a thin diaphragm that is moved by the pressure of the sound waves. The movements of the diaphragm cause a variation in the spacing and therefore in the capacitance of the device. This variation in capacitance is, in turn, reflected in a similar variation in the charge carried by each plate. The consequent current to and from one plate is carried by a resistor, the varying potential difference across which constitutes the device's output signal. It was formerly known as a condenser microphone

capacity

capacitance was formerly known as capacity.

capacity cell

capacitance type device used to measure the dielectric constant of gases, liquids or solids. Capacitanoe type device used to monitor certain composition changes in flowing streams.

capacity of parallel plate condenser

it is given by

$$C=\frac{K.A}{4nd}$$

Where A = area of plate in sq. cm.

d = distance between plates in cm.
k = dielectric constant of the medium

capacity of spherical conductor

it is equal to its radius.

C = r.e.s.u.
Where r cm is the radius

capicitative reactance

It is the opposition offered by a capacitance to the flow of aleternatinig current. It is given by

$$X_c = \frac{1}{\omega.c} = \frac{1}{2\pi.f.c}$$

Where, X_c = capacitative reactance in ohms
f = frequency in cycles/sec
c = capacitance in farads

capillarity

a term to describe the rise or fall of liquids in vertical capillary tubes. The election of a liquid in a capillary tube is given by Juvin's rule.

capillary

a tube of small diameter, such as the narrowest type of blood vessel in the vertebrate circulatory system.

capillary action (capillarity)

the phenomenon of rise or fall of a liquid in a capillary tube when it is dipped in the liquid. Due to this the portion of the surface of the liquid coming in contact with a solid is elected or depressed.

capillary attraction

the force of adhesion existing between a solid and a liquid in capillarity.

capillary electrometer

is an electrolye cell. It can be conveniently used as a nul instrument.

capillary pressure

the difference in pressure across the interface of two missile fluid passes.

capilary rise

it refers to the rise of a liquid in a capillary tube times the radius of the tube.

capillary tube

a tube with a very small internal diameter.

capsule

a small, sealed and pressurised cabin in which a man or animal mayride in flight above the earth's atmosphere.

capture

the absorption of a particle by an atomic or nuclear system.

carat

1. a measure of fineness (purity) of gold. Pure gole is described as 24-carat gold. 14-carat gold contains 14 parts in 24 of gold, the remainder usually being copper. 2. A unit of mass equal to 0.200 gram, used to measure the masses of diamonds and other gemstones.

carbon arc

an electric arc between two electrodes at least one of which is made of carbon; used in welding and high intensity lamps such as in search lights and photography lamps.

carbon arc lamp

an arc lamp in which an electric current flows between two electrodes of pure carbon, with incandescence at one or both electrodes and some light from the luminescence of the arc.

carbon cycle or carbon nitrogen cycle

is a cycle of nuclear reactions that result into the conversion of hydrogen nuclei into helium nuclei giving out a large amount of energy. Carbon acts as a catalyst. Energy generated by the sun and stars is explained on the basis of this cycle.

carbon dating or radiocarbon dating

is a method of determining the age of materials that contain matter of living origin. The ratio of ${}_6C^{12}$ to ${}_6C^{11}$enables us to determine the time when the death of the sample had occurred.

carbon dioxie gas laser

a continuously operating powerful laser in the infrared which gives out several hundred watts of power at a wavelength of 10.6 micrometer.

carbon fibres

fibres of carbon in which the carbon has an oriented crystal structure. Carbon fibres are made by heating textile fibres and are used in strong composite materials for use at high temperatures.

carbon film resistor

it is a resistor made by depositing a thin carbon film on a ceramic form.

carbon lamp

an arc lamp with carbon electrodes.

carbon monoxide laser

a molecular gas laser in which the active laser molecule is carbon monoxide, and the strongest wavelengths are 4.9 to 5.7 micrometers. Also known as co laser.

carbon 13

a heavy isotope of carbon having a mass number of 13.

carbonize

means to enrich with carbon.

carburettor

a device in the internal-combustion petrol engine for mixing air with petrol prior to explosion.

cardinal points

for a thick lens or a coaxial system of lenses, the position and size of the image of an object can be determined if the position of few points, called cardinal points of the system, is known. The two focal points, the two principal points and the two nodal points constitute the six cardinal points for such a system.

carey foster bridge

it is a modified form of a slide wire bridge. It has four gaps instead of two in the slide wire bridge. P, Q are two approximately equal resistances. R is a known resistance and X is the unknown resistance whose value is to be determined. It is very accurate for determination of low resistances.

carnot—clausius equation

for any reversible closed system the total change in the entry of the system, dq/T, is zero; dq is the quantity of heat absorbed by the system during an infinitesimal reversible change of state and T is the absolute temperature of the system during this change.

carnot cycle

it is a reversible cycle and consists of two isonthermal ($A \rightarrow B$ and $C \rightarrow D$) and two adiabatic ($B \rightarrow C, D \rightarrow A$) changes.

$A \rightarrow B$ is an isothermal expansion at constant temperature T_2.

$$\therefore Q_2 = W_2 = nRT_2 \log \frac{VB}{VA} > 0.$$

$B \rightarrow C$ is an adiabatic change in which temperature changes from T_2 to T_1.

$$\therefore W = -n.c. \Delta T = -n.c. (T_1 - T_2) > 0$$

$C \rightarrow D$ is an isothermal

compression at constanc temperature T_1

$\therefore Q_1 = W_1 = nRT_1 \log \frac{VD}{VC} < 0.$

D→A is an adiabatic compression

$\therefore W = - n.c.DT = - n.c. (T_2 - T_1) < 0$

For complete cycle

$DE = Q_1 = W_{BC} + W_{DA} = 0$

$^{Q}cycle = Q_2 + Q_1 = W_2 + W_1 = {}^{W}cycle$

$= nR (T_2 - T_1) \log \frac{V_2}{V_1}$

= area of the cycle.

Efficiency η = $\frac{W}{Q} = \frac{Q_2 - Q_1}{Q_2} = \frac{T_2 - T_1}{T_2}$

$= 1 - \frac{Q_1}{Q_2} = 1 - \frac{T_1}{T_2}$

carnot's principle or carnot's theormen

(i) the efficiency of a reversible heat engine working between any two temperatures is greater that the efficiency of any other heat engine working between the same two temperatures.

(ii) The efficiency of a reversible heat engine depends only on the temperatures of the source and the sink and is totally independent of the working substance.

carnot's theorem

all machines working reversible between the same temperatures of source and sink have the same efficiency.

carrier

the electrons or holes whose movements are responsible for current in a semi-conductor.

carrier density

it indicates the density of electrons and holes in a semiconductor.

carrier line

any transmission line used for multiple-channel carrier communication.

carrier mobility

it is the mean drift velocity of the charge carrier per unit electric field.

carrier wave

a continuous electro-magnetic radiation of constant amplitude; oscillating electric currents caused by sounds at the transmitting end are conveyed by it to the receiver.

cartridge fuse

a type of electric fuse in which the fusible element is connected between metal ferrules at either end of an insulating tube.

cartridge lamp

a pilot or dial lamp that has a tubular glass envelope with metal ferrule terminals at each end.

cascade

it is an arrangement of component devices, such as critical temperature. Another gas already below its critical temperature, is liquified and evaporated at a reduced pressue in order to cool the first gas to below its critical temperature. In practice, a series of steps is often used, each step enabling the critical temperature of the next gas to be reached.

cascade liquefier

a gas liquefier where in the critical temperature of the gas, below which it must be cooled before it can be liquefied in steps. The steps use a series of gases having successively lower boiling points.

cascade network

two networks in tandom such that the output of the first feeds the input of the second.

cascade particles

the perticles Xi-hyperon, Xi minus hyperon etc., are called cascade particles.

cascade process

any process that takes place in a number of stages.

cascade shower

a cosmic-ray shower of electrons, positrons and gamma rays which grows by pair production and B bremsstralung events.

case hardening

the hardening of the surface layer of steel, used for tools and certain mechanical components. The commonest method is to carburize the surface layer by heating the metal in a hydrocarbon or by dipping the red hot metal into molten sodium cyanide. Diffusion of nitrogen into the surface layer to form nitrices is also used.

cassegrain telescope

a reflecting telescope in which a small hyperbolical mirror reflects the convergent beam from the paraboloidal primary mirror through. See newtonian telescope.

casting stress

the stress set up in a casting due to its geometry and casting shrinkage is known as casting stress.

casting

the process of pouring a liquid or suspension into a mold, or the object produced by this process.

catadioptric

involving both reflection and refraction of light.

catenary

a curve formed when a chain or rope of uniform density hangs from two fixed points. If the lowest point on the curve passes through the origin, the equation is $y = c(\cosh x/c)$, where c is the distance between the x-axis and the directrix.

cathetometer

a telescope mounted on a graduated vertical pillar along which is can move. Used for measuring displacements at a distance of a few feet.

cathode

negative electrode in a cell. The source of electrons in a thermionic valve.

cathode dark-space

a dark region following the first cathode layer in a gas discharge tube.

cathode drop

an abrupt fall of electric potential at the cathode of an electrolytic cell or vacuum tube.

cathode glow

refers to the luminosity which appears at the cathode of a gas discharge tube and envelops it.

cathode ray

refers to a stream of electrons emitted from the cathode of an evacuated tube, or from the ionized region in its proximity, under the influence of an applied voltage.

cathode ray tube

refers to a special form of vacuum tube which is used in various electronic applications, as in the television picture tube and as an oscilloscope tube.

cathode ray oscillograph

it gives a visual structure of waveform of different waves on a screen. In this instrument, the electrons are emitted from an electron gun which are accelerated and deflected subsequently by electromagnetic fields to obtain Lissajous figures on the oxide coated screen. The outline of a C.R.O.

cathode-ray oscilloscope

an instrument which is used for investigating electrical signals. An electron beam gets directed at a cathode-ray tube forming a small spot. The beam can be deflected in he horizotal and vertical directions by an electrostatic field from two sets of plates. The signal to be investigated gets amplified and applied to the vertical deflecting plates. Thus, a graph of the signal would be 'drawn' on the screen.

cathode ray tube

a vacuum tube generating a focused beam of electrons that can be deflected by electric and magnetic fields.

cathoyte

refers to the portion of an electrolyte in an electrolytic cell which is adjacent to a cathode.

cation

positively charged ion, which during electrolysis, is attracted towards the negatively charged cathode.

catoptric light

light reflected from a mirror, for example of light from a filament, concentrated into a parallel beam by means of a reflector.

catoptrics

the branch of optics dealing with the formation of images by mirrors.

cauchy dispersion formula

a formula for the dispersion of light of the for : $n = A + (B/\lambda^2) + (C/\lambda^4)$, where n is the refractive index, λ the wavelength, and A, B, and C are constants. Sometimes only the first two terms are necessary.

cauchy number

a dimensionless number used in the study of compressible flow, equal to the density of a fluid times the square of its velocity divided by its bulk modules. Also known as hobo number.

causality

the relating of causes to the effects which they produce. Many contemporary physicists believe that no coherent casual description can be given of events which occur on the subatomic scale.

caustic

the curve or surface formed by the reflection of parallel rays of light in a large-aperture concave mirror. The apex of the caustic lies at the principal focus of the mirror. Such a curve can sometimes be seen on the surface of the liquid in a cup as a result of reflection by the curved walls of the cup. A similar curve is formed by a convex lens with spherical surfaces refracting parallel rays of light.

cave

a heavily shielded or protected chamber in which some highly radioactive material can be handled by remote control. It is commonly known as a hot cell.

cavitation

refers to the formation of cavities in fluids, when at some point in a flowing fluid the velocity reaches a magnitude that causes the pressure to approach zero.

cavitation noise

noise resulting from the formation of vapour-or gas-filled cavities in liquids by mechanical forces, as occurs near a propeller.

cavity radiator

a heated enclosure with a small opening which allows some radiation to escape or enter; the escaping radiation approximates that of a black body.

cavity resonance

the resonant vibration of a cavity.

c-battety

an electric battery for supplying a constant voltage bias to the control electrode of a vacuum tube.

celestial mechanics

the study of the motions of and forces between the celestial bodies. It is based on Newton's laws of motion and Newton's law of gravitation. Refinements based on the general theory of relativity are also included in the study, although the differences between the two theories are only important in a few cases.

celestial meridians

great circles of the celestial sphere passing through the poles. They are the earth's meridins projected on the celestial sphere.

celestial sphere

the imaginary sphere of infinite radius within which celestial bodies appear to lie. The earth, and the observer, are visualized as being at the centre of the sphere and the sphere as rotating once every sidereal day. The sphere is used to describe the position of celestial bodies with respect to the earth.

cell

in a electrolytic cell, an e.m.f. is developed across the two electrodes by a chemical reaction.

cell constant

the constant obtained by dividing the area of the electrode in an electrolytic cell with the distance between the electrodes.

cell, primary

they supply electric current directly at the expense of chemical reaction going on inside the cell.

cell, secondary

in this case current has to be passed from external source before they can supply current themselves. In this type of cells the interacting substances may be restored to their original chemical form by sending a direct current of electricity through the cell in reverse direction to that of the discharge.

celo

a unit of acceleration. The defloration of a body is one celo when its velocity changes uniformly by one foot per second in one second.

celon laws system

an anastigmatic lens system consisting of two air-spaced achromatic doublet lenses one on each side of the stop. Also known as gauss lens system gauss objective lens.

celsius scale

a temperature scale in which the fixed points are the temperatures at standard pressure of ice in equilibrium with water (0°C) and water in equilibrium with steam (100°C). The scale, between these two temperatures, is divided in 100 degrees. The degree Celsius (°C) is equal in magnitude to the kelvin.

celsius temperature scale

a temperature scale in which the melting point of ice is taken as 0°C and the boiling point of water as 100^{0}C. These are taken as lower and upper points of the termomenter which is graduated by dividing this in 100 equal parts. Each part is 1^{0}C.

cementation

any metallurgical process in which the surface of a metal is impregnated by some other substance, especially an obsolete process for making steel by heating bars of wrought iron to red heat for several days in a bed of charcoal. See also case hardening.

cenctigrade scale

celsius scale.

cent

the interval equal to 1/1200 of the interval of two frequencies having the ratio 2:1, viz. The octave.

centi

symbol c. A prefix used in the metric system to denote one hundredth. For example, 0.001 metre = 1 centimetre (cm).

sentigrade temperature scale

it i the celsius temperature scale on which the temperatures are measured in ^{0}C.

centimetre

it is a unit of length equal to 0.01 cmetre.

centimetre gram-second system

short called C.G.S. system where metric unit centimetre, gram and second are the basic units.

centipoise

a standard unit of viscosity equal to 0.01 poise the c.g.s, unit of viscosity. Water at 20 degree c has a viscosity of 1.002 centipoise or 0.01001 poise.

centrad

a small angle unit, one hundredth of a radian.

central field approximately

the approximation that the electrons in an atom or the nucleons in a nucleus move in the potential of a central force which is the same for all the particles.

central force

a force whose line of action is always directed towards a fixed point. The force may be attractive or repulsive.

centre of curvature

of a spherical mirror or lens. The centre of the sphere of which the mirrorlens forms a part.

centre of buoyancy

it is the point through which the resultant of the buoyancy forces on a submerged body act, it coincides with the centre of gravity of the displaced fluid.

centre of gravity

a point where the whole mass of the body may be supposed to be concentrated.

centre of inertia

a synonym for centre of mass.

centre of mass

a point at which the whole mass of the body may be supposed to be concentrated. It coincides with the centre of symmetry of the body if the body has a uniform density.

centre of moments

it is the point about which lever in equilibrium is free to move. The reference axis used in calculating the moments of forces.

centre of oscillation

point in a physical pendulum, on the line through the point of suspension and the centre of mass, which moves as if all the mass of the pendulum were concentrated there.

centre of percusion

refers to that point of an oscillating body at which that body may be struck without producing any jar.

centre of pressure

it is the point at which the resultant pressure over the entire surface immersed in a fluid may be assumed to act.

centre of suspension

the intersection of the axis of rotation of a pendulum with a plane perpendicular to the axis that passes through the centre of mass.

centre of symmetry

it is point inside a crystal so located that all lines passing through it contact opposite faces of the crystal in corresponding points at equal distances.

centre top

it indicates a terminal at the midpoint of a resistor, coil or any other device.

centrifugal

this term is used for acting in a direction away from the centre of a circle along which a body is revolving.

centrifugal force

a force that acts radially outwards on a body moving in a circle of radius r with speed v. The magnitude of this force is given by $\frac{mv^2}{r}$ where, m is the mass of the body.

centrifugal moment

the total moment of the centrifugal forces of all the particles of a rotating body about any line.

centrifugal separation

separation of isotopes by spinning a mixture in gas or vapour form at high speed.

centrifuge

refers to an instrument which is used for separating liquids of different specific gravities by the use of centrifugal force.

centripetal

the term is used for acting or moving towards the axis or centre of circle along which a body is revolving.

centripetal acceleration

the radical component of the acceleration of a particle of object moving around a circle, which can be shown to be directed toward the centre of circle.

centripetal force

refers to the force which restrains a body in rotation. A force equal, but opposite in sign, to the centrifugal force.

centrobaric

pertaining to the centre of gravity, or to some method of locating it. Possessing a centre of gravity.

centroid

the centre of mass of a uniform solid with the same shape as the volume.

centrosymmetry

having symmetry with respect to a point. Crystals that are centrosymmetrical have their faces arranged in parallel pairs. These pairs are alike or enantiomorphous in surface properties.

ceramic capacitor

a capacitor whose dielectric is a ceramic material such as statute or barium titanate the composition of which can be varied to give a wide rang of temperature coefficients.

ceramic magnet

a permanent magnet made from pressed and sintered mixtures of ceramic and magnetic powders. Also known as ferromagnetic .

cerenkov counter

an apparatus for detecting high energy charged particles by observation of the cerenkov radiation produced.

cerenkov radiation

electromagnetic radiation, usually bluish light, emitted by a beam of high-enegry charged particles passing through a transparent medium of a speed greater than the speed of light in that medium. It was discovered in 1934 by the Russian physicist Pavel Cerenkov (1904). The effect is similar to that of a sonic boom when an object moves faster than the speed of sound; in this case the radiation is a shock wave set up in the electromagnetic field. Cerenkov radiation is used in the Cerenkov counter.

cermet

abbreviation of ceramic and metal. A very strong mixture of a ceramic substance and sintered metal, used in places where resistance to high temperature, corrosion and abrasion is required.

cetane number

a number that provides a measure of the ignition characteristics of a Diesel fuel when it is burnt in a standard Diesel engine.

c.g.s. system

a system of units based on centimetre, gram, second as the fundamental units.

chain fission yield

it is the sum of the independent fission yields for all isobars of a particular mass number.

chain reaction

refers to a any self-sustaining process, whether molecular or nuclear the products of which are instrumental in, and directly contribute to the propagation of the process.

change of phase

a change of matter in one physical phase into another. The change is invariably accompanied by the evolution or absorption of energy, event if it takes place at constant temperature.

change of state

a change from one state of

matter to another. See also latent heat.

channel

in communication a specified band of frequencies, or a particular path, used in the transmission and reception of electric signals.

channel selector

a control used to tune in the desired channel in a radio or television receiver.

channelling radiation

the radiation emitted by energetic charged particles that pass through a solid.

chapman jougue condition

a detonation in which the velocity of the shock front with respect to the material behind it is equal to the corresponding sound velocity.

characteriatic function

a set of functions that satisfy a particular equation with specified boundary conditions. In wave mechanics, characteristic functions are well-behaved solutions of Schrodinger's wave equation for an atomic particle, function.

characteristic radiation

radiation originating in an atom following removal of an electron, whose wavelength depends only on the element concerned and the energy levels involved.

characteristic spectrum

the atomic spectrum.

characteristic x-radiation

the characteristic spectrum of an element may be obtained by making it the target in an x-ray tube.

characteristic x-rays

monochromatic x-rays which are characteristic of a particular element and emitted by it, in addition to heterochromatic x-radiation, when it gets exposed to cathode rays or x-rays of a sufficiently high energy.

characteristics

graph showing change of current with voltage of an electrode in a valve. For example, a plate voltage-plate current variation graph.

charge

symbol: Q . A property of some elementary particles which causes them to exert forces on one another. Charge is the integral or electric current with time and is measured in couloombs. The electron has a charge of 1.602 192 $\times 10^{-19}$.

charge carrier

a mobile conduction electron or mobile hole in a semiconductor.

charge congugate parity

it is a quantum number associated wit elementary particles which have zero charge, baryon number and strangeness. It implies whether the wave function describing the particle is unchanged (c = + 1) or changes sign (c = –1) when the particle is replaced by antiparticle.

charge conjugation

symbol C. A property of elementary particles that determines the difference between a particle and its antiparticle. The property is not restricted to electrically charged particles.

charge conservation

states that in an isolated system, the total charge of the system remains conserved i.e.,

$$Q = \sum_{j-1}^{n} q_j$$

charge density

the charge per unit volume of a material, per unit area of a surface or per unit length of a line. They are respectively called volume, surface or line charge density.

charge eliminator

a barrery charge with a low-noise, low-impedance output which can either charge a storage battery or supply a load directly, without a storage battery in parallel.

charge exchange

the transfer of electric charge from one particle to another during a collision between the two particles.

charge neutrality

the condition in which electrons and holes are present in equal number in a semi conductor.

charged particle

a particle whose charge in not zero.

charging current

the current that flows into a capacitor when a voltage is first applied.

Charles, Jacques Alexandre Cesar

French chemist and physicist, who became professor of

physics at the Paris Conservatoire des Arts et Metiers.

Charles' law

mass of gas at constant pressure, the volume increases by a constant fraction of the volume at 0^0C for each Celsius degree rise in temperature.

chatter

also known as contact chatter. It involves prolonged undesirable opening and closing of electric contacts, as is done on a relay.

cheese antenna

an antenna having a parabolic reflector between two metal plates.

chemical energy

energy stored in the chemical substance. It can change into another form. When a chemical substance burns, chemical energy is converted into heat.

chemical hygrometer

it is an apparatus with water flowing from the aspirator 0 which causes a known volume of air to be drawn through B. The moisture content is removed in drying uses C, B and A. The process is repeated with tube RS ratio of increase in weight of C and B before RS is attached is measured. It gives relative humidity of the atmosphere.

chemical potential

symbol m. For a given component in a mixture, the coefficient ¶G/¶n, where G is the Gibbs free energy and n the amount of substance of the component. The chemical potential is the change in Gibbs free energy with respect to change in amount of the component, with pressure, temperature, and amounts of other components being constant.

chemical shift

a change in the position of a spectrum peak that result from a small change in energy level due to a chemical effect.

chemical shutdown

addition of a dissolved poison to the coolant of a nuclear reactor to achieve shotdown.

chemical tracer

a tracer having chemical properties similar to those of the substance with which it is mixed.

chemiluminescence

emission of light during chemical

reaction.

chemosphere

atomospheric layer.

chief ray

refers to the central or representative ray of a pencil from an object point on or off the axis, to the centre of the entrance pupil.

chi-meson

a boson resonance of mass 958 Me V/c^2. Denoted by η ('eta-dash'). It has zero isospin and charge, negative parity and positive G-parity. The spin is probably zero.

chimney effect

the phenomenon by virtue of which air or some other gas has a tendency to rise through a vertical passage on heating, is called chimney effect.

chip

a very small semiconductor having a component or an integrated circuit.

chirality

the property of existing in left- and right-handed structural forms. See optical activity.

chiron

a minor planet discovered in 1977. It has an orbit of 50.68 years that, unlike other known minor planent, lies almost entirely outside that of Saturn. Its diameter is uncertain, but appears to be of the order of 300 km.

chladni's plates

refers to flat plates used to investigate vibrations in solids. Various patterns can be obtained by clamping and exciting the plate in different positions.

choke

an indictor which presents a relatively high impedance to alternating current.

chock filter

it is a choke used as an input filter for removing the AC traces from the DC output obtained across a diode.

choked flow

flow in a duct or passage such that the flow upstream of a certain initial section connot be increased by a reduction of downstream pressure.

choking

the condition prevailing in compressible fluid flow when the upper limit of mass flow is reached, or when the speed of sound is reached in a dect.

chord

a combination of three or more different tones sounded simultaneously.

choroid

the second coating inside the sclerotic of the eye. It is the opaque membrane which seems to darken the interior of the eye.

christinaser filter

a type of colour filter, a solid-in-liquid suspension, which scatters all incident energy except that of a narrow frequency range of the direct beam.

chroma

the attribute of a visual sensation which helps us to judge the amount of pure colour, irrespective of the quantity of white or grey present.

chromascope

an instrument used to determine the optical effects of colour.

chromatic

relating to colour.

chromatic aberration

a defect of the image for example, when a single lens is used red colour is focused farther away from the lens than the violet colour, which is nearest, to the lens. Can be corrected making use of a suitable combination of lenses.

chromatic resolving power

it is the ability of resolution between two closure wavelength spectral lines. If λ and $\lambda + d\lambda$ are the wavelengths of two lines, the resolving power will be $\lambda / d\lambda$.

chromatic sensitity

refers to a property of the eye which enables it to distinguish colour hues; its numerically expressed magnitude equals the smallest change in wavelength of the radiation which still registers on the eye as a perceived dirrerence in hue.

chromaticity

refers to the quality of a colour as determined by its wave length and its purity.

chormatography

one of various methods used for the chemical analysis of liquid or gaseous mixtures.

chromatoscope

this refers to an optical device in which light beams are used to mix colour stimuli.

chrominance

the difference in colour quality between a colour and a reference colour that has an equal brightness and a specified chromaticity.

chromium steel

any of a group of stainless steels containing 8-25% of chromium. A typical chromium steel might contain 18% of chromium, 8% of nickel, and 0.15% of carbon. Chromium steels are highly resistant to corrosion and are used for cutlery, chemical plant, ball bearings etc.

chromoscope

an instrument for analysing colour values and intensities.

chromosphere

layer of the sun's atmosphere surrounding the photosphere, which is visible during a total eclipse. The chromosphere is several thousand miles thick and has an estimated temperature of 20,000 k.

chronometer

any highly accurate time piece.

chronometry

a device which measures the time between two events by measuring the positions on a transmission line of pulses initiated by the events.

chronograph

an accurate time-recording instrument.

chronon

a hypothetical 'particle' of time defined as the time taken for electromagnetic radiation to cross an electron; i.e. the diameter of an electron divided by the speed of light. This value is approximately 2×10^{-23} second.

chronoscope

an electronic device used for measuring very short time intervals.

chronotron

an device used for measuring the time interval between events.

cinematograph

a projector used for projecting motion pictures on a screen.

circle

a closed curve every point on which is a fixed distance within the curve. The diameter is a centre: the diameter is twice the radius (r). The circumference of a circle is equal to 2pr; the area is pr^2, where p is a constant with the value 3.141592. In analytical geometry the equation of a circle, centred at the origin, is $x^2 + y^2 = r^2$.

circle of confusion

the blurred circular image of a point object which is formed by a camera lens event with the best focusing. Also known as circle of least confusion.

circuit

refers to a number of electrical conductors connected together to form a conducting path. When they form a continuous closed path through which a current can circulate it is said to be closed circuit when the circuit is not closed it is said to be open.

circuit-breaker

a device used for making and breaking an electric circuit under normal or under fault conditions, e.g., switch ; tripping device.

circuit diagram

a diagram, using standardized symbols, of the arrangement and interconnections of the conductors and components of an electrical or electronic device or installation.

circuit element

refers to any device that is used in an electric circuit. It may be a resistance, capacitor, inductance etc.

circuitry

the complete combination of circuits used in an electrical or electronic system or equipment.

circular current

an electric current which moves along a circular path.

circular electric wave

a transverse electric wave for which the lines of electric force form concentric circles.

circular flow method

a method to determine viscosity of new tanian fluids.

circular measure

measurement of angles in radians.

circular motion

refers to motion of an object moving in circle of radius r with a speed v.

circular velocity

at any specific distance from the primary, the orbital velocity required to maintain a constant-radius orbit.

circularly polarized wave

an electromagnetic wave for which the electric or magnetic field vector or both at a point describe a circle. This term is generally applied to transverse waves.

circulation

when the vector field $\vec{a}$ and a closed line 'l' are given the circulation of $\vec{a}$ is said to be line integral

$$C = \oint a.dl$$

extended around the entire closed path. If the field is conservative

$$\oint \vec{a} dl = 0$$

cladding

the process of bonding one metal to another in order to prevent corrosion of one of the metals, used in nuclear reactors to prevent corrosion of a fuel element by the coolant and the escape of fission products.

clamping diode

catching diode.

clapeyron equation

refers to a mathematical expression of the rate of the change in the vapour pressure of a liquid with the temperature, or of the boiling points of liquids depending on the pressure.

clark cell

a type of voltaic cell consisting of an anode made of zinc amalgam and a cathode of mercury both immersed in a saturated solution of zinc sulphate. The Clark cell was formerly used as a standard of e.m.f.; the e.m.f. at 15^{0}C is 1.4345 volts.

classical physics

refers to physics developed prior to quantum theory.

classical mechanics

the branch of mechanics based on Newton's laws of motion. It is applicable to those systems which are so large that in their case Plank's constant can be neglected.

claude process

the liquefaction of air in stages, the expanding gas being cooled by performing work on pistons.

clausius-clapeyron equation

the equation :

$$\frac{dp}{dT} = \frac{L}{T(v_2 - v_1)'}$$

where v_1 and v_2 are the specific volumes of the substance in two different phases L is the specific latent heat for the change from one of these states to the other.

clausius's equation

The equation :

$$c_2 - c_1 = T\frac{d}{dT}\left(\frac{L}{T}\right),$$

where c_1 and c_2 are the specific heat capacities or the liquid and vapour phases respectively and L is the specific latent head of vaporization at the thermodynamic temperature T.

clausius' theorem

in an arbitrary heat cycle.

clausius law

the law that the specific heat of an ideal gas at constant volume does not depend on the temperature.

cleavage

the breaking up of a crystal along atomic planes so that smooth surfaces result.

cleavage plane

plane of easy splitting or a characteristic crystallogram plane where fracture takes place easily.

clinilcal thermometer

thermometer, for clinical use.

clock frequency

refers to the master frequency delivered by an electronic device, known as a clock, at fixed intervals to synchronize operations in a computer, and to monitor and measure properties of the circuits involved.

clock pulses

refers to the regular pulses delivered to the elements in a logic circuit to effect logical operations.

clocks

the ancient clocks were based on processes taking place at a constant rate sophisticated clocks use periodic processes of constant frequency.

clonimeter

it is an instrument that is used for determining angle of inclination or slope.

close-packed

structure with the highest possible packing factor.

closed

a system, whose component parts, have no interactions with anything outside the system. In such a system, the energy, momentum and angular momentum are conserved.

closed circuit

a thermodynamic cycle in which thermodynamic fluid does not leave or enter the system but is used over and over again.

closed circuit television

a television system having all the parts (camera, control system and receiver) physically linked by cables and there are no aerials or open circuits.

closed end organ pipe

in these cases one end of the pipe is closed. In them first harmonic is given by $\frac{\lambda_1}{4}$. In such cases only the odd harmonics are produced and even harmonics are missing.

$$\text{Fundamental frequency} = \frac{V}{.4\ell}$$

closed shell

an atomic or nuclear shell containing the maximum number by electrons or nucleons allowed by the Paul exclusion principle.

closed system

a system, whose component parts do not interact with any thing outside the system for such a system, the energy, momentum and angular momentum are conserved.

cloud chamber

a device for making visible the paths of particles of ionizing radiation. The Wilson cloud chamber consists of a container containing air and ethanol vapour, which is cooled suddenly by adiabatic expansion, causing the vapour, which is cooled suddenly by adiabatic expansion, causing the vapour to become supersaturated.

clusius column

a device for separating isotopes by thermal diffusion. One form consists of a vertical column some 30 metres high with a heated electric wire running along its axis.

clustering

the preferential grouping of like atoms together.

clutch

a mechanism for readily

engaging or disengaging a shaft with or from another shaft or rotating part.

coated lens

a lens whose surfaces have been coated with a thin, transparent film having an index of refrectionth at minimizes light loss by reflection.

coaxial

having common axis of radial symmetry.

coaxial cable

a cable consisting of a central conductor surrounded by an insulator, which is in turn contained in an earthed sheath of another conductor. The central conductor and the outer conductor are coaxial. They are used to transmit high-frequency signals as they produce no external fields and are not influenced by them.

coaxial combination of lenses

the focal length of the coaxial combination of lenses of focal length f_1, f_2 at disanced is given by

$$\frac{1}{f} = \frac{1}{f_1} + \frac{1}{f_2} - \frac{d}{f_1.f_2}$$

coaxial hybrid

it refers to a hybrid junction of coaxial transmission lines.

cobalt steel

any of a group of alloy steels containing 5-12% of cobalt, 14-20% of tungsten, usually with 4% of chromium and 1-2% of vanadium. They are very hard but somewhat brittle. Their main use is in high-speed tools.

code

a system for communication by elegraph, or heliograph, using long and short sounds, light flashes, coloured flags etc to symbolise letters, words or pharases.

coefficient

1. A number or other known factor by which a variable quantity is multiplied, e.g. in $ax^2 + bx + c = 0$, a is the coefficient of x^2 and b is the coefficient of x. 2. A measure of a specified property of a particular substance under specified conditions, e.g. the coefficient of friction of a substance.

coefficient of comprehensibility

the decrease in volume per unit volume of a substance resulting from a unit increase in pressure. It is the reciprocal of the bulk modulus.

coefficient of expansion

it is a coefficient associated with linear, superficial and volumetric (α, β, γ) expansions of a substance respectively.

coefficient of friction

$$\mu = \frac{f}{R}$$

where f = sliding friction
R = Normal reaction.
Also μ = than θ
where θ = angle of friction

coefficient of mutual inductance

(i) It is numerically equal to the magnetic flux linked with one circuit when unit corrent flows through it. The effective flux Ns linked with secondary circuit is given be Ns = M.i.

(ii) It is numerically equal to the e.m.f. induced in one circuit when the rate of change of current in the other is unity. The e.m.f. inducted in a secondary coil, when the rate of change of current with time in primary is $\frac{di}{dt}$ is given by

$$e_s = M. \frac{di}{dt}$$

coefficient of restitution

in the collision of two solids, this term refers to the ratio of the difference in velocity after the impact to the difference before the impact.

coeficitne of rigidity

refers to the ratio of shearing stress to shearing strain.

coefficient of thermal conductivity (K0)

it is the amount of heat flowing in one second across the opposite faces, of a 1 cm cube, maintained at a temperature difference of 1°C.

coefficient of self-induction

(i) it is numerically equal to t e magnetic flux linked with the coil when the unit current flows through it. The effective flux N is given by N = L. i.

Where i = current flowing n rough the circuit.

(ii) It is numerically equal to the e.m.f. induced in the circuit when the rate of change oa current is unity.

(iii) It is numerically equal to twice the work done against the induced e.m.f. in establishing unit current in the coil.

coefficient of thermal expansion

the ratio of the change of length

per unit length or change of volume per unit volume, to the change of temperature.

coefficient of viscosity

it is the tangential force required to maintain a unit velocity gradient between two layers of unit area. Its units are NSm^{-2} or poiseulle or decapoise.

coelostat

a device that enables light from the same area of the sky to be continuously reflected into the field of view of an astronomical telescope or other instrument. It consists of a plane mirror driven by a clockwork or electrical mechanism so that it rotates from east to west to compensate for the apparent west-to-east rotation of the celestial sphere.

coercive force

the magnetic field intensity h that d the magnetic flux density in a material to zero. The maximum value of this forces is called corrosively.

coercivity

refers to the property of a substance of a substance which could be measured by the maximum magnitude of the coercive force.

coherence time

the mean time required for the relative phase of two waves, or the phase of a single wave, to fluctuate appreciably is called its coherence time.

coherent

refers to waves that are in phase both temporally and spatially. The laser is a source of coherent radiation.

coherent light

radiant electromagnetic energy of the same, or almost the same wavelength, and with definite phase relationships between different points in the fields.

coherent radiation

electromagnetic radiation in which two or more sets of waves have a constant phase relationship, i.e. with peaks and troughs always similarly spaced.

coherent scattering

scattering in which there is a definite phase relationship between incoming and scattered particles or photons.

coherent sources

sources which are always in phase. Such sources are

essential to be able to see interference effects.

coherent units

a system of units, such as si units, in which the quotient or product of any two units gives the units of the resultant physical quantity.

coherent

a beam of light or other electromagnetic radiation is said to be coherent if its waves are in phase. See laser.

cohesion

it is the force of attraction between the similar molecules or molecules of the same substance.

cohesive energy

it refers to the energy difference between per atom of a system of free atoms at rest far apart from each other and the energy of the solid.

coil

a conductor wound in a spiral or other form.

Coil spring

any spring of wire coiled helically, having a cylindrical or conical outline.

coincidence circuit

a circuit having input terminals and is designed to produce an output pulse only when both input terminals receive a pulse within a specified time inverval.

cold cathode

refers to the cathode of an electronic tube which is caused to emit electrons by having a sufficiently high voltage gradient.

cold emission

emission of electrons from a solid by a process other than thermionic emission. The term is usually used to describe either field emission or secondary emission.

cold light

the visdible light, having no infrared radiation associated with it, is called cold light. Such a light produces almost no heating effect.

cold stress

forces tending to deform steel and other materials, resulting from low temperatures.

cold trap

refers to a tube, cooled with liquid air or dry-ice in acetone, it will condense vapour passing into it.

coleman-gross theorem

the theory that non-Abelian gauge theories with unbroken gauge theories are the only renormalizable quantum field theories able to have asymptotic freedom. The Coleman-Gross theorem was stated by the US physicists Sidney Coleman and David James Gross in 1973.

collapse properties

strength and dimensional attributes of piping, tubing or process vessels related to the ability to resist collapse from exterior pressure or internal vacuum.

collar

a short ring formed on or fastened over a rod or shaft, as a locating or holding part.

collector

the electrode in a stransistor through which carriers leave the interelectrode region.

collective excitation

a quantized mode in a many-body system, occurring because of cooperative motion of the whole system as a result of interactions between particles. Plasmons and phonons in solids are examples of collective excitations. Collective excitations obey Bose-Einstein statistics.

collective transition

it stands for a nuclear transition from one state of collective motion to another.

collector

it is an electrode in a transistor through which primary carriers leave the interelectrode region.

colliding-beam experiments

see particles that depend on the concentration of particles present in a solution, and not on the nature of the particles.

collimating lens

a lens on a collimator used to focus light from a source near one of its focal points into a parallel beam.

collimator

a horizontal tube at the one end of which an achromatic lens is fitted. The other end is fitted with a second brass tube which can slide inside the first tube. It is use to produce a parallel beam of light to be incident on an optical like a prism or a grating.

collinear array

it refers to a linear array.

collision

a collision refers to the natural action of molecules, atoms, etc., when they encounter one another.

collision density

the total number of a specified type of collision that occur per unit time per unit volume of material.

collision excitation

the process of excitation of a gas by the impact of charged particles.

collision frequency

the average number of collisions undergone by a particle travelling through a material, such as an electron travelling through a gas, in a unit time.

collision of the first kind

an inelastic collision in which some of the kinetic energy of translation motion is converted to internal energy of the colliding systems. Also known as endoergic collision.

collision of the second kind

an inelastic collision in which some of the internal energy of the colliding systems is converted to kinetic energy to translation. Also known as exoergic collision.

colloid

a substance containing very small particles. Sol, gels, and emulsions are examples of colloids.

cologarithm

the logarithm of the reciprocal of a number.

colorimetry

the science of specifying and reproducing colours as a result of measurement.

colour blindness

inability to differentiate different colours.

colour circle

an arrangement of hues about the circumference of a circle in the order in which they appear in the electromagnetic spectrum, with pairs of complementary colours at opposite ends of diameters.

colour code

a system of colours used to indicate the electrical value of a component or to identify terminals and leads.

colour disc

a rotating circular disc having three filter sections to produce the individual red, green and blue pictures in a field-sequential colour television system.

colour saturation

the degree to which a colour is mixed with white; high saturation means little white, low saturation means much white. Also known as chroma and saturation.

colour temperature

the temperature of a nonblack body's indicated by the temperature of a black body having appromately the image of a point lying off the axis has a comet-shaped appearance.

colour vision

the ability of the human eye to distinguish between different colours. A person is colour blind to a particular colour if he/she cannot distinguish the colour from others.

colourimetry

it refers to the science of specifying and reproducing colours as a result of the measurement.

coma

an aberration of spherical lenses, occurring in the case of oblique incidence, when the bundle of rays forming the image is unsymmetrical. The image of a point is comet shaped, hence the name.

combinations

see permutations and combinations.

combustion

a chemical reaction in which a substance reacts rapidly with oxygen with the production of heat and light. Such reactions are often free-radical chain reactions. See also flame.

comet

a heavenly body, moving under the attraction of the sun. Consists of a hazy gaseous cloud containing a brighter nucleus and a fainter tail.

common-collector connection

a technique used in the operation of some transistors in which the collector is common to both the input and output circuits, the input terminal is the base, and the output terminal is the collector.

commutation

it stands for a process of current reversal in the armature of a D.C. rotating machine to provide D.C. at the brushes.

commutative law

the mathematical law stating that the value of an expression is independent of the order of combination of the numbers, symbols, or terms in the expression.

commutator

a part of the dynamo to change a.c. current into d.c.

comparator

a device used for measuring horizontal distances by comparison with a standard scale.

compass

a magnet free to set itself along the lines of force of the earth's magnetic field. It usually, carries a scale divided into degrees and marked with the cardinal points.

comparison lamp

an incandescent lamp whose luminous intensily is constant and which is compared against other lamps in a photometer.

comparison spectrum

a line-spectrum whose wavelengths are accurately known and which is matched with another spectrum to determine the wavelengths of the latter.

compensated pendulum

a type of pendulum in which the distance between the support and the centre of gravity of the bob is independent of temperature.

compensating eyepiece

a type of Huygens eyepiece in which the eye lens is achromatized to compensate for the colour errors of the objective.

compiler

a computer program taking a high level programming language as its input and capable of converting it to a set of machine instructions.

complementarity

it indicated a principle according to which a system, such as an electron, can be discussed interms of particles or waves.

complementary

the principle according to which a system, such as an electron, can be described either in terms of particles or in terms of wave motion.

complementary colours

a pair of colours which, when combined give the effect of white light. A large number of such pairs are possible.

complementary wave

it is a wave brought into existence at the ends of a coaxial cable, or two-conductor transmission lines or any discontinuity along the line.

complex conjugate

symbol Z. The quantity given by Z = x − iy, when the complex number Z, is given by Z =x + iy. The polar form of Z is number is a reflection of the complex number about the real axis. The sum and product of Z and Z satisfy $Z + Z = 2x$, $ZZ = x^2 + y^2$.

compliance

it indicates the linear displacement of a vibrating mechanical system under a unit force.

component vectors

refers to two or more vectors into which a given vector can be resolved. The effect of these vectors is equal to that of the given vector.

composite balance

an electric balance made by modifying the kelvin balance to measure amperage, voltage or wattage.

composite cable

cable in which conductors of different gauges or types are combined under one sheath.

composition of forces

the determination of a force whose effect is the same as that of two or more given forces acting simultaneously; all forced are considered acting at the same point.

compound lens

a lens system consisting of two or more lenses. Such a lens system is used as the objective or eyepiece of a telescope or microscope.

compound microscope

it utilizes two lenses or a lens system. One lens forms an enlarged image of an object and the second lens magnifies the image formed by the first.

compound pendulum

pendulum.

compressed air

air whose density is increased by subjecting it to a pressure

++greater than atmospheric pressure.

compressibility

it is the reciprocal of the bulk modulus of a material.

compression

it is region of large pressure along the direction of propagation of a longitudinal wave.

compressive stress

it is the force (stress) which causes an elastic body to shorten in the direction of the applied force.

comptom electron

an electron set in motion through interaction with a photon in the complin effect.

Compton, Arthur Holly

(1892-1962) US physicist, who became professor of physics at the University of Chicago in 1923. He is best known for his discovery (1923) of the Compton effect, for which he shared the 1927 Nobel Prize with C.T.R. Wilson. In 1938 he demonstrated that cosmic radiation consists of charged particles.

compton effect

refers to the decrease in frequency and increase in wavelength of x-rays or gamma rays when scattered by free electrons.

compton electron

an electron ejected from its orbit in the extranuclear structure of an atom and possessing a momentum as a result of an impact with a photon or other high-energy quatm of radiatin.

compton-getting effect

the sidereal variation of cosmic radiation of extra-galactic origin due to rotation of the earth's galaxy.

compton scattering

it is the elastic scattering of photons by electrons.

concave

a concave mirror is one with a concave reflecting surface. A concave lens is either a biconcave or a plane-concave lens.

concavo-convex

a lens having one surface concave and the other convex.

concentration

the quantity of a substance in kg or moles contained in unit volume.

concentric lens

a lens whose two spherical surfaces have the same centre.

conchoidal fracture

fracture of a solid in which the surface of the material is corved and marked by concentric rings. It occurs particularly in amorphous materials.

concord

combination of two or more sites sounded together that produce a pleasing effect on the ear is known as a concord.

conde spectrograph

a stationary spectrograph that is attached to the tube of a conde telescope.

condensation

a change of state from vapour to liquid. It results when the vapour pressure becomes equal to the maximum vapour pressure of the liquid at that temperature.

condenser

capacitor.

conductance

the reciprocal of resistance, units are ohm or mho.

conduction

in electrical conduction, it means the flow of charge from +ve to –ve terminal. In general, it is the mode of energy transfer from one part of a substance to another where the substance does notmove.

conduction band

the range of inertness in a semiconductor cor-responding to states in which the electrons can be made to flow by an applied electric field.

conduction current

it is a curent due to flow of conduction electrons through a body.

conduction electron

the electrons in the conduction band of a solid which are free to move under the influence of an electric field.

conductivity, electrical

the reciprocal of the resistivity or specific resistance of a conductor. The ratio of electric current density of electric field strength.

conductor

it is a sustance having a large

value of conductivity.

conductor, electrical

a substance that offers little resistance to flow of electrical current.

conductor, thermal

a substance with a large value of the coefficient of thermal conductivity.

cones

the cells in the rating of the eye that are important for vision in normal light. They are also responsible for colour vision.

configuration

1. the arrangement of atoms or groups in a molecule. 2. The arrangement of electrons in atomic orbitals in an atom.

conical antenna

a specially designed antenna in which the driven element is conical in shape.

conjugate particle

it is a particle with the existence of antiarticles.

conjugate points

refers to a pair of points on either side of a lens such that an object placed at one will produce an image at the other.

conjugate impedances

impedances having equal resistance components, and equal reactance components, the latter with opposite signs.

conpernic

an, alloy of nickel and iron used in magnetic shielding.

consequent poles

refers to magnetic poles in excess of the usual pair in any magnetized body.

conservation law

according to this law, some physical quantity associated with an isolated system always remains constant or conserved.

conservation of angular momentum

when no external torque is present the total angular momentum of a system is conserved or remains constant.

conservation of charge

in a closed system, the total charge remains constant.

conservation of energy, low of

energy can neither be created nor destroyed. It can, however, be changed from one form to another form.

conservation of linear momentum, law of

if no external force acts on a system, the total linear momentum of the system must remain constant.

conservation of mass

states that the mass can neither be created nor destroyed but the form can be changed.

conservative field

it is that vector field for which the line integral depends on the end points of the path only and is independent of the path. A conservative field can be always expressed as the gradient of a scalar field.

conservative force

it is a force which does the work in such a way that the work done depends on the final and initial points but not on the path along which the object moves.

consolute temperature

the temperature at which two partially miscible liquids become fully miscible as the temperature is increased.

consonance

a combination of two or more notes generally accepted as giving a satisfying effect in itself.

constactor

a device for making and breaking an electric circuit designed for frequent use.

constant

1. a component of a relationship between variables that does not change its value, e.g. in $y = ax + b$, b is a constant. 2. A fixed value that has to be added to an indefinite integral. Known as the constant of integration, it depends on the limits between which the integration has been performed. 3. See fundamental constants.

constantan

an alloy having an electrical resistance that varies only very slightly with temperature. It consists of copper and nickel and is used in resistance wire, thermocouples, etc.

constant angular momentum, law of

the total angular momentum of a system cannot change unless a net outside torque acts.

constant energy, law of

the total energy of a system

cannot change unless energy is take from or given to the outside.

constant momentum law of

the total linear momentum of a system cannot change unless a net outside force acts.

constant of motion

a dynamical variable of a system which remains constant in time is called a constant of motion.

constrain

refers to limit to a predetermined position or path. Constrains reduce the number of degree of freedom of the system.

contact

it refers to a surface between two immiscible fluids contained in a reservoir.

contact angle

the angle between the tangent plane to the surface of a liquid and the tangent plane to the surface of a solid at any point where they are in contact.

contact force

it is the force exerted by the moving contact of a switch or relay on a stationary contact.

contact lens

a thin lens fitted over the cornea to correct vision. A similar lens or prism is used with a gonioscope in eye examinations.

contact potential

the difference of potential produced when two conductors of different material are placed in contact.

contactor

it is an electric device for making and breaking an electric circuit.

contact potential difference

potential difference between two solids placed in contact.

containment

1. The prevention of the escape of radioactive materials from a nuclear reactor. 2. The process of preventing the plasma in a thermonuclear reactor from touching the walls of the vessel by means of magnetic fields.

containment vessel

a gas tight sheil or other enclosure around a reactor.

containment

the process of containing radioactive material within a shield for safety reason. The process of containing the plasma in a turion reactor so that it does not come in contact with the walls of the vessel.

contiuity

refers to a continuous effective contact of all components of a circuit to give it a high conductance by providing a low resistance path.

continuous function

a function f(x) is continuous at x = a if the limit of f(x) as x approaches a is f(a). A function that aoes not satisfy this condition is said to be a discontinuous function.

continuous spectrum

spectrum consisting of continuous range of wavelengths.

continuous wave

electromagnetic wave generated or transmitted continuously over a period of time and not in short pluses.

continuum

a system of axes that form a frame of reference. The three dimensions of space and the dimension of time together can be taken to form a four-dimensional continuum; this was sugested by Minkowski in connection with special relativity.

control drive

the system of control rods which regulate the rate of reaction of a nuclear reactor is known as control drive.

control rods

neutron-absorbing rods made of boron, cadmium etc. Which can be moved up or down their axis and thus control continuously the rate of nuclear fission reaction in a reactor.

control unit

the part of the central processor of a computer that supervises the execution of a computer program.

controlled fusionit is a fusion reaction in a controlled manner to generate power.

controlled thermonuclear reactor

a fusion reaction generated in a controlled manner for research purpose or for production of useful power.

convection

1. it is a method of heat transfer in which there is movement of molecules of the liquid or gas. It may also refer to the

transmission of energy or mass by a medium involving movement of the medium itself.

conventional current

is a current due to transfer of negatively changed electrons.

convergent beam

a beam of light meeting at a point.

converging lens

a lens that converges a beam of light incident on it parallel to its axis, at a point on its axis.

converter

1. An electrical machine for converting alternating current into direct current, or less frequently, vice versa. 2. The reaction vessel in the Bessemer process or some similar steel-making process. 3. A computer device for jcoverting information coded in one form into some other form.

converter reactor

a nuclear reactor that converts fertile material into fissile material. A converter reactor can also be used to produce electrical power.

convertor

a device which converts a.c. to d.c. current and vice versa.

convex

a convex mirror is one with a convex reflecting surface. A convex lens is either a biconvex lens or a plano-convex lens.

cooke objective

a three lens objective consisting of one biconcave lens, the dispersive component, between two biconvex lens, the collective components, used in astronomical cameras.

coolant

a fluid that removes energy from a source, for example, an engine, by convention.

coolidge tube

a type of x-ray tube invented by W.D. Coolidge which employs a thermionic cathode and an air-water-cooled anode.

cooling

setting aside a highly radioactive material until the radioactivity has diminished to a desired level.

cooling correction

a correction applied in experiments involving temperature changes as, some heat is lost due to temperature difference between the body and the air. So a correction has to be applied for that.

cooling stress

it refers to a stress resulting from uneven contraction during cooling of metals and ceramics due to nonuniform temperature distribution.

coordination lattice

a lattice in which each ion bears the same relation to the neighbouring ions in all directions, thus the identity of the molecules becomes ambiguous.

coordination number

the number of equidistant nearest neightbour atoms surrounding a given atom in a crystal.

coplanar forces

forces which act in the same plane.

copper loss

power loss in a winding due to current flow through the resistance of the copper conductors.

corbino effect

if current is passed from the centre to the circumference of a metal disc having its surface at right angles to a magnetic field, a current will flow round the circumference.

core

refers to either a magnetic material used to concentrate the magnetic lines of force as in a transformer. The central part of a nuclear reactor where the chain reaction takes place.

corona current

the current of electricity equivalent to the rate of charge transferred to the air from an object experiencing corona discharge.

corona discharge

a luminous discharge which appears round the surface of a conductor due to unionization of the air by the voltage gradient exceeding a critical value, but not being sufficient to cause sparking.

corona failure

high-voltage failure initiated by corana discharge at areas of high-voltage stress such as metal inserts or terminals.

corona shield

a shield placed about a point of high potential to redistribute electrostatic lines of force.

corpuscle

a particle of light in the corpuscular theory, corresponding to the photon in the quantum theory.

corrosion

deterioration by chemical attack by its environments.

corruated lens

a lens having circular sections cut out from the surface to reduce its weight without lowering its focal power.

cosine rule

in any triangle, with sides of length a, b, and c, $c^2 = a^2 + b^2 - 2ab\cos q$, where q is the angle between sides a and b.

cosmic rays

high-energy radiation, consisting of mainly protons with some particles, electrons and other atomic nuclei and y-rays reaching the earth from space.

cosmogeny

refers to the study of the origin and development of the universe or of a particular system in the universe, i.e. the solar system or a satellite system of a planet.

cosmology

the branch of astronomy that deals with the evolution, general structure, and nature of the universe as a whole.

cosmotron

a proton accelerator containing a very large ring-shaped electromagnet. It is capable of imparting energies of billions of electron volts.

cottrell precipitator

an electrostatic precipitator used to remove dust particles from industrial waste gases, by attracting them to charged grids or wires.

coulomb

si units of electric charge. It is the quantity of electricity transferred by 1 ampere in one second.

coulomb antenna

an antenna electro-magnetically coupled to another.

coulomb field

the electric field created by a stationary charged particle.

coulomb force

the electrostatic force of attraction or replusion exerted by one charged particle on another.

coulomb friction

a collision of two charged particles in which the coulomb force is the dominant interaction.

coulomb

si unit of electric charge, defined as the quantity of electricity transferred by 1 ampere in one second.

counter

a device used for detecting and counting of particles and electromagnetic radiation.

counting rate

it is exhibits the average rate of occurrence of events as observed by means of a counting system

couple

two equal and opposite parallel forces applied to the same body that do not act in the same line. The forces create a torque, the moment of which is equal to the product of the force and the perpendicular distance between them. See moment of a force.

coupled oscillators

a set of alternating-current circuits which interact with each other.

coupled wave

a surface wave which is being continuously generated by another wave having the same phase velocity.

covelent bond

atomic bonding by sharing electrons resulting in reduction of energy.

CP invariance

the symmetry generated by the combined operation of changing charge conjugation (C) and parity (P). CP violation occurs in weak interactions in kaon decay. See also CPT theorem; time reversal.

CPS

is a prefix used for cycles per second.

CPU (central processing unit)

the main operating part of a computer; it includes the control unit (CU) and the arithmetic/logic unit (see ALU). Its function is to fetch instructions from memory, decode them, and execute the program. It also provides timing signals.

creep

a slow deformation of a solid as a result of a continuous applied stress.

creep rupture strength

the stress which at a given temperature, will cause a material to rupture at a given time.

crinal

a unit of force. 1 crinal = 0.1 n.

critical assembly

an assembly of sufficient fissionable and moderator material to sustain a fission chain reaction at a low power level.

critical damping

this term is used for damping in a linear system on the threshold between oscillatoryand exponential be haviour.

critical damping resistance

the resistance of a galvanometer at which the oscillations just stop. If C.D.R. < resistance, galvanometer is oscillatory, and if C.D.R.> Resistance, it is dead beat.

critical facility

a facility where critical experiments are conducted.

critical frequency

it is the limiting frequency below which a radio wave is reflected by an ionospheric layer at vertical incidence at a given time.

critical mass

the minimum amount of fissile material that is required in a nuclear reactor to sustain a chain-reaction.

critical potential

the minimum energy required to raise the energy level of an orbital electron or to remove it from the atom. See ionization potential and radiation potential.

critical pressure

the pressure of the saturated vapour of a substance at the critical temperature.

critical speed

it is the speed above which the motion of a fluid becomes turbulent. Below it, the motion is streamlined.

critical state

the state of a fluid in which the liquid and gas phases both have the same density. The fluid is then at its critical temperature, critical pressure, and critical volume.

critical temperature

the temperature above which a gas cannot be liquified by pressure alone.

critical velocity

the velocity at which the flow of a liquid ceases to be streamlined and becomes turbulent.

critical volume

the volume occupied by unit mass of a substance at its critical temperature and critical pressure.

crombar

a device or action that in effect places a high overload on the actuating elements of a circuit breaker or other protective device, thus triggering it.

crooke's darks space

it appears near the cathode in a discharge tube when an electric discharge is allowed to pass through it, at a pressure 0.5 mm of Hg. At 10^{-2}mm of Hg, it appears between the cathode and negative glow.

Crookes, Sir William

(1832-1919) British chemist and physicist, who in radiometer. He also developed an improved vacuum tube for studying gas discharges.

crossed lens

a lens designed with radii of curvature which give minimum spherical aberration for parallel incident rays.

cross section

the term is used for apparent are which is to be attributed to an atom for its interaction with an incident beam of bombarding particles. This term can also be used for the area of cylindrical (hollow and solid) bodies.

cross over

a point at which two conductors cross, with appropriate insulation between them to prevent contact.

crucible

a dish or other vessel in which substances can be heated to a high temperature.

crushing strain

compression which causes the failure of a material.

cryogenics

refers to the study of materials and phenomenon at very low temperatures close to absolute zero.

cryohydrate

a eutectic mixture of ice and some other substance (e.g. an ionic salt) obtained by freezing a solution.

cryometer

a thermometer especially designed for measuring low temperatures.

cryopumping

the technique of removing gas from a system by condensing it on a surface maintained at very low temperatures.

cryoscopy

the determination of freezing points.

cryostat

a cryostat is a device used for maintaining temperatures below 0°C in a given space for definite period.

crystal

a substance whose constituents are arranged in a definite geometrical form.

crystal analysis

X-ray crystallography is used for this.

crystal base

refers to the entire content of the unit cell, whether considered as a symmetrical arrangement of atoms or as a symmetrical distribution of electron density.

crystal controlled oscillator

this makes use of a mechanically vibrating quartz cyrstal for generating electrical oscilations of constant frequency. Piezoelectric effect of quartz cyrstals plays an important role in coupling vibrations with the electric circuit.

crystal counter

a counter tube which depends upon a crystal in which the electrical conductivity is momentarily increased by an ionizing event.

crystal cut

crystal sections may be cut in particular crystallographic directions which are specified as cuts and designated by letters such as x-cut, AT cut and so on.

crystal defect

an imperfection in the regular lattice pattern of a crystal. See Feature (pp 100-101).

crystal detector

its action depends upon its

properly of rectification of current, when placed in contact with a metal. It was used in earlier days in Radios as a detector for separating the single information from the carrier frequency.

crystal diffraction

the constructive and destructive interference of waves scattered by the periodic arrangement of electrons, nuclei, or field of force in a crystal giving a pattern of discrete spectra.

crystal filter

a filter having one or more piezoelectric crystals forming resonant or antiresonant circuits in the filter.

crystal grating

the symmetrical arrangement of the atoms in a crystal in a series of parallel planes which enables the crystals to act as a three dimensional diffraction grating for x-rays.

crystal laser

a laser that uses a pure crystal of ruby or other material for generating a coherent beam of light.

crystal lattice

the regular pattern of atoms, ions, or molecules in by repeated translations of a unit cell of the lattice. See also crystal system.

crystallography

the study of crystal form and structure. See also X-ray crystallography.

crystal optics

the study of the propagation of light, and associated phenomena, in crystalline solids.

crystal oscillator

a fixed-frequency oscillator in which the output is derived from a crystal of rochelle salt or quartz specially cut so that its raturel frequency of mechanical vibration is the derived value.

crystal rectifier

a semiconductor used as a diode; its action is similar to that of a diode.

crystalline

a solid with a crystal structure, a regular internal arrangement of atoms, ions or molucules.

crystalline field

it stands for an internal E–field in a solid due to localized charges (especially ions) inside.

crystallogram

ıethod used to study structure f crystals.

tr

ee controlled thermonuclear ɘactor.

ubec

unit of valume flow rate, used rimarily to describe pumps, qual to a uniform flow of 1 cubic ot in 1 second.

ubical antenna

ı antenna array, the elements which are positioned to form cube.

ıbical expansion

e increase in volume of a ıbstance with a change in mperature or pressure.

ıbic crystal

crystal in which the unit cell is cube (see crystal system). ıere are three possible ıckings for cubic crystals: mple cubic, face-centred bic, and body-centred cubic. ɘe illustration.

bic equation

equation in which the highest wer of the variable is three. It s the general form $ax^3 + bx^2$ $x + d = 0$ and, in general, is tisfied by three values of x.

cumulative dose

the total dose resulting from repeated exposures to radiation.

cumulative excitation

process by which the atom is raised from one excited state to a higher state by collision, for example, with an electron.

cumulative, ionization

it is a process f ionization of an excited atom in the metastable state by means of cumulative excitation.

curie

the former unit of activity. It is named after Marie Curie.

curie point

the temperature above which a ferromagnetic substance becomes paramagnetic.

curie temperature

it exhibits transition between ferromagnetism and paramagnetism or between ferroelectric phase and paraelectric phase.

curi-weiss law

it states a relation between magnetic or electric susceptibilities and absolute temperatures, non-polar ferroelectric, antiferro-electrics and some paramagnets.

current

it is the flow of charge across a point and is measured in amperes (a) la = 1 coulomb/sec.

current antinode

a point at which current is a maximum along a transmission line, antenna, or other circuit element having standing waves.

current balance

an instrument used for accurately measuring electric current. It involves the measurement of force between two conductors carrying the current.

current-carrying capacity

the maximum current that can be continuously carried without causing permanent deterioration of electrical or mechanical properties of a device or conductor.

current density

1. the current flowing through a conductor per unit area. It is expressed in amperes per square metre. 2. (In electroly) is the current flowing per unit area of electrode.

current divider

a decide used to deliver a desirec fraction of a total currant to a circuit.

current drain

the amount of current extractec from a voltage source by a loac is called current drain.

current intensity

the magnitude of an electric current.

current relay

it is a relay that operates at a specified current value rathe than at a specified voltag source by a load.

curtain

a very thin shield which surrounds the nuclear reactor to completely stop the flow of slov neutrons from it, is called its curtain.

curve resistance

the force opposing the motion of a railway train along a trac due to track curvature.

currvilinear motion

motion along a curved path.

cusp

a point at which two arcs of

curve intersect.

customer substation

a distribution substation located on the premises of a larger customer, such as a shopping centre, or industrial plant.

cutoff

technique used when the contribution to the value of a physical quantity by integration over a certain variable is absurd.

cutout

an electrical device that is used to interrupt the flow of current through any particular instrument, either automatically or manually.

cw laser

cutaneous wave laser; a laser that radiates its energy in an uninterrupted beam.

cyanometer

an instrument designed to measure or estimate the degree of blueness of light, as of the sky.

cybernetics

the theory of communication and control mechanisms in living being and machines.

cycle per minute

a unit of frequency of action, equal to 1/60 hertz.

cycle

a set of changes or operations which a system undergoes, finally coming back to its original position.

cycloid

the curve traced by a point on the circumference of a circle as it rolls without slipping along a straight line. The length of the arc formed by one revolution of the circle is 8r, where r is the radius of the circle. The horizontal distance between cusps is 2pr.

cyclostropic flow

a form of gradient flow in which the centripetal acceleration exactly balances the horizontal pressure force.

cyclotron radiation

the electromagnetic radiation emitted by charged particles as they orbit in a magnetic field, at a speed which is not close to the speed of light.

cylindrical antenna

it is an antenna in which a hollow cylinere serves as the radiating element.

cylindrical cavity

a cavity resonator in the shape of a right circular cylinder.

cylindrical atenna

an antenna in which hollow cylinders serve as radiating elements.

cylindrical reflector

a reflector that is a portion of a cylinder.

cylindrical winding

the current carrying element of a core-type transformer, consisting of a single coil of one or more layers wound concontrically with the iron core.

d'alembert's paradox

the paradox that no forces act on a body moving at constant velocity in a straight line through a large mass of incompressible fluid which was initially at rest, or in uniform motion.

d'alembert's principle

according to this principle the resultant of the external forces and the kinetic reaction acting on a body is always equal to zero.

dagor lens

a specially designed anastingmatic lens. It has tw lens systems which are nearl symmetrical with respect to th stop.

daily variation

the small variations of th horizontal intensity, magneti declination and dip recurring ove a period of a day.

dalitz pair

an electron positron pair as car be produced by the decay of a neutral x-meson.

dalitz plot

in nuclear physics, a graphica method of obtaining informatior on the spin and intrinsic parity of a charged particle decaying into three particles.

dalton's law

the total pressure of a mixture of gases or vapours is equal to the sum of the partial pressures of its components, i.e. the sum of the pressures that each component would exert if it were present alone and occupied the same volume as the mixture of gases.

damaging stress

the minimum unit stress for a given material and area that will cause damage to the member and make it unfit for its expected length of service.

damped oscillation

an oscillation whose amplitude decreases with time.

damped wave

a wave in which amplitude of each sinusoidal component decreases with time.

damping

a decrease in the amplitude of an oscillation or motion with time.

damping capacity

a material's capacity in absorbing vibrations.

damping factor

the ratio of the logarithmic decrement of any underdamped harmonic motion to its period.

damping ratio

the ration of the actual resistance in damped harmonic motion to that required to produce critical damping.

daniell cell

refers to a type of primary cell which consists of two electrodes in different electrolytes separated by a porous partition. The positive electroe has been copper immersed in copper (II) sulphate solphuric acid the e.m.f. has bee about 1.08 volts; with zinc sulphate it has been about 1.11 volts.

At the copper electrode copper ions in solution gain electrons from the metal and get deposit as copper atoms:
$Cu^{2+} + 2e^{-}$ ® Cu
The copper electrode thus gains a positive charge. At the zinc electrode, zinc atoms from the electrode use electrons and dissolve into solution as zinc ions, leaving a net negative charge on the electrode:

Zn® $2e^{-} + Zn^{2:}$.

darey's law

the law that the rate at which a fluid flows through a permeable substance per unit area is equal to the permeability.

dark conduction

electrical conduction in a photosensitive material which is not exposed to radiation.

dark fringes

$$\frac{x.d}{D} = (2n+1)\frac{\lambda}{2}, n = 0, 1, 2, 3$$

distance between two dark fringers]

$x_2 - x_1 = \frac{\lambda D}{2}$, width of frings

$\beta = \frac{\lambda D}{d}$.

dark-line spectrum

the absorption spectrum that results when white light passes through a substance, consisting of dark lines, against a bright background.

dark space

the comparatively non-luminous portion of an electrical discharge through a gas.

dasejemeter

a thin glass globe used time-share the density of gas by weighing the globe in the gas.

daspun antenna

satellite directional antenna pointed continuously at earth by electrically or mechanically despinning the antenna at the same rate that the satellite is spinning for stabilizing.

DAT (digital audio tape)

a type of magnetic tape original designed for audio recording but now adapted for computer storage and backup use. The recording method allows a capacity of about 1 gigabyte.

database

a large collection of information that has been coded and stored in a computer in such a way that it can be extracted under a number of different category headings.

data transmission line

a system of electrical conductors such as a coaxial cable or pair of wires used to send information from one place to another or one part of a system to another.

daughter

1. a nuclide produced by radioactive decay of some other nuclide. 2 An ion or free radical produced by dissociation or reaction of some other ion or radical.

daughter nucleus

a nucleus resulting from the radioactive decay of another nucleus, called parent nucleus.

Davy, Sir Humphry

(1778-1829) British chemist, who studied gases at the Pneumjatic Institute in Bristol, where he discovered the anaesthetic properties of dinitrogen oxide.

day

the time taken for the earth to complete one revolution on its axis. The solar day is the interval between two successive returns of the sun to the meridian. The mean solar day of 24 hours is the average value of the solar day for one year.

dawes' limit

the resolving power of a telescope, limited by diffraction effects is 4.5/a seconds of arc, where a is the aperture in inches.

day

the time taken by the earth to complete one rotation about its axis. The time between two successive transits of the sun across the meridian is called the solar day.

daylight lamp

an incandescent or fluorescent lamp that emits light whose spectral distribution is approximately that of daylight.

dc-to-dc converter

an electronic circuit which converts one direct-current voltage into another.

dead beat galvanometer

a galvanometer which is damped so that its oscillations die away very quickly. In such galvanometer its resistance is less than its critical damping resistance.

dead earth

this term is used in electricity and is referred to the connection between any line conductor and earth by means of a path of low resistance.

dead-end

the end of a sound studio that has the greater sound-absorbing characteristics.

dead-end switch

a switch used to short-circuit unused portions of a tapped coil to prevent dead-end effects.

dead time

the time interval immediately following a stimulus during which it is insensitive to another stimulus.

de broglie equation

is the relations given by $l = \frac{h}{m\nu}$,

Here l is the wavelength, h is plancke's constant, m is the mass of the particle and v is the velocity of the particle.

debye

a unit of electric dipole moment

in the electrostatic system, used to express dipole moments of molecules. It is the dipole moment produced by two charges of opposite sign, each of 1 statcoulomb and placed 10^{-18} cm apart, and has the value 3.33564×10^{-30} coulomb metre.

debye frequency

the maximum allowable frequency in the computation of the debye specific heat.

debye length

refers to the maximum distance at which the coulomb field of charge particles in a plasma can interact.

deca

symbol: da. the prefix meaning 10, e.g. 1 decametre = 10 metres.

decaliter

a unit of volume equal to 10 litres.

decametre

a unit of length in the metric system equal to 10 metres.

decay constant

if N_0 is the number of nuclei at t =0 and N at any time t. Then we have $N = N_0 e^{-\lambda . t}$.

decay curve

a graph showing the variation of the concentration of a radioactive sample with time.

decay heat

the amount of heat given out by the decay of a radioactive include is called its decay heat.

deceleration

the rate of decrease of speed of motion.

decentered lens

a lens whose optical centre does not coincide with the geometrical centre of the rim of the lens.

deci

symbol d. A prefix used in the metric system to denote one tenth. For example, 0.1 coulomb = 1 decicoulomb (dC); 0.1 metre = 1 decimetre (dm).

deciare

a unit of area equal to 10 square metres.

decibar

a metric unit of pressure equal to one-tenth bar.

decibel

a unit used to express they

intensity of a sound wave. It is measured on a logarithm scale.

declination

1. the angle between the magnetic meridian and the geographic meridian at a point on the surface of the earth see geomagnetism. 2. The angular distance of a celestial body north of the celestial equator.

declination, angle of

refers to the angle between the magnetic meridian and the geographic meridian at a point on the surface of the earth.

declination angle of

the angle between the magnetic meridian and the geographic meridian at a point on the surface of the earth.

decomposition voltage

the maximum potential difference which can be applied to the electrodes of an electrolytic cell without giving rise to a permanent current through the cell.

decoupling

preventing transfer or feedback of energy from one circuit to another.

decrement

the ratio of the amplitudes of an underdamped harmonic motion during two successive oscillations. Also known as damping factor; numerical decrement.

deergize

to disconnect from the source of power.

deerhorn antenna

a dipole antenna whose ends are swept back to reduce wind resistance when mounted on an airplane.

defect

an irregularity in the ordered arrangement of particles in a crystal littice.

defect conduction

conduction due to the presence of holes in the valence band of a semi-conductor.

definition

the sharpness of focus of an image. No image can be perfectly sharp because of diffraction, even with a perfect optical system.

deflection galvamound

(i) End on position or tan A or Gauss A position

$$\tan\theta = \frac{2Mr}{H(r^2 - \ell^2)^2}.$$

(ii) Broad side on position or tan B or Gauss B position

$$\tan\theta = \frac{M}{H(r^2 - \ell^2)^{3/2}}.$$

deformation curve

a curve showing the relationship between the stress or load on a structure, structural member or a specimen and the strain or deformation that result. Also known as stress strain curve.

deformation potential

the electric potential due to deformation of the crystal lattice of semiconductors and conductors.

degaussing

neutralisation of magnetisation of mass of magnetic material.

degeneracy

in a resonant device, the condition where two or more modes have the same frequency.

degenerate gas

a gas in which, because of high density, the particle concentration is so high that the Maxwell–Boltzmann distribution does not apply and the behaviour of the gas is governed by quantum statistics.

degenerate level

an energy level of a quantum-mechanical system that corresponds to more than one quantum state.

degenerate matter

matter that has been stripped of its orbital electrons, so the nuclei are packed close together.

degenerate semiconductor

a heavily doped semiconductor in which the Fermi level is located in either the valence band or the conduction band causing the material to behave as a metal.

degenerate states

quantum states of a system that have the same energy.

degradation

loss of energy of a particle, such as a neutron photon, through a collision.

degress of freedom

refers to the number of independent co-ordinates required to define the state of a system.

deionized water

water from which dissolved ionic salts have been removed by ion-exchange techniques. It is used for many purposes as an alternative to distilled water.

dekatron

a neon-filled tube with a central anode surrounded by ten cathodes and associated transfer electrodes. As voltage pulses are received by the tube a glow discharge moves from one set of electrodes to the next enabling the device to be used as a visual counting tube in the decimal system. The tube can also be used for switching.

del (nabla)

symbol Ñ;. The differential vector operator i ¶/¶x + j ¶/¶y + k ¶/¶z.

delayed alpha particle

an alpha particle emitted by an excited nucleus that was formed an appreciable time after a beta disintegration process.

delayed neutrons

neutrons produced from nuclear fission and are not directly formed in the fission process but are produced from excited fission products by beta decay.

delay line

a transmission line or any other device which introduce a known delay in the transmission of a signal.

delay time

the time taken for a pulse to traverse device or circuit.

delbnick scattering

elastic scattering of gamma rays by a nucleus caused by virtual electron positron pair production.

deliquescence

the absorption of water from the atmosphere by a hygroscopic solid to such an extent that a concentrated solution of the solid eventually forms.

dellinger fade-out

a failure of short-wave radio communication caused by a highly absorbing d layer in the ionosphere associated with a sunspot.

delta connexion

connexion of a three-phase electrical system so that the corresponding findings of the transformers form a triangle.

delta current

electricity going through a delta connection.

delta network

the term is commonly used in electricity and comprises a set of three branches connected in series to form a mesh.

delta-ray

a low energy electron emitted by a substance after bombardment by high energy particles (e.g.α-particles).

degeneracy

the state of matter when it is at such a high temperature that all the electrons have been stripped from the atoms. The materials is made up of atomic nuclei and electrons and found in neutron stars.

degrees of freedom

the number of independent co-ordinates needed to define the state of a system.

dekatron

a cold cathode scaling tube having ten cathodes arranged in a circle, and associated transfer electrodes surrounding the anode.

del

syn,. nabla, Summbol ∇. The differential operator i $(\delta/\delta x)$ + j $(\delta/\delta y)$ + k $(\delta/\delta z)$, i, j, and k are unit vectors along the x–,y–, and z–axes respectively. The Laplace operator is it $\nabla 2^0$.

demagnetization curve

refers to a curve which shows the relation between the magnetic flux density and the magnetizing force for values of the latter decreasing from saturated to zero induction.

demagnetization energy

the energy which would be released when a magnetized body is completely demagnetized.

demand factor

the ratio of the maximum demand of a building for electric power to the total connected load. Also known as demand.

demand rate

the maximum amount of electric power that must be kept available to a customer is known as demand rate.

demodulation

the process of separation of the audio signal from the modulated signal wherein the audio signal is superposed on the carrier wave.

denature

to add another isotope to a fissile material to make it unsuitable for use in a nuclear weapon.

dendrite

skeleton crystal.

densitometer

instrument for the measurement of the density of an image produced by light, gamma rays etc., on a photographic plate.

density

1. the mass of a substance per unit of volume. In SI units it is measured in kg m^{-3}. See also relative density; vapour density. 2. See charge density. 3. See photographic density.

density bottle

an accurately calibrated thin glass bottle. It is used for determining the density of liquids.

density of gases

it is directly proportional to the pressure ($d \propto p$) and inversely proportional to the absolute temperature

$$\left(d \propto \frac{1}{T}\right)$$

density of states

it refers to the number of electronic states per unit volume having energies in the range from E to E + dE. It is an important concept of band theory of solids.

depleted

denoting a material that contains less of a particular isotope than it normally contains, especially a residue from a nuclear reactor or isotope-separation plant containing fewer fissile atoms than natural uranium.

depletion layer

the region of a semi-conductor in which the density of mobile carriers is too low to neutralize the fixed charge density of donors and acceptors. This layer is also called as barrier.

depolarization

the prevention of polarization in a primary cell. For example, maganese (IV) odixe (the depolarizes) is placed around the positive electrode of a Leclanche cell to oxidize the hydrogen released at this.

depolarizer

a substance like manganesian dioxide used to prevent polarization in a voltaic cell.

depth dose

the amount of radiation dose delivered at a particular depth beneath the surface of a body is known as depth dose.

depth magnification

the ratio of the distance between two nearby points of the axis on the image side of an optical system to the distance between their conjugate points on the object side.

depth of field

depth of focus. The range over which a camera or other optical instrument, will produce a distinct image of an object.

derived units

the units of physical quantities other than those of length, mass and time.

desorption

the removal of adsorbed atoms, molecules, or ions from a surface.

detached shock wave

a shock wave not in contact with the body which originates it.

detector

1. an instrument which responds to a physical effect. It is used to detect the presence of the effect or to measure it. 2. A circuit for separating the original modulating signal from a modulated wave.

detonation wave

a shock wave in a combustible mixture, which originates as a combustion wave.

detonating rate

the velocity at which the explosion wave passes through a cylindrical charge.

deuterated compound

a compound in which some or all of the hydrogen—1 atoms have been replaced by deuteriunm atoms.

deuteron

nucleus of deuterium atom consisting of a proton and a neutron.

deuteron accelerator

an accelerator that produces a flux of slow neutrons by bombarding a metal tritium target with deuterons.

deuteron capture

the absorption of a deuteron by a nucleus, giving rise to a compound nucleus which subsequently decays.

deviation

refers to bending of a light ray or other form of radiation from its original path, as measured by the angle between the diections of the incident ray and of the diffracted or refracted ray.

dew

water droplets produced due to condensation of water vapour in the air when the temperature of air falls so that the amount of vapour present at that temperature reaches saturation.

dewcap

an open tube attached to the end of a refracting telescope to prevent moisture from condensing on the objective.

dew point

refers to the temperature at which dew begins to form.

dew point hygrometer

it is instrument used for determination of relative humidity.

dewar flask

a double walled glass glask, the space between walls being evacuated and sealed. The inner surfaces of glass walls are silvered to minimise transfer of heat by radiation.

dextrorotatory

denoting a compound that rotates the plane of polarization of plane-polarized light to the right. See optical activity.

dextrorotatory compound

refers to optically active substance which turns the plane of polarization of light to the right.

diabatic

involving a thermodynamic change of state of a system in which there is a transfer of heat across the boundaries of the system.

dial key

key unit of the subscribers cord circuit used to connect the dial into the line.

dial lamp

a small lamp used to illuminate a dial.

diamagnetic faraday effect

faraday effect at frequencies near an absorption line which is split due to the splitting of the upper level only.

diamagnetic substances

refers to those substances that have a negative value of suscoptibility. They are repelled when placed in a magnetic field.

diamagnetism

refers to the behaviour of diamagnetic substances.

diamagnetism

the behaviour of diamagnetic substance. See diamagnetic substances.

diamonds

the pattern of shock waves often visible in a rocket exhaust which resembles a series of diamond shapes placed end-to-end.

diaphragm

a device to control the aperture of an optical system so that a desired amount of light enters the system. They also help reduce defects of images resulting from the light incident over a wide part of the opening of the system.

diascope

an optical projector for translucent objects the name is rather old fashioned.

diastereoisomers

stereoisomers that are not idential and yet not mirror images. For instance, the d-form of tartaric acid and the meso form constitute a pair of diastereoisomers. See optical activity.

diathermanous

substances that allow the radiation to pass through are known as diathermanous.

diatomic

substances whose molecules consist of two atoms.

diatonic scale

a musical scale in which the octave is divided into intervals of two different sizes, five of one and two of other, with adjustments in turning systems other than equal temperament.

dichoric mirror

colour selective mirror. Such a mirror reflects a particular band of spectral energy and trnsmits all others.

dichroism

some crystals have different absorption for the two polarised components of a doubly refracted beam. The phenomena is called dichroism and rich crystals are called dichroic crystals.

dichromate cell

syn. bichromate cell. A orimary cell having poles of carbon and amalgamated zinc immersed acid. A two flud form, in which the zinc is in dilute suplhuric acid and the carbon in an aqueous solution of dichromate, the two being separated by a porous partition, has also been used. Its e.m.f. is 2.03 volts.

dielectric

an insulator; a nonconductor of electricity. Refers to those substances in which an electric field produces a displacement of charges but there is no net flow of charge.

dielectric absorption

the persistence of electric polarization in certain dielectrics after removal of the electric field.

dielectric antenna

an antenna in which a dielectric is the major component used to produce a desired radiation pattern.

dielectric current

the current flowing at any instant through a surface of a dielectric that is located in changing electric field.

dielectric hyterisis

the polarisation of a dielectric depends on its previous variation in addition to the applied electric field. It leads to a power loss with alternating currents.

dielectric lens

a lens made of a suitable dielectric to refrect radiowaves before they reach a microwave aerial.

dielectric lens antenna

an aperture antenna in which the beam width is determined by the dimensions of a dielectric lens through which the beam passes.

dielectric loss

the electric energy that is converted into heat in a dielectric subjected to varying electric field. Also known as dielectric absorption.

dielectric phse angle

it is the angle between the applied electric field and the corresponding conduction current vector. The cosine of this angle is the power factor of the dielectric.

dielectric polarisation

it refers to the phenomenon that is explained by the formation of doublets (dipoles) of elements of dielectric ender stress.

dielectric shielding

the reduction of an electric field in some region by interposing a dielectric substance, such as polystyrene glass or mica.

dielectric strength

the maximum electric field that a dielectric is capable of withstanding without a breakdown.

dielectric wave guide

a waveguide in which the waves travel through solid dielectric material.

diesel cycle

diesel was dissatisfied with the low efficiency of the onto engine and was led to investigate certain continuances whereby the efficiency of the carnot cycle may be reached.

diesel engine

an internal combustion engine which uses heavy oil as a fuel.

difference tone

a combination tone whose frequency equals the difference of the frequencies of the pure tones producing it.

differential

means involving the difference of two or more motions, forces etc.

differential amplifier

an amplifier with two inputs which the output is a function of the difference between the inputs.

differential antenna

an antenna which receives or radiates radiowaves more effectively in some direction as compared to others is known as differential antenna.

differential calorimetry

technique for measurement of and comparison of process heats for a specimen and a reference material.

differential gear

it is an epicyclic train of gears that is designed in such a way so as to allow two or more shafts to revolve at different speeds e.g. a set of gears in an automobile allowing the rear wheels to be driven at different speeds when the car is turning.

differential geometry

the branch of geometry concerned with the applications of differential calculus to geometry. Differential geometry has important applications in gauge theories, the general theory of relativity, and some problems in the theory of condensed matter.

differential pressure

the difference in pressure between two points of a system, such as between the well bottom and well head or between the two sides of an orifice.

differential pulley

it is sa syste of two blocks– one the upper one, consisting of two sheaves of different diameters and cast together to form one piece and the other, the lower one containing one sheave only. The links of the endless chain fit into the projections on the rims of the sheaves. The mechanical advantage of such a pulley is slightly less than one half of velocity ratio. Its efficiency is less than 50%.

differential relay

a two winding relay that operates when the difference between the currents in the two windings reaches a predetermined value.

diferential transducer

a transducer that simultaneously senses two separate sources and provides an output proportional to the difference between them.

differential transformer

a transformer used to join two or more sources of signals to a common transmission line.

differential voltmeter

a special type of voltmeter which measures only the difference between a known voltage and an unknown voltage.

differential winding

a winding whose magnetic field opposes that of a nearby winding is known as differential winding.

differential wound field

type of motor or generator field having both series and shunt coils that are connected to oppose each other.

differentiating circuit

a circuit whose output voltage is proportional to the rate of the change of the input voltage. Also known as differentiating network.

diffluence

a region of fluid flow in which the fluid is diverging from the direction of flow.

diffracted wave

a wave whose front has been changed in direction by an obstacle or other non-homogeneity in a medium, other than by reflection or refraction.

diffraction pattern

pattern produced on a screen or plate by waves which have undergone diffraction.

diffraction propagation

propagation of electromagnetic waves around objects or over the horizon by diffraction.

diffraction ring

circular light pattern which appears to surround particles in a microscope field.

diffraction scattering

elastic scattering that occurs when inelastic process remove particles from a beam.

diffraction spectrum

parallel light and dark or coloured bands of light produced by diffraction.

diffraction zone

the portion of a radio propagation path which lies outside a line of sight path.

diffractometer

an instrument used to study structure of matter by means of the diffraction x-rays, electrons, neutrons of other waves. Also known as diffraction instrument.

diffuse illumination

lighting so arranged that the object is illuminated from many directions or sources.

diffuse radiation

radiant energy propagating in many different directions through a given small volume of space.

diffuse reflection

scattering at all angles from the point of reflection.

diffuse reflector

any surface whose irregularities are so large compared to the wavelength of the incident adiation that the reflected rays are sent back in a multiplicity of directions.

diffuse series

refers to series of spectral lines observed in the spectra f alkali metals. Energy levels for which quantum orbital number is two are designated d –levels.

diffuse sound

sound that has uniform energy density in a given region so that all directions of energy flux at all parts of the region are equally probable.

diffuse spectrum

any spectrum having lines which are very broad even when there is no possibility of line broadening by collisions.

difuse-cutting filter

a colour filer that gradually changes in absorption with wavelength.

diffusion

it is the process of free inter-mixing of molecules, ions etc. It is due to thermal agitation.

diffusion coefficient

the weight of a material in grams, diffusing across an area of 1 square centimetre in 1 second in a unit concentration gradient.

diffusion constant

the diffusion current density in a homogeneous semi-conductor divided by the charge carrier concentration gradient.

diffusion gradient

the graphed distance of penetration or diffusion versus concentration of the material diffusing through a second material.

diffusion length

it is the average distance that is travelled by minority carriers between generation and recombination in a semiconductor.

diffusion limited aggregation

a process of aggregation dominated by particles diffusing and having a nonzero probability of sticking together irreversibly when they touch. The clusters formed by DLA are fractal in type.

diffusion plant

a plant which separates isotopes by isotopic diffusion or thermal diffusion

diffusivity

symbol α. It is equal to the thermal conductivity divided by thespecific heat capacity at constant pressure and the density, i.e. $\alpha = \lambda/pc_p$. It is measured in $m^2\ s^{-1}$.

digit

a symbol used to represent a single number. For example, the number 479 consists of three digits.

digital

using numerical digits for representing discretely all variables occurring in a problem.

digital circuit

any circuit that responds to discrete values of input voltage and produces discrete output voltage levels. Usually only two values of voltage are recognized, as in binary logic circuits.

digital recording

it refers to a method of recording sound in which the sound itself is not recorded, but the pressure in the sound wave is sampled at least 30,000 tines per second and the successive values represented by numbers which are then recorded.

digital voltmeter

a voltmeter that displays the measured values as numbers composed of digits.

digitron

an electronic gas-discharge tube that provides a digital display in calculators, counters, etc. It usually has 10 cold cathodes shaped into the form of the digits 0–9. The cathode selected receives a voltage pulse causing a glow discharge to illuminate the digit.

dihedral

formed by or having two intersecting planes or sides. For example, the angle between two intersecting plane faces of a crystal is a dihedral angle.

dilation

a change in volume.

dilatometer

any apparatus eased for studying thermal expansion.

dilution

reducing the intensity of a colour by adding white.

dimensional analysis

a method of checking an equation or a solution to a problem by analysing the dimensions in which it is expressed. It is also useful for establishing the form, but not the numerical coefficients, of an empirical relationship. If the two sides of an equation do not have the same dimensions, the equation is wrong.

dimensional constant

a physical quantity whose numeric value depends on the units chosen for fundamental quantities but not on the system being considered.

dimensional formula

the expression of a derived quantity as a product of powers of the fundamental quantities.

dimensionless group

any combination of dimensional or dimensional quantities possessing zero overall dimesions.

dimensions

the product of powers of fundamental quantities which are used to define a physical quantity.

dimensional equation

it is an equation in which dimensional formula is equated with the physical or derived quantity e.g. for power, we have $[P] = [M^1 L^2 T^{-3}]$.

dimensional formula

it is an expression that shows how and which of the fundamental units of length, mass and time occur in the derived unit of the given physical quantity e.g. the dimensional formula of force is $(M^1 L^1 T^{-2})$.

dimensiona lanalysis

a method used to check whether a given relation between various physical quantities is correct. The principle used is that dimensions of the fundamental quantities must be same on both sides of an equation.

dimmer

an electrical or electronic control for varying the intensity of a lamp or other light source.

dimorphism

the property of some substances by virtue of which they crystallise in two chemically identical but crystallographically different forms e.g. carbon can crystallise as graphite or diamond.

dimorphous

existing in two different crystalline forms.

dineutron

a combination of two neutrons which has a transitory existence in certain nuclear reactions.

diode

an electronic device with two electrodes. In the obsolescent thermionic diode a heated cathode emits electrons, which flow across the intervening vacuum to the anode when a positive potential is applied to it.

dioptometer

an instrument for determining ocular refraction.

dioptre

unit of power of a lens, it is the reciprocal of focal length of the lens expressed is metres.

dioptometer

it is a device that is used to measure the refraction of the eye.

dip, (inclination), ϕ

the dip at a place is the angle which the earth's field makes wit earth's surface at a place.

dip circle

it is an instrument that is used to measure the angle of dip at a place. It consists of a magnetic needle mounted in such a way that it can rotate in a vertical plane. The angle is measured on a circular scale.

diplex reception

simultaneous reception of two signals which have some features in common, such as a single receiving antenna.

diplexer

a system of coupling which enables a communications transmitter and a radar to be used with the same aerial.

dipole

refers to two equal and opposite electric charges (or magnetic poles) separated by a distance.

dipole disk feed

antenna, consisting of a dipole near disk, used to reflect energy to the disk.

dipole moment

product of the pole strength and length of a magnetic dipole.

dipole radiation

the electromagnetic radiation generated by an oscillating electric or magnetic dipole.

dipole sound field

a sound field generated by an oscillating dipole source.

dipole transition

a transition of an atom or nucleus from one energy state to another in which dipole radiation is emitted or absorbed.

diproton

a hypothetical bound state of two protons, which probably does not exist.

dirac fields

operators arising in the second quantization of the theory, which correspond to the dirac wave functions in the original theory.

direct aperture antenna

an antenna whose conductor or dielectric is a surface or solid, such as a horn, mirror or lens.

direct current

an electric current flowing in one direction only.

direct current circuit

any combination of dc voltage or current sources, such as generators and batteries in conjunction with transmission lines, resistors and motors.

direct current circuit theory

an analysis of relationship within a dc circuit.

direct motion

1. the apparent motion of a planet from west to east as seen from the earth against the background of the stars. 2. The anticlockwise rotation of a planet, as seen from its north pole. Compare retrograde motion.

direct route

in wire communications, the trunks that connect a pair of switching centres, regardless of the geographical direction the actual trunk facilities may follow.

direct stroke

a lightning stroke that actually strikes one part of a power or communication system.

direct vision prism

a compound prism made up of two glasses having different dispersive powers and cemented together in such a way that light passing through the combination suffers no deviation.

direct vision spectroscope

a spectroscope in which the middle portion of the spectrum remains underviated.

direct-current continuity

property of a circuit in which there is an established pathway for conduction of current from a direct-current source.

direct-current generator

a rotating electric machine that converts mechanical power into dc power.

direct-current motor

an electric rating machine energized by direct current and used to convert electric energy to mechanical energy.

direct-current power supply

a power supply that provides one or more dc output voltages such as a dc generator.

direct-current signalling

a transmission method that uses direct current.

direct-current working volts

the maximum continuously applied dc voltage for which a capacitor is rated.

direct-cycle reactor

a nuclear power plant in which the heat transfer fluid circulates through the reactor and then passes directly to the tubing in a continuous cycle.

direct-electromotive force

unidirectional electromotive force in which the changes in values are either zero or so small that they may be neglected.

direct-view finder

a view finder in which the user views the subject directly through a lens or sight.

direct vision spectroscope

a spectroscope in which the middle portion of the spectrum remains undeviated.

direct-voltage

a voltage that forces electrons to move through a circuit in the same direction continuously, thereby producing a direct current. Also known as direct current voltage.

directional antenna

an antenna that radiates or receives radiowaves more effectively in some directions than others.

directional beam

a radio or radar wave that is concentrated in a given direction.

directional counter

a counter that is more sensitive to nuclear radiation from some directions than from others.

directional relay

relay which functions in conformance with the direction of power, voltage, current, pulse, rotation and so on.

director

a parasitic element placed a fraction of a wavelength ahead of a dipole receiving antenna to increase the gain of the array in the direction of the major lobe.

directrix

1. a plane curve defining the base of a cone. 2. A straight line from which the distance to any point on a conic is in a constant ratio to the distance from that point to the focus.

dischange

a silver impregnated cotton wick encased in a flexible plastic tube with an aluminium mounting bug, used in aircraft to reduce precipitation static.

discharge

meəns to remove an electric charge.

discharge key

device for switching a capacitor suddenly from a charging circuit to a load through which it can discharge.

discomposing effect

changes in physical or chemical properties of a substance caused by discomposing. Also known as wigner effect.

disconnect

to open a circuit by removing wires or connections, as distinguished from opening a switch to stop current flow.

disconnect fitting

an electrical connection that can be disconnected without tools.

disconnecting switch

a switch that isolates a circuit or piece of electrical apparatus after interruption of the current. Also known as disconnecter.

disconnecter release

device which disengages the apparatus used in a telephone connection to restore it to its original condition when not in use.

discontinuity

an abrupt change in the shape of a waveguide.

discrete spectrum

a spectrum in which the component wavelengths constitute a discrete sequence of values rather than a continuum of values.

discriminator

an electronic circuit that can discriminate between and select desired electrical single.

disintegration

refers to the break up of a nucleus into fragments, either due to spontaneous decay, or as a result of a collision by external particles.

disintegration constant

decay constant.

dispesion

the splitting up of a ray of light of mixed wavelengths by refraction into its components. Dispersion occurs because of deviation for each wavelength is different on account of the different speeds at which waves of different wavelengths pass through the refracting medium.

disk armature

the armature in a motor that has a disk winding or is made up of a metal disk.

disk telescope

a telescope designed for observations of the brilliant solar disk. e.g., tower telescope and horizontal fixed telescope.

dislocation

a crystal imperfection which facilitates slip. A line defect in a crystal, the result of slip along a surface of on e or more lattice constants.

dispersive line

a delay line that delays each frequency a different length of time.

dispersive medium

a medium in which the phase velocity of an electromagnetic wave is a function of frequency.

dispersive power (ω)

dispersive power of the material of the prism is given by

$$\omega = \frac{\mu_v - \mu_r}{\mu - 1} \text{ for blue \& red rays.}$$

where μ_v and μ_r are the refractive indices of blue and red rays respectively and μ is the refractive index for yellow rays.

displacement

a vector drawn from the initial position to the final position of a particle.

dissecting microscope

either of two types of optical microscope used to magnify materials undergoing dissection.

dissipation factor

the inverse of Q the storage factor.

dissipation loss

a measure of the power loss of a transducer in transmitting signals, expressed as the ratio of its input power to its output power.

dissonance

also known as discord is an unpleasant combination of harmonics heard when certain musical tones are played simultaneously.

distance

the length of the path between two points.

distance ratio

velocity ratio.

distance relay

protective relay, the operation of which is a function of the distance between the relay and the point of fault.

distant field

the electromagnetic field at a distance of five wavelengths or more from a transmitter, where the radial electric field becomes negligible.

distortion

lacking the true proportion orclarity of the original image, sound etc.

distributed constant

a circuit parameter that exists along the entire length of a transmission line. Also known as distributed parameter.

distributed inductance

the inductance that exist along the entire length of a conductor, as distinguished from inductance concentrated in a coil.

distribution cable

cable extending from a feeder cable into a specific area for the purpose of providing service to that area.

distribution centre

in an alternating current power system, the pot at which control and routing equipment is installed.

distribution switch board

power switchboard used for the distribution of electrical energy at the voltage common for each distribution within a building.

distribution transformer

an element of an electric distribution system located near consumers which changes primary distribution voltage to secondary distribution voltage.

distributor points

cam-operated contacts, the opening of which triggers the ignition pulse in an internal combustion engine.

distributive law

the mathematical law stating that one operation is independent of being carried out before or after another operation. For example, multiplication is distributive with respect to addition and subtraction, i.e. x(y +z) = xy + xz. Compare associative law; commutative law.

diurnal

dialy; denoting an event that happens once every 24 hours.

diurnalmotion

refers to the motion of celectial bodies across the sky from east to west. It is caused due to the rotation of the earth.

devergent beam

a beam of light rays moving away from a point. The separation between the rays increases as it moves in space.

divergent beam

a beam of light moving away from a point.

diverging lens

a lens that renders a parallel beam of light falling onto it into a divergent beam. A concave lens is a diverging lens; its focal length and power is negative.

diverging mirror

a mirror that renders a parallel beam of light falling onto it into a divergent beam. A convex mirror is a diverging mirror.

diverging mirror

a mirror which renders a parallel beam of light falling onto it into a divergent beam. A convex mirror is a diverging mirror.

d-lines

two close lines in the yellow region of the visible spectrum of sodium, having wavelengths 589.0 and 589.6 mm. As they are prominent and easily recognized they are used as a standard in spectroscopy.

dolter

a worker who uses a centring machine to locate the optical centre and optical axis of a lens for the guidance of workers who will cut, edge, trim and mount the lens. Also known as spotter.

domain

refers to a bounded region of uniform or unidireftional magnetization or electric or magneric polarization within a ferroelectric or ferromagnetic body.

dominant wave

an electromagnetic wave having the minimum cut off frequency in a given unconductor wave guide, is called a dominant wave.

dominant wavelength

the single wavelength of light that, when combined in unsuitable proportions with a reference standard light, matches the colour of a given sample.

donkey power

a unit of power equal to 250 watts; it is approximately 1/3 hrs. power.

donohue equation

equation used to determine the heat-transfer film coefficient for a fluid on the outside of a baffled shell and tube heat exchanger.

donor

imperfection or impurity added to a semi-conductor to increase the number of charge carriers.

donor level

an intermediate energy level close to the conduction band in the energy diagram of an extrinsic semi-conductor.

doorknob capacitor

a high voltage plastic encased capacitor resembling a doorknob in size and shape.

doping

the process of adding impurity to a semiconductor to achieve desired characteristics, normally to increase its conductivity.

doping level

it refers to the extent of doping in a semi conductor.

doppler broadening

the broadening of spectral lines on account of the motion of particles emitting or absorbing the radiations corresponding to these lines.

doppler effect

according to this effect, the apparent or observed frequency of a wave motion changes as the distance between its source and the observer changes, regardless of whether the source is stationary and the observer approaches it or recedes from it or the source approaches or recedes from the stationary observer. It the distance between source ad observer decreases, the frequency of the wave increase, and if the distance increases, the frequency of the wave increase, and if the distance increases, the frequency of the wave decreases. This effect is applicable to sound, light, as well as the other electromagnetic radiations.

doppler shift

the amount of the change in the observed frequency of a wave due to doppler effect, usually expressed in hertz. Also known as doppler frequency.

doroid

a coil resembling half a toroid, using a removable cone segment to simplify the winding process.

dose

energy imparted by an ionising radiation to living organism and absorbed by it.

dose rate

the rate at which nuclear eradiation is delivered.

dose-rate meter

an instrument that measures radiation dose rate.

dosimeter

any instrument which measures radiation dose.

dosimetry

the measurement of radiation doses. Also known as radiation dosimetry.

dot product (scallar product)

the scallar product of two vectors $\vec{a}$ and $\vec{b}$ is given by the number

$\vec{a}\vec{b} = ab \cos\theta,\ 0 \leq \theta \leq \pi$

where θ is the angle between two vectors. For rectangular vectors $\theta = 90$ so $\cos\theta = 0$ and is such a case, we get

$$\vec{a}\vec{b} = 0$$

For components of a vector along the cartesion axis, the scalar product becomes

$\vec{a}\vec{b} = a_x.b_x + ay.\ by + a_z.b_z$

where $\vec{a} = a_x.\vec{i} + ay\,\vec{j} + a_z.\vec{k}$

and $\vec{b} = bx.\ \vec{i} + by\vec{j} + by.\vec{k}$

double bond

a bond formed between atoms sharing two pairs of electrons.

double break switch

switch which opens the connected circuit at two points.

double bus-double breaker

a situation switching arrangement having two common buses and two breakers per connection.

double bus-single breaker

a substation switching arrangement that involves two common buses and only one breaker per connection.

double mirror

two plane mirrors inclined at an angle to each other.

double refraction

when a beam of light is incident on certain materials, it breaks it into two plane polarised beams with their plane of polarisation perpendicular to each other. The two beams have different velocities in the medium. This phenomenon is called double refraction.

double-current generator

machine which supplies both direct and alternating current from the same armature winding.

double-doublet antenna

two half-wave doublet antennas crisscrossed at their centre, one being shorter than the other to give broader frequency coverage.

double-pole switch

a switch that operates simultaneously in two separate electric circuits or in both lines of a single circuit.

double-shield enclosure

type of shielded enclosure or room in which the inner wall is partially isolated electrically from the outer wall.

double slit experiment

young's double slit.

doublet

1. a pair of associated lines in a spectrum whose wave length are usually very close to each other.
2. A compound lens consisting of two lenses in contact. The arrangement is sometime used forminimizing aberrations.

douling time

the time required for a breeding reactor to double its fuel inventory.

downdraft

a current of air or other gas that travels downward, as during a thunderstorm.

downwash

the downward deflection of air, relative to the direction of motion of an airfoil.

draft differential

the difference in static pressure

between two locomotions of gas flow.

drain

refers to the electrode in a field-effect transistor through which carriers leave the inter-electrode region.

drang

resistance caused by friction in the direction opposite to the direction of motion of airfoil.

draft differential

the difference in static pressure between two locomotions of gas flow.

drag

resistance caused by friction in the direction opposite to that of the motion of the centre of gravity of a moving body in a fluid.

dram

a unit of mass, formerly used in the United Kingdom, equal to 1.77185 grams.

drift

the movement of current carriers in a semiconductor under the influence of an applied voltage.

drift mobility

in a semi-conductor, the average velocity of excess minority carriers per unit electric field.

drift speed

average speed at which electrons or ions progress through a medium.

drit transistor

syn. A transistor in which the impurity concentration in the base changes across the base region. A high doping level at the emitter-base junction reduces across the base to a low doping level at the collector-base junction. They have a very high frequency response.

driver

a circuit whose output provide the input of one or more other circuits.

driver element

antenna array element that receives power directly from the transmitter.

driving point impedance

the ratio of the r.m.s. value of the sinusoidal voltage applied to two terminals of an electrical net work to the r.m.s. value of the current flowing between the terminals as a result of the applied voltage.

drop weight

the term is associated with the weight of the largest drop which can hang from the end of a tube of given radius.

drude's theory of conduction

Drude gave a formula for the specific resistance of a substance, based on classical mechanical considerations.

drum

syn. magnetic drum. A direct access strategy device used in computing which consists of a rapidly rotating cylinder coated with a magnetic iron oxide.

drum winding

a type of winding used in electrical machines, consisting of coils, generally former-wound, which are housed in slots either on the outer periphery of a cylindrical core or on the inner periphery of a core having a cylindrical bore.

dry and wet-bulb hygrometer

in it two thermometers are mounted side by side. The bulb of one of the thermometers is wrapped in a muslin cloth which is kept moist. It is used for determination of relative humidity.

dry battery

a battery made up of a series, parallel or series- parallel arrangement of dry cells in a single housing to provide derived voltage and current values.

dry cell

a leclanche cell in which the electrolyte is in the form of paste instead of being liquid. It is used as source of energy in portable electronic appliances and flash lights.

dry contact

a contact that does not break or make current.

dry criticality

reactor critically achieved without a coolant.

dry friction

resistance between two dry solid surfaces.

dryice

solid carbon dioxide.

dry measure

a measure of volume for commodities that are dry.

dry well

the first containment tank surrounding a water-cooled

nuclear reactor that uses the pressure suppressing containment system.

dry-bulb temperature

the actual air temperature as measured by a dry-bulb thermometer.

dual radioactive decay

property exhibited by a nucleus which has two or more independent and alternative modes of decay.

dual-purpose reactor

any nuclear reactor which both acts as a source of heat energy for a power plant and produces fissionable material.

duane and hunt's law

the maximum photon energy in continuous x-ray spectrum is equal to the kinetic energy of the electrons producing the x-ray.

dubnium

symbol Db. A radioactive transactinide element; a.n. 105. It was first reported in 1967 by a group at Dubna near Moscow and was confirmed in 1970 at Dubna and at Berkeley, California. It can be made by bombarding californium-249 nuclei with nitrogen-15 nuclei. Only a few atoms have ever been made.

ductility

property of substance, usually metals, of being capable of being drawn in wires.

dulong and petit's law

states that the product of the atomic weight and specific heat of a solid element, called its atomic heat is constant for all elements and is nearly 6.4.

dump power

electric power, generated by any source, which is in excess of the needs of the electric system and which cannot be stored or conserved.

dust

a loose term applied to solid particles predominately larger than colloidal size and capable of temporary gas suspension

dwarf star

a stare, such as the sun, that lies on the main sequence in a Hertzsprung–rusell diagram. See also white dwarf.

dynamic behaviour

the behaviour of a control system or an individual component in relation to operational time.

dynamic braking

a technique of electric braking in which the retarding force is supplied by the same machine that originally was the driving motor.

dynamic creep

creep resulting from fluctuations in a load or temperature.

dynamic height

the amount of work done when a water particle of unit mass is moved vertically from one level to another.

dynamic metre

the standard unit of dynamic height expressed as 10 square metres per second per second.

dynamic resistance

a device's electrical resistance when it is in operation.

dynamics

branch of mechanics dealing with the study of the behaviour of bodies under that action of forces that change their motion.

dynamo

an electric generator, especially one designed to provide direct current. Alternating=current generators can be called dynamos but are more often called alternators.

dynamo action

the generation of electrical current and magnetic field by the motion of an electrically conducting fluid. It is generally believed that the magnetic fields of the earth and the sun are produced by dynamo action in the molten iron-nicl\kel core of the earth and in the plasma of the solar interior.

dynamometer

1. an instrument used to measure a force, often a spring balance. 2. A device used to measure the output power of an engine measuring electric current.

dynamic resistance of a diode

it is the ratio of a small change in volume, Δv, to a small change in current $\Delta \ell$. Thus $r_d = \frac{\Delta V}{\Delta \ell}$

dynatoson oscillator

an oscillator using a tetrode in such a way that the anode current increases as the anode voltage is reduced.

dyne

the c.g.s unit of force; the force

required to give a mass of one gram an acceleration of 1 cms^2. 1dyne = 10^{-5} newton.

dynode

an electrode in an electron tube, its primary function is to provide secondary emission of electrons.

dystectic mixture

a mixture of substances that has a constant maximum melting point.

e

the irrational number defined as the limit as n tends to infinity of $(1+1/n)^n$. It has the value 2.71 28 .... It issue as the base of natural logarithms and occurs in the exponential function, e^x.

e-beam

an intense burst of fast electrons from a small particle accelerator, used to excite a pulsed gas laser in which the gas pressure is too high to permit an electric discharge.

e-cell

a timing device that converts the current time integral of an electrical function into an equivalent mass integral up to a maximum of several thousand microampere hours.

e-plane

of electromagnetic waves, a plane containing the direction of maximum radiation.

eachelon

a type of grating used for very high resolution spectroscopy. It consists of a number of glass plates of equal thickness arranged on a slant in a stepwise formulation. The arrangement gives a very large value of the grating element and produces very high spectral orders.

eamshow's theorem

according to this theorem, a charge cannot be held in stable equilibrium by an electrostatic field.

earth

to join an object to earth by a conductor so that it will share any net charge it has with the earth. Because the earth is so large, this effectively means that the earthed object can not keep charge. To earth an object it is connected to a metal plate or stake in the ground.

earth current

also known as grand current, it is associated with the return or fault or leakage of current passing through the earth from some electric equipment.

earth inductor

refers to a type of fluxmeter which is used for measuring large uniform fields.

earth plate

a plate of conducting material buried in the earth to serve as an earth electrode.

earthing

connecting an electrical conductor to earth which is assumed to have zero electric potential.

earthquake

a sudden movement or fracturing within the earth's lithosphere, followed by the series of shocks generated by this movement. This may range from a mild tremor to a large-scale earth movement causing extensive damage over a wide area. The point at which the earthquake originates is known as theseismic focus; the point on the earth's surface directly above this is the epicentre (or hypocentre). Earthquakes result from a buold-up of stresses within the rocks until they are strained to the point beyond which they will fracture. They occur in narrow continuous bolts of activity, which correspond with the junction of lithospheric plates, including the circum-Pacific belt, the junction of lithospheric plates, including the circum-Pacific belt, the Alpine—Himalayan belt, and thew mid-ocean rides. The scale of the shock of an earthquake is known as the magnitude; the most commonly used scale for comparing the magnitude of earthquakes is the logarithmic Richter scale (8.9 is the highest recorded magnitude on the scale).

earthshine

sunlight reflected from the surface of the earth. An observer in space may see nearby objects dimaly illuminated by earthshine, as things on earth may be illuminated by moonlight. Under certain conditions near new moon the dark disc of the moon can be seen faintly illuminated by earthshine - a phenomenon called 'the old moon in the new moon's arms'.

earth's magnetism

the earth shows a magnetic field at points on or near its surface and behaves as if a huge bar magnet were located inside it along nearly the north south direction.

ebullition

the process of boiling or bubbling up of a liquid.

eccentricity

the distance of the geometric centre of a revolving body from the axis of rotation

echelon grating

a diffraction grating, consisting of 20-40 parallel plates of equal thickness arranged in optical contact, staggered to form a row of steps about one millimetre wide each. The grating of this type have very high powers of resolution, ranging as high as 1,000,000.

echo

the reflection of a wave by a surface or object so that a weaker version of it is detected shortly after the original. The delay between the two is an indication of the distance of the reflecting surface. An echo sounder is an apparatus fordetermining the depth of water under a ship.

echo chamber

an enclosure or a reverberant room which is used in a studio to add echo effects to sound waves for radio or television programmes.

echo location

a method used by some animals (e.g. bats) to detect objects in the dark.

echo sounder

a device for estimating the depth of the sea beneath a ship by measuring the time taken for a sound pulse to reach the sea bed and for its echo to return.

echo ranging

refers to the determination of the distance and direction of under-water objects by the same process used in sonar.

eclipse

the total or partial obscuring of light from a celestial body as it passes behind or through the shadow of another body. A lunar eclipse occurs when the sun, earth, and moon are in a straight line and the shadow of the earth falls on the moon. A solar eclipse occurs when the shadow of the moon falls on the earth.

ecliptic

the great circle formed by the intersection of the plane of the earth's orbit with the celestial sphere.

eddy currents

a current at variance with the main current particularly one having rotatory or whirling motion.

eddy resistance

resistance or drang of a ship resulting from eddies that are shed from the hull or appendages of the ship and carry away energy.

eddy velocity

the term is commonly used in fluid mechanics. It is equal to the difference between the mean velocity of fluid flow and its intantaneous velocity at that point.

edison accumulator

nickel-iron cell.

edison battery

a storage battery composed of cells having nickel and iron in an alkaline solution. Also known as nickel iron battery.

edison effect

the phenomenon, first discovered by Edison, of electrical conduction between an incandescent filament and an independent cold electrode in the same envelope, when the cold electrode is made positive with respect to the filament. See thermionic emission.

edser and buter's bands

dark bands, with constant frequency separation, in the spectrum of white light which has traversed a thin parallel-sided plate of a transparent material.

effective aperture

the diameter of the image of the aperture stop of an optical system, as viewed from the object.

effective capacitance

total capacitance existing between any two given points of an electric circuit.

effective current

the value of alternating current that will give the same heating effect as the corresponding value of direct current. Also known as root mean square current.

effective height

the height of the centres of radiation of a transmitter above the ground is called its effective height.

effective launcher line

the line or path along which a rocket would go if it were not affected by the gravity of earth is called the effective launcher line.

effective resistance

the resistance of a conductor or other element of an electric circuit when used with alternating current.

effective value

root mean value of an a.c. quantity.

effervescence

the escape of small gas bubbles from a liquid, usually as the result of chemical action.

efficiency

the ratio of the useful energy output to the total energy input in any energy transfer. It is often given as percentage and has no units.

efficiency of an accumulator

it is the ratio of the energy, measured in watt-hour, received from the cell during discharge to the energy supplied to it in the process of charging.

Thus, Efficiency

$$= \frac{\text{Output of energy}}{\text{Input of energy}}$$

effusion

the flow of gas molecules through relatively large holes.

ehf

extremely high frequency.

ehrenhaft effect

a helical motion of fine particles along the lines of force of a magnetic field during exposure to light, resulting from radiometer effects.

eigen function

a solution of equation which satisfies a set of boundry conditions. In quantum mechanics a possible solution of Schrodinger's equation.

einstein

a unit of light energy used in photochemistry. It is equal to the product of avogadro's number and the energy of one photon of light of a given frequency.

einstein number

a dimensionless number, equal to the ratio of the velocity of a fluid to the velocity of light.

einstein static universe

a non-vacuum globally static solution to einsteins equations of general relativity with cosmological term.

einstein's equation

refers to the equation, maximum (K.E.)= $hf - \omega$ for the kinetic energy of electrons which are emitted in photo–electric effect, f the frequency of incident radiation and ω the work function of the photomaterial upon which the radiation is incident.

einstein's law

mathematically it can be expressed as $E = mc^2$.

einstein's principle of relativity

a theory of dynamics involving a space-time continuum and based on two major postulates.

elastance

the reciprocal of capacitance.

elastic after effect

the delay of certain substances in regaining their original shape after being deformed within their elastic limits. Also known as elastic lag.

elastic body

after being deformed, if a body regains its original state on removal of the deforming force, it is called elastic.

elastic buckling

an abrupt increase in the lateral deflection of a column at a critical load while the stresses acting on the column are wholly elastic.

elastic collision

a collision in which the momentum as well as the kinetic energies of the colliding bodies are conserved on collision.

elastic constant

constants such as Youngs mojulus (K) and the Poission ration relating stress to strain in a homogeneous medium.

elastic failure

the inability of a body to recover to its original shape and size after a stress is removed, is called an elastic failure.

elastic limit

it is the maximum stress that a solid can sustain without undergoing permanent deformation.

elastic ratio

the ratio of the elastic limit to the ultimate strength of given solid is called its elastic ratio.

elastic scattering

scattering due to an elastic collision.

elasticity

the property of a body due to which it returns to its original shape and size when a deforming stress is removed.

elastodynamics

a branch of physics which deals with the study of the mechanical properties of elastic waves.

electret

a permanently electrified dielectric that has a positive charge at one end at a negative charge at the other. It has permanent dipole moment.

electrical analog

an electrical circuit whose behaviour may be described by the same mathematical equations as some physical system under study.

electrical conductivity

it is the amount of electricity transferred per unit time across unit area per unit potential gradient.

electrical line of force

a curve in an electric field the tangent to which at every point gives the direction of the electrical field at the point.

electrical energy

a form of energy related to the position of an electric charge in an electric field. For a body with charge Q and an electric potential V, its electrical energy is QV. If V is a potential difference, the same expression gives the energy transformed when the charge moves through the p.d.

electric arc

a luminous discharge between two electrodes. The discharge raises the electrodes to incandescence, the resulting thermal ionization largely providing the carriers to maintain the high current between the electrodes.

electric braking

a method of barking an electric motor by causing it to act as a generator. It has a particular application in electric traction.

electric charge

charge.

electric connection

a direct wire path which allows the flow of current between two points in circuit is commonly known as an electric connection.

electric current

current.

electric dipole

two equal and opposite charge very close together.

electric displacement

refers to the electric flux density in a dielectric medium. It is proportional to the electric field strength e in the medium.

electric field

a region in which a charged particle experience a force. It is completely defined if one knows the magnitude and direction of the force experienced by a unit positive charge placed at that point.

electric flux

symbol y. In an electric field, the product of the electric flux density and the relevant area. See electric displacement.

electric intensity

electric field strength.

electricity

any effect resulting from the existence of stationary or moving electric charges.

electric motor

a device that converts electrical energy into mechanical energy. An electric current is passed through a coil which is placed in a magnetic field. The coil rotates on passing electric current.

electric polarization

relative displacement of positive and negative charge in an atom or dielectric whin it is placed in an electric field.

electric spark

the transient passage of an electric current through a gas between two points of high opposite potential, with the emission of light and sound. Lightning consists of a spark between a cloud and earth or between two oppositely charged parts of the same cloud.

electrocardiogram

a tracing or graph of the electrical activity of the heart. Recordings are made from electrodes fastened over the heart and usually on both arms and a leg. Changes in the normal pattern of an ECG may indicate heart irregularities or disease.

electrochemical equivalent

symbol z. The mass of a given element liberated from a solution of its ions in electrolysis by one coulomb of charge. See faraday's laws.

electrochemistry

the study of chemical properties and reactions involving ions in solution, including electrolysis and electric cells.

electrode

a conductor that emits or collects electrons in a cell, thermionic valve, semiconductor device, etc. The anode is the positive electrode and the cathode is the negative electrode.

electrodeposition

the process of depositing one metal on another by electrolysis, as in electroforming and electroplating.

electrode potential

the potential developed on an inert-metal, such as platinum, when it is inserted in a reversible oxidation-reduction system.

electrodynamics

the study of electric charges in motion, the forces created by electric and magnetic fields, and the relationship between them. Compare electrostatics.

electroencephalograph

it is a device which records the voltage waveform associated with the brain. The traces are known as electroencephalograph.

electroendosmosis

it mainly indicates the use of electricity to cause diffusion of a liquid through an organic membraine.

electroforming

a method of forming intricate metal articles or parts by electrodeposition of the metal on a removable conductive mould.

electrolysis

the production of a chemical reaction passing an electric current through an electrolyte. In electrolysis, positive ions migrate to the cathode and negative ions to the anode.

electrolytic cell

a cell in which electrolysis occurs; i.e. one in which current is passed through the electrolyte from an external source.

electrolytic gas

the highly explosive gas formed by the electrolysis of water. It consists of two parts hydrogen and one part oxygen by volume.

electrolytic separation

a method of separating isotopes

by exploiting the different rates at which they are released in electrolysis. It was formerly used for separating deuterium and hydrogen. On electrolysis of water, hydrogen is formed at the cathode more readily than deuterium, thus the water becomes enriched with deuterium oxide.

electrometallurgy

the uses of electrical processes in the separation of metals from their ores, the refining of metals, or the forming or plating of metals.

electrometer

a device for measuring potential differences between two points in a circuit, drawing very little current in the process.

electron affinity

symbol A. The energy change occurring when an atom or molecule gains an electron to form a negative ion. For an atom or molecule X, it is the energy released for the electron-attachment reaction $X(\gamma) + e \rightarrow X^{-}(\gamma)$

Often this is measured in electronvolts. Alternatively, the molar enthalpy change, ΔH, can be used.

electron biprism

an arrangement of fields that splits a beam of electrons or other charged particles in an analogous way to an optical biprism.

electron charge

refers to the charge of an electron.

electron density

it is the number of electrons per unit volume of a material. As quantum mechanical effects are significant, probability of finding an electron in a unit volume becomes significant.

electron diffraction

it is associated with interference occurring when electrons are scattered by atoms in crystals to form diffraction patterns.

electron flow

it is actually a current resulting due to flow of tree electrons moving towards the +ve terminal, the current moves towards the – ve terminal.

electron gas

it stands for the concentration of electrons whose behaviour is not governed by the forces.

electron gun

a device used in cathode-ray

tubes electron microscopes, etc., to produce a steady narrow beam of electrons. It usually consists of a heated cathode, control grid, and two or more annular anodes inserted in an evacuated tube.

electronics

it is the branch of science which deals with the study, development and application of electronic devices and other electronic components.

electron magnetic moment

it refers to the magnetic dipole moment which an electron posses on account of its spin.

electron microscope

it produces a magnified image of an object by using an electron beam instead of light rays. Optical lenses are replaced by electron lenses. Magnification $\approx$ 200,000 can be obtained by this device.

electro-optical effect

the interaction between the refractive properties of some transparent dielectrics and a strong electric field in which they are placed.

electroballistics

the measurement of the velocity of projectiles by electronic methods.

electroncapillarity

the phenomena of variation of surface tension of a liquid resulting from an electric field at its surface.

electrocardiograph

ecg; an instrument for recording current and voltage waveforms associated with the contraction of the heart muscle.

electrochemical equivalent

of an element is defined as the mass of the element deposited when one coulomb of charge flows through an electrolyte containing the element.

electrochemistry

the study of the formation and behaviour of ions in solutions. It includes electrolysis and the generation of electricity by chemical reactions in cells.

electrode

a device for emitting, collecting, or deflecting electric charge carriers. In certain electrolytic cells a liquid mercury electrode is used.

electrode dissipation

the heat dissipated by a

specified electrode of a thermionic valve in unit time due to bombardment by electrons and/or ions.

electrode potential

a measure of the tendency of a metal to lose electrons to a surrounding solution. It is the potential difference, at equilibrium between the metal and a solution of its ions.

electrodynamics

branch of physics that deals with the relationships between electric and magnetic forces on one hand and mechanical forces on the other.

electroencephalograph

a sensitive instrument that records the voltage waveforms associated with the brain. The trace obtained is known as an electroecephalogram.

electroendosmosis

electrosmosis.

electrofluorescence

the production of fluorescence on a solid by conversion of electrical power independently of irradiation or other excitation. Cf. electroluminescence.

electrogen

a molecule that emits electrons on being illuminated.

electrokinetic potential

zeta potential.

electroluminescence

luminescence resulting from the application of an electric potential to certain solids, e.g., a dielectric phosphor, as in the electroluminescent lamp.

electrolysis

the chemical decomposition of a substance on passing an electric current through it. The substances usually decompose into positive and negative ions and these travel towards negative and positive electrodes respectively.

electrolysis, faraday's laws of

faraday's laws of electrolysis.

electrolytic capacitor

a capacitor in which one plate is a thin metal plate coated with a thin oxide layer immersed in a suitable electrolyte H_2SO_4.

electrolytic separation

the separation of isotopes by electrolysis.

electromagnet

a magnet formed by winding a coil of wire around a piece of soft iron. It behaves as a magnet as long as a current passes through the coil. A temporary magnet.

electromgnetic pulse

a pulse of electromagnetic radiation generated by some large thermonuclear explosion is called and electromagnetic pulse.

electromagnetic wave filter

any device to transmit electromagnetic waves of desired frequencies while substantially attenuating all other frequencies.

electromagnetic lens

an electron lens which employs electromagneting focusing technique.

electrometer

a device for measuring potential differences between two points in a circuit. It draws very little current in the process.

electromotive force of a cell

potential difference across the terminals of cell when no current is flowing in it. It is a measure of the energy supplied by the cell and is measured in volts.

electron diffraction analysis

the phenomenon of examination of a solid surface by observing diffraction of a steam of electrons by the surface

electron gas

the concept of the free electrons in the solid or liquid state as a gas may be compared with that of gas dissolved in a solid or liquid. This model has found application in theories of electric and thermal conduction, thermionic emission, etc.

electron gun

refers to a heated cathode in a vacuum tube, that produces a stream of electrons by thermionic emission, with an anode to which the electrons are attracted and focusing electrode.

electron lens

a combination of electric and magnetic field used for focusing a beam of electrons like an optical lens focusing a beam of light.

electronic angular momentum

the total angular momentum associated with the orbital motion and spins of all the electrons of an atom is called its electronic angular momentum.

electronics

a branch of science that deals with the study and development of circuits involving thermionic valves, semiconductors and other electrical components such as resistances, capacitors, inductances etc.

electron micrograph

a photograph of an object obtained with an electron microscope.

electron optics

it is the study of the behaviour and control of an electron beam in magnetic and electrostatic fields.

electron paramagnetic resonance

paramagnetic resonance in which the renounce effect is due to conduction of electrons in metals of semiconductors.

electron probe microanalysis

a method of analysing a very small quantity of a substance. The method consists of directing a very finely focused beam of electrons on to the sample to produce the characteristic X-ray spectrum of the elements present. It can be used quantitatively for elements with atomic numbers in excess of 11.

electron synchrotron

synchrotron.

electron temperature

the electron temperature of the plasma is that temperature at which gas molecules would have the same average knietic energy as the electrons of the plasma.

electron transfer

the passage of an electron from one constituent of a system to another is referred to as electron transfer.

electron trap

a chemical impurity in a insulator or in a semiconductor which captures or mobile electrons is known as an electron trap.

electron tube

a device where in the movement of electrons between two electrodes, through a gas or a vacuum, takes palace in a sealed or continuously exhausted envelope.

electron volt

symbol eV. A unit of energy equal to the work done on an electron in moving it through a potential difference of one volt. It is used as a measure of particle energies although it is not an SI unit. 1 eV = 1.602 $\times$ 10^{-19} joule.

electron wave

the de brogue wave associated with an electron is commonly known as an electron wave.

electropathology

the study of human diseases by electrical means.

electrophonic effect

the aural sensation produced when alternating current of certain frequencies and magnitudes is passed through the human body.

electrophoresis

it is the process of the migration of fine particles of solid suspended in liquid to the anode or cathode when an electric field is applied to the suspension.

electrophorus

a laboratory demonstration apparatus for showing electrostatic charging induction.

electroplating

the process of depositing a thin layer of a metal on a solid surface by means of electrolysis.

electropositive

describing elements that tend to lose electrons and form positive ions. The alkali metals are typical electropositive elements.

electroscope

an instrument for the detection of electrical potential differences. An instrument capable of accurate quantitative indication is known as an electrometer.

electrosmosis

electroendosmosis. Refers to the passage of an electrolyte through a membrane or porous partition under the influence of an electrometer.

electrostatic accelerator

an accelerator which depends on an electrostatic field due to a high direct voltage.

electrostatic deflection

a method used for deflecting an electron beam making use of the electrostatic fields produce between two metal electrodes.

lectrostatic field

electric field produced by stationary charges or charges at rest.

electrostatic generator

refers to a machine for the continuous separation of electric charge, e.g., wimshurst machine and vender graff generator.

electrostatic generator

a device used to build up electric charge to an extreme potential usually for experimental purposes. The electrophorus and the Wimshurst machine were early examples; a more usual device now is the Van de Graaff generator.

electrostatic precipitation

a method of removing solid and liquid particles from suspension in a gas. The gas is exposed to an electric field so that the particles are attracted to and deposited on a suitably placed electrode. Electrostatic precipitation is widely used to remove dust and other pollutants from waste gases and from air.

electrostatics

refers to the study of the effects of static charges in their neighbourhood. The study of the electric fields and potential produced by them.

electrostatic units

a system of electrical units in the c.g.s. system. The e.s.u. of electric charge is the statcoulomb. The statcoulomb is the quantity of electric charge that will repel an equal quantity 1 centimetre distant with a force of 1 dyne. In e.s.u. the electric constant is of unit magnitude. The system has now been replaced for most purposes by SI units. Compare electromagnetic units; Gaussian units; Heaviside–Lorentz units.

electrostriction

the change in the dimensions of a dielectric when it is placed in an electric field.

electrotyping

the production or reproduction of printing plates by electrofarming.

electrum

a natural alloy of gold 55%-85% and silver.

element

a single lens forming a part of doublet or other compound lens.

elementary particles

the particles which at the present time it is assumed to be impossible to resolve into further components, as the proton, neutron, electron, positron, neutrino, meson photon or g-ray. Although the x-particle and the deuteron are composite particles, they are usually included under this collective term, due to the important part which they play in nuclear reactions.

elements, magnetic

the three quantities, magnetic declination, angle of dip and horizontal intensity, which define completely the earth's magnetic field at any point.

elements of an orbit

six parameters that can be used t define the path of a celestial body. The shape of the orbit is defined by its eccentricity and semima jor axis. The orientation of the orbit is specified by the inclination of the orbital plane to the reference plane and by the longitude of the ascending node. The position of the body in its orbit is defined by its eccentric anomaly and the position as a function of time is calculated from the time of periapsis passage.

elevation of boiling point

an increase in the boiling point of a liquid when a solid is dissolved in it. The elevation is proportional to the number of particles dissolved and is given by $Dt = k_B C$, where C is the moral concentration of solute. The constant K_B is the ebullioscopic constant of the solvent and if this is known, the relative molecular mass of the solute can be calculated from the measured value of Dt. The elevation is measured by a Beckmann thermometer. See also colligative properties.

elinvar

trade name for a nickel–chromium steel containing about 36% nickel, 12% chromium, and smaller proportions of tungsten and manganese. Its elasticity does not vary wit temperature and it is therefore used to make hairsprings for watches.

elipse of the moon

refers to an obstruction of the Moon by the shadow of the Earth when the Earth is between the Sun and the Moon and on a straight line with both.

ellipsoid

a solid figure traced out by an ellipse rotating about one of it two axes.

ellipsometry

the phenomenon of measuring the degree of ellipticity of polarized light.

elliptically polarized wave

a polarized wave in which the

direction of displacement at a point rotates about a point in a plane and the magnitude of displacement varies as the radius of an ellipse.

elopse of the Sun

refers to a partial or complete obstruction of the Sun by the shadow of the Moon when the Moon comes between the Sun and the Earth and on a straight line with both.

elster and geitel effect

in the presence of a gas, a heated conductor assumes a charge either positive or negative. In a vacuum the charge is always negative.

elutriation

the process of suspending finely divided particles in an upward flowing stream of air or water to wash and separate them into sized fractions.

emanation

radium emanation. The gas formed by the radioactive disintegration of certain substances, consisting principally of radon, thorn, and action.

emery

a granular mineral substance. It consists of corundum mixed with magnetite or haematite.

emission

a measure of number of electrons emitted by heated filament or cathode of a vacuum tube.

emission spectrum

the spectrum observed when light coming directly from a source is examined with a spectroscope.

emissive power

the total energy emitted from unit surface area of body per second.

emissivity

symbol e. The ratio of the power per unit area radiated by a surface to that radiated by a black body at the same temperature. A black body therefore has an emissivity of 1 and a perfect reflector has an emissivity of 0. The emissivity of a surface is equal to its absorptance.

emitter

one of the three electrodes in a transistor.

emiprical

based upon the results of

experiment and observation only.

emulasion

the coating on a film or plate which is sensitive to the light illuminating it.

enabling pulse

a pulse which opens an electrical gate which is normally closed.

enantiomorphism

the occurrence of substances in low crystalline forms one being a mirror image of the other.

end correction

the correction required in the reading of balance point in a slide wire bridge to correct the error due to the resistances at the ends of the bridge wire.

endothermic process

a process in which heat is absorbed.

end rule

when looking at the end of the bar if the current is seen in he coil in anticlockwise motion, the end will be north pole.

energy

the capacity of a body to do work. It is measured in joules. The exists in various forms and can be converted from one form to another but can neither be created not destroyed.

energy band

a range of energies that electrons can have in a solid. In a single atom, electrons exist in discrete energy levels. In a crystal, in which large numbers of atoms are held closely together in a lattice, electrons are influenced by a number of adjacent nuclei and the sharply defined levels of the atoms become bands of allowed energy this approach to energy levels in solids is often known as the band theory. Each band represents a large number of allowed quantum states. Between the bands are forbidden bands. The outermost electrons of the atoms form the valence band of the solid. This is the band, of those occupied, that has the highest energy.

energy gap

gap in the allowed energy state- a measure of separation in energy, of the valence and conduction bands in semi-conductors and insulators.

energy levels

in accordance with quantum

theory, atoms or molecules can exist only in certain discrete energy states. These are known as the energy levels of atoms or molecules.

engine

a device that can convert one form of energy into mechanical energy.

enrich

refers to increase in the percentage of a particular isotope in a mixture of isotopes.

ensemble

a set of systems of particles used in statistical mechanics to describe a single system. The concept of an ensemble was put forward by the US scientist Josiah Willard Gibs (1839-1903) in 1902 as a way of calculating the time average of the single system, by averaging over the systems in the ensemble at a fixed time. An ensemble of systems is constructed from knowledge of the single system and can be represented as a set of points in phase space with each system of the ensemble represented by a point. Ensembles can be constructed both for isolated systems and for open systems.

enthalpy

it is given by h=u + pv, where u is the internal energy, p the pressure, and v is the volume. It is also a state function.

entropy

a measure of the degree of disorder of a system.

ephemeris time

a time system that has a constant uniform rate as opposed to other systems that depend on the earth's rate of rotation, which has inherent irregularities. It is reckoned from an instant in 1900 (Jan 0d 12h) when the sun's mean longitude was 279.696 677 8^0. The unit by which ephemeris time is measured is the tropical year, which contains 31 556 925.9747 ephemeris seconds. This fundamental definition of the second was replaced in 1964 by the caesium second of atomic time.

epicenter

the point on the surface of the earth which lias directly above the focus of an earthquake.

epidiascope

an optical projector for throwing an enlarged image of either an opaque objector a transparent object upon a screen. It is used to illustrate lectures.

epitaxy

the process of growing a thin layer of material upon a single crystal substrate so that the lattice structure is identical to that of the substrate.

epidiascope

an optical projector for throwing an enlarged image of either an opaque object or a transparency on a screen.

epithermal neutron

a neutron having energy just above thermal energies, generally in the range from 10^{-2} eV($1.6 \times 10^{-21}$to 1.6×10^{17} joule). Epithermal neutrons have energies of the same order as the energies of chemical bonds.

equalization

in electronics, the introduction of networks which compensate for a particular type of distortion over the frequency band required and thus reduce distortion in a system.

equation of motion

$$S = ut + \frac{1}{2}at^2$$

$$V^2 - u^2 = 2as.$$

equation of state

an equation which describes how the pressure, volume and temperature of a substance are related. The equation of state for an ideal gas is PV =nRT.

equation of time

the length of time that must be added to the mean solar time, as shown on a clock, to give the apparent solar time, as shown by a sundial. The amount varies during the year, being a minimum of –i4.2 minutes in February and a maximum of +16.4 minutes in October. It is zero on four days (April 15/16, June 14/15, Sept. 1/2, Dec. 25/26). The difference arises as a result of two factors: the eccentricity of the earth's orbit and the inclination of the ecliptic to the celestiai equator.

equation of wave

$$S = A \cos 2\pi\left(\frac{1}{T} \pm \frac{x}{\lambda}\right)$$

where S = instantaneous displacement of equilibrim of the point of abscissa.
A = Amplitude of wave
λ = Wave length
T = Time period.

equator

1. the great circle around the earth that lies in a plane perpendicular to the earth's axis.

It is equidistant from the two geographical poles. 2. The magnetic equator is a line of zero magnetic dip (see geomagnetism) that is close to the geographical equator but lies north of it in Africa and south of it in America. 3. The celestial equator is the circle formed on he celestial sphere by the extension of the earth's equatorial plane.

equator, terrestrial

great circle of earth. It lies in a plane perpendicular to the axis of the earth and is equidistant from the two poles.

equilibrant

a force which is equal and opposite to the resultant of forces acting on a body. Acting on the body along with this set of forces, it brings the body to equilibrium.

equilibrium

any state of rest or balance due to equal action of opposing forces.

equinox

the moment at which the sun apparently crosses the celectical quarter; the point of intersection of the ecliptic and the celestial equator.

equipartition of energy

the theory, proposed by Ludwig Boltzmann and given some theoretical support by James Clerk Maxwell, that the energy of gas molecules in a large sample under thermal equilibrium is equally divided among their available degrees of freedom, the average energy for each degree of freedom being kT/2, where k is the Boltzmann constant and T is the thermodynamic temperature. The proposition is not generally true if quantum considerations are important, but is frequently a good approximation

equipotental

a line or surface such that all points on it are at the same potential. Equipotentials in a field cut the lines of force at right angles.

equipotential

surfaces having same potential.

equipotential surface

a surface in which all points are at the same potential. The lines of force of the corresponding field are at right angles to such a surface.

equivalent circuit

an arrangement of simple circuit

elements which has the same electrical characteristics as a more complicated circuit or device under specified conditions.

equivalent focal length

the distance from a principal point its corresponding principal focal point.

equivalent length of a magnet

the poles of a magnet are not situated at its ends. An equivalent length 21 can be chosen such that 21 times the pole strength is equal to the moment. This length is commonly about 5/6 of the geometrical length for simple bar magnets.

equivalent network

an electrical network that can be connected in place of another without changing in any way the conditions in the other parts of the system.

equivalent positions

refers to a complete set of points in any given space group that is obtained by performing the symmetry operations of the space group on a single point.

equivalent resistance

the resistance that, when concentrated at a point in electrical circuit, would dissipate power equal to the total of various smaller resistance at different points in the circuit.

equivalent sine wave

a sine wave with the same root-measquare value as the given wave and also the same fundamental frequency.

eracting prism

system of prisms which converts the inverted image into an erect image.

erect

describing an image that is the same way up as the object.

erecting prism

a right-angled optical prism used in optical instruments to render an inverted image upright.

erio meter

an instrument for measuring the amount for energy produced or the work done by any device.

erg

unit of energy in the C.G.S. system.

1 erg = 10^{-7} joule.

ergodicity

a property of a system that obeys the ergodic hypothesis. The ergodicity of systems has been discussed extensively in the foundations of statistical mechanics, although it is now thought by man physicists to dynamics, since the behaviour can be very complex even for simple dynamical systems. Systems, such as spin glasses, in which ergodicity is thought not to hold are described as having broken ergodicity in systems. See also KAM theorem.

ergon

a quantum of energy of an oscillator and is equal to the product of the frequency of oscillation and the plank constant.

ergor

a quantum of energy of an oscillator and is equal to the product of the frequency of oscillation and the Planck constant.

error equation

the equation given below :

$y = h\pi^{\frac{-1}{2}} \exp(-h^2(x-a)^2)$.

escapement

a device in a clock or watch that controls the transmission of power from the spring or falling weight to the hands. It is usually based on a balance wheel or pendulum. It thus allows energy to enter the mechanism in order to move the hands round the face, overcome friction in the gear trains, and maintain the balance wheel or pendulum in continuous motion.

escape velocity

$$V_0 = \sqrt{2G.\frac{M}{r}} = 11.2 \times 10^3 \text{m/sec.}$$

e.s.u.

electrostatic units.

etalon

an interferometer used for studying fie spectrum lines based on the interference effects produced by multiple reflection between fixed, parallel half silvered glass or quartz plates.

ether

a hypothetical medium once believed to be necessary to support the propagation of electromagnetic radiation. It is now regarded as unnecessary and in modern theory electromagnetic radiation can be propagated through empty space. The existence of the ether was first called into question as a result of the

Michelson–Morley experiment.

ether drift

hypothetical motion of the ether relative to the earth. The concept of ether was rejected by michelson-morley's experiment.

ether

an imaginary fluid supposed to permeate all space and introduced as a medium through which light as electromagnet waves were assumed to propagate.

ettingshausen effect

a conductor carrying current in a magnetic field develops a transverse temperature gradient perpendicular to the field and current.

eudiometer

an apparatus for measuring changes in volume of gases during chemical reactions. A simple example is a graduated glass tube sealed at one end and inverted in mercury. Wires passing into the tube allow the gas mixture to be sparked to initiate the reaction between gases in the tube.

eutectic

a term applied to the solid solution of two or more substances which has the lowest melting point of all the possible mixtures which can be formed using the components.

evaporation

the change of state of a liquid into a vapour at a temperature below the boiling point of the liquid. Evaporation occurs at the surface of a liquid, some of those molecules with the highest kinetic energies escaping into the gas phase. The result is a fall in the average kinetic energy of the molecules of the liquid and consequently a fall in its temperature.

even-even nucleus

a nucleus in which there are an even number of protons and even number of neutrons.

even-old nucleus

a nucleus that contains an even number of protons but an odd number of neutrons.

evershed effect

spectrographic evidence that the general motion of gases in the penumbrae regions of sunspots is readily outwards. The radial velocities are greatest near the solar limb and least at the centre of the disc.

exaction

a non-conducting, non-localized, excited state in semiconductor. A bound hole-electron pair which results from an injection of holes into a crystal.

exchange current

the amount of current flowing through a galvanic cell when it is operating in a reversible manner.

exchange force

a force existing between two particles which results due to the exchange of another particle between them. E.g. the nuclear force between two nucleons, results from the exchange of masons between them.

excitation

1. a process in which a nucleus, electron, atom, ion, or molecule acquires energy that raises it to a quantum state higher than that of its ground state. The difference between the energy in the ground state and that in the excited state is called the excitation energy. See collective excitation; energy level; quasiparticle. 2. The process of applying currant to the winding of an electromagnet, as in an electric motor. 3. The process of applying a signal to the base of a transistor or the control electrode of a thermionic valve.

excitation energy

the energy needed to change the energy level of an atom or molecule to a higher energy level. It is equal to the difference in energy of the levels and is the difference in energy between the ground state of the atom and a specified excited state.

excited state

refers to the state of a system, such as an atom or molecule, when it has a higher energy level than its ground state.

exciter

an auxiliary generator that supplies energy for the excitation of another electric machine.

exciton

an electron in combination with a hole in a crystalline solid. Exciton may migrate through the solid. In semiconductors it is important.

exclusion area

the domain or area around a nuclear reactor where human habitation is totally prohibited.

excursion

any abrupt increase in the power level of a nuclear reactor.

exhaust velocity

the velocity with which the burnt gas is expelled from the rocket is called exhaust velocity.

exitance

the radiant or luminous flux decimated from a surface per unit area.

exoerigic

denoting a nuclear process that gives out energy.

exoergic process

refers to a nuclear reaction in which energy is given out.

exothermic

denoting a chemical reaction that releases heat into its surroundings.

exotic atom

1. an atom in which an electron has been replaced by another negatively charged parged particle, such as a muon or meson. In this case the negative particle eventually collides with the nucleus with the emission of X-ray photons. 2. a system in which the nucleus of an atom has been replaced by a positively charged meson. Such exotic atoms have to be created artificially and are unstable.

expansion

the writing of a function or quantity as a series or terms. The series may be finite or infinite.

expansion of the universe

the hypothesis, based on the evidence of the redshift, that the distance between the galaxies is continuously increasing. The original theory, which was proposed in 1929 by Edwin Hubble (1889–1953), assumes that the glasxies are flayin apart like fragments from a bomb as a consequence of the big bang with which the universe originated. Several variants have since been proposed.

expansivity (thermal expansion)

1. linear expansivity is the fractional increase in length of a specimen of a solid, per unit rise in temperature. If a specimen increases in length from P_1 P_2 when its temperature is raised $\theta^{0,}$ then the expansivity (α) is given by :

$$\ell_2 = \ell_1(1+\alpha\theta).$$

This relationship assumes that α is independent of temperature. This is notkl in general, the case and a more accurate relationship is :

$$\ell_2 = \ell_1(1+\alpha\theta + b\theta^2 + c\theta^3 ...)$$

where a, b, and c are constants.

2. Superficial expansivity is the fractional increase in area of a solid surface caused by unit rise in temperature, i.e.
$A_2 = A_1 (1 + \beta\theta)$,
where β is the superficial expansivity. To a good approximation $\beta = 2\alpha$. 3. Volume expansivity is the fractional increase in volume of a solid, or gas per unit rise in temperature, i.e.
$V_2 = V_1 (1 + \gamma\theta)$,
where γ is the cubic expansivity and $\gamma = 3\alpha$. for liquids, the expansivity observed directly is called the apparent expansivity as the onstaner will also have expanded with the rise in temperature. The absolute expansivity is the apparent expansivity plus the volume expansivity of container.

exploring coil

syn. search coil. A coil used for measuring magnetic flux.

exponent

a number or symber or symbol that indicates the power to which another number or expression is raised. For example, $(x + y)^n$ indicates that the expression $(x + y)$ is raised to the nth power; n is the exponent. Any number or expression in which the exponent is zero is equal to 1 i.e. $x_o = 1$.

exponential

a function the varies as the power of another quantity. If y = $x^{x,}$ y varies exponentially with x The function e^x is called the exponential function (see e). It is equal to the sum of the exponential series, i.e.

$e^x = 1 + x + x^2/2! + x^3/3! + ... + x^n/n!$

exponential growth

a form of population growth in which the rate of growth is related to the number of individuals present. Increase is slow when numbers are low but rises sharply as numbers increase. If population number is plotted against time on a graph a characteristic J-shaped curve results. In animal and plant population, such factors as overcrowding, lack of nutrients, and disease limit population increase beyond a certain point and the J-shaped exponential curve tails off giving an S-shaped curve.

exposure meter

a photo-electric cell operating a suitable indicating meter, used in photography to assess the amount of light.

extensive variable

a quantity in a macroscopic

system that is proportional to the size of the system. Examples of extensive variables include the volume, mass, and total energy. If an extensive variable is divided by an arbitrary extensive variable, such as the volume, an intensive variable results. A macroscopic system can be described by one extensive variable and a set of intensive variables.

extensometer

a device for measurement of linear strain.

extinction

the process in which a plane polarized light is fully absorbed by a polarize.

extinction coefficient

a measure of the extent by which the intensity of a beam of light is reduced by passing through a distance d of a solution having a molar concentration c of the dissolved substance. If the intensity of the light is reduced from I_1 to I_2, the extinction coefficient is $[\log(I_1/I_2)]/cd$.

extrapolation

an approximation technique for finding the value of a function or measurement beyond the values already known. If the values $f(x_0), f(x_1)...f(x_n)$ of a function of a variable x are known in the interval $[x_0,x_n]$, the value of f(x) for a value of x outside the interval $[x_0,x_n]$ can be found by extrapolation. The techniques used in extrapolation are usually not as good as those used in interpolation.

extremely high frequency

a radio frequency in the range between 300 gh and 30 gh.

extrinsic semi-conductor

a semi-conductor in which the carrier concentration is dependent upon extent of impurities.

eye

a sense organ able to produce optical images and to send corresponding nerve signals to the brain.

eye glass

a device to aid defective vision or to protect the eye from light, dust etc.

eye lens

the lens which is nearest to the eye in a compound eye place.

eye piece

a magnifier, usually a combination of lenses to give a magnified, aberration free image in a telescope or a microscope. It consists of two lenses – eye lens and field lens.

f.p.s.system

the foot-pound-second system of units in which the fundamental quantities length, mass and time are measured in these units.

faber flaws

regions of strain in superconductors that act as nucleation centres for growth of superconducting regions.

fabry–perot interferometer

a type of interferometer in which monochromatic light is passed through a pair of parallel half-silvered glass plates producing circular interference fringes. One of the glass plates is adjustable, enabling the separation of the plates to be varied. The wavelength of the light can be determined by observing the fringes while adjusting the separation. This type of instrument is used in spectroscopy.

face

a plane surface of a crystalline volume.

face-centred

a crystal is said to be face-centred when there is a lattice point at the centre of each face as well as at the corners.

factor of safety

the ratio between the breaking load on a given membrane and the safe permissible load applied upon it.

factorial

the product of a given number and all the whole numbers below it. It is usually written n! , e.g. factorial 4 = 4! = 4 × 3 × 2 × 1 = 24. Factorial 0 is defined as I.

fade chart

a graph in which the null areas of an air-search reader antenna are plotted as an aid to locating the target altitude.

fahrenheit scale

a temperature scale in which the temperature of boiling water is taken as 212 degrees and the temperature of melting ice as 32 degrees. It was invented in 1714 by G.D. Fahrenheit, who set the zero at the lowest temperature he knew how to obtain in the laboratory and took his own body temperature as 96°F. The scale is no longer in scientific use. To convert to the Celsius scale the formula is C = 5(F – 32)/9.

fall out

radioactivity precipitated from the atmosphere, usually originating from nuclear explosions, occasionally from releases of radioactivity from nuclear establishment.

fall time

the time required for the amplitude of fall from 90% to 10% of its peak value.

falling body

a body whose motion is accelerated toward the centre of the earth by the force of gravity, other forces acting on it being negligible by comparison.

fan-in

refers to the maximum number of inputs to a logic circuit.

fan-out

the maximum number of inputs to other circuits which can be driven by the output of a given circuit.

farad

symbol F. The SI unit of capacitance, being the capacitance of a capacitor that, if charged with one coulomb, has a potential difference of one volt between its plates. 1 F = 1 CV^{-1}. The farad itself is too large for most applications; the practical unit is the microfarad (10^{-6}F). The unit is named after Michael Faraday.

faraday

the quantity of electricity required to liberate or deposit 1 gram-equivalent of an ion. 96.49-coulombs.

faraday constant

symbol F. The electric charge carried by one mole of electrons or singly ionized ions, i.e. the product of the Avogadro constant and the charge on an electron. It has the value 9.648 5309(29) $\times$ 10^4 coulombs per mole. This number of coulombs is sometimes treated as a unit of electric charge called the faraday.

faraday dark space

in a discharge tube, the dark space occurring between the positive column and the negative glow.

faraday effect

the rotation of the plane of polarization of electromagnetic radiation on passing through anisotropic medium exposed to a magnetic field. The angle of rotation is proportional to Bl, where l is the length of the path of the radiation in the medium and B is the magnetic flux density.

faradays laws of electromagnetic induction

(i) whenever the number of lines of force linket (flux) with any closed circuit changes and induced current flows through the circuit which lasts only so long as the change lasts.

(ii) The magnitude of indicted e.m.f. produced in a coil is directly proportional to the rate of change of lines of force threading the coil.

$$e \,\alpha\, \frac{d\theta}{dt} \text{ e.m.u.}$$

where ϕ = flux (number of lines of force threading the circuit)

faraday's laws of induction

there are three which are describing the electromagnetic induction of an e.m.f. in a conductor by a changing magnetic flux: (1) If number of lines of force linked with a conducting circuit has been changing, a current is induced in the circuit. (2) The direction of the induced current has been such that the magnetic field it produces tends to keep the flux linkage constant. (3) The total quantity of electricity passing round the circuit has been directly proportional to the total change in lines of force.

far infrared

the part of the spectrum that lies towards the end of the infrared region of the electromagnetic spectrum and is near the rediowave region.

far point

the farthest point from the eye where an object can be seen clearly by the eye. For an object placed of this point, the image is formed at the retina.

fast effect

the increase in the number of neutrons due to fissions caused by fast neutrons in a thermal reactor.

fast neutrons

neutrons produced in nuclear fission. They have energies in excess of 0.1 Me V and travel at high speeds. Such neutrons are reduced to lower speed or thermmalised by making them to collide with suitable substances.

fast reactor

a nuclear reactor in which little

or no moderator is used and in which, therefore, the nuclear fissions are generated by fast neutrons.

fatigue

the failure of a material by cracking resulting from some cyclic stress is known an fatigue.

fault

a defect such as an open circuit, short circuit or ground in a circuit component or line.

feed back

a method of control in which part of the outright signal is returned as the input signal.

feeder

a conductor, or group of conductors, connecting primary equipment in an electric power system.

femto

symbol f. A prefix used in the metric system to denote 10^{-15}. For example, 10^{-15} second = 1 femtosecond (fs).

fermat's principle

the path taken by a ray of light between any two points in a system is always the path that takes the least time. This principle leads to the law of the rectilinear propagation of light and the laws of reflection and refraction. It was discovered by the French mathematician, Pierre de Fermat (1601–65).

fermi

a unit of length former used in nuclear physics. It is equal to 10^{-15} metre. In SI units this is equal to 1 femtometre (fm). It was named after the Italian–born US physicist Enrico Fermi (1901-54).

fermi age theory

method of calculating the slowing–down density or neutrons in a nuclear reactor. The age equation :

$$\nabla^2 q - \frac{dq}{d\tau} = 0,$$

relates the slowing–down density q to neutron age τ.

fermi-dirac distribution function

the probability that an electron will occupy a particular quantum state when thermal equilibrium is reached.

fermi-dirac statistics

is fermi-statistics or quantum mechanics.

fermi energy

at the absolute zero of temperature, the maximum kinetic energy that a free electron can have is called the fermi energy.

Fermi, Enrico

(1901–54) Italian-born US physicist. He became a professor at Rome University, where in 1934 he discovered how to produce slow neutrons. He used these to create new radioisotopes, for which he was awarded the 1938 Nobel Prize. In 1938 he and his Jewish wife emigrated to the USA. In 1942 he led the team that built the first atomic pile in Chicago.

femi gas

it is a nuclear Model in which the neutrons and protons are considered as independent particles obeying F~D statistics, but confined in a cube like volume of nucleus.

fermi gas model

a model of the nucleus wherein the neutrons and protons are considered as independent particles obeying fermidirac statistics but confined within a cube of volume equal to that of the nucleus.

fermi-level

the highest occupied energy level at absolute zero. It lines in the conduction band in conductors, in valence band in the insulators and in the forbidden gap in semi-conductors.

fermion

an elementary particle (or bound state of an elementary particle, e.g. an atomic nucleus or an atom) with half-integral spin; i.e. a particle that conforms to Fermi-Dirac statistics (see quantum statistics). Compare boson.

fermium

symbol Fm. A radioactive metallic transuranic element belonging to the actinoids; a.n. 100; mass number of the most stable isotope 257 (half-life 10 days). Ten isotopes are known. The element was first identified by A. Ghiorso and associates in debris from the first hydrogenbomb explosion in 1952.

ferranti effect

the phenomenon of abrupt increase in voltage occurring at the end of a long transmission line when its load is removed.

ferrimagnetism

the existence of alternate unequal magnetic moments aligned antiparallel to each other roducing a net weak magnetisation.

ferrites

a group of iron compounds having weak but permanent magnetism or that are ferrimagnetic in nature. Used as cores in high-frequency electrical circuits as they do not suffer from eddy-current power losses.

ferrite-rod antenna

is a metallic conductor with a coil wound on a rod of ferrite used for receiving the electromagnetic signals.

ferroelectric domain

a domain in ferroelectric materials within which the spontaneous polarization remains constant.

ferroelectrics

certain dielectric materials whose electric properties resemble some properties of ferromagnetic substances, like hysteresis.

ferromagnetic

possessing a magnetic permeability considerably higher than unity, and being therefore attracted by a magnet.

ferromagnetic substances

these are the substances which on being placed in a magnetic field get strongly magnetised in the direction of the magnetic field e.g. Iron (Fe), Nickel (Ni), Cobalt (C0(, Magnetite (Fe_3O_4) etc.

ferromagnetism

the phenomena of the existence of a large magnetism is some substances such as iron, cobalt and nickel. These sustenance are called ferromagnetic.

fertile material

substaces that can be converted to fissile material by absorption of neutrons.

fiber

it is transparent thread like material made of glass or plastic and is highly usable in the conduction of light.

fiber gass

it is a material made up of extremely thin filaments of glass. It is used as a thermal or acoustical insulator.

fiber optics

deals with transmission of light along fine transparent fibres, involving a series of internal reflections along the length of the fibres.

fidelity

the degree to which an electrical transmission system reproduces at its output the characteristics of signal applied to its input.

field

a region in which a given influence can be experienced. An electric field is thus a region wherein an electric charge will experience a force.

field coil

the winding (or coil) used in an electric motor or generator that produces the magnetic field when a current is passed through it.

field emission

the emission of electrons from an unheated surface due to strong electric field existing at that surface.

field intensity

is the intensity of a field usually called field strength.

field-ionization microscope

a type of electron microscope that is similar in principle to the field-emission microscope, except that a high positive voltage is applied to the metal tip, which is surrounded by low-pressure gas rather than a vacuum. The image is formed in this case by field ionization: ionization at the surface of an unheatd solid as a strong electric field creating positive ions by electron transfer from surrounding atoms or molecules. The image is formed by ions striking the fluorescent screen. Individual atoms on the surface of the tip can be resolved and, in certain cases, adsorbed atoms may be detected.

field lens

refers to the lens farthest from the eye, in the eye-piece system of optical instruments.

field magnet

a magnet which provided a magnetic field in the dynamo electric motor, or other electrical appliances.

field of view

this term is commonly used in optical instruments. It is defined as the area which can be seen through an optical instrument.

field scan

in television, the vertical

movement of electron beam downwards across the face of the picture tube, in order to scan alternate lines of the picture.

field shift

it is the portion or the mass shift produced by the charge distribution when neutrons are added to the nucleus.

field theory

it gives a detailed mathematical description of the distribution and movement of matter under the influence of one or more fields.

filament

a thin wire of tungsten or other metal having high melting point, used in incandescent electric light bulbs and thermionic valves which is heated by passing an electric current.

file

a collection of data stored in a computer. It may consist of program instructions or numerical, textual, or graphical information. It usually consists of a set of similar or related records.

filled band

is an energy band, completely occupied by electrons.

filter

is an optical element partially absorbing electromagnetic radiations in VIS, UV, IR spectra. In electrical circuits, the combination of capacitors and coils is also called filer.

filler band

the valence band in the energy level diagram of a solid, which has its full complement of energy levels.

film badge

a device worn for the purpose of indicating the absorbed dose of radiation received by the mirror.

filter

a device or electronic circuit that permits only certain frequencies to pass through and reduces the effect of or stops other frequencies.

filter choke

an iron-core coil which is used in a power-supply filter system. It offers very high resistance to pulsating or alternating current but very low resistance to direct current.

filter pump

a simple laboratory vacuum pump in which air is removed

from a system by a jet of water forced through a narrow nozzle. The lowest pressure possible is the vapour pressure of water.

filtration

the process of separating solid particles using a filter. In vacuum filtration, the liquid is drawn through the filter by a vacuum pump. Ultrakiltration is filtration under pressure; for example, ultrafiltration of the blood occurs in the nephrons of the vertebrate kidney.

fine structure

the splitting up of certain spectrum lines on being examined under high resolution. Each line can be resolved into a number of closely spaced lines.

fireball

a highly dense luminous sphere of hot gases which lasts for a very short time after a nuclear explosion.

first law of thermodynamics

states that the total amount of energy in an isolated system remains constant, i.e., dQ =dU + dW, where dQ is the small amount of heat given to the system, dU is the increase in its internal energy and dW is the small amount of work done by the system.

fissile

it is the material which is fissionable.

fissile material

substances which ace capable of undergoing nuclear fission, generally upon impact with a thermal neutron.

fission

this the a process of disintergratig a heavy nucleus into light elements along with emission of enormous energy.

fission nuclear

nuclear fission.

fission neutron

the name given to neutrons emitted during nuclear fission.

fission products

refers to both the stable and the unstable isotopes produced as a result of nuclear fission.

fission reactor

is a kind of Nuclear Reactor in which enriched uranium is used as a fuel.

fission threshold

the minimum amount of kinetic

energy of the bombarding neutron which enables the fission of a nucleus.

fission yield

the amount of energy released by fission in nuclear explosion, as distinct from that released by fusion.

fixed capacitor

a capacitor having a fixed definite capacitance value and which cannot be further adjusted.

fixed point

an accurately reproducible, equilibrium temperature like the ice point, the steam point, etc.

fixed resistor

a resistor whose resistance always remains the same.

fixed star

one of very many heavenly bodies that does not appear to alter its position on the celestially sphere. They were so called to distinguish them from the planets, which were once known as wsndering stars. The discovery of the proper motion of stars in the 18th century established that stars are not fixed in the sky although, because of their immense distances from the solar system, they may appear to be so.

fizeau fringes

interference fringes observed in a wedge shaped film due to interference between waves reflected from the two surfaces.

fizeau's method

a method of measuring the speed of light, invented by Armand Fizeau in 1849. A cogwheel rotating at high speed enables a series of flashes to be transmitted to a distant mirror. The light reflected back to the cogwheel is observed and the speed of light calculated from the rates of rotation of the wheel required to produce an eclipse of the returning light.

flame laser

a molecular gas laser in which gases such as carbon disulphide and oxygen are mixed at low pressures and ignited.

flare spot

a small diffused, brightly illuminated region produced by multiple reflections of light from the various surfaces of an optical system.

flash barrier

a structure of fire-proof material so as to minimize the formation of electric arc between conductors or to minimize the damage caused by such an arc in an electrical machine.

flash over

indicates the abnormal formation of an arc between two electrical conductors.

flash photolysis

a technique for studying free-reactions in gases. The apparatus used typically consists of a long glass or quartz tube holding the gas, with a lamp outside the tube suitable for producing an intense flash of light. This dissociates molecules in the sample creating free radicals, which can be detected spectroscopically by a beam of light passed down the axis of the tube. It is possible to focus the spectrometer on an absorption line for a particular product and measure its change in absorption line for a particular product and measure its change in intensity with time using an oscilloscope. In this way the kinetics of very fast free-radical gas reactions can be studied.

flash point

the temperature at which the vapour above a volatile liquid forms a combustible mixture with air. At the flash point the application of a naked flame gives a momentary flash rather than sustained combustion, for which the temperature is too low.

flash test

this test is used for checking the insulation of a material. In this test we apply a much higher voltage than the rated working voltage, for a very short duration.

flashover

syn. sparkover, refers, to an abnormal formation of an arc between two electrical conductors.

flash point

the lowest temperature at which a substance ignite upon the application of small flame.

flat

the term is used in acoustics and denotes a musical note which is half step lower than a specified note.

flat trajectory

when a projectile moves with relatively high velocity, its trajectory is nearly flat and is referred to as a flat trajectory.

fleming's left hand rule

stretch the fore–finger, the middle finger and the thumb of left hand mutually perpendicular to each other, if the fore finger represents the direction of magnetic field (magnetic conductor, then thumb gives the direction of motion of the fleming's right hand rule.

fleming's right-hand rule

if the forefinger, middle finger and the thumb of the right hand are stretched mutually perpendicular to each other then if the middle finger points towards current, forefinger points towards field then thumb points towards force acting on the conductor.

flicker

is a visual sensation produced by periodic fluctuations.

flicker photometer

photometer used for comparing illuminating powers of different sources of light. In this light falls on two surfaces from the two sources in rapid succession.

fint glass

a type of glass containing lead silicate. Used as an optical glass for making lenses, prism etc.

fleming's rules

fleming's left-hand rule applies to motors. If the left hand is held with the thumb and first two fingers all mutually at right angles, the thumb shows motion (force); the first finger, field; and the second finger, current. Fleming's right-hand rule is similar but with the fingers of the right hand showing the operation of an electrical generator.

float

to rest or remain on the surface of a liquid.

floatation

according to principle or floatatin, "a body floating in a liquid/fluid displaces a mass of fluid which is equal to its own mass."

floating charge

when the battery is idle, the application of a constant voltage to the storage battery, to maintain a constant charge is a phenomena of floating charges.

floation , law of

a body floating in a fluid displaces a mass of the fluid which is equal to its own mass.

flourescence

the absorption of radiant energy by a substance followed immediately by its re-emission in the form of visible light of a greater wavelength.

flow rate

the weight or volume of a fluid flowing in a unit time is called its rate of flow or flow rate.

flow stress

the stress along one axis at a given value of strain that is required to produce plastic deformation.

fluctuations

Random deviations in the value of a quantity about some average value. In all systems described by quantum mechanics fluctuations, called quantum fluctuations, occur – even at the absolute zero of thermodynamjic temperature as a result, ultimately, of the Heisenberg uncertainty principle. In any system above absolute zero, fluctuations, called thermal fluctuations, occur. It is necessary to take fluctuations into account to obtain a quatitative theory of phase transitions in three dimensions. The formation of structure in the early iniverse can be regarded as a result of quantum fluctuations.

fluid

a general term used for a liquid or a gas. A substance which can flow.

fluid dynamics

is the science which deals with the motion of the fluids.

fluid resistance

the force exerted by a fluid opposing the motion of a body moving through it.

fluid stress

stress associated with plastic deformation in a solid material.

fluidics

the use of jets of fluid in pipes to perform many of the control functions usually performed by electronic devices. Being about one million times slower than electronic devices, fluidic systems are useful where delay lines are required. They are also less sensitive to high temperatures, strong magnetic fields, and ionizing radiation than electronic devices.

fluidity

the reciprocal of viscosity.

fluorography

photography of an image on a

fluorescent screen.

fluoroscence

the luminescence produced when certain substances absorb radiation of one wave length and emit light of another wave length.

floroscent lamp

glass tube coated inside with a fluorescent susbtance, that acts as a light source. The tube contains mercury vapour and contains two electrodes.

flute

a modified form of an organ pipe. It consists of a pipe with six holed drilled along its length. The air blown into the mouth-piece is set into vibration inside the flute. Different notes are produced when fingers are removed from the holes in different combinations.

flux

rate of flow of mass per unit area perpendicular to the direction of flow. Number of lines of force of a field.

flux density, magnetic

the number of magnetic lines of force per unit are at a point.

flux leakage

it is the measure of the maghetic flux which doesn't pass through an air gap or other part of a magnetic circuit, where the requirement exists.

fluxmeter

an instrument used to measure magnetic flux. It consists of a coil connected to galvanometer.

flux of energy

the amount of energy passing through a given surface per unit area per unit time.

flywheel

a heavy wheel of a large moment of inertia. It maintains constant speed in engines and machines even when there are fluctuations in the torque causing motion.

f-number

is also called focal ratio or stop number and is the ratio of focal length to diameter of a lens. f-number varies inversely with the aperture.

focal distance (focal length)

when a parallel beam of light is allowed to fall on a lens or mirror, it converges to a point, or appears to diverge from a point on its principal axis.

focal length

when a parallel beam of light

becomes incident on a mirror or lens, it converages or diverges on the axis. The distance between this point, called as focus and the optical centre, is known as focal distance or focal length.

focal plane

a plane perpendicular to the principal axis of a lens or mirror and entered at its focus.

focus

the point at which a beam of converging rays meet, or from which a beam of diverging rays seem to originate from.

fog

the effect produced due to condensation of water vapour in the atmosphere or a atmospheric particles.

fogtrack

is a line of condensasion produced in supersaturated water vapours when charged particles are passed through it.

foot

the unit of length in f.p.s. units. It is equal to one-third of a yard and is now therefore defined as 0.3048 metre. Several units based on the foot were formerly used in science, including the units of work, the foot-pound-force and the foot-poundal, and the illumination units, the foot-candle and the foot-lambert. These have all been replaced by SI units.

foot candle

it is a unit of luminance equakl to the illumination of a surface, all points of which are at a distance of 1 foot from a uniform point source of 1 candela.

foot pound

practical unit of work in the F.P.S. system. It is the work done by a force of 1 pound acting through a distance of 1 foot.

foot-poundal

unit of work in the foot pound second system. It is the work done by force of 1 poundal acting through a distance of 1 foot.

forbidden band

a range of energy levels in a crystalline solid which is not tainted by any electron in the crystal. In the energy level diagram forbidden bands appear as gaps between allowed bands.

forbidden transition

a transition of an atom or molecule between energy levels involving a change of quantum number which is not allowed by the selection rules.

force

symbol F. The agency that tends to change the momentum of a massive body, defined as being proportional to the rate of increase of momentum. For a body of rnass m travelling at a velocity v, the momentum is mv. In any coherent system of units the force is therefore given by F = d(mv)/dt. If the mass is constant F = mdv/dt = ma, where a is the acceleration (see Newton's laws of motion). The SI unit of force is the newton. Forces occur always in equal and opposite action- reaction pairs between bodies, though it is often convenient to think of one body being in a force field.

force constant

is the ratio of force and the deformation of a system.

force ratio

for a machine, the ratio of the output force to the input force. There is no unit, the ratio is, however, often given as percentage.

forced convection

ventilated cooling in a strong draught.

forced oscillation

oscillation of a system or object induced by an external periodic force. Its frequency is the same as the frequency of the external force.

formula

any statement of a relationship, expressed in terms of symbols of quantities involved, is called a formula. For example, for time period of a simple pendulum,

$$T = 2p\sqrt{\frac{1}{g}}$$

forward bias or voltage

a voltage applied to a circuit in such a direction so as to produce the larger current.

fossil fuel

coal, oil, and natural gas, the fuels used by man as a source of energy. They are formed from the remains of living organisms and all have a high carbon or hydrogen content. Their value as fuels relies on the exothermic oxidation of hydrogen to form water ($H_2 + ½O_2 \rightarrow H_2O$).

foucault current

a current induced in the interior of conductors by variations of magnetic flux. Another name for eddy currents.

foucault's pendulum

it is a pendulum consisting of a heavy weight attached to a long wire and free to swing in any direction. The slow turning of the rotation of the earth.

fovea

an area about half a millimetre across in the centre of the yellow spot of the human retina. Here the cones are most dance and greatest visual acuity but has low sensitivity to dim light.

f.p. s. system

the foot pound second system of units.

frame of reference

a set of reference axes to define the position of a point of body in space.

frank-condon principle

electronic transitions in molecules occur in times which are very short in comparison with the period of vibration of the nuclei.

Franklin, Benjamin

(1706-90) American scientist and statesman who held various government posts. As an amateur scientist he experimented with electricity, introducing the concepts of 'positive' and 'negative'. In 1752 he carried out the extremely dangerous experiment of flying a kite during a thunderstorm and proved the electrical nature of lightning. He also invented the lightning conductor.

francis formula

is an equation for the calculation of water flow rate in terms of length and head.

franz-keldysh effect

a shift to longer wavelengths, in the absorption edge of semiconductors, produced by a strong electric field.

frasch process

a method of obtaining sulphur from underground deposits using a tube consisting of three concentric pipes. Superheated steam is passed down the outer pipe to melt the sulphur, which is forced up through the middle pipe by compressed air fed through the inner tube. The steam in the outer casing keeps the sulphur molten in the pipe. It is named after the German-born US chemist Hermann Frasch (1851-1914).

fraunhoffer diffraction

diffraction observed when both

the source of light and the screen are effectively an infinite distance away from the slit or obstacle. See also diffraction.

fraunhoffer lines

dark lines in the sun's spectrum caused by the absorption of some wavelengths by elements in the outer colder regions of the sun.

free atom

this is an atom, as in a gas, whose properties, such as spectrum and magnetic moment are not significantly affected by other atoms, ions or molecules.

free electron

an electron that is free to move under the influence of an electric field.

free energy (gibb's function, g).

the energy that is absorbed or evolved during a reversible thermodynamics process.

free fall

motion resulting from a graviational field that is unimapeded by a medium that would provide a frictional retarding force or buoyancy. In the earth's gravitational field, free fall takes place at a constant acceleration known as the acceleration of free fall.

free-flight tajectory

the path followed by a body in free fall.

free space

a region in which there is no matter and no electromagnetic or gravitational fields. It has a temperature of absolue zero, unit refractive index, and the speed of light of light is its maximum value. The electric constant and the magnetic constant are defined for free space.

free space propagation

is propagation of electromagnetic waves in space without obstruction.

free surface

it is a boundary between two homogeneous fluids.

freeze drying

a process used in dehydrating food, blood plasma, and other heat-sensitive substances. The product is deep-frozen and the ice trapped in it is removed by reducing the pressure and causing it to sublime. The water vapour is then removed, leaving an undamaged dry product.

freezing

change of state from liquid to solid, it takes place at a constant temperature, called freezing point for any given substance at a given pressure.

freezing mixture

a mixture of two substances to produce a low temperature e.g. a mixture of ice and salt.

freezing point

is the temperature at which any liquid begins to solidify.

frenkel defect

a defect in a crystal lattice formed because of an atom of ion being removed from its normal position in the lattice and taking up an interstitial position.

frenkel imperfection

a closely associated cation interstitial and cation vacancy.

frequency

for a body revolving about a fixed point, frequency refers to the numbers of complete revolutions made by the body in a unit time i.e. one second.

$$n = \frac{1}{T}$$

frequency band

a range of frequencies of electromagnetic radiations that fall within prescribed limits.

frequency divider

an electrical apparatus or circuit the output frequency of which is an exact integral sub-multiple of the frequency of the input.

frequency meter

an instrument for measuring the frequency of an alternating current. A common type consists of a cavity resonator that measures the frequency of an electromagnetic wave.

frequency modulation

modulation of the frequency of a carrier wave in accordance with the audio or visual signal to be transmitted.

frequency spectrum

is a plot of the distribution of intensity of some type of electromagnetic or acoustic radiation as a function of frequency.

frequency of a vibrating string

the fundamental frequency, f, of a stretched string of length i, under tension t, is given by

$$f = \frac{1}{2e}\frac{t}{m}$$

Where m is the mass per unit

length of the wise.

fresnel

a unit of frequency equal to 10^{12} hertz. In SI units this is equal to 1 terahertz (THz). It was named after of French physicist A. J. Fresnel (1788-1827).

fresnel's biprism

a glass prism with a large angle ($\approx 178^0$) which produces two coherent virtual sources and interference patterns when monochromatic light is passed through it.

fresnel diffraction

a form of diffraction in which the light source or the receiving screen, or both, are at finite distances from the diffracting object, so that the wavefronts are not plane, as in Fraunhofer diffraction. It was studied by A. J. Fresnel

fresnel's frings

is one of the series of light and dark bands that appear near the edge of a shadow in Fresnel's diffraction.

fresnel lens

a lens having a surface made up of a large number of smaller lenses to produce a short focal length lens.

freanel theory of double refraction

fresnel accounted for the phenomenon of double refraction in a crystal by assuring non-spherical wave surfaces inside the crystal.

frinction

it is an effect that opposes the motion of one surface over another. For two solid bodies, sliding friction and rolling friction are generally considered.

friction, rolling

when a body is allowed to roll over any surface, the friction between the two is known as rolling friction. It is much smaller than the sliding friction between the same two surfaces.

friedel's law

every crystal diffracts x rays as if a centre of symmetry were present.

fringes

alternate dark and light region obtained by interference or diffraction of light.

frost

it is a degree or state of coldness that is sufficient to cause the freezing of water.

froth flotation

a method of separating mixtures of solids, used industrially for separating ores from the unwanted gangue. The mixture is ground to a powder and water and a frothing agent added. Air is blown through the water. With a suitable frothing agent, the bubbles adhere only to particles of ore and carry them to the surface, leaving the gangue particles at the bottom.

frustum

a solid figure produced when two parallel planes cut a larger solid or when one plane parallel to the base cuts it.

fuel

a substance which is used for producing heat energy either by means of the release of its chemical energy by combustion or its nuclear energy by nuclear fission.

fuel assembly

a combination of fuel and structural materials used in some nuclear reactors to facilitate assembly of the core.

fuel calorific value of

the amount of energy produced when a unit mass of the fuel is completely burned.

fuel cell

a cell in which electricity is produced by oxidation of a fuel thus converting chemical energy into electrical energy.

fuel element

the smallest unit of fuel assembly containing fissile nuclides for powering a nuclear reactor.

fuel indection

the spraying of liquid fuel into the cylinder or combustion chambers to an engine.

fuel reprocessing

the processing of nuclear reactor fuel to recover the unused fissionable material.

fuel wave rectifier

a rectifier that coverts the negative half wave of an alternating current into a positive half wave, so that both halves of the swing deliver a undirectional current.

fuels, calorific value of

the energy produced when a unit mass of the fuel is completely burned.

fugacity

the thermodynamic reactions a

measure of the tendency of a substance to escape by some chemical process from the phase in which it exists.

fulcrum

it is the support or the point of rest on which a lever turns in a moving body.

full back

the part of the material which is scattered into the air due to an atomic explosion and which finally drops back to the earth or water at the place of explosion, is called full back.

full load

the maximum output of an electrical machine under certain specified condition.

full wave rectifier

a rectifier which converts the negative half wave of an alternative current into a positive half-wave, so that both halves of the swing are able to deliver a unindirectional current.

full-wave rectification

rectification in which both halves of the alternating current cycle are transmitted as unidirectional current.

function generator

a signal generator that produces specific waveforms that may be used for test purposes, over a wide range of frequencies.

fundamental

generally that component of a complex vibration which describes the pitch of a note. In a given note it is generally the tone with the lowest frequency.

fundamental constants (universal constants)

some quantities that do not change as the environment changes e.g. planck's constant, velocity of light in vacuum.

fundamental units

a set of independently defined units of measurement that forms the basis of a system of units. Such a set requires three mechanical units and, in some systems, one electrical unit; it has also been found convenient to treat certain other quantities as fundamental, even though they are not strictly independent. In the metric system the centimetre-gram-second (c.g.s.) system was replaced by the metre-kilogram-second (m.k.s.) system; the latter has now been adapted to provide the basis for SI units. In British Imperial units the foot-pound-second (f.p.s.) system was formerly used.

fuse

a device in an electric which melts and cuts off the supply of electricity if the current becomes too large.

fuse alarm

an electric circuit which produces an audible or visual signal to indicate a blown fuse, is known as fuse alarm.

fuse electrical

a device that prevents a high electric current from passing through a circuit.

fusibility

refers to the property of a substance of being converted from solid to liquid on being heated.

fusible metal

alloys or metals which melt at comparatively low temperatures. Such alloys are used for making various safety devices.

fusion

the interaction of light nuclei are produced.

fusion reactor

syn. thermonuclear reactor. A device wherein nuclear fusion takes place and where there is a net evolution of usable energy.

Gabor, Dennis

(1900-79) Hungarian-born British physicist, who worked as a research engineer from 1927 until 1933, when he joined the British Thomoson-Houston company. In 1948 he joined the staff of Imperial College, London. In that same year, while working on electron microscopes, he invented holography, for which he was awarded the 1971 Nobel Prize.

gadget

any mechanical device.

gaging

the process of measurement of density, thickness or quantity of material by the amount of radiation absorbed by the material. It is of great significance in industry.

gain

ratio of the output signal developed across a load to the input signal, for an amplifier.

galactic radio waves

electromagnetic waves which are emanating from the milky way galaxy.

galaxy

an organization of gas, stars, and dust as a separate independent system. Most galaxies are members of a group sharing a common motion.

galaxy noise

electrical noise from interstellar space, mainly from certain areas in milky way.

gallon

1. the volume occupied by exactly ten pounds of distilled water of density 0.998 859 gram per millilitre in air of density 0.001 217 gram per millilitre. 1 gallon = 4.546 09 litres. 2 A unit of volume in the US Customary system equal to 0.832 68 Imperial gallon, i.e. 3.785 44 litres.

galvanic

means caused by electric current.

galvanic cell

a cell containing two dissimilar metals and an electrolyte.

galvanic current

a stabilised direct current is also known as galvanic current.

galvanism

the therapeutic use of direct current.

galvano effects

named after L.A. Galvani, these are effects occurring when an electric current is passed through a conductor.

galvanometer

an instrument that is used to detect small electric currents ($\approx 10^{-6}$ amp.).

galvanostat

an electric device which produces a constant current from a high-voltage.

gamma

the ratio of the principal specific thermal capacity of a gas at constant pressure to that at constant volume.

gamma radiations

high energy electromagnetic waves produced during the decay of certain nuclei. They can pass through matter very easily.

gamma radiography

radiography by means of gamma rays.

gamma rays (gamma radiation)

electromagnetic radiation having very short wave length.

gamma ray spectrum

a series of wave length lying in the gamma ray region, given out by a given radioactive source.

gamma ray spectrometer

an instrument for determining the energy distribution of gamma rays.

gamma ray tranformation

a radioactive disintegration that is accompanied by the emission of gamma rays.

gamut

the interval between a note and its octave is generally divided into seven smaller intervals. The eight notes so formed constitue a musical scale or a gamut.

ganeneow barrier

the potential barrier which retards the escape of alpha particles from the nucleus.

ganged circuits

two or more circuits having variable elements mecnanically coupled by a single control so that the circuit can be tuned.

gas

a substance whose molecules or atoms occupy the entire volume of the containing vessel. The intermolecular forces in a gas are very weak in comparison to the forces in a liquid or solid.

gas activeted battery

a reserve battery which is activated by introducing a gas which reacts with a material between the electrodes of the battery to form an electrolyte.

gas cell

a cell whose action depends on the absorption of gases by its electrodes.

gas constant (R)

$$R = \frac{PV}{T}$$

gas equation

an equation that relates the pressure p, volume v and temperature t of an ideal gas. For n moles of the gas, pv = nrt.

gas laws

laws describing the changes in volume of gas when the pressure and/or temperature of the gas is changed e.g. boyle's law and charles's law.

gas maser

a maser in which microwave radiation interacts with gas molecules.

gas oil

diesel oil. The oil left after petrol and kerosene have been distilled from crude petroleum. Used as a fuel for diesel engines and for carburetting water gas.

gas thermometer

a thermometer that is used to measure temperature by observing the variation in the properties of a gas as a function of temperature.

gas turbine

an engine in which the chemical energy of a liquid fuel is converted into mechanical energy. Used in aeroplanes, locomotives and motor cars.

gassing

the process of evolution of a gas in the form of small bubbles in a storage battery when the charging of the battery continues even after the battery has been completely charged, is called gassing.

gate

1. an electronic circuit with a single output and one or more inputs; the output is faunction of the input or input or inputs. In the transmission gate the output waveform is a replica of a selected input during a specific interval. In the switching gate a constant output is obtained for a specified combination of inputs. These gates are the basic components of digital computers. See logic circuits. 2 The electrode in a field-effect transistor that controls the current through the channel.

gauge

a device that is used for measuring or testing some thing.

gauss

unit of magnetic induction. It is the induction when a magnetic field of 1 oersted intensity exists in a medium of unit magnetic permeability.

gauss's theorem

it states, "The total electric flux through the closed surface enclosing the change 'q' is given by $\phi = \frac{q}{\varepsilon_0}$."

$$\text{Total flux} = \frac{\text{Change}}{\text{Permittivity of free space}}$$

gaussmeter

a magnetometer, especially one calibrated in gauss.

gay lussac's law

it states, "The density of an ideal gas at constant pressure varies inversely with the absolute temperature of the gas."

gegenschein

(Germon : counterglow) a faint elliptical patch of light visible on a moonless night on the ecliptic at a point 180^0 from the position of the surn. It is caused by the reflection of sunlight by meteoric particles.

geiger counter (geiger muller counter)

an instrument used for detecting ionizing radiation and counting individual particles.

Geiger, Hans Wilhelm

(1882-1945) German physicist, who carried out research with Rutherford at Manchester University before returning to Germany in 1912. In 1908 he and Rutherford produced the Geiger counter, improved in 1928 as the Geiger-Muller counter. In 1909 his scattering experiments with alpha particles led to Rutherford's nuclear theory of the atom.

geissler pump

a simple vacuum pump made of glass which uses a jet of water to create a low vacuum to facilitate filtration.

geissler tube

it is a gas discharge tube particularity designed for demonstrating the luminous effect of an electric discharge through a rarefied gas.

gel

a lyophilic colloid that has coagulated to a rigid or jelly–like solid. In a gel, the disperse medium has formed a loosely–held network of linked molecules through the dispersion medium. Examples of gels are silica gel and gelatin.

generation time

the average timer that elapses between the creation of a neutron by fission in a nuclear reactor and a fission in a nuclear reactor and a fission produced by that neutron.

generator

a machine that produces electrical energy from mechanical energy. It is made up of two sets coil windings, one of these is fixed and the other, known as rotor, rotates.

geocentric

having the earth as a centre; measured from the centre of the earth.

geodesic

a geodesic line also called a 'geodesic' is the shortest distance between two points on a curved surface.

geoid

the geoid is a surface in the earth's gravitational field and is approximately an oblate spheroid in shape.

geometrical optics

study of optical phenomena that can be discussed in terms of light rays and in which the wave nature of light does not play an important part.

geometrical resolving power

the smallest angle subtended at the instrument, whose resolving power is being defined, by two objects which can be seen as just separate and distinguishable.

geophysics

the study of the earth and its atmosphere by physical methods. Examples seismology, meteorology, hydrology, terrestrial magnetism.

geopotential

the difference between the potential energy of a mass at a given altitude and the potential energy of an idential mass at sea level, equivalent to energy needed to move the mass from sea level to given altitude.

geostationary orbit

it refers to a circular orbit around the earth and lies in the plane of the equator and has a period equal to the period of earth's rotation on axis. The altitude of such an orbit is about 35780 km.

geostationary satellite

it is a satellite which revolves around the earth with the same angular speed in the same direction as that of the earth around its axis. Such a satellite is also called a geosynchronous satellite.

geothermal energy

heat within the earth's interior that is a potential source of energy. Volcanoes, geysers, hot springs, and fumarols are all sources of geothermal energy. The main areas of the world in which these energy sources are used to generate power include Larderello I(Italy), Wairakei (New Zealand), Geysers (California, USA), and Reykjavik (Iceland). High–ten perature porous rock aiso occurs in the top few kilometres of the earth's crust. Thermal energy from these reservoirs can be tapped by drilling into them and extracting their thermal energy by conduction to a fluid. The hot fluid can then be used for direct heating or to raise steam to drivea turbogenerator.

german silver

an alloy of copper, zince and nickel in varying proportions, approximating to 5 parts cu, 2 of zn, and 2 of ni.

getter

a material having a strong chemical affinity for other materials.

gev

gega electron volt, a unit of energy

1 Gev = 10^9 ev.

ghost

image formed by reflection from the front surface of glass. Also, a false line appearing in the spectrum produced by a diffraction grating due to imperfections in the grating.

giant star

a very large star that is highly luminous. Lying above the main sequence on a Hertzsprung–Russel diagram, giant stars represent a late stage in stellar evolution.

gibbs' paradox

one might expect that, as two diffusing gases become more and more alike, the change in entropy due to diffusion should get smaller and smaller, approaching zero as the gases become identical.

gibbs' phenomenon

in considering the transient response of an electrical network to a unit step function, the wider the band of frequencies passed by the network the better will be the response.

giga

symbol G.A. prefix used in the matric system to denote one thousand million times, for example, 10^9 joules = 1 gigajoule (GJ).

Gilbert

a unit of magnetomotive force on C.G.S. system.

1 Gilbert = 0.7958 ampere turns.

Gimbal

a type of mount for aninstrument (such as a gyroscope or compass) in which the instrument is free to rotate about two perpendicular axes.

giorgi system

a system of measurement in which the units are the metre, the kilogram, the second and the ampere.

giorgi units

units based on the metre, kilogramme, and second as fundamental units along with one electrical unit of practical size, now superseded by si units.

glass

an amorphous material which the dimensional primary bonds and possessing no long-range crystalline structure.

glass fibres

melted glass drawn into thin fibres some 0.005 mm–0.01 mm in diameter. The fibres may be spun into threads and woven into fabrics, which are then impregnated with resins to give a material that is both strong and corrosion resistant for use in car bodies and building.

glass laser

a solid laser in which glass serves as the host for laser ions of such materials as erbium, holmium etc.

glass resistor

an electrical resistance which consists of a glass tube with a helical carbon resistance element painted on its surface.

glass wool

a material consisting of very fine glass threads, resembling cotton wool. Used for filtering absorbing corrosive liquids and heat insulation.

glide

refers to the movement of one atomic plane over another in a crystal. It is by this process that a solid undergoes plastic deformation.

glide plane

a plane upon which glide can take place upon application of a suitable shearing stress.

glint

a small region which is specially designed to strongly reflect light from a target.

global radiation

the total of direct solar radiation and diffuse sky radiation received by a unit horizontal surface.

globar lamp

a lamp whose illuminating element is a silicon carbide rod which gives off black body radiation when heated.

globars

trade name for silicon carbide resistor.

globular cluster

an approximately spherical cluster of stars, usually containing between 10^4 and 10^6 stars. Globular clusters appear to move in elliptical orbits around the galaxies. The Milky Way system has about 200 such clusters moving around it.

gloss

the ratio of the amount of light specularly reflected from a surface to the total amount of light reflected is commonly known as glois. It has no units, being the ratio of the similar quantities.

glove box

a metal box the\at has gloves fitted to ports in its walls. It is used to manipulate mildly radioactive materials and in laboratory techniques in which an inert, sterile, dry, or dust–free atmosphere has to be maintained.

glow discharge

generally an electric discharge through a gas, at a low pressure, in which the gas becomes luminous.

glue

a general name for adhesives, particularly those made by extracting hides, bones, cartilages, etc., of animals with water.

gluon

hypothetical particle exchanged between quarks that bind them together.

gold leaf electroscope

an instrument used for detecting the presence of an electric discharge. It consists of two rectangular leaves of gold foil attached to a conducting rod of metal held by an insulating plug.

gold point

the temperature of the freezing point of gold at a pressure of 1.

goldschmidt's law

after consideration of the crystal structures of a large number of inorganic compounds, v. Goldschmidt postulated in 1929 the fundamental law of crystal chemistry.

goniometer

an instrument for the measurement of angles.

gradient operater

the operator

Ñ = i¶/¶x + j¶/¶y + k¶/¶z, where i, j, and k are unit vectors in the x, y, and z directions. Given a scalar function f and a unit vector n, the scalar product n. Ñf is the rate of change of f in the direction of n. See also curl; divergence.

graham's law of diffusion

the rate of diffusion of gas is inversely proportional to the square root of its density.

grain

$$1 \text{ grain} = 0.648\text{g} = \frac{1}{7000}\text{pound.}$$

gram molecule

molecular weight of a substance expressed in grams.

gram weight

a unit of force. It is equal to the force experienced by a unit mass due to the earth's attraction. 1 gm. wt. = g newton.

graticule

a grid of squares used with the eyepieces of many optical instruments to provide easier measurement and/or reference.

gravitation (G)

it refers to the force of attraction that exits between any two bodies that possess mass.

gravitation, newtons law of

newton's law of gravitation.

gravitional energy

$$\text{it is equal to} = \frac{G.M.m}{R}$$

gravitational field

it is the region that surrounds a mass of such a size that we can detect the gravitational field caused by the mass.

gravitational force

one of that four fundamental forces. It influences all matter and acts over an infinite range.

gravitational mass

the mass of the body as determined by the force of attraction between two bodies given by newton's law of graviation.

gravitational red shift

a displacement of spectral lines towards the red when the graviational potential at the observer of the light is greater than at its source.

graviton

a hypothetical particle responsible for the effects of gravity.

gravity

the attractive force of earth, or other celestial body, on an object.

gravity cell

a primary electric cell wherein two electrolytes are kept apart due to their different densities.

gravity vector

the ratio force of gravity per unit mass at a given point under consideration.

gravity wave

a wave occurring on the surface of a liquid the wave being controlled by gravity and not by the surface tension of the liquid. For example, for shallow sea waves the velocity v depends on the wavelength λ according to v=(gλ) 1/2, where g is the acleration of free fall.

gray

symbol gy. the derived si unit of absorbed ionizing radiation dose; equivalent to an absorption per unit mass of one joule per kilogram of irradiated material.

grasing angle (PHYS)

it is the term used for a very small glancing angle.

grease spot photometer

a photometer in which the light sources whose intensifies are to be compared illuminate a thin sheet of opaque paper with a translucent spot at the centre.

great circle

any circle on a sphere formed by a plane that passes through the centre of the sphere. The equator and the meridians of longitude are all great circles on the earth's surface.

greenhous effect

1. the effect within a greenhouse in which solar radiation mainly in the visible range of the spectrum passes through the glass roof and walls and is absorbed by the floor, earth, and contents, which re-emit the energy as infrared radiaticn. Because the infrared adiation cannot escape through the glass, the temperature inside the greenhouse rises. 2. A similar effect in which the earth's atmosphere behaves like the greenhouse and the surface of

the earth absorbs most of the solasr radiation, re-emitting it as infrared radiation. This is absorbed by carbon dioxide, water, and ozone in the atmosphere as well as by clouds and reradiated back to earth. At night this absorption prevents the temperature falling rapidly after a hot day, especially in regions with a gigh atmosphere water content.

gregorian telescope

an early type of reflecting telescope similar to the cassegrainian arrangement, except that both mirrors were converging.

greninger net

a net used for interpreting back-reflection laue photographs.

grid [ELEC]

1. it is a metal plate with holes or ridges, used in a storage cell or battery. 2. It can also be used as a control electrode between anode and cathode in triode valves.

grid bias

voltage applied between the cathode and the control grid of a thermionic valve; the value of the gird bias determines the operating conditions of the system.

grid circuit

the part of a circuit which consists of the grid and cathode of a vacuum tube.

grid current

the current that moves with in a vacuum tube from grid to the cathode.

grind

means to sharpen.

grinding stress

it is a residual tensile or compressive stress or both on the surface of a material due to grinding.

ground

a conducting connection between an electric circuit or equipment and earth or to a body at zero potential with respect to the earth.

ground clutter

clutter on a ground or air borne radar due to reflection of signals from the ground or objects on the ground.

ground circuit

is a telephone or telegraphic circuit, a part of which passes through the ground.

ground conductivity

is the effective conductivity of the ground which is used in calculating the alternation of radio waves.

ground fault

the process in which the grounding of a conductor takes place accidentally is known popularly as ground fault.

ground glass

refers to that glass from whose surface polish has been removed by fine grinding. Such a glass is used to diffuse light.

ground plane

it is an arrangement of radial wires required with a ground mounted antenna.

ground rod

a conducting rod properly driven into the earth to provide a good ground connection.

ground state

the least energy state of a system, which may be a nucleus, an atom or a molecule. If the system is disturbed from this state, it tends to return to its ground state.

ground wave

refers to a radio wave that is propagated on or near the earth's surface and affected by the ground and troposphere.

ground wire

a conductor used to connect an electric equipment to a grounded object.

ground zero

it is the point on the surface of earth or water directly below/above at which an atomic/hydrogen bomb explodes.

group velocity (phys)

is the velocity with which a group of waves travel. It is related to the phase velocity b the equation.

$$V_g = V_p - \lambda \frac{dV_p}{d\lambda}$$

where l is wavelength and V_g, V_p are ground velocity and group velocity respectively.

grown junction

refers to a pn junction formed in a single crystal of a semiconductor by varying in a precise manner, the types and qualities of impurities added to the semiconductor while the crystal is being ground from the melt.

gruneisen's law

the ratio of the coefficient of expansion of a metal to its specific heat capacity at constant pressure is constant at all temperatures.

guard band

while allocating the bands of frequencies in a frequency spectrum to various communication channels, it is desirable that frequency bands of adjacent channels be separated by narrow bands of frequencies. They reduce the possibility of mutual interference between the bands.

guided missile

a missile which is directed towards its target, either by pre-set or self-reacting devices inside it or by radio command from outside.

guided wave

a wave whose energy is concentrated substantially within the boundaries between materials of different properties and which is propagated along the path so defined. See wave guide.

guillemin effect

a magnetostrictive effect in which, if a bar of ferromagnetic material is elastically or permanently bent, it tends to straighten upon mechanization.

guinier-preston zones

in the solid state, a phase of a material may contain micro-constituents which do not show definite boundaries within the phase.

gun camera

a camera used in gunnery training that records the image of the target at which it is aimed on a strip of motion picture film.

gun metal

an alloy of copper, zince, tin etc. used for chains, belt buckes etc.

gun reaction

is the force exerted on the gun by the backward movement of the gun resulting from the forward motion of the projectile and hot gases.

gust load

the wind load on an antenna due to gusts.

gut

grand unified theory - a theory that would produce a single mathematical equation unifying all fundamental interactions.

gutta-percha

an insulating material with properties similar to those of the natural rubber.

gyrate

means to move in a circle or spiral.

gyration

the motion of a body around a fixed centre or axis.

gyrocompass

a non magnetic compass that uses a gyroscope fitted with a pendulous weight or some equivalent to induce precession due to gravity.

gyrodynamics

the study of rotating bodies, on being subjected to precession.

gyromagnetic effect

the phenomenon of inducing rotation in a substance due to alteration in its magnetization or vice versa.

gyromagnetic ratio

it is the ratio of the magnetic moment to the angular momentum of an atom or a nucleus.

gyroscope

a rotating heavy wheel that tends to resist any change in its axis of rotation.

gyrostat

a gyroscope, especially a conversion intended primarily to indicate or to use the constancy of direction of axis of a fast running gyroscope.

gyrostatics

the branch of science that deals with the laws of rotating bodies.

h

symbol used for the planck constant.

h-bend

in waveguides, a smooth change in the direction of the axis which is maintained perpendicular to the plane of polarization.

h.t.

high tension. (voltage)

h.t.g.r.

high temperature gas cooled reactor. See gas cooled reactor.

ha

indicates the measurement of land i.e., hectare.

hardron

it is an elementary particle with strong interactions with other particles.

haidinger interference fringes

fringes: produced by the interference of light reflected from or transmitted by two plane parallel surfaces of a thick transparent plate.

hair hygrometer

a hygrometer which depends for its action on the increase in length of a hair taking place when the relative humidity of the surrounding air increases.

halation

the luminous patch which surrounds the spot on the screen of a cathode ray tube, usually resulting from internal reflections in the glass of the screen.

half bridge

it is a bridge with two power supplies, located in two of the bridge arms to replace the single power supply.

half-cell

a metal electrode in contact with a solution of the metal ions.

half-life

the time required for half of a given amount of a radioactive substance to decay is called its half-life. The larger the half-life of a substance, the more stable is the substance.

half-life period

the time it takes for a measure, whose decay is exponential, to fall to half of its value. Half-life is often used in connection with number of parent radioactive nuclei in a sample.

half-period zones

the term used for circular bands o a spherical wavefront required in the analysis of Fresnel diffraction.

half tap

a specially designed bridge which is placed across conductors without affecting their continuity.

half-value thickness

the thickness of uniform sheet of material which when interposed in a beam of radiation will reduce the intensity or some other specified property of the radiation passing through it to one half. This is generally used for defining the quality of radiation.

half wave

it exhibits half of one cycle of a

wave. It is also related to the electrical length of half a wavelength.

half-wave dipole

refers to the conductor tuned at ends, which receives the singles to be supplied to the receiver sets. It is fitted with the antenna.

half-wave plate

refers to a thin plate of quartz or mica cut to the proper thickness to produce a phase difference of 180^0 between the ordinary and extraordinary rays into which it splits an incident beam of light.

half wave rectifier circuit

a rectifier circuit in which only alternate half-waves of the single phase a.c. input waves are effective in delivering a unidirectional current to the load.

half wave vibrator

is a kind of vibrator having only one pair of contacts. It hinders the D.C. through the primary of a power transformer but does not reverse the current.

half-width

the wavelength region during which the relative intensity as a function of wavelength for an electromagnetic radiation lies between 0.5 and 1.

hall coefficient

a coefficient associated with the hall effect where this results in a transverse potential grandient in a conductor.

hall effect

if an electric current is passed through a conductor and a magnetic field is applied at right angles, a potential difference is produced between two opposite surface of the conductor.

hall mobility

a measure of the flow of charged particles perpendicular to both a magnetic and electric field.

halley's comet

a bright comet that takes about 76 years to orbit the sun; last seen in 1986. Named after Edmund Halley, who first calculated its orbit.

hallwach's effect

a negatively charged body in a vacuum is discharged by exposing it to ultraviolet light.

halo

a luminous ring sometimes observed surrounding the sun or the moon. Caused by the refraction of light by ice crystals in the atmosphere.

halogen counter

a geiger counter in which the self-quenching action is provided by a halogen gas.

hamiltonian

symbol H. A function used to express the energy of a system in terms of its momentum and positional coordinates. In simple cases this is the sum of its kinetic and potential energies. In Hamiltonian equations, the usual equations used in mechanics are replaced by equations expressed in terms of momenta. These concepts, often called Hamiltonian mechanics, were formulated by Sir William Rowan Hamolton (1805-65).

hamiltonian function

syn. Hamiltonian. symbol: h. A function which expresses the energy of a system in terms of momenta, p, and the positional coordinates, q. It is much used in wave mechanics.

hand generator

a manually cranked dynamo or alternator usually used as the prima mover emergency radio transmitters.

hand rule

hold the thumb of right hand at right angles to the fingers. Place the hand on wire with the palm facing the bar and fingers pointing in the direction of the current, the thumb will point towards the north pole of the bar.

hand viewer

an optical magnifying device small enough for hand use.

hard radiation

radiation whose particles or photons have a high energy and as a result readily penetrate all kinds of materials including metals.

hard vacuum

a vacuum tube in which the residual gas has a negligible effect upon its electrical characteristics.

hardness

resistance to penetration.

hardon

an elementary particle that has strong interactions with other elementary particles.

hardware

refers to the those mechanical equipment that are necessary for carrying out an activity.

harmonic

it is one of the series of sound corresponding to a frequency which is an integral multiple of the fundamental frequency. It is a sinusoidal component of a periodic wave with same type of frequency.

harmonic frequency

it is the frequency which is an integral multiple of the fundamental frequency.

harmonic generator

an oscillating device, controlled by a tuning fork, which is capable of producing a large range of odd and even harmonics of the fundamental tuning fork frequency.

harmonic motion

simple harmonic motion.

hormonic oscillator

also known as linear oscillatorkit is a physical system that is bound to a position of stable equilibrium by a restoring force of torque proportional to the linear or angular displacement from this position.

harmonics

waves, with frequencies that are an integral multiple of the fundamental frequency, superposed on the fundamental frequency.

harness

wires and cables so arranged and tied together that they may be inserted and connected, or may be removed after disconnection as a unit.

hartman flow

is a steady flow of an electrically conducting fluid between two parallel places when there is a uniform magnetic field normal to the plates.

hartree fock technique

a method for calculating the effect of interactions between many bodies. It takes into account the exchange interaction between the bodies, although calculation of this interaction is laborious and usually requires approximations.

hash

electric noise which is produced in a generator by the contacts of brushes.

Hawking, Stephen William

(1942-) British cosmologist and physicist, who in 1979 became a professor of mathematics at Oxford University. Working with

Roger Penrose (1931-), who had shown how a singularity results from a black hole, he postulated that the original big bang must have come from a singularity. He also showed how black holes can emit particles by the hawking process.

haze

the term is associated with the degree of cloudiness in a solution.

h-bar

it is a fundamental cost. equal to $\frac{h}{2\pi}$, where h is planck's constant.

head of liquid

difference of level between the free surface of a liquid and that of the delivery pipe through which the liquid is supplied. It is measured in metre.

health physics

the branch of physics which deals with the effects of ionizing radiation on living organisms, with particular reference to the protection of human beings from the ill effects caused thereby.

heat

a magnetic device that reads, writes and erases data on a medium such as a magnetic tape, disc etc.

heat balance

it is an equilibrium which exists when all sources of heat gain and loss for a given region or body are accounted for.

heat capacity

it is the heat required to raise the temperature of a body through $1^{\circ}C$.

heat convection

is the thermal energy transferred by actual physical movement of a substance in which thermal energy is stored.

heat death

it is the condition of an isolated system corresponding to maximum entropy. If the universe is a closed system, it fetches this state hence called as head death of the universe.

heat calorific theory of

the earliest theory of heat according to which heat is an elastic imponderable yield called calorie. It is assumed to pervade all substances and is considered as indestructible and uncreatable.

heat death of the universe

the condition of the universe when entropy is maximized and all larfe-scale samples of mater are at a uniform temperature. In this condition no energy is available for doing work and the universe is finally unwound. The condition was predicted by Rudolph Clausius, who introduced the concept of entropy. Clausius's dictum that "the energy of the universe is constant, its entropy tends to a maximum" is a statement of the first two laws of thermodynamics. These laws apply in this sense only to closed systems and, for the predicted heat death to occur, the universe must be a closed system.

heat engine

a device that converts heat energy into mechanical work. Energy is transferred from a source at high temperature, part of it is converted into work and the rest is transferred to sink at a lower temperature.

heat exchanger

a device for transferring heat from one fluid to another without permitting the two fluids to contact each other . A simple industrial heat exchanges consists of a bundle of parallel tubes, through which one fluid flows, enclosed in a container, through which the other fluid flows in the opposite direction.

heat filter

special glass in condenser lens system to keep heat from film.

heat flux or thermal flux

the amount of heat energy passing through a unit area of a surface per unit time.

heat of combustion

heat of combustion of a substance is the amount of heat evolved by the combustion of 1 gm mol wt. of the stance.

heat pipe

a device for conducting energy.

heat pump

a device for transferring energy from a low temperature region to a high temperature region by doing work externally. A refrigerator is an example of a heat pump.

heat reactor

a specially designed nuclear reactor used to supply heat for industrial purposes.

heat release

the amount of heat energy given

out by a furnace per second per unit volume is called its heat release.

heat transmission coefficient

any one of a number of coefficients used in the calculation of heat transmission by conduction, convection, and radiation, through various materials and structures.

heat waves

infrared radiations which have much larger frequency than radiowaves.

heaviside layer

heaviside suggested that an ionized layer in the air, concentrate with the earth's surface, might serve as a reflecting surface which would confine radiation between it and the earth.

heavy hydrogen

an isotope of hydrogen with mass number 2.

heavy-side layer

a region of the ionosphere about 55 to 85 miles from the earth's surface which maintains its ionized conditions night and day.

heavy-water

water in which hydrogen has been replaced by deuterium. The ratio of heavy water to ordinary water in natural water is 5000.

hefner

the hefner, a unit of linctus intensity, is the lamp of specified design burring amyl acetate called the hefner lamp. 1 hefner = 0.9 international candle.

heisenberg forces

an exchange force between nucleons in which charge (equivalent to spin plus position) is exchanged.

Heisenberg, Werner Karl

(1901-76) German physicist, who became a professor at the University of Leipzig and, after World War II, at the Kaiser Wilhelm Institute in Gottingen. In 1923 he was awarded the Nobel Prize for his work on matrix mechanics. But he is best known for his 1927 discovery of the uncertainty principle.

heisenberg's uncertainty principle

the principle deals with the impossibility of making simultaneous measurements of both the position and the momentum of a subatomic particle like and electron, with unlimited accuracy. It arises from the wave-particle duality of particles and radiation. In one direction the uncertainty in position Dx and momentum Dp_x have been related by DxDp ~ h/4p, where h is the Planck's constant.

helical antenna

an antenna which has the shape of a helix. It is also known as helix antenna.

heliocentric

having the sun as a centre : measured from the centre of the sun.

heliometer

a specially designed split- lens telescope. It is used for measuring the sun's diameter. It can also be used for measuring the distances between stars.

helioscope

a telescope used to observe the sun. It is designed in such a manner as to protect the observer's eyes from the sun's glare.

helium neon laser

an atomic gas laser which makes use of helium and neon gases.

helix

a spiral. Many large natural molecules (e.g. proteins and nucleic acids) are helical in shape.

helmholtz coils

a pair of similar coils designed to produce nearly uniform field in the region between them when a current is passed through them. They are connected in series and are placed parallel to each other at a distance equal to their radius.

helmholtz function (f)

a thermodynamic function defined by the equation f = u - ts, where u is the internal energy, t the absolute temperature and s the entropy of the system.

helmholtz reasonators

a set of vessels, each resonating at particular frequency. They can be used to detect the frequency at which each resonates.

helmhotz's theorem (for fluids)

in the absence of body forces (when entropy is constant), individual vortices in a non viscous fluid always consist of the same fluid particles.

henry (h)

si unit of self inductance as well as of mutual inductance.

1 h = 1 weber/ampere.

hertz (hz)

si unit of frequency, 1 hz is equal to 1 cycleper second.

hertz effect

the enhancement of a spark discharge by passing ultraviolet light to promote ionization.

Hertz, Heinrich Rodolph

(1857-94) German physicist, who worked as an engineer before attending Berline University. He is best known for his 1888 discovery of radio waves, as predicted by James Clerk Maxwel. The SI unit of frequency is named after him.

hess's law

if reactants can be convered into products by a series of reactions, the sum of the heats of these reactions (with due regards to their sign) is equal to the heat of reaction for direct conversion from reactants to products. More generally, the overall energy change in joint from reactions to products does not depend on the route taken. The law can be use to obtain thermodynamic data that cannot be found by considering the ractions:

$2C(s) + 3H2(g) + 3½\ O_2(g) \rightarrow 2CO_2(g) + 3H_2O(l)$

The heat of this reaction is $2\Delta Hc + \Delta H_{H,}$ where ΔH_C and ΔH_H are the heats of combustion of carbon and hydrogen respectively whech can be measured. By Hess' law, this is equal to the sum of the energies for two stages :

$2C(s) + 3H_2(g) \rightarrow C_2H_6(g)$ (the heat of formation ethane, ΔH_f) and $C_2H_6(g) + 3½\ O_2 \rightarrow 2CO_2(g) + 3H_2O(l)$ (the heat of combusiton of ethance, ΔH_E). As ΔH_E can be measured and as $\Delta H_f + \Delta H_f = 2\Delta H_c + 3\Delta H_{H.}$ DH_f can be found. Another examples is the used of the Born-Haber cycle to obtain lattice energies. The law was first put forward in 1840 by the Russian chemist Germain Henri Hess (1802-50). It is sometimes called the law of conservation of energy.

heterodyne

to mix radio signals of different frequencies to produce a third signal which is of lower frequency; viz, to produce beating.

heterodyne detection

detection using the heterodyne principle.

heterogeneous radiation

a particular type of radiation like x rays or gamma rays, having a variety of wave lengths or quantum energies.

heterogeneous reactor

a type of nuclear reactor wherein the fuel is separated from the moderator.

heteropolar generator

a generator wherein the active conductors pass through magnetic fields of opposite sense in succession.

hexagonal crystal

a crystal with three chaplanar axes at 120 degree angles.

hexagonal system

type of crystal systems.

hexode

a thermionic valve having four grids between the cathode and anode, generally employed as a frequency changer.

high tension

term generally used for high voltage.

high voltage direct current

a long-distance direct- current power transmission system that uses direct current voltages up to about 1 magi volt to keep transmission losses down.

high voltage insulation

electrical insulation designed to prevent breakdown in a circuit operating at high voltages.

hoffman electrometer

an extremely sensitive form of quadrant electrometer.

hoie

a vacancy due to a missing electron in a crystalline semi-conductor. When an electron from a neighbouring atom fills this vacancy, a new vacancy or hole is created at the neighbouring atom.

hologram

the intermediate photographic record which contains the information for reproducing a three dimensional image by holography.

holomicrography

the use of holography to produce three dimensional images with various types of microscopes.

holoscope

an apparatus for tracing the path of charged particles (usually a cosmic ray particle).

homogeneous reactor

a nuclear reactor in which the fissionable material and the moderator are properly mixed to form an effectively homogeneous medium for neutrons.

homopolar crystal

a crystal having only covalent bonds is known as a homopolar crystal.

homopolar generator

a direct current generator. It consists of a metal disc rotating in a magnetic field at right angles to the plane of the disc. The e.m.f. Is induced between the centre of the disc and the edge.

hooke's law

if a body is strained by applying an external force, the strain produced is directrly proportional to the applied stress within elastic limit.

horizontal component of earth's magnetic field (h)

the value of the earth's magnetic field in a horizontal direction at a given point on the earth's surface.

horizontal intensity

symbol: B_H may be defined as the strength of Earth's magnetic field in a horizontal direction at a given point on or near the surface.

horse power

a measure of power, defined as equal to 33,000 foot pounds min. or 746 watts.

hot

the term is mostly associated with highly radioactive substances.

hot atom

an atom which has very high kinetic energy as a result of a nuclear process.

hot cathode tube

a discharge tube wherein the supply of electron for carrying the discharge is provided by thermionic emission from a heated element.

hot laboratory

the name is given to a specially designed laboratory where research with radioactive materials is carried out. These radioactive materials have a much larger reactivity and require special handling precautions.

hot spot

it is a localized region whose temperature is much higher as compared to that of its surroundings.

hot wire instrument

an electrical measuring instrument which depends on the change in the resistance of, or expansion of a wire when it is heated by passing an electric current through it.

hot wire gauge

a pressure gauge depending on the cooling by the gas of a hot filament.

hot wire microphone

a device for the measurement of the intensity and amplitude of sound waves, based on the decrease in the resistances of an electricity heated wire on being subjected to sound waves.

h.t.

high tension (voltage).

htgr

high-temperature gas-cooled reactor.

hubbard model

this is a highly simplified model which attempts to account for magnetic ordering in metals.

hue

a pure colour in the visible spectrum, relating to one visible wavelength.

hum

extraneous alternating currents that appear in the output of the amplifier having their origin in an associated or nearby electric power circuit.

humidifier

a device for increasing the amount of water vapour in the air of a room or a building.

humidity

it is a measure of the amount of water vapour present in the air. Absolute humidity is defined as the amount of water vapour present per unit volume of air.

hundred weight

an empirical unit of mass equal to 112 lbs. (50.802 kg). It is sometimes called long hundred weight to distinguish it from U.S. Short hundred weight (100 lbs).

huygen's principle (huygens fresnel principle)

every point of a wave can be considered as the centre of a new elementary wave.

hunting

variation of temperature of a thermostat above and below the desired value. It can be eliminated by damping.

huygen's construction

every point of a wave from any itself be considered as a source of secondary waves. Thus knowing the position of a wave front at any instant, a simple construction of its position can be drawn at any subsequent time.

hybrid balance

loss between two conjugate sides of a hybrid set less the same loss when one of the other sides is open or shorter.

hydralulic press

a machine based on pascal's law. In this device, a force applied over a small area by a piston is transmitted through a fluid to another piston having a large area.

hydraulics

the practical application of hydro dynamics to engineering.

hydro electric power

electrical energy obtained from water power, the latter being used to drive a dynamo.

hydrodynamics

mathematical study of the forces, energy, and pressure of liquids in motion.

hydrogen bond

a secondary bond arising due to the attraction of dipoles where the hydrogen is the positive end.

hydrogen electrode

an electrode based on hydrogen and assigned zero electrode potential, so that elements may be compared with it.

hydrogen laser

a molecular gas laser in which hydrogen is used to generate coherent wavelengths near 0.6 micrometer in the vacuum ultravoilet region.

hydrogen ion

a positively charged hydrogen atom; a proton. The general properties of acids in solution are due to the presence of hydrogen ions.

hydrology

the study of water with reference to its occurrence and properties in the hydrosphere and atmosphere.

hydromagnetics

the study of conducting fluid (plasma) when subjected simultaneously to the laws of electromagnetics and hydrodynamics. It is also known as magnetohydrodynamics. (m.h.d.).

hydrometer

an instrument used for measuring the density or specific gravity of a fluid. A common type of hydrometer consists of weighted bulb with a graduated stem.

hydrometrograph

an instrument for determining and recording the quantity of water discharged from a pipe, orifice, etc., in a given time.

hydrophone

an electro-acoustic transducer which responds to waterborne sound waves and delivers essentially equivalent electric waves.

hydrostatics

the study of fluids (liquids and gases) in equilibrium.

hygrograph

an instrument used for measuring and recording the relative humidity of the air.

hygrometer

an instrument for measuring the relative humidity of the atmosphere.

hygroscope

an instrument that indicates variations in the relative humidity of air. It uses a substance that changes colour in the presence of moisture.

hygroscopic

having a tendency to absorb moisture.

hygrsitor

an electronic component with an electrical resistance that varies with humidity.

hyperbola

a conic with eccentricity $e > 1$. It has two branches. For a hyperbola centred at the origin, the transverse axis runs along the x-axis between the vertices and has length 2b. There are two foci on the x-axis at (ae,0) and (-ae, 0). The latus rectum, the chords through the foci perpendicular to the transvers axis, have length $2b^2/a$. The equation of the hyperbola is:

$x^2/a^2 - y^2/b^2 = 1$,

and the asymptotes are $y = \pm bx/a$.

hyperbolic functions

a set of functions; sinh, cosh, and tanh, that have similar properties to trigonometric functions but are related to the hyperbola in the manner that trigonometric functions are related to the circle. The hyperbolic sine (sinh) of the angle x is defined by:

$sinhx = ½(e^x – e^{-x})$. Similarly,
$coshx = ½(e^x – e^{-x}$
$tanhx = (e^x – e^{-x})/(e^x + e^{-x})$
Hyperbolic secant (sech), cosecant (cosech), and cotangent (coth) are the reciprocals of cosh, sinh, and tanh, respectively.

hypercopia

long sight caused if the distance between the lens and the back of the eyeball is too short.

hypermetropia (long sightedness)

defect of the eye to see near objects distinctly. It can be corrected by using convex lens spectacles.

hypersonic

pertaining to hypersonic flow. Also pertaining to speeds of mach 5 or greater.

hypersonic flow

in aerodynamics, flow of a fluid over a body at speeds much greater than the speed of sound and in which the shock waves start at a finite distance from the surface of the body.

hypsometer

an apparatus for measuring the boiling point of a liquid. Since the boiling point of a substance depends on the altitude, it can be used for the measurement of altitude above sea level.

hysterisis (magnetism)

if a ferromagnetic substances is magnetized by an external applied field h and then demagnetized, the flux density lags behind the field h.

ic

integrated circuit.

iceland spar

a transparent calcite ($CaCO_3$) which has the property of producing double refraction and polarization of light.

ice line

a curve expressing the relation between the melting point of ice and the applied pressure.

ice point

the temperature of equilibrium between water and ice at one

atmospheric pressure; the melting point of ice. It is assigned the value 0 degree c.

iconoscope

a television camera tube in which a high velocity electron beam scans a photoactive mosaic which has the capacity for electrical storage.

ideal crystal

a crystal whose lattice is perfectly regular and which contains no foreign atoms or ions or other defects or imperfections.

ideal flow

fluid flow which is incompressible.

ideal gas

syn. perfect gas. A gas that obeys boyle's law and has an internal energy independent of the volume occupied.

ideal transformer

a hypothetical transformer that neither stores nor dissipates energy.

identity

symbol º. A statement of equality that applies for all values of the unknown quantity. For example, 5y º 2y + 3y.

ignition temperature

1. the temperature to which a substance must be heated before it will burn in air. 2. the temperature to which a plasma has to be raised in order that nuclear fusion will occur.

ignitron

it is a heavy duty recitifer tube. It contains a pool of mercury.

illuminance

symbol E. The energy in the form of visible radiation reaching a surface per unit area in unit time; i.e. the luminous flux per unit time. It is measured in lux (lumens per square metre).

illuminance of a surface

the amount of luminous energy falling on unit area of the surface per unit time. Its units are lumen/ m.

illumination

symbol: E. Rerers to a measure of the visible-radiation energy reaching a surface in unit time.

image

a point or region where rays of light from an object meet or appear to meet after reflection or refraction from a reflecting or refracting surface.

image converter

an electronic device in which an image formed be in visible radiation (usually gamma rays, X-rays, ultrviolet, or radiation is focused on to a photocathode which emits electrons when it is illuminated. These electrons fall on a fluorescent anode screen, after acceleration and focusing by a system of electron lenses. The fluorescent screen produces a visible image. The device is used in fluorescent scene produces a visible image. The device is used in fluoroscopes, infrared telescopes, ultraviolet microscopes, and other devices.

image force

the force on a charge due to the charges which it may induce on conductors of dielectrics near it.

image intensifier

a device used to produce a brighter optical image than an initial image. An image intensifier can be used at very low levels of brightness without introducing no is into the brightness levels of the intensified image. The principle is similar to that of the image converter.

image plane

the plane perpendicular to the axis centred on the image.

image space

a region of space where the real or virtual images are formed by an optical system.

imaginary number

a number that is a multiple of Ö – 3 = iÖ3.

imaging

the formation of images of objects.

immersion heater

an electric device for heating a liquid by direct immersion in the liquid.

immersion objective

an objective used in high powered microscopes. The space between the lens and the microscope slide to be examined is filled with a suitable liquid.

impact strength

the ability of substance to resist shock loading..

impact stress

the force per unit area imposed upon a substance by a suddenly applied load.

impact test

a test to determine the resistance of a material to a suddenly applied stress , i.e. shock.

impact velocity

also known as striking velocity. The is the velocity of a projectile at the instant of impact.

impedance

the total opposition to the flow of an alternating current, i.e., the combined effect of resistance and reactance.

impedance bridge

an electrical device which is quite similar to whetstone bridge. It is used to compare impedances. An impedance may comprise of inductance, capacitance and resistance.

imperial units

the system of measurement based on the yard and the pound, formerly used in the U.K. The f.p.s. System was a scientific system based on imperial units.

impetus

refers to the force by virtue of which a moving body tends to maintain its verlocity and overcome resistance to its motion.

implosion

a bursting inwarding as the inward collapse of an evacuated container or the compression of fissionable material by ordinary explosives in a nuclear weapon.

impulse

the product of the force and the (short) time during which the force acts. Impulse given to the body is equal to the change in the momentum of the body.

impulsive force

a force acting for a very short time as in a collision.

in vacuo

the term is commonly used in physics to denote vacuum.

incandescence

the emission of light by surface heated to a high temperature.

incandescent lamp

an electric lamp wherein light is produced by the heating effect of a filament of carbon, osmium, tantalum, or tungsten.

incident radiation

the radiation which arrives at a

given point or surface.

incident ray

with reference to refraction, diffraction, etc., a ray which arrives at a given point or surface from thesource of the radiation, in contradistinction to a refracted ray, etc.

inclination (angle of dip)

the angle between the earth's magnetic field and the horizontal at any point on the earth's surface is called the angle of dip at the point.

inclined plane

a plane at an angel (to the horizontal). A type of simple machine which can be used to raise a weight vertically by movement up an inclined path.

inclinometer

an instrument used for measuring the magnetic inclination.

incoherent

not coherent. Radiation from any source other than a laser is incoherent.

incoherent holography

holograms produced initially from conventional photographs or incoherent optical assembly.

incoherent light

electromagnetic radiant energy not all of the same phase, and possibly also consisting of various wavelengths.

incompressible flow

fluid motion without any change in density.

incubator

a box designed to maintain a constant internal temperature by the use of a thermostat, used for rearing chickens and prematurely born infants, and in bacteriology.

indeterminancy principle

uncertainlly principle.

index

a numerical quantity which is usually dimensionless. It is introduced to denote the magnitude of a physical effect e.g., refractive index of a substance.

index error

syn. zero error. A scale error on a measuring instrument so that the instrument shows a reading x when it should show zero reading.

indicator diagram

it is the cycle traced out during the motion of a piston in the cylinder of an engine.

induced current

electric current in a conductor which is caused by e.m.f. set up by a changing magnetic field surrounding it.

inductance

e.m.f. Induced in a circuit due to a changing electric current in the circuit or in neighbouring circuit when the rate of change of current is unity.

inductance meter

it is an electric device used to find the self inductance of a circuit or the mutual inductance of two coupled circuits.

induction

the process which sets up electric currents in a conductor when it is placed into an electromagnetic field.

induction balance

a bridge to measure the inductance of a coil or device.

induction coils

an instrument for production of high voltage impulses from a source of low e.m.f.

induction, electromagnetic

development of an e. m. f. Induced in a circuit when the magnetic flux linked with the circuit varies.

induction furnace

a device to convert electrical energy to heat by electromagnetic induction.

induction heating

a form of heating in which electrically conducting material is heated as a result of the electric current induced in it by an alternating magnetic field.

induction motor

an electric motor in which an a.c. Current passed through the primary winding induces electric current in the secondary of the rotor.

induction, electromagnetic

development of an e.m.f. Induced in a circuit when the magnetic flux inked with the circuit changes.

inelastic collision

a collision in which the linear momentum is conserved but kinetic energy is not conserved. Some of the kinetic energy may be converted into internal energy.

inelastic scattering

scattering that results from inelastic collisions.

inert gases

the elements he, ne, ar, kr, xn and ra whose outermost orbit is completely filled.

inertia

the property of a body due to which it opposes any change in its state of rest or of uniform motion. The property is implied by newton's first law of motion which is, therefore, also called the law of inertia.

inertial force

the force produced by the reaction of a body to an accelerating force.

inertial frame

a frame of reference in which newton's laws of motion are valid is called an inertial frame.

inertial mass

refers to the mass of an object as measured by he property of inertia.

inertial system (inertial frame of reference)

frame of reference for which acceleration is zero. Two frames of reference are inertial with respect to each other, if there is no relative acceleration between them.

infra sound

sound of pressure waves having frequency below 20 hz.

infrared (ir)

electromagnetic radiation past the red end of the visible spectrum. The range of wavelengths is approximately 0.7 mm to 1mm. Infrared is some times called thermal radiation, most of the energy radiated by surfaces below 6000 k is the infrared.

infrared astronomy

the study of radiation from space o\in the infrared region of the spectrum. Some infrared radiation k is absorbed by water and carbon dioxide molecues in the atmosphere but there are sevral narrow atnmospheri windows in the near–infrared (1.15 –1.3 μm, 1.5 – 1.75 μm, 2–2.4 μm, 3.4 – 4.2 μm, 4.6 – 4.8 μm, 8 – 13 μm, and 16 – 18 μm,) Longer wavelength, observiations must be mad from balloons, rockets or statellites. Infrared sources are either thermal, i.e., emitted gy gas or dust atoms or moloecules in the temperatrure range 100 – 3000 K, or electrnic i.e. emitted by high–energy electrons interacting with magnetic fields as in Synchrotrn radiation. Deterctors are either modified reflecting telescopesor solid-state photon detectors, usually incorportaing photovoltaic devices.

infrared detector

a thermal device for observing and measuring infrared radiation.

infrared emission

the process of emission of infrared radiations by a body.

infrared filters

a device which is highly transparent to infrared radiation at certain wavelengths while absorbing other types of electromagnetic radiation.

infrared laser

a specially designed laser capable of emitting infrared radiations, generally in the near and intermediate infrared regions of the spectrum.

infrared maser

an optical maser which employs an infrared frequency for stimulation and radiates or detects signals of millimetre wavelengths.

infrared optical material

a material which is transparent to infrared radiation.

infrared radiation

refers to the thermal radiations. These can be detected by blackened thermomenters, skin nerve cells, thermoplies and photograhic films. All matter rafistwes infra-red at all times.

infrared stars

celestial bodies whose principle emission is infrared radiation, believed to consist of stars surrounded by dust clouds. In some cases the light from the central star penetrates the dust so that it can be seen with optical telescopes.

infrasonic

of a frequency below the range of audible sound.

infrasound

vibrations in a medium having frequencies below about 16 hertz.

inhibit

means to restrain, hinder or arrest an action, impulse etc.

inhour

a unit of reactivity of a nuclear reactor. One inhour is the reactivity which will provide the reactor a period of one hour.

injection laser

a laser in which a forward biased gallium arsenide diode converts direct current input power directly into coherent light, without optical pumping.

inline holography

hologram produced by single reference beam interference with waves diffracted or scattered from a small object.

insolation

(from incoming solar radiation) The solar radiation that is received at the earth's surface per unit area. It is related to the solar constant, the duration of daylight, the altitude of the sun, and the latitude of the receiving surface. It is measured in MJ m^{-2}.

instantaneous power

the product of instantaneous voltage and instantneous current for a circuit.

instantaneous value

the value of a varying physical quantity at a particular instant.

instrument

refers to any mechanical device, tool, implement etc.

insulation, electrical

the use of non conductors to coat or separate electrical conductors (for safety or prevention of short circuits). Rubber, pvc, and ceramics are common insulators.

insulator

a substance that does not conduct electricity e.g. wood plastic etc.

insulator, thermal

a material that does not readily transmit heat. Many insulators, such as asbestos, are porous or fibrous solids that trap small pockets air within them.

integral dose

the total energy imported to an irradiated body by an ionizing radiation.

integrated circuit

micro circuit. A microelectronic circuit is incorporated into a chip as semi-conductor, usually crystalline silicon (a silicon chip).

intensifier

a substance that strengthens the image on a negative or positive photographic medium.

intensifying screen

a screen, coated with calcium tungsten crystals. It emits light under the action of x rays and reduces the exposures needed in radiography by a factor of about 100.

intensity

1. the rate at which radiant energy is transferred per unit area. See radiant intensity. 2. The rate at which sound energy is transferred as measured relative to some reference valvue. See decibel. 3. magnetic intensity. See magnetic field. 4. Electric intensity. See electric field. 5. See luminous intensity.

intensity level

the tenfold of the logarithm of the ratio of the intensity of a given sound to an intensity chosen as standard of reference. The intensity of a sound is expressed in units called bel and decibel.

intensity of an electric field

the force which would act on a unit positive charge placed at the given point of the electric field.

intensity of magnetization

magnetic moment per unit volume i.e., the magnetic moment of a magnet or magnetized body divided by its volume.

intensive variable

a quantity in a macroscopic system that has a well defined value at every point inside the system and that remains (nearly) constant when the size of the system is increased. Examples of intensive variables are the pressure, temperature, density, specific heat capacity at constant volume, and viscosity. An intensive variable results when any extensive variable is divided by an arbirary extensive variable such as the volume. A macroscopic system can be described by one extensive variable and a set of intensive variables.

interference

the effect produced due to superposition of waves. If the crest of one wave falls on the crest of another, an increased effect is produced at that point.

interference fringes

refers to the pattern of alternate dark and light bands produced by the interference of light owing to the fact that the interfering beams weaken each other or cancel each other out at some places, while reinforcing each other at others.

interferometry

the technique of producing interference patterns and using these for accurate wavelengths measurements. Measuring small distance changes, testing flat surfaces, etc.

interferometer

an instrument which is used for measuring wave-lengths of light and for analyzing spectra.

intergalactic space

the space between galaxies, in which intergalactic matter may occur.

intergrating meter

a measuring instrument which integrates the measured quantity with reference to time.

intermediate reactor

it is a special type of nuclear reactor in which the nuclear chain reaction is sustained due to intermediate neutrons.

intermediate frequency (i- f)

in superheterodyne reception, a frequency resulting from the combination of the received modulated carrier frequency and the local oscillator frequency.

intermolecular forces

forces between molecules and atoms. These force are attractive in nature.

internal combustion engine

an engine in which the fuel is burnt inside the cylinder of the engine and the gases thus produced constitute the working substance.

internal energy (u)

the total energy of a system, which is a function of its temperature t, and which is the sum of the kinetic and potential energy of its molecules. It increases when the temperature of the system is increased or work is done on the system externally.

internal resistance (r) of a cell

resistance offered to the flow of current in a cell.

internal work

the work done in separating the molecules of system against their force of attraction. Its value is zero for an ideal gas.

international ampere

the unvarying electric current which deposits silver from a standard solution of silver nitrate at the rate of 0.001118000 gram per second. One international ampere equals 0.999835 absolute ampere.

international angstrom

a unit very nearly equal to the angstrom unit (10^{-8} cm) but defined as being such that the red cadmium line at 15°C and 760 mm pressure would have a wave-length of 6438.4696 I.A.

international candle

a former unit of luminous intensity, approximately equal to 1.0183 candela. It was originally defined in terms of the light emitted per second by a specified electric lamp, but after 1946 was superseded by the candela, now the si base unit.

international coulomb

the quantity of electricity which passes any section of an electric circuit in one second, when the current in the circuit is one international ampere. One international coulomb equals 0.99985 absolute coulomb.

international farad

the capacitance of a capacitor of a charge of one international coulomb produces a potential difference between the terminals of one international volt. One international farad equals 0.99952 absolute farad.

international henry

the indectance which produces an electromotive force of one international volt when the current is changing at the rate of one international ampere per second. One international henry equals 1.00048 absolute henrys.

international joule

the energy required to transfer one international coulomb between two points having a potential difference of one international volt. One international joule equals 1.00048 absolute joules.

international ohm

defined as the resistance at zero degree centigrade of a column of mercury of uniform cross-section, having a length of 106.300 centimetres and a mass of 14.4521 grams. Experimental results show that one international ohm equals 1.00048 absolute ohms.

international practical temperature scale (ipts)

a scale of temperature (1968)

based on a number of fixed points, with agreed methods of measuring temperatures over particular ranges.

international system

an old system of units for measuring electrical quantities based on the international ohm and the international ampere.

international system of units (si)

the metric system of units based on the meter, kilogram, ampere, kelvin degree and candela. Also called mska system.

interplanetary space

the space between the planets within the solar system.

interpolation

estimation of the value of a function, y (x), for a value of the variable, x that lies between those for which the function is known.

interrupter

a device which periodically interrupts the flow of a continuous current to produce pulses.

interstellar space

the space between stars within a galaxy, in which interstellar matter may occur.

interval

the ratio of frequencies of two notes. When the interval is 1, the notes are said to be in unison.

intesifying screen

a screen, coasted with calcium toungstate crystals, it emits light under the actions of x-rays and reduces the exposures needed in radio–graphy by a factor of about 100.

intensity of magnetic field

(i) along the axis of a circular coil

$$B \frac{\mu o.n.I.r^2}{2(r^2+x^2)^{\frac{3}{2}}}$$

where x is the distance of the point (p) from the centre of the coil.
(ii) At the centre of the long solenoid.
Intensity of wave :
$I = 2\pi^2 f^2 V pA^2$ (Wm-2)
where I = Intensity of wave power
f = frequency of wave
v = speed of propagation of wave
A = amplitude
p = density of medium.

interaction

an effect involving a number of

bodies, particles, or systems as a result of which some physicakl or chemical change takes place to one or more of them.

interface

a surface that is considered as a common boundary between two bodies or spaces.

interference

waves which are propagated in the same direction (transvers or longitudinal polarisation) with the same amplitude and frequency, then we have

$$S_1 = A \cos 2\pi\left(\frac{1}{T} - \frac{x}{\lambda} + \frac{\phi}{2\pi}\right)$$

$$S_2 = A \cos 2p\left(\frac{1}{T} - \frac{x}{\lambda}\right)$$

ϕ = phase of S_1 with respect to S_2, for t = 0 and x = 0. $S_1 = A \cos\phi$ and $S_2 = A$.
At any point in time 't', the two waves are displaced with respect to each other along the x–axis by a constant length.

$$\Delta x = \frac{\varphi}{2\pi}.l$$

Resultant amplitude = $S_1 + S_2$

$$= \left(2A\cos\frac{\varphi}{2}\right)\cos 2\pi\left(\frac{t}{T} - \frac{x}{\lambda} + \frac{\varphi}{4\pi}\right)$$

For $\phi = 2$ k. π, Δx = k. λ
The amplitude of a resultant wave have a maximum value equal to 2A (constructive interference)

The interference is said to be constructive when the resultant amplitude of two waves reaching a point in the same phase is equal to the sum of the amplitude due to each wave fraction of integers neither of them being large.
The effect is not related to the difference between frequencies but to their ratio.
The ratio of frequencies of two notes is called interval. The simplest interval in one. In this case the two notes are said to be in unison. Again for $\phi = (2k+1)\pi$, where have

$$Dx = (2k + 1)\frac{\lambda}{2}$$

In this case the amplitude of resultant wave is zero. It is known as destructive interference.

intrinsic (itype) semiconductor

a pure semiconductor wherein the electron and hole densities are equal under conditions of thermal equilibrium.

invar

an alloy of iron containing 36% of nickel. It has a very small coefficient of thermal expansion. It is used in making clocks and accurate standards of length.

inverse gain

of a transistor. The gain of a bipolar junction transistor when it is connected with the emitter as the collector, and vice versa.

inverse network

two networks are regarded as inverse if the product of their impeadances is independent of frequency within the required range.

invers piezoelectric effect

the contraction and expansion in quartz and certain other asymmetric crystals along an electric axis as a result of the mechanical strain set up in them as they are subjected to an electric field in that direction.

inverse square law (light)

the illuminance of a surface is inversely proportional to the square of its distance from the (point) source.

inverse square law of illumination

the illumination of a surface by a point source of light varies directly with the intensity of the sourceand inversely as the square of the perpendicular distance from the source of the surface.

inverse zeeman effect

the zeeman effect observed ir absorption spectra is known as the inverse zeeman effect.

inverter

a device for converting direc current into alternating current.

ioffe bars

heavy current carrying bars used in experimental fusior devices to increase plasma stability.

ion

a charged particle consisting o an atom, or group of atoms, tha has either lost or gainec electrons.

ion current

the magnitude of electric curren which arises due to the motior of ions.

ion density

the number of ions present in a unit volume. It is commonly called ion concentration.

ionic bond

atomic bonding by coulombic attraction of unlike ions.

ionic radius

a value assigned to the radius of an ion in La crystalline solid based on the assumption that ions are spherical with a definite size. X-ray diffraction can be use to measure the inter nuclear distance in crystalline solids. For example, in NaF the Na – F distance is 23.1 nm, and this is assumed to be the sum of the Na and F^- radii. By making certain assumptions about the sheilding effect that the inner electrons have on the outer electrons, it is possible to assign individual values to the ionic radii Na^+ 9.6 nm; 13.5 nm. In general, negative ions have larger ionic radii than positive ions. The larger the negative charge, the larger the ion; the larger the positive charge, the smaller the ion.

ionization

the formation of ions by ionizing radiation, by collision with fast moving particles or by chemical reactions.

ionization chamber

an apparatus for measuring the amount of ionization produced by radioactivity in air or some other gaseous medium.

ionization energy

ionization energy of an atom is equal to energy required to be supplied to the atom to remove an electron from it; also called ionization potential.

ionization gauge

a high vacuum gauge in which the pressure of the gas in the gauge is measured by its degree of ionization.

ionization potential

ionization potential is the potential required to give an electron just sufficient energy to ionize the atom, viz., to knock out an electron.

ionizing radiation

radiation which has enough energy to cause ionization and produce ions in a system.

ionsphere

a region in the earth's upper atmosphere that reflects radios wave and makes radio transmission possible. It contains ions and electrons that reflect electromagnetic waves.

ionosphere f-region

the region of the ionosphere about 85 to 220 miles above the surface of the earth.

ionospheric wave

a radiowave may travel from transmitting aerial to receiving aerial by one of two paths; either directly along the ground, or by reflection from the ionosphere. In the latter case it is called a sky wave or ionospheric wave.

ipts

international practical temperature scale.

ir

infrared.

iris

an arrangement able to vary the amount of light that enters an optical instrument. In the mamalian eye, this is a circular muscle that changes the size of the pupil.

iris diaphragm

it is a variable aperture made of a number of moveable overlapping plates.

irradiance

symbol: E. Refers to the rate of energy reaching unit area of a surface, i.e., the radian flux per unit area.

irreversible process

a process which cannot be returned to its original state through the same series of stages. In such processes, the system is not in equilibrium throughout the change.

isemtropic

of equal entropy.

isenthalpic

of equal enthalpy.

isenthalpic process

a process taking place without any change of enthalpy i.e. so that the total heat energy remains constant.

ising model

used, for instance, if ferromagnetism and phase transformation theory, it is a model for a system of interacting particles.

iso

prefix indicating "the same".

isobars

nuclides in which the number of nucleons (neutrons plus protons) is the same but which differ in the number of protons they contain.

isobaric process

it refers to the process that occurs at constant pressure $\Delta p = 0$

Thus $w = P\Delta V = nR\,\Delta T$

$Q = n.\,C_p.\,\Delta T.$

isochore

a curve that represent two variables involved in an isometric (constant volume) thermodynamic change e.g. pressure/temperature, temperature/entropy.

isochoric process

process carried out at constant volume.

isochronous circuits

two electric circuits are said to be isochronous to each other if they have the same resonant frequency.

isoclinal

a curve drawn in such a manner that all places on the curve have the same magnetic dip.

isoclinic line

imaginary line on the earth's surface which joins points of same angle of dip (inclination).

isodiapheres

two or more nuclides having the same isotopic number.

isodynamic

a curve drawn in such a manner that the total magnetic field strength of the earth's magnetic field is identical at all points on the curve.

isodynamic line

a line passing through points of equal horizontal intensity of the earth's magnetic field.

isogam

a line on a map joining points at which the acceleration of free fall is constant.

isogonal

a curve drawn in such a manner that the magnetic declination is the same at all places on the curve.

isogonal line

a line passing through points of equal magnetic declination.

isogonic line

an imaginary line of the Earth's surface which is joining points of equal declination.

isolating transformer

a transformer that is used to isolate any circuit or a device from its power supply.

isolator

a device which allows microwave energy to pass in one direction while absorbing power in the reverse direction.

isomagnetic lines

lines that join points at which the magnetics force is equal.

isomers

compounds having same olecular weight and percentage composition but differing in some or all their chemical and physical properties.

isometric

exhibiting isomerism.

isometric change

a change in a gas which takes place at constant volume.

isotherm

a line or graph joining points having the same temperature.

isothermal change

refers to a process that takes place at a constant temperature.

isothermal process

a process in which the temperature remains constant. In such a process, the system is in equilibrium with its surroundings throughout.

isothermal transformation

the term is very commonly used in thermodynamics and involves the transformation of a substance at constant temperature.

isotones

nuclides having the same number of neutrons but the number of protons is different.

isotope seperation

the process of separating the different isotopes of an element according to their atomic masses. Most methods depend on small differences in physical properties between isotopes.

isotopes

atoms of the element having the same atomic number but different mass number. The nuclei of such species have the same number of protons but different physical properties.

isotope separation

the term used for the process of separating the different isotopes of an element according to their atomic masses.

isotopic mass (isotopic weight)

the mass number of given isotope of an element.

isotopic number

neutron excess. The difference between the number of neutrons in an isotope and the number of protons.

isotropic

exhibiting identical properties in all directions.

isotropic crystal

crystals having the same properties in all the three directions along the three axis of the crystal.

isotropic dielectric

a dielectric material which has only one dielectric constant which is therefore independent of the direction of the applied field.

isotropic radiator

any source of energy which radiates uniformly in all possible directions.

isotropy

a medium is isotropic if the value of a measured physical quantity does not depend on the direction.

j

the symbol represents the mechanical equivalent of heat.

jack

a connecting device into which a plug can be inserted to make circuit connections; may also have contacts that open or close to perform switching functions when the plug is inserted or removed.

jacket

a thin container for one or more fuel slugs; used to prevent the fuel from escaping into the coolant of a reactor. Also known as can, cartridge.

jaeger method

a method of determining surface tension of a liquid in which one measures the pressure required to cause air to flow from a capillary tube immersed in the liquid.

jamin refractometer

used to find refractive index.

jamming

interference in radio reception caused due to an undesired signal that is so strong that the signal cannot be understood.

jansky noise

any high–frequency static disturbance of cosmic origin.

jaw

two or more parts of a machine hold something.

jet (joint European Torus)

a large Tokomak experiment at Culham, England, carried out in collaboration by various European nations in the search for thermonuclear energy by nuclear fusion.

jet engine

an aircraft engine. It produces forward motion due to the rearward exhaust of a jet of fliud or heated air/gases.

jet plane

an aeroplane having a jet engine.

jet propulsion

propulsion where in the propulsive force is the reaction of one or more jets of hot gases coming out at high velocity from backwardly directed nozzles.

jet propelled

any thing that is propelled by a jet engine.

jet stream

refers to the exhaust of a rocket engine.

jet tones

the unsteady tones formed when a steam of air is projected into stationary air from an orifice.

jitter

a short-term instability in either the amplitude or phase of a signal specifically the signal on a cathode ray tube.

joffe effect

an observed decrease in brittleness or rock salt on dissolution of the surface. The effect is probably associated with the disıocations in the crystal.

jogging

the phenomenon of rapidly repeated closing and opening of an electric circuit in order to cause mobility of a driven machine.

johnson noise

in electronics, noise arising from thermal agitation of electrons in conductors.

johnson–rahbeck effect

when a semiconducting plate of material like slate agate is placed against a metal plate, the two hold strongly together during the application of a potential of about 200 volts. The plate and stone are only in actual contact at a few points through which a very small current flows that equalize a high potential difference and the forces of attraction are correspondingly great.

joint

a juncture of two wires or other conductive paths for current.

joint pole

pole used in common by two or more utility companies.

joliot-curin, Irene

(1897-1956) French physicist, daughter of Marie and Pierre Curie, who was educated by her mother and her scientist associates. In 1921 she began work at the Radium Institute, becoming director in 1946 Nobel Prize for chemistry for their discovery of artificial radioactivity the previous year.

joly steam calorimeter

an apparatus for measuring the specific thermal capacity of a gas at constant volume.

joly's steam calorimeter

a calorimeter used for the determination of the specific heat capacities of solids.

jones zone

this is similar to, and in certain cases equal to, the brillouin zone for a solid and the distinction is not always made.

josephson effect

if two superconductors are connected by a thin layer of ihsulating material with no electrostatic potential present, there is a quantum mechanical penetration, through the layer, of electrons existing as cooper pairs.

joshi effect

a fall (negative effect) or rise (positive effect) in the low frequency alternating current passing through a gas dielectric condenser when the gas is irradiated continuously with visible light.

joule (j)

unit of work in the system. 1 joule is equal to the work done by a force of 1 newton when it moves an object through a distance of 1 meter along the direction of force.

joule calorimeter

an electrically heated calorimeter.

joule effect

the heating effect produced by the flow of current through a resistance. Also a change in the length of a ferromagnetic substance which occurs parallel to an applied magnetic field.

joule heat

the phenomenon of production of heat in a medium having electrical resistance, through which an electric current is passed.

joule-keliven effect

refers to a temperature change that takes place when a gas expands through a porous barrier into a region of lower pressure.

Ioule's equivalent

symbol: J. Refers to a constant, 4.1855×10^7 ergs per calorie (15^0).

joule's law

1. the heat (Q) produced when an electric current (I) flows through a resistance (R) for a time (t) is given by $Q = I^2Rt$. 2. The internal energy of a given mass of gas is independent of its volume and pressure, being a function of temperature alone. This law applies only to ideal gases (for which it provides a definition of thermodynamic temperature) as in a real gas intermolecular forces would cause changes in the internal energy should a change of volume occur. See also Joule-Thomson effect.

joule's mechanical equivalent of heat (j)

$W = JH$.

Value of J

$J = 4.2$ J/Cal

$= 4.2 \times 10^3$ J/K Cal

joule meter

an integrated wattmeter calibrated in joules.

joule-thomson effect

a change in temperature due to expansion of a gas through porous plug into a region of lower pressure. It may either result in heating or cooling effect. If the initial temperature is less than the inversion temperature then cooling is produced otherwise heating effect is produced.

joule thomson expansion

the adiabatic irreversible expansion of a fluid flowing through a porous plug or partially opened valve. Also known as joule thompson process.

joy stick

it refers to the control stick of an aeroplane.

juke box

it is a phonograph that is operated by a coin. The push button provided can be used to select fronma variety of records available.

jumper

a short length of the conductor used to make a connection (generally temporary) between terminals of a circuit or to bypass a circuit.

junction

in a semi-conductor device, a region of transition between semi conducting regions of different electrical properties.

junction detector (soli–state detector)

a sensitive detector of ionizing radistion in which the output is a current pulse proportional to the energy falling in or near the depletion region of a reverse-biased semiconductor junction. The first types were made by evaporating a thin layer of gold on to a polished water on n-type germanium; however, gold-superseded the germanium type, which have to be operated at the temperature of liquid nitrogen to reduce noise.

junction laser

a laser in which a junction in a semi-conductor serves as the source of the coherent laser beam.

junction pole

pole at the end of a transposition section of an open-wire line or the pole common to two adjacent transposition sections.

junction rectifier

a rectifier based on a semi-conductor junction.

junction rule (or kirchhof's first law)

it states, "the algebraic sum of the currents at any given function in a circuit is zero".

$\Sigma i = 0$

$i_1 + i_2 + i_3 + i_4 + i_6 + i_7 + i_8 = 0$

Thus there could be no accumulation of current at any point in a circuit.

just scale

a diatomic scale rendered in the just tuning system.

junction transistor

a transistor having a base electrode and two or more electrodes connected to semi-conductor junctions.

just tuning

a tuning system generated by octave rearrangement of the notes of three consecutives triads, each having the frequency ratio 4 : 5 : 6, with the highest note of one triad sewing as the lowest note of the next.

k

the symbol represents the boltzmann constant.

k band

an optical absorption band which appears together with an f-band and has a lower intensity and shorter wavelength than the latter.

k-capture

refers to an sbsorption of electron from the innermost (K–shell) shell of an atom into its nucleus.

k-lines

the characteristic X–ray frequency from atoms because of excitation of electrons from K–shell (n=1).

k shell

the innermost shell of electrons surrounding the atomic nucleus, having electrons characterised by the principal quantum number 1.

k-electron

one of the two electrons in the orbits which are closet to the nucleus of an atom.

k/l ratio

the ratio of the number of internal conversion electrons emitted from the k shell of an atom during de-excitation of a nucleus to the number of such electrons emitted from the l shell.

kaiser effect

an effect observed in most metals in which acoustic emissions are not observed during the reloading of a material until the stress exceeds its previous high value.

kaleidoscope

an optical instrument in which small pieces of glass beads of different colours are loosely held. On rotating the instrument various patterns are formed by reflections in two or more mirrors set at suitable angles to each other.

kane band

a form of energy band which commonly occurs in semiconductors which have a narrow gap between the valence and conduction bands.

kaon (k meson)

a type of meson. There are four types of meson : positively charged, negatively charged and two types of neutral particles. They are strongly interacting bosons of zero spin with several alternative modes of decay.

kaonic atom

the name is associated with an atom having a negatively charged kaon orbiting around an ordinary nucleus.

kapp line

a unit of magnetic flux equal to 6000 maxwells.

karat

it is a unit used to specify the purity of gold. A pure gold is 24 Karat gold.

kater's pendulum

a complex pendulum designed by Henry kater (1777-1835) to measure the acceleration of free fall. It consists of a metal bar with khife edges attached near the ends and two weights that can slide between the knife edges. The bar is pivoted from each knife edge in turn and the positions of the weights are adjusted so that the period of the pendulum is the same with both pivots. The period is then given by the formula for a simple pendulum, which enalesg to be calculated.

kater's reversible pendulum

a gravity pendulum designed to measure the acceleration of gravity and consisting of a body with two knife edge supports on opposite sides of the enter of mass.

katharometer

a device for detecting small quantities of a gas within a gaseous mixture, based on the great differences between the thermal conductivities of the different gases.

keeper

syn. armature. The regions near the ends of a magnet produce an induced flux within it that opposes the original magnetizing flux, the effect being maximum for the shortest magnets.

keldysh theory

a theory of multiphoton ionization in which an atom is ionized by rapid absorption of a sufficient number of photons.

kellner eyepiece

a type of eyepiece having a cemented eye lens that corrects chromatic aberration and distortion. It is commonly used as an eyepiece in prism binoculars.

kelvin: symbol k

the si base unit of

thermodynamic temperature. It is defined as the fraction of the thermodynamic temperature of the triple point of water. Zero kelvin (ok) is absolute zero.

kelvin balance

an electrodynamic ammeter, voltmeter or wattmeter, in which the electromagnetic forces are balanced against gravity by a travelling weight.

kelvin body

an ideal body whose shearing stress is the sum of a term proportional to its deformation and a term proportional to the rate of change of its deformation with time.

kelvin bridge

a bridge embodying two similar sets of ratio coils, designed for measurement of low values of resistance.

kelvin contacts

a method used for testing or measuring electronic circuits or components.

kelvin scale

the basic scale used for temperature definition; the triple point of water (comprising i.e., liquid and vapour) is defined as 273.16 k.

kelvin, degree (k) **unit of temperature**

the kelvin scale of temperature is based on the triple point of water, which is assigned the temperature 273.16 k.

kelvin skin effect

a non-uniform distribution of variable currents in solid conductors, resulting in an increase in current density near the surface.

kenotron

a high-vacuum diode; specially designed to serve as a powerful current.

keplerian telescope

a telescope that forms a real intermediate image in the focal plane and can be used for introducing a reticule or a scale into the focal plane.

kepler's laws

the three laws of planetary motion discovered by Kepler (1571-1630) that explain the movements of planets in terms of the Copernican concept. These laws are: 1. The orbit of every planet about the sun is an ellipse, the sun occupying one focus. 2. A line from each planet to the sun sweeps over equal areas in equal times. 3. the squares of the lines required for the different planets to complete their orbits are proportional to the cubes of their mean distances from the sun.

kerma

the kinetic energy imparted to charged particles in a unit mass of material by uncharged particles such as neutrons; it may be expressed as joules per kilogram or per gram.

kernel

an atom which has lost all its valency electrons is known as its kernel.

kerr effect

1. an electro-optical effect in which certain transparent isotropic substances become doubly refracting when subjected to the effect of an electric field at right angles to a beam of light. 2. The conversion of plane-polarized light into ellipticall polarized light when it is reflected from the polished end of a magnet.

kerr magneto optic effect

light, plane polarized in or normal to the plane of incidence, becomes elliptically polarized when reflected from the polarized pole of an electromagnet.

ke v

kiloelectronvolts; 10^3 electronvolts.

key

a device that is used for opening and closing electrical contacts. A key can switch one or more parts of a circuit.

key boart\d

it consista or a set of keys for example on a piano, type writer etc.

key stroke

refers to one stroke of any key on machine operated by a key board.

keyes equation

an equation of state of a gas which is designed to correct the van der waals equation for the effect of surrounding molecules on the term representing the volume of a molecule.

keying

the forming of signals, such as for telegraph transmission by modulating a direct current or other carrier between discrete values of some characteristic.

keylock switch

an electric switch which can be

operated only by inserting and turning a key.

kiln

a furnace or oven for burning, baking or drying.

kilo

symbol: k. A prefix which denotes 10^3. For example, 1 kilometre (km) = 10^3 metres (m).

kiloampere

a metric unit of current flow equal to 1000 amperes. Abbreviated ka.

kilobar

a unit of pressure equal to 1000 bars. Abbreviated kb.

kilocalorie

a unit of heat energy equal to 1000 calories. Abbreviated kg cal. Also known as kilogram calorie (kg cal).

kiloelectronvolt

a unit of energy eqúal to 1000 electronvolts. Abbreviated kev.

kilogram (kg)

si unit of mass. Mass of the international prototype made of a plantinum iridium alloy kept in France.

kilogram force

a unit of force equal to the weight of a 1 kilogram mass at a point on the earth's surface where the acceleration of gravity is 9.80665 metres/sec. Abbreviated kgf.

kilogramme

an alternative spelling of kilogram.

kilohertz

a unit of frequency equal to 1000 hertz. Abbreviated khz. Also known as kilocycle (kc).

kilojoule

a unit of energy or work equal to 1000 joules. Abbreviated kj.

kilolitre

a unit of volume equal to 1000 litres or 1 cubic meter. Abbreviated kl.

kilometer

a unit of length equal to 1000 metres. Abbreviated km.

kiloton

a unit used in specifying the yield of a fission or fussion bomb; equal to the explosive power of 1000 metric tons of trinitro toluence (tnt). abbreviated kt.

kilovar

a unit equal to 1000 volt amperes reactive. Abbreviated kvar.

kilovolt

a unit of potential difference equal to 1000 volts. Abbreviated kv.

kilovolt ampere

a unit of apparent power in an alternating current circuit equal to 1000 volt amperes. Abbreviated kva.

kilovolt meter

a voltmeter which measures potential differences on the order of several kilovolts.

kilowatt

a unit of power equal to 1000 watts. Abbreviated kw.

kilowatt-hour

symbol: kwh. A unit of energy. It is equal to the energy which gets transferred by one kilowatt of power in one hour. It is the same as the Board of Trade unit and has a value of 3.6×10^6 joules.

kinematics

branch of mechanics, that deals with the study of motion of objects without reference to mass or force.

kinescope

a television picture tube.

kinetic effect

a chemical effect that depends on reaction rate rather than on thermodyamics. For example, diamond is thermodynamical less stable than graphite; its apparent stability depends on the vanishingly slow rate at which it is converted. Overvoltage in electrolytic cells is another example of a kinetic effect. Kinetic isotope effects are changes in reaction rates produced by isotope substitution. For example, if the slow step in a chemical reaction is the breaking of a C–H bond, the rate for the deuterated compound would be slightly lower because of the lower vibrational frequency of the C–D bond.

kinetic energy (K.E.)

it is the energy possessed by a body by virtue of its motion. The K. E. of a body of mass 'm' moving with a

velocity 'v' cm./sec is equal to

$\frac{1}{2} mv^2$

Kinetic energy per molecule of

gas K.E. (E) = $\frac{3}{2}$ RT.

kinetic, friction

the force of friction that acts on a body when it is moving over a second body.

kinetic momentum

the momentum possessed by a particle because of its motion is called kinetic momentum of the particle.

kinetic pressure

the kinetic energy per unit volume of a fluid is known as its kinetic pressure.

kinetic reaction

the negative of the mass of a body multiplied by its acceleration.

kinetic stress

a stress which arises in a theory taking the motions of individual molecules into account, from the existence of a velocity distribution of molecules, an example is the pressure of an ideal gas.

kinetic theory of gases

the mathematical explanation of the behaviour of gases on the assumptio that gases consist of molecules which are in ceaseless motion in space, the kinetic energy of the molecules depending upon the temperature of the gas. The pressure exerted by a gas on the walls of the vessel is due to the collisions of the molecules with it.

kenetic theory of matter

according to this theory matter is considered to be made of small particles in randiom motion.

kinetic viscosity

symbol v. the ratio of a fluids viscosity to its density.

kinetics

the dynamics of material bodies.

kip

a 1000 pound (435.6 kilogram) load.

kirchhoff's formula

a formula for the dependence of vapour pressure p on temperature t, valid over limited temperature ranges. It may be written log p=log t, where a, b and c are constants.

kirchhoff's law (heat)

for a given temperature and wavelength the ratio of the emissive power of a substance to its absorptive power is the same for all substances and is equal to the emissive power of a perfectly black body at that temperature.

kirchhoff's laws electric circuits

the algebraic sum of the electric currents meeting at any point i a circuit is zero. 2. In a closed electrical circuit the algebraic sum of the products of the current ad resistance in each part of the circuit equals the electromotive force present in the circuit.

kirchhoff's radiation law

the ratio of the emissive power to the absorption coefficient is the same for all substances, and is affected only by the temperature and the frequency of the radiation.

kirkendall effect

if inert marker wires are embedded at the common face of a copper and a brass (cuzn) block, which is held at a high temperature, the wires markings the original interface move into the brass.

klein–gordon equation

an equation in relativistic quantum mechanics for spin-zero particles. The Klein–Gordon equation has the form

$[\bullet - (mc/h)^2]\ y = O,$

where $\bullet = Ñ^2 - (1/c^2)(¶/¶t^2)$, and $Ñ^2$ is thelaplace operator, m is the mass of the particle, c is the speed of light, h is the Dirac constant, and y is the wave function of the particle. This equation was discovered by several authors independently, including Oskar Klein (1894 – 1977) and Walter Gordon (1893-1940) in 1926.

klystron

an instrument for producing electromagnetics waves in the microwave region.

knife edge

a sharp wedge used as a fulcrum or support as in a kater's pendulum, balance etc. The area of contact between the two parts is reduced to a minimum by using a sharp tip.

knob and tuberwiring

an electric wiring method used for light and power circuits that uses open insulated wiring on solid insulators; now obsolete and illegal in most countries.

knocking

The most effective method is to use high–octane fuel which has a longer self-ignition delay than low–octane fuels. This is usually achieved by the addition of lead tetraethy (IV) to the fuel.

knot

unit of speed : one nautical mile per hour. (1.15 statue miles per hour roughly).

knudsen flow

that flow which occurs when the mean free path of molecules is grater than the dimensions of the apparatus. The ratio of the latter to the former is often called knudsen's number.

knudsen number

the ratio of the mean free path length of the molecules of a fluid to a characteristic length, used to describe the flow of low density gases.

kohlrausch's law

when ionization is complete, the conductivity of an electrolyte is equal to the sum of the conductivities of ions which the substance dissociates.

konig

the x tristinulus value.

konowalof 's rule

the vapour from a mixture of two liquids is relatively richer in the component whose addition to a liquid mixture results in an increase of total pressure.

kopp's law

the specific heat of a solid element is the same whether free or combined. In general this is not true.

kossel lines

these are analogous to kikuchi lines in electron diffraction and occur when a point source of x radiation is used.

kossel sommerfeld law

the arc spectrum of an element having an odd atomic number shows even multiplicity, whereas the arc spectrum of an element having an even atomic number shows odd multiplicity.

koster effect

plastic deformation of a material lowers the elastic modulus by introducing free dislocations.

kovar

a tradename for an alloy of iron, cobalt, and nickel with an expansivity similar to tat of glass. It is therefore used in making glass-to-metal seals, especially in circumstances in which a temperature variation can be expected.

kramer's theorem

in electron paramagnetic resonance in solid materials, a twofold spin degeneracy is not removed by electric fields or spin-orbit coupling if the spin is half integral.

krchoff's equations

equations that state that the partial derivative of the change of enthalpy during a reaction, with respect to temperature, at constant pressure equals the change in heat capacity at constant pressure (or volume).

kronig-penny model

an approximate one dimensional method of obtaining features of electron propagation in crystal by considering the crystal as having a periodic square-well type of variation of electric potential.

krypton lamp

an arc lamp filled with krypton, one type pierces fog for 1000 feet (300 meters) or more and is used to light airport runways at night.

krypton 86

an isotope of krypton, atomic mass 86, used in measurement of the standard meter.

kundt's constant

a constant used to measure the faraday effect. It is similar to verdet's constant, but is for rotation per unit magnetization in place of rotation per unit magnetic field.

kundt's rule

the refractive index of a medium on the shorter wavelength side of an absorption band is abnormally low and on the longer wavelength side abnormally high. The phenomenon of anomalous dispersion is due to this effect.

kundt's tube

a divice which is used for showing statonary waves in a gas. A horizontal rod, clamped at its midpoint, is having a flat disc on one end.

kymograph

an instrument for recording periodic movements, especially in muscles.

l-mesons

a collective designation for the μ-mesons and pl-mesons.

l.t.

low tension (voltage).

label

a stable or radioactive nuclide used to investigate some process, such as a chemical reaction.

lactometer

it is an instrument that is used to find out the specific gravity of milk.

lactoscope

it is an optical device that is used for determination of the quantity of cream present in a given sample of milk.

ladder filter

a network made up of a succession of series and shunt impedances, generally acting as a transmission line with a known attenuation or delay.

laevorotatory

syn. laevorotary. capable of rotating the plane of polarized light in an anticlockwise direction as viewed against the direction of motion of the light.

lag

the angle, time or phase by which one periodic quantity lags behind another.

lagging current

an alternating current that, with respect to the applied e.m.f. producing it, has a lag.

lagging load

syn. inductive load. a reactive load that takes a lagging current.

lalande cell

a primary cell having zinc and iron electrodes in caustic soda solution as electrolyte and copper oxide as depolarizor.

lamb wave

an electromagnetic wave propagating over the surface of a solid, provided the thickness of the solid surface and the wavelength of the wave are comparable to each other.

lambda particle

uncharged elementary particle, hyperon, which can replace a neutron in a nucleus to form an extremely unstable hypernucleus.

lambda point

symbol l. The temperature of 2.186 K below which helium - 4 becomes a superfluid. The name derives from the shape of the curve of specific heat capacity against temperature, which is shaped like a Greek latter lambda (l) at this point.

lambert (l)

a unit of luminance. The average luminance of surface emitting or reflecting light at the rate of one lumen per sq cm. For practical purposes the mililambert (0.001 lambert) is used.

lambert's law of absorption

as an electromagnetic radiaton passes through a homogeneous absorption medium, each layer of an equal hickness absorbs an equal fraction of it.

lambert's law of emission (lambert's cosine law)

the intensity of the light emitted from a perfectly defusing surface is proportional to the cosine of the angel between the normal to the surface and the direction of observation.

lambert's law of illunination

the illumination on a surface from a point source of light is proportional to the cosine of the angle b the light ray with the normal at the point of incidence, but inversely proportional to the square of the distance between the surface and the source when the light insides at right angles.

lamb shift

a small energy difference between two levels ($^2S_{½}$ and $^2P_{½}$) in the hydrogen spectrum. The shift results from the quantum interaction between the atomic electron and the electromagnetic radiation. It was first discovered by Willis Eugene Lamb (1913–). It was explained using renormalization in quantum electrodynamics by the US physicists Richard Feynman (1918-88) and Julian Seymour Schwinger (1918-94) and the Japanese physicist Sinitiro Tomonaga (1906-79).

lami's theorem

if three forces act on a particle in equilibrium, each is proportional to the sine of the angle between the other two.

laminar flow

the turbulence free flow of a fluid along a streamlined surface.

laminate

a product made by bonding together two or more layers of materials.

laminated core

a core for a transformer or other electrical machine in which the ferromagnetic alloy is made into thin sheets (laminations), which them. This has effect of reducing eddy currents, which occur when alternating are used.

laminated iron

a piece of iron consisting of thin sheets of iron used for cores of transformers to minimize loses due to eddy currents.

lamination

a thin stamping of ferromagnetic material used in the assembly of magnetic cores, for transformers etc.

land line

the term is associated with a communication cable, which may be on or under the surface of the earth.

landau damping

the damping of space charge wave by electrons which move at the phase velocity of the wave and gain energy transferred from the wave.

landau diamagnetism

this is the net non-vanishing magnetization which is produced antiparallel to an applied magnetic filed as a result of coupling of the magnetic field with orbital electronic motion.

landau fluctuations

experimental determination of the energy loss of a fast particle frequently involves measurement of the energy lost in a thin detector in which the particles suffer many ionizing collisions but do not lose much of their initial energy.

landolt fringe

if a brilliant source of light is viewed through two nicol prisms oriented with their principal axes perpendicular to one another, the field is not quite dark when exact adjustment is made.

lane's law

if a star contracts, its internal temperature must rise. The law is independent of the source of energy but assumes that the material of the star behaves as a perfect gas.

langmuir effect

an ionization produced when atoms of low ionization potential come into contact with hot metal of high work function.

langmuir probe

a small metallic conductor or pair of conductors inserted within a plasma in order to sample the plasma current.

laplace's coefficients

spherical harmonics which are the analogues in three dimensions of legendre polynomials.

lapse rate

the rate of change of atmospheric temperature with light.

large dyne

it is an old name for newton (symbol : n) which is a unit of force.

larmor diamagnetism

an alternative name for langevin diamagnetism.

larmor precession

the orbital motion of the electrons about the nucleus of an atom is such as to give the atom a resultant angular momentum and a magnetic moment, which causes it to process about the direction of the applied magnetic field.

larygophone

a throat microphone.

laser

(light amplification by stimulated emission of radiation). A highly powerful, coherent, monochromatic light source.

latent heat

the quantity of heat required to change a unit mass of substance from one state without any change of temperature.

lateral

pertaining to the side.

lateral inversion

refers to the type of inversion produced in the image formed by a plane mirror. The left hand side appears as right side and vice versa.

lateral velocity

the component of celestial body's velocity perpendicular to the line of sight velocity.

lathe

a machine for use in working pieces of wood, metal etc. by rotating them against tool that shapes them.

latitude

the angular distance of a point from the equator measured upon the curved surface of the earth. The celestial latitude is the angular distance between the celestial body and ecliptic.

lattice

a regular network of geometrical points about which atoms, molecules or ions move in a crystal.

lattice constant

the length of edge of the angle between the axes of the unit cell of a crystal. It is generally the edge length of a cubic unit cell.

lattice energy

the amount of energy required to separate the ions of a crystal to an infinite distance from each other.

lattice parameter (lattice spacing)

the lengths of the edges of a unit cell in a crystal. The characteristic intercepts (a. b. c.) and interfacial angles are called as lattice parameters of a unit cell.

lattice vibrations

the periodic vibrations of the atoms, ions, or molecules in a crystal lattice about their mean positions. On heating, the amplitude of the vibrations increases until the are so energetic that the lattice breaks down. The temperature at which this happens is the melting point of the solid and the substance becomes a liquid. On cooling, the amplitude of the vibrations diminishes. At absolute zero a residual vibration persists, associated with the zero-point energy of the substance. The increase in the electrical resistance of a conductor is due to increased scattering of the free conduction electrons by the vibrating lattice particles.

latitude

refers to the angular distance north or south from the equator of a point on the earth's surface, measured on the meridian of the point.

laue diagram

when a heterogeneous beam of X–rays, electross, or neutrons is allowed on to a thin crystal, the different atomic planes give rise to a series of symmetrically arranged spots on a photographic plate placed behind the crystal. This pattern, known as a Laue diagram, is used to determine the type of crystal structure.

Laue, Max Theodor Felix von

(1879-1960) German physicist, who became a professor at Berline in 1919, moving in 1943 to the Max Planck Institute at Gottinagen. He is best known for his discovery in 1912 of X-ray diffraction, for which he was awarded the 1914 Nobel Prize for physics.

laue pattern

x ray diffraction pattern of a single crystal is known as laue pattern.

launch pad

it is the platform from which a rocket is launched.

launch vehicle

a rocket used to launch a satellite, spaceprobe space station, etc. Multistage rockets are usually used, the empty tanks and engine of the first two stages being jettisoned before the desired orbit is reached. The launch window is the time interval during which the vehicle must be launched to achieve the orbit.

lauritsen electroscope

an electroscope in which a metal wire carries a metalcoated quartz fibre, that is attached to the wire when under charge. A t-piece on the fibre is seen by a microscope with an eyepiece scale.

law of conservation of energy

energy can neither be created nor destroyed, and the sum total of all energies in a closed system always remains constant, and merely a transformation of energy from one form to another can be take place.

law of conservation of mass

the total quantity of mass and energy in a system always remains constant. Thus, in ordinary molecular reaction, the total mass of the reactants must always equal the mass of the products, and in nuclear reactions the total mass plus energy of the reactants must always equal the total mass of the products plus the energy liberated.

law of conservation of matter

the law of conservation of mass as it applies to ordinary molecular reactions in which the quality of mass transformed into energy is negligible.

law of conservation of momentum

in any reaction involving collisions of particles, vector som of the momentums of the colliding particles must be the same before and after the collision.

law of gravitation

according to it, all bodies and particles in universe exert gravitational force on one another. The force of gravitation between any two bodies is directly proportional to the product of their masses and inversely proportional to the distance between them.

law of intermediate temperature

the e.m.f. of a themrmocouple

between any two, temperatures is equal to the sum of the e.m.f. of an number of successive steps in which the given range of temperature is divided. Thus if $E_{t_1}^{1}$ n is the thermos e.m.f. between two temperatures t_1 and t_n, $E_{t_1}^{1_n} = E_{t_1}^{1_2} + E_{t_2}^{1_3} + E_{t_3}^{1_4} + E_{t_{n-1}}^{1_n}$

where the given temperature range is divide between the steps t_1, t_2, t_3,.........t_n.

law of magnetic poles

the rule which describes the forces between nearby poles-like poles repel each other; unlike poles attract each other.

law of motion

first law :- A body continues to remain in its state of rest of uniform motion in the same direction in a straight line unless acted upon by some external force.

Second law :- The rate of change of mometum of a body is directly proportional to the implied force and takes place in he direction of the force

$F = m \times a$.

third law :- To every action there is equal to and opposite reaction.

$F_1 = -F_2$

law of resistances

(i) $R \alpha \ \ell$, l = length of conductor

(ii) $R \alpha \ \frac{1}{a}$, a = area of cross–section of conductor

Thus $R \ a \ \frac{\ell}{a}$

$= \rho.\frac{\ell}{a}$

Where l = specific resistance of the material. Specific resistance is also called resistivity.

law of radioactive disintegration:-

$-\frac{dN}{dt} \alpha \ N$

Where N_0 = Number of atoms present at t =0

N = Number of atoms present after time t

dN = Number of atoms disintegrated in time dt.

$\text{or} -\frac{dN}{dt} = \lambda N$

Where λ =Decay constant of disintegration constant. Rate of decay

$R(t) = \left|\frac{dN}{dt}\right| = \lambda N(r)$

law of reflection

the angle of reflection equals the angle of incidence.

law of the refraction of light

when light passes from a rarer medium into a denser, its path is deviated toward the normal;

when it passes from a denser medium into a less dense one, its path is deviated away from the normal. The ratio of the sine of the angle of incidence to the sine of the angle of refraction is constant; this constant is called the index of refraction, also referred to as Snell's law.

laws of thermodynamics

first law of thermodynamics: Energy can neither be created nor destroyed. Second law of thermodynamics: All systems tend to approach a state of equilibrium. Hence, heat cannot pass spontaneously from one body to another, hotter body). Third law of thermodynamics: The entropy of a perfect crystalline substance at 0^0 K is zero.

lawson criterion

the product of the particle density of plasma and the containment time at or above its ignition temperature, such that the fusion energy given out equals the energy required to form and confine the plasma.

l c r

a circuit containing expressed in henrys divided by its capacitance expressed in farads is commonly called the lc ratio.

l-capture

refers to a absorption of an electron from the L-shell on atomic number of the element.

lead

refers to an electrical conductor or the interval of time or the angle by which a particular phase in one wave is in advance of the similar phase in another wave.

lead acid accumulator

refers to a type of electrical accumulator which used in vehicle batteries. It is having two sets of plates; spongy lead plates connected to the positive terminakl of the electrodes is kept in a hard lead-alloy grid. The plates get interleaved. The electrolyte has been dilte sulphuric acid. The e.m.f. when fully charged in about 2.2 V. This falls to a steady 2 V when current is drawn. As the accumulator starts to run down, the e.m.f. fals further.

The electrolyte is having hydrogen ions (H^+) and sulphate ions (SO_4^{2-}). During discharge, H^+ ions react with the lead (IV) oxide to yield lead (II) oxide and water

$PbO_2 + 2H^+ + 2e \rightarrow PbO + H_2O$

This reaction takes electrons from the plate, making the positive charge. There has been a further reaction to yield soft lead sulphate:

$PbO + SO_4^{2-} + 2H^+ \rightarrow PbSO_4 + H_2O + 2e^-$.

Electrons get released to the electrode, producing the negative charge.

During charging the reactions, get reversed:

$PbSO_4 + 2e^- \rightarrow Pb + SO_4^{2-}$

$PbSO_4 + 2H_2O \rightarrow PbO_2 + 4H^+ + SO_4^{2-} + 2e$.

lead equivalent

a measure of the absorbing power of a radiation screen expressed as the thickness of metallic lead which could give the same protection as the given material under similar condition.

leader stroke

the initial discharge which establishes the track of a lightning flash.

leading current

an alternating current which, with respect to the applied e.m.f. Producing it, has a lead.

leading load

capacitive load. A reactive load which takes a leading current.

league

a unit of length. 1 league = 4828.032 m.

leakage

refers to the flow of an electric current, on account of imperfect insulation, in a path other than that intended. The current is small compared to that of a short circuit.

leakage current

a stray current of relatively small value which flows through or across the surface of an insulator when a voltage is impressed on the insulator.

leakage flux

in electrical machines and transformers in which there is a magnetic circuit, flux whose circuit is outside the useful flux circuits. Lost flux.

least action principle

in a dynamic system, the motion between two points is stationary for the actual path in comparison with various paths between the same points for which the total energy has the same constant.

least energy principle

a dynamic system is in equilibrium if the potential energy of the system is a minimum.

least squares, method of

a technique for determining the equation which gives the best results for experimental data. The best result is considered to occur for a value of a at which the sum of the squares of these deviations is a minimum.

le chatelier's rule

when a constraint is applied to a system in equilibrium, a change takes place within the system, that opposes the constraints and tends to restore equilibrium.

leclanche cell

it is a primary voltaic cell which consists, in its 'wet' form, of a carbon rod anode and a zinc cathode, with a 10-20% solution of ammonium chloride as electrolte. Manganese dioxide mixed with crushed carbon in a porous bag or pot surrounding the anode has been acting as a depolarizing agent. The dry form has been widely used fortorch batteries, transistor radios, etc. It is having a mixture of ammonium chloride, zinc chloride, flour, and gum forming an electrolye paste.

led (light emitting diode)

This is a p–p junction diode and is usually made from gallium arsenide phosphide. Energy is released with the LED and this is given off as light. The junction is made near to the surface so that the emitting light can be seen. No light is emitted with a reverse bias. LED are generally coloured red, yellow or green. They are widely used in a variety of electronic devices.

leed

low energy Electron Diffraction.

lees' disc

refers to an apparantus which is used for measuring the thermal conductivity of a poor conductor. The sample has been a thin flat disc of known area (A) and thickness (l) placed between two discs of brass (or other good conductor)., each having a thermometer in a hole in its side. The apparatus can be modified for use with liquids, these being contained in a narrow insulating ring held between the two metal discs.

left-hand rule

a method of determining direction of magnetic lines of force. The first three fingers of the left hand are spread so as to form rectangular axis. Then pointing the centre finger of the left hand in the direction of the current and the forefinger with the flux, the thumb will the direction of thrust. Using the right hand in the same manner will give the direction of induced current.

lenard rays

cathode rays which have passed outside a lenard tube.

lenard tube

a discharge tube with a thin window opposite the cathode to allow the cathode rays to pass outside.

lens

an optical device that bends transmitted light by refraction.

Converging (convex) lens bring the rays together at a point called focus. They are thicker at the centre than at the edge.

Diverging (concave) lens spread the rays out. They appear to be coming from one point, the focus. Such a lens is thin at the centre but get thicker towards the outside.

Lens are used for correction of defects of vision.

lens markers formula

$$\frac{1}{f} = \frac{1}{u} + \frac{1}{v} = (u-1)\left[\frac{1}{R_1} + \frac{1}{R_2}\right]$$

Where μ is the refractiveindex of the material of lens, R_1 and R_2 are the radius of curvature of its surfaces.

lenz's law

for currents induced by motion in a magnetic field, the induced currents have such a direction that their reaction tends to oppose the motion which produces them.

leptons

name of the groups of light elementary particles such as electron, neutrino, and muon.

leslie's cube

a cube-shaped can with the four sides painted in different colours or given different finishes (polished rough etc.). It is filled with hot water and used in experiments on the effect of surface or emissivity.

lethargy

symbol. refers to the negative natural logarithm of the ratio of the energy of a neutron to a specified reference energy.

lever

a rigid bar which can be turned about a fixed point, known as fulcrum. Depending upon the position in the middle, of the fulcrum, the effort or the load. The levers are classified into various kinds.

lever arm

the distance of a weight or line

of action of a force from the fulcrum of the lever.

leverage

it refers to the action of lever, the mechanical advantage gained due to the use of a fever.

lewis number

symbol : A dimensionless number used in problems that involves both heat and mass transfer. It is equal to $\lambda/p\ Dc$, λ is the thermal conductivity, p is the density, D is the diffusion coefficient, and c is the specific heat capacity.

lewis-randall rule

at a given temperature the fugacity of a constituent of a mixture of gases is proportional to its mole fraction. Up to 25 atmospheres this rule appears to hold, and is a great, improvement on dalton's law of partial pressures.

leyden battery

a number of leyden jars arranged in parallel.

leyden jar

it is a parallel plate capacitor consisting of two cylindrical tin-foil coatings separated by a medium, usually glass.

libration

the phenomenon the enables 59% of the moon's surface to be observed from each over a 30-year period, in spite of its synchronous rotation. Physical libration arises from slight variations in the rotation of the moon on its axis, caused by minor distortions in its physical shape. Geometric liberation are apparent oscillations arising from the fact that the moon is observed from slightly different directions at different times. The geometric libration in longitude results from the nonuniform orbital motion of the moon. The geometric libration in latitude arises because the moon's axis of rotation is not perpendicular to its orbital plane; it enables more of the lunar polar regions to be observed.

lichtenberg figur

a complex symmertical star–shaped pattern which is formed by dust particles adhering to a solid dielectric when it is under a high potential. It can also be produced on a photographic plate placed between electrodes.

lifetime

the mean time interval between generation and recombination of charge carrier.

lift coefficient

for a body and a fluid of density p in a motion having relative velocity V, the lift coefficient of the body is the ratio of the component of resistance force perpendicular to the direction of relative motion. (lift) t the quantity $p\ell^2 V^2$ where ℓ is some characteristic length of the body. The coefficient is dependent on the circulation round the body.

ligand-fieldtheory

an extension of crystal-field theory describing the properties of compounds of transition-metal ions or rare-earth ions in which covalent bonding between the surrounding molecules and the transition-metal ions is taken into account. This may involve using valence-bound theory or molecular-orbital theory. Ligand-field theory was developed extensively in the 1930s. As with crystal-field theory, ligand-field theory indicates that energy levels of the transition-metal ions are split by the surrounding ligands, as determined by group theory. The theory has been very successful in explaining the optical, spectroscope, and magnetic properties of the compounds of transition-metal and rare-earth ions.

light (visible radiation)

a form of electromagnetic radiation able to be detected by the human eye. Its wavelength range is between about 400 mm (far 'red') and about 700 mm (far 'violet').

light emitting diode (led)

a semi conductor diode made from certain materials (e.g., gallivne arsenide) in which light is emitted in response to the forward-bias current.

lightening

refers to the luminous electric discharge caused in the atmosphere by electric charge separation produced in thunder storms, clouds etc.

lightening arrester

it is a device that is used for preventing damage to radio, telephonic or other electric equipment from lightning or other high voltage currents.

light ray

a beam of light having a very small cross section is known as a light ray.

light watt

a term used in optics to express luminous power of light source.

light water reactor

a special type of nuclear reactor in which ordinary water is used as a moderator.

light year

a unit of distance used in astronomy; the distance travelled by light in a vacuum during one year. It is equal to 9.4650 $\times$ 10^{15} metres or 5.8785 $\times$ 10^{12} miles.

lighting arrestor

a device with the property of reducing the voltage of a surge applied to its terminals.

lightning

refers to a discharge of electricity between two clouds or between charged cloud and the earth. It takes place when the potential difference between two charged clouds or between a cloud and the earth becomes quite large.

lightning conductor

an electrical conductor, normally installed in buildings and other structures to save them from damage due to lightning.

lightening flash

a complete lightning discharge along a single discharge path. It may be made up of more than one lightning stroke, in which case it is known as multiple stroke.

lightning surge

any transient disturbance in an electric circuit due to lightning is called a lightning surge.

limiter

an instrument which automatically prevents some output characteristic from exceeding a certain value. E.g. in a frequency modulation receiver it is used for elimination or reducing any amplitude modulation of the recèived signal.

limiting current

in electrolysis the rate of diffusion of ions toward the electrodes can not keep pace with their deposition. Thus there is a limiting value of current which can be passed under the particular conditions of ionic concentration and characteristics of the electrolyte.

limiting friction

the maximum force of resistance which comes into play when one body moved over the surface of another body.

linde process

a method used for the production

of liquid air. It is based on the joule thomson effect. Air is compressed and expanded by passing it through a nozzle.

line of force (electric)

an imaginary line in an electric or magnetic field, the tangent to which at any point gives the direction of the electric field at that point. Lines of force never cross each other.

line spectrum

an emission or absorption spectrum of single lines, each of which corresponds to a well defined wavelength.

line strength

the intesity of a spectrum line is generally known as its line strength.

line width

the width of a spectral line in wavelets terms. The usual measure is the half width of the line.

linear accelerator (linac)

an accelerator consisting of a series of cylindrical electrodes in a row having a common axis and separated by small gaps.

linear amplifier

an amplifier in which there is a linear relation between instantaneous anode current and grid voltage.

linear distortion

any form of distortion which is independent of the amplitude of the signal.

linear energy transfer

the energy transferred per unit path length b a moving high-energy charged particle (such as an electron or a proton) to the atoms and molecules along its path. It is of particular importance when the particles pass through living tissue as the LET modifies the effect of a specific dose of radiation. LET is proportional to the square of the charge on the particle and increases as the velocity of the particle decreases.

linear equation

an equation between two variables that gives a straight line when plotted on a graph. It has the general form $y = mx + c$, where m is the gradient of the line and c is the intercept of the line on the y-axis (in Cartesian coordinates.).

linear expansion

the change in length of a substance on heating.

Coefficient of linear expansion is defined as the change in length per unit length per degree rise of temperature.

linear magnification

$$m = \frac{v}{u} = \frac{\text{size of image}}{\text{size of object}}$$

It is also known as Lateral magnification

linear modulation

modulation in which the change in the modulated characteristic of the carrier signal is proportional to the value of the modulating signal over the range of the audio frequency range.

linear motor

a form of induction motor, in which the stator and rotor are linear instead of cylindrical, and parallel instead of co axial.

linearity

it is the relationship which exists between two quantities in such a way that any change in one of them produces a directly proportional change in the other.

lines of force

imaginary lines in a field of force that enable the direction and strength of the field to be visualized. They are used primarily in electric and magnetic fields; in electric fields they are sometimes called tubes of force, to express their characteristic of being perpendicular to a conducting surface. The tangent to line of force at any point gives the direction of the field at that point and the number of lines per unit area perpendicular to the force represents the intensity of the field.

liquefaction

refers to a change of state to a liquid. The term is often used for the conversion of gases to their liquid state.

liquefaction of gases

a gas can be liquefied by the application of external pressure on it if its temperatures is below its clinical temperature.

liquid

refer to state of matter.

liquid air

a pale blue liquid, containing mainly oxygen, boiling point 183 degree c, and liquid nitrogen. bp 196 degree c.

liquid crystal

a substance that flows like a liquid but has some order in its arrangement of molecules. Nematic crystals have long molecules all aligned in the same direction, but otherwise randomly arranged. Cholesteric and smectic liquid crystals also have aligned molecules, which are arranged in distinct layers. In cholesteric crystals, the axes of the molecules are parallel to the plane of the layers; in smectic crystals they are perpendicular.

liquid–crystal display

a digital display unit used in watches, calculators, etc. It provides a source of clearly displayed digits for a very low power consumption. In the display unit a thin film of liquid crystal is sandwiched between two transparent electrodes (glass with a thin metal or oxide coating). In the commonly used field–effect display, twisted nematic crystals are used . The nematic liquid crystal cell is placed between two crossed polarizer. When an electric field is applied the molecular alignment in the liquid crystal is altered, the polarization of the entering light is unchanged, and no light is therefore transmitted. In these circumstances, a mirror placed behind the second polarizer will cause the display to appear black. One of the electrodes, shaped in the form of a digit, will then provide a black digit when the voltage is applied.

liqiud–drop model

a model of the atomic nucleus in which the nucleons are regarded as being analogous to the molecules in a liquid, the interactions between which maintain the droplet shape by surface tension. The model has been useful in the theory of nuclear fission.

liquid fire

refers to flaming petroleum used against an enemy in a war.

liquid oxygen

oxygen gas compressed to give a liquid. It is used as an oxidises in liquid rocket propellants.

lissajous figures

a curve in one plane traced by a point moving under the influence of two independent harmonic motions. In the common case the harmonic motions are simple, perpendicular to each other, and have a simple frequency ratio. They can be displayed by applying sinusoidal alternating potential to the X-and Y-inputs of a cathode-ray oscilloscope. They are named after Jules Lissajous (1822-80).

litre (i)

unit of volume. 1l = 1000.028 cc. It is defined as the volume of 1 kg of pure water at 760 mm pressure and at 4 degree c.

live

electrically connected to a source of potential difference.

live room

the term is used in acoustics and refers to an enclosure which has minimum of sound absorbing material.

lloyd's mirror

an optical arrangement to study interference of light. Light incident on a mirror at grazing incidence after reflection is made to interfere with direct light from the source.

load

a device or material wherein signal power is dissipated or received. Also refers to the power delivered by a machine, generator, or electronic circuit or device.

load impedance

refers to the impedance presented by a load to the driver circuit.

load line

a line drawn on the graph of a family of characteristics, that shows graphical relationship between voltage and current for the particular load of the circuit under consideration.

load line

the load is a graphic presentation on the distribution of the plate supply voltage across the load and internal resistance of the tube. It is used in determining the power output and distortion of the tube.

loaded concrete

concrete made up of material of high atomic number or capture cross section, such as barium, iron, or lead, to increase its effectiveness as a radiation shield in nuclear reactors.

local action

the voltaic effect produced in one of the plates of a primary cell owing to the impurities in the plate.

local oscillator

the oscillator in heterodyne or superheterodyne radio receiver which produces the radio frequency oscillations with which the received wave is combined.

Lodge, Sir Oliver Joseph

(1851-1940) British physicist, who became principal of the new Birmingham University in 1900. His best-known work was in radio, particularly his invention in 1894 of the 'coherer,' used as a detector in early radio receivers. After 1910 he became increasingly interested in spiritualism and reconciling science and religion.

logarithmic decrement

of an underdeveloped harmonic system, the natural logarithm of the ratio of the excursions during two successive oscillations, with no external forces applied to maintain the oscillations.

logic gate

an electronic circuit that can be used to perform simple logical operations. Example of such operations are 'and', 'either or', 'not' 'neither-nor', etc. Logic gates operate on high or low input and output voltage.

lone pair of electrons

a pair of unshared valency electrons which are responsible for the formation of coordinate bonds.

longitudinal

lengthwise; in a line with the length of the object under consideration.

longitudinal wave

a wave in which the particle displacement is in the same direction in which the wave travels. Sound wave is an example of a longitudinal wave.

looming

an optical illusion in which the images of objects normally hidden below the horizon are seen in the sky, sometimes upside down.

lorentz equation

a set of equations for correlating space and time coordinate in two frames of reference, especially at relativistic velocities named after Hendrik Lorentz (1853 to 1928).

lorentz-fritzgerald contraction

refers to a reduction in the length of a body which is moving with a velocity v relative to an observer, as compared with the length of an identical object at rest relative to the observer. The object has been supposed to contract by a factor $\sqrt{(1 - v^2/c^2)}$, c being the speed of light. The contraction was given to account for the negative result of the Michelson-morley experiment in classical terms.

lorenz force

refers to an aspect of the motor effect; the force on a charge Q, moving at velocity v across a magnetic field B.

$f = BQv \sin\theta$

θ refers to the angle between v and B.

lorenz's law

the ratio of the thermal and electrical conductivities of all metals is proportional to the absolute temperature.

lorentz's theory of light sources

when maxwell showed that light was an electromagnetic wave it was necessary to identify some electrical oscillator of atomic proportions to account for these waves.

lorentz-fitzerald contraction

the shortening or contraction in the length of an object along its direction of motion is known as the lorentz fitzgerald contraction.

loss angle

the angle by which the angle of lead of the current is less than 90 degree when the applied voltage is sinusoidal.

loss factor

the ratio of the average power loss to the peak load power loss during a specified period of time.

lossy

relating to a material or instrument such as a dielectric or transmission line, which dissipates energy wit a high degree of attenuation.

loudness

the sensation that a sound produces in a listener corresponding to its intensity (i.e. the energy flow per unit area).

loudness level

the sound pressure level in decibel, relative to 0.0002 microbar, or a simple tone of frequency 1,000 hertz, which is judged by the listeners to be equivalent in loudness to the sound under measurement.

loudness of sound

the sensation produced by a source of sound in a listner. It depends on the intensity of sound for a given frequency. It also depends on the frequency of the sound.

loudspeaker

a device which converts electric signals into sound vibrations loud enough to be heard. It essentially consists of a small coil through which the signal flows and which is attached to the centre of a diaphragm.

lowering of vapour pressure

a reduction in the saturated vapour pressure of a pure liquid when a solute is introduced. If the solute is a solid of low vapour pressure, the decrease in vapour pressure of the liquid is proportional to the concentration of particles of solute; i.e. to the number of dissolved molecules or ions per unit volume. To a first approximation, it does not depend on the nature of the particles. See colligative properties; Raoult's law.

low frequency

frequency in the range of 30-300 hz.

lubricant

a soft, readily deformed material with weak secondary bonds. It also fills the depressions present in the surface of contact and reduces friction.

lumen

refers to the luminous flux emitted by a point source of light of one candela in a solid angle of one steradion.

luminance (I)

of an extended source of light in a given direction is the luminous intensity per unit area projected at right angles to that direction.

luminescence

the emission of light radiation by a body when an electron of the atoms jumps from an excited state to the ground state.

luminosity

brightness. The amount of light emitted by a star.

luminous (energy)

energy whose wavelength is such that the eye is sensitive to it.

luminous exitance

symbol : m, m. The luminous flux that leaves a surface per unit area. Previously called the luminous emittance. Measured in lumen per square metre.

luminous flux

through an area is the amount of light passing through the area per unit time. It is measured in lumens.

luminous intensity

the amount of light in a unit solid angle emitted per second by a source. It is measured in candela.

luminous paint

paint prepared from phosphorescent compounds such as calcium sulphide etc., which glows after exposure to light.

lunar eclipse

eclipse of moon.

lunminosity

brightness. Refers to the among of light emitted by a star.

lux (lx)

si unit of illuminance 12 x = 1 lumen/sq metre.

luxmeter

an optical instrument for measuring illuminance, calibrated in lux units.

lyman series

a series of line in the ultraviolet region in the hydrogen spectrum. They are produced when an electron from higher orbits jumps to the first permitted orbit of hydrogen.

m.k.s. system

a system of units based on the metre, kilogram and second. Now superseded for scientific purposes by the sI units which are based on the m.k.s. system.

mach

a unit of speed measurement for a moving object equal to the speed of sound in the medium in which the object moves.

machine

a device capable of making the performance of mechanical work easier, usually by overcoming a force of resistance at one point by the application of a more convenient force at some other point. In physics, the six so-called simple machines are the lever, wedge, inclined plane, screw, pulley, and wheel and axle.

mach line or surface

the line or surface dividing the regions of subsonic and supersonic flow is called the mach line.

mach number

the ratio of the speed of fluid or body to the local speed of sound. The speed of a fluid or body is therefore said to be supersonic if its mach number is greater than unity.

macleod equation

the fourth root the surface tension of a liquid is directly proportional to the difference between the densities of the liquid and its vapour. This equation is known as macleod equation.

macromolecule

a very large molecule, generally of a polymer.

magic numbers

atomic nuclei containing 2,8,20,28,50,82 and 126 neutrons or protons are found to be exceptionally stable. These numbers, mentioned above are called magic numbers.

magn

this term is used in electromagnetism. It is the unit of absolute permeability of a medium. 1 magn = 1 henry per metre.

magnesium cell

a special type of primary cell. The negative electrode of this cell is made of magnesium or one of its alloys.

magnet

a body having the property of magnetism.

magnet power

the term is used in electromagnetism and refers to the electric power supplied to the coil of an electromagnet.

magnet wire

insulated wire of copper or aluminium employed in the coils of all types of electromagnetic devices.

magnet, permanent

a substance which has a permanent magnetic moment and a magnetic field associated with it.

magnetic anisotropy

according to this phenomenon, the magnetic properties of some substances depend upon direction.

magnetic balance

a device used for the direct determination of attraction or repulsion between poles.

magnetic bottle

any configuration of magnetic fields used to confine a plasma, specially a lunare device whose ends are stoppered with magnetic mirrors.

magnetic bubble memory

a form of computer memory in which a small magnetized region of a substance is used to store information. Bubblememories consist of materials such as magnetic garnets, that are easily magnetized in one direction but hard to magnetize in the perpendicular direction. A thin film of these materials deposited on a nonmagnetic substrata constitutes a bubble–memory chip. When a magnetic field is applied to such a chip, by placing it between two permanent magnets, cylindrical domains (called magnetic bubbles) are formed.

magnetic circuit

refers to the completely closed path described by a given set of lines of magnetic flux.

magnetic compass

a compass that depends entirely on the earth's magnetic field for its directive force, without the aid of any elaborate mechanism. Its indicator needle always points in the direction of the earth's magnetic lines of force, and therefore to the magnetic north pole.

magnetic declination

declination, angle of.

magnetic dip

inclination.

magnetic dipole

dipole magnetic.

magnetic drum

a revolving cylinder in a computer, having a magnetised surface on which information can be stored as small polarized spots.

magnetic elements

magnetic declination, magnetic dip and the horizontal component of earth's magnetic field which completely define the earth's magnetic field at any point on the earth's surface.

magnetic equator

an isolclinic line of zero magnetic dip that lies near the geographic equator.

magnetic field

a region in which a small magnet or a loop of wire carrying current will experience a force. The field is said to be uniform in the region if a given magnet experiences the same force at every point of the region.

magnetic field strength

symbol : h. The force that would be exerted on a unit n-pole at a given point in a magnetic field. The unit is the ampere per meter (am).

magnetic flux

magnetic flux through a surface is equal to the total number of lines of induction passing through the surface held normal to the lines.

magnetic flux density

the normal magnetic flux induced by a magnetizing force. It is the product of the field strength and the permeability, expressed in terms of x lines of magnetic flux per unit area; the unit is the gauss (1 gauss = 1 line of flux per square centimetre).

magnetic focusing

focusing of charged-particle beams by making use of shaped magnetic fields. The method is made use of in accelerators, cathode ray tubes and electron miceroscopes.

magnetic force

may be defined as the force which produces the magnetic field density at any point of a magnetic field. Synonymous with magnetic field strength.

magnetic hysteresis

refers to the lagging of the magnetic flux density behind the magnetizing force during reverse magnetization.

magnetic induction

the force experienced by a unit n-pole placed at a point in a magnetic field is known as magnetic intensity at that point. Its unit is ampere per metre. Also known as magnetic field strength.

matnetic intensity

the magnetic intensity produced by an electric current at any point in the neighbourhood of a circuit in which an electric current is flowing.

magnetic line of force

an imaginary line in a magnetic field which at every point has the direction of the magnetic flux at that point.

magnetic meridian

a vertical plane that contains the direction of the earth's magnetic field.

magnetic monopole

a hypothetical unit of magnetic charge similar to electric charge. No definite evidence has been found for the existence of a separate magnetic pole; they are always found in pairs.

magnetic pendulum

a simple bar magnet which is hung by a thread so that it starts executing oscillations when released in a magnetic field having a horizontal component.

magnetic permeability

this term is used to refers to a measure of the ease with which the magnetic lines of force can pass through a substance for a given magnetizing force.

magnetic pole

pole, magnetic.

magnetic probe

a small conducting coil used for measuring the change in the strength of a magnetic field by inserting coil into the field.

magnetic resistance

reluctance.

magnetic scattering

the phenomenon of acattering of neutrons due to the interaction of the magnetic moment of the neutron with the magnetic moments of atoms.

magnetic screening

an area may be screened from magnetic effects by enclosing it with material having high permeability.

magnetic shell

a very thin sheet of ferromagnetic material having opposite polarity on the two sides.

magnetic shielding

a screen made of high permeability material used to isolate why devices from unwanted magnetic fields.

magnetic shunt

a piece of magnetic material mounted near a magnet in an electrical measuring instrument, and having means so that its position relative to the magnet can be adjusted where by the useful magnetic flux of the magnet can be changed.

magnetic storm

a disturbance in the earth's magnetic field, associated with abnormal solar activity, which can affect both radio and wire transmission.

magnetic tape

a ribbon of material (generally plastic base) coated on one side (single tape) or both sides (double tape) with substances containing iron oxide, to make it sensitive to impulse from an electromagnet.

magnetic variation

variations in the magnetic elements at a point on the surface or earth with sine. Such changes may take place suddenly due to a magnetic stone or may be slow continuous changes with passage of time.

magnetic viscosity

there is some time lag between application of magnetic field and the resulting magnetization in most ferromagnetic substances which is accounted for by the eddy currents induced in the substance. In some materials, however, the persistence and magnitude of the change of magnetization are great to be accounted for in this way, and this phenomenon is called magnetic viscosity.

magnetic well

a configuration of magnetic fields for storing a plasma in experimental fussion devices.

magnetism

deals with the study of the nature and cause of magnetic force fields, and how different substances are affected by them.

magnetization curves

the magnetic properties of ferromagnetic substances are generally studied by plotting curves relating the magnetization of the material to the strength and changes of the magnetizing field.

magneto

an electrical generator, generally one in which the magnetic field is provided by a permanent magnet.

magnetocaloric effect

refers to the change of temperature.

magnetodamping

refers to an increase is internal damping of acoustic vibrations in a metal like mikel when it is subjected to a strong magnetic field.

magnetoelectricity

refers to the electricity developed by the action of magnets.

magnetohydrodynamics

deals with the study of how magnetic fields interact with conducting fluids.

magnetometer

an instrument used for measuring the magnitude and

sometimes also the direction of a magnetic force.

magnetometer, deflection

it is a type of magnetometer which is used for comparison of magnetic moments or magnetic fields of two magnets. It consists of a small bar magnet which is pivoted just above the centre of a circular scale graduated in degrees. A long pointer is attached to the magnet at right angles to it.

magnetocaloric effect

the process by virtue of which the magnetization of a ferromagnetic material changes by varying the temperature of the material is known as magnetocaloric effect. It is a reversible effect.

magnetomotive force

refers to the integral of the magnetic field strength around a closed path. Analogous to e.m.f. in an electric circuit. Measured in ampere turn.

magneton

a term used for atomic, molecular or nuclear magnets to represent their respective magnetic moment.

magneton number

the ratio of the magnetic moment per atom of magnetic material to the magneton.

magneto-optical effects

changes of the optical behaviour of matter when the external field changes. Examples are the faraday effect and the kerry effect.

magnetoresistance

the phenomenon of variation of electrical resistance of a current carrying conductor by the application of a magnetic field is known as magneto resistance.

magnetoresistive effect

the change of electrical resistance of a sample when the external field changes. The hall effect is related to this.

magnetosphere

the space surrounding the earth, or any celestial body, in which there is a magnetic field associated with that body.

magnetostatics

study of the effect of stationary magnetic poles. Although free magnetic poles are known not to exist, the results have some validity.

magnetostriction

the change in length of a ferromagnetic rod with change in external field. The effect is the result of domain boundary changes.

magnetron

an electron tube used for producing microwaves. Electrons emitted from a hot cathode circle under the influence of an externally applied magnetic field and generate electromagnetic oscillations.

magnification

the ratio of the size of the image to the size of an object.

magnifying glass

a convex lens, microscope simple.

magnitude

a measure of the relative brightness of a star or other celestial object. The apparent magnitude depends on the star's luminosity, its distance, and the absorption of light between the object and the earth. In 1856 the astronomer N.R. Pogson devised a scale in which a difference of five magnitudes corresponds to a brightness ratio of 100 to 1. Two stars that differ by one magnitude therefore have a brightness ratio of $(100)^2.1 = 2.512$, known as the Pogson ratio.

magnox

a type of alloy containing magnesium aluminium and traces of other elements, used for canning the uranium rods in many British and a few foreign nuclear reactors.

main spring

refers to the principal spring in any mechanism

magnus effect

if a cylinder or sphere rotates about its axis while at the same time it is in relative motion with a fluid, there is a resultant force on the cylinder or sphere perpendicular to the direction of motion.

majorana effect

when light is palled through certain liquid or crystalline materials in a direction perpendicular to an applied magnetic field, the material becomes double refracting.

majority carrier

the type of carrier forming more than half of the total charge carrier concentration.

majority carriers

in a semiconductor, the type of carriers which constitute more than half the total number of carriers.

make

the term is associated with the closing of a relay, a key or some other contact.

make-and-break

the term used for an arrangement by which a circuit is alternately opened and closed.

making-current

circuit-breaker, or similar apparatus. The peak value of the current during the first cycle after the circuits closed on a short-circuit.

maksutov telescope

an astronomical telescope developed by D.D. Maksutov in 1944. It consists of a concave spherical mirror the aberration of which is refused by a meniscus lens.

malus' theorem

a system of rays normal to a wave front remains normal to the wave front after any number of refractions and reflections.

manganin

an alloy containing 15-25% mn, 70-86% cu, and 205% ni. It has a high electrical resistivity and low temperature coefficient of resistance. It is used for electrical resistances.

manometer

a device used for measurement of pressure. In a simple form, it consists of a u-shaped glass tube containing some liquid. The difference in the heights of the liquid in the two arms indicates the pressure difference between the arms.

marconi aerial

a vertical aerial one quarter of a wavelength long earthed at its lower end through an inductive capacitative reactance.

mark space ratio

the ratio of the duration of the pulse to the time between pulses.

marx effect

the energy of photoelectrons emitted from any illuminated surface gets reduced when the surface is simultaneously illuminated by light waves of lower frequency than that causing emission. This phenomenon is known as marx effect.

maser

microwave Amplification by Stimulated Emission of Radiation.

mass

symbol: m. Refers to a measure of the quantity of matter in an object. The SI unit of mass is the kilogram.

mass action

the law of mass action states that the rate at which a chemical reaction takes place at a given temperature is proportional to the product of the active masses of the reactants. The active mass of a reactant is taken to be its molar concentration. For example, for a reaction

xA + yB® products
the rate is given by
$R = k[A]^x[B]^y$
where k is the rate constant. The principle was introduced by C. M. Guldberg and P. Waage in 1863. It is strictly correct only for ideal gases. In real cases activities can be used.

mass defect

the difference between the mass of a nucleus and the sum of the masses of nucleus. Its constituents.

mass-energy equation

the equation $E = mc^2$, where E is the total energy of a mass m, c being the velocity of light. The equation has been a consequence of Einstein's Special theory of relativity; mass has been a form of energy and energy also has mass.

mass formula

the equation which expresses the atomic mass of a nuclide as a function of its atomic number and mass number, is commonly referred to as its mass formula.

mason's hygrometer

a hygrometer of the wet and dry bulb type used as the standard British instrument. The instrument must be exposed to an air draught of 1 to 1.5 metres/second.

mass-luminosity law

a law relating the mass m and luminosity, l of normal stars : log l = 3.3 log m, where m and l are in solar units.

mass number

syn. nucleon number. symbol : a. The number of nucleons in the nucleus of particular atom. It is the whole number nearest to the atomic mass of a nuclide.

mass of earth

the gravitational fore on the

surface of earth felt—by a body of mass, m, is given by

$$f = \frac{G.m.M}{R^2} \text{ ....(i)}$$

Where M = mass of earth
R = radius of earth
Aslo F = m.g..........(ii)
where 'g' is acceleration due to gravity.
From (i) and (ii), we have

$$mg = \frac{G.m.M}{R^2}$$

$$\text{or } M = \frac{g.R^2}{G}$$

Substituting the values of g, R and G, we get

$$M = \frac{9.8 \times (6.38 \times 10^6)^2}{6.67 \times 10^{-11}}$$

$=5.91 \times 10^{24}$ kg.

mass reactance

reactance (accoustic)

mass resistivity

refers to the product of the mass and electrical resistance of a conductor, divided by the square of its length.

mass spectrograph

a n apparatus for the determination of the exact masses of individual atoms, i.e., isotopic weights, by photographing the mass spectrum produced.

mass spectrometer

refers to an instrument which is used for producing ions in a gas and analysing them according to their charge/mass ration.

mass-transfer rate

the term is usually associated with the measurement of the movement of matter as a function of time.

massieu function

symbol : j. It is equal to the negative of the helmholtz function divided by the thermodynamic temperature.

master oscillator

an oscillator having high inherent frequency stability, used to establish the carrier frequency in radio transmission.

matched

having no reflected waves at a termination or, in a wave guide, at any of the transverse sections.

materialization

the process of the direct conversion of energy E into mass m according to Einstein's equation $E = mc^2$ (c = velocity of light)

mathiessen's rule

the product of the resistivity and temperature coefficient of resistance of a metal is the same whether the metal be pure or impure.

matrix mechanics

a formulation of quantum mechanics using matrices to represent states and operators. Matrix mechanics was the first formulation of quantum mechanics to be stated and was developed by Heisenberg and Max Born and the German physicist Pascual Jordan. It was shown by Erwin Schrodinger in 1926 to be equivalent to the wave mechanics formulation of quantum mechanics.

matter

the term matter is commonly used very loosely and was formerly regarded as synonymous with substances.

maximum ordinate

the difference in altitude between the origin and highest point of the trajectory of a projectile.

maxwell

sumbol: Mx. A unit of magnetic flux which is used in the C.G.S. system. It is equal to 10^{-8} Wb.

maxwell distribution

the term used for a distribution of velocities among the particles of a gas. The curve of number of molecules against velocity is having a characteristic shape that depends on temperature. The equation:

N = Noexp –W/RT

gives the number of molecules N with energy greater than W. No. refers to the total number of molecules.

maxwell's formula

a formula that connect the relative permittivity ε_r of a medium and its refractive index n. If the medium is not ferromagnetic the formula is $\varepsilon_r = n^2$.

maxwell's rule

every part of an electric circuit is acted upon by a force which tends to move it is such a direction as to enclose the maximum amount of magnetic flux.

mayer's relationship

$C_p - C_v = R$

Where C_p = Molar specific heat of gas at constant pressure

C_v = Molar specific heat of gas at constant volume.

R = Gas constant (8.314 Jk^{-1} mol^{-1})

The C_p and C_v are measured in Jk^{-1} mol^{-1}.

$$C_v = \frac{\lambda}{2}.R \text{ and } Cp = \left(\frac{\lambda}{2}+1\right) R$$

$$T = \frac{C_p}{C_v} = 1 + \frac{2}{\lambda}$$

Where λ = number of degrees of freedom of gas under consideration.

mcleod gauge

a vacuum pressure gauge in which a relatively large volume of a low–pressure gas is compressed to a small volume in a glass apparatus. The volume is reduced to an extent that causes the pressure to rise sufficiently to support a column of fluid high enough to read. This simple device, is suitable for measuring pressures in the range 10^3 to 10^{-3} pascal.

mean deviation

it is a measure of dispersion. It is computed by taking the arithmetic mean of the absolute values of the deviations of the functional values from some central value, generally the mean or the medium.

mean free path

the average distance travelled by a particle between two collisions. For a gas, it is obviously, inversely proportional to the pressure or density of the gas.

mean free time

the average time that elapses between the collisions of the molecules in a gas, the electrons in a crystal, the neutrons in a moderator, etc.

mean life

reciprocal of the decay constant of a radioactive substance.

mechanical advance

the ratio of the output to the input of a machine, i.e., of the force exerted by the machine to the force applied to it.

mechanical equivalent of heat

joule's equivalent.

mechanical ohm

a unit of mechanical resistance, reactance or impedance. It is equal to the ratio of force applied to the velocity.

mechanical properties

mechanical properties are those which are assciated with stress and strain.

mechanics

branch of science that deals with the behaviour of bodies when they are subjected to forces.

mechanomotive force

the root-mean-square value of the force developed in any machine developing an alternating force.

median

refers to the middle number in a given sequence. For a sequence with even numbers it is the average of two middle numbers.

medical physics

refers to the application of physics to medicine, as in radiotherapy, nuclear medicine, and medical electronics.

medium

the nature of the space through which something tansmitted or propagated. It may be solid, liquid, gas or a vacuum.

medium frequency

a radio frequency in the range between 3 MHz and 0.3 MHz (wavelength 100-1000 m).

mega

symbol: M. A prefix which denotes 10^6. for example, 1 megahertz (MHz) = 10^6 hertz (Hz).

megaphone

an acoustical instrument which is used to amplity or direct the sound of speaker's voice.

megaton

a unit to express the explosive power of nuclear weapons,. One magaton is an explosive power equivalent to that of one million tons of tnt.

meissner effect

the falling off of the magnetic flux within a superconducting metal when it is cooled to a temperature below the critical temperature in a magnetic field. It was discovered by Walther meissner (1882-1974) in 1933 when he observed that the earth's magnetic field was expelled from the interior of tin crystals below 3.72K, indicating that as superconductivity appeared the material became perfectly diamagnetic. See magnetism.

meitnerium

symbol Mt. A radioactive transactinide element; a.n. 109. It was first made in 1982 by Peter Armbruster and a team in Darmstadt, Germany, by bombarding bismuth-209 nuclei with iron-58 nuclei. Only a few atoms have ever been detected. It is named after Lise Meitner.

melde's experiment

an experiment for verification of laws of transverse vibration of strings.

melody

the pleasing effect on the ear produced when two notes that produce concord are sounded one after the other.

melt strength

the term is usually associated with the strength of a molten plastic.

melting

change of state of a substance from solid to liquid state. The temperature at which this happens depends on the pressure and is called the melting point of the substance.

melting point

the fixed temperature at which a solid changes into the liquid state. The melting point of ice is 0°C. Melting point of a solid depends upon pressure. It is also calledfussion temperature of the liquid.

memory

the part of a computer in which data is stored while it is being worked on. A typical microcomputer, for example, has a comparatively small amount of read-only memory (see ROM) and a large amount of random-access memory (see RAM). Only data in ROM is preserved when the machine is switched off; any data in RAM must be saved to disk if it is wanted again.

meniscus

the curcved surface of a liquid in a vessel. A liquid which wets the surface of the vessel, e.g., water, has a depressed meniscus; other liquids, e.g., mercury, have a raised or convex meniscus.

mercury barometer

a barometer in which the weight of a column of mercury in a glass tube having a sealed top is balanced against that of atmosphere pressing on an open vessel of mercury at the base of the column. The height of mercury column changing with changing with change in atmospheric pressure.

mercury cell

a primary electrolytic cell consisting of a zince anode, a cathode of mercuric oxide and koh as electrolyte. Its e.m.f. is 1.3 v.

mercury thermometer

refers to a liquid-in-glass thermometer that uses mercury as its working substance.

mercury vapor lamp

an evacuated gas tube which contains mercury which is vaporized by heat; the mercury vapour gives an incandescent arc between the electrodes, serving as a source of ultraviolet radiation as ell as of an intense visible light.

meridian

a great circule on the surface of the earth or another heavely body, which passes through the north and south poles.

mesh

refers to any arrangement of interlocking metal links.

mesons

elementary particles that are thought to be responsible for the exchange forces between nucleons in a nucleus. Their masses are more than that of electrons and less than those of nucleons.

mesoscopic

designating a size scale intermediate between those of the microscopic and the macroscopic states. Mesoscopic objects and systems require quantum mechanics to describe them. Many devices in electronics are mesoscopic.

meta centre

it is the point of intersection between two vertical lines, one through the centre of buoyancy of a hull in equilibrium and other through the centre of buoyancy when the hull is slightly inclined to one side or towards one end.

metachromatism

change of colour because of change of temperafure.

metallic bond

a bond, characteristic of atoms in a metal, which allows free passage of the valence electrons through out the metal lattice and therefore accounts for the fact that metals are good electrical conductors.

metallic circuit

the term is frequently used in electricity and referees to any wire circuit which does not include the ground as its part.

metallic insulator

a mechanical support consisting of a short length of transmission line, and odd number or quarter wavelengths long, used at ultra-high frequencies.

metallography

the study of crystalline structure of metals and alloys.

metamict state

the amporphous state of a substance that has lost its crystalline structure as a result of the radioactivity of uranium or thorium. Metamict minerals are minerals whose structure has been disrupted by this process. The metamictization is caused by alphaparticles and the recoil niclei from radioactive disintegration.

metastable state

refers to a state of a system in which it is apparently in as stable equil'brium; however, if slightly disturbed the system changes to a new state of lower energy.

meteor

a lump of matter from space that enters the earth's atmosphere and is detected either optically on account of its luminosity or by ratio means on account of the trial of ionized gas left in its wake.

meteorograph

an instrument for recording some or all of the following: temperature, relative humidity, pressure, and wind force. It is generally carried into the upper air by a balloon or kite.

meteorology

the science of the atmosphere, particularly with respect to weather and climate.

meter

any instrument that measures automatically and resisters a quantity used up, distance travelled etc.

method of mixtures

a method of determining the specific heat capacities of liquids or a liquid and a solid by mixing known masses of the substances at different temperatures and measuring the final temperature of the mixture.

metre bridge

refers to a metre length of uniform resistance wire which is mounted above a scale marked in millimetres, with suitable terminal points added to make the device adaptable either as a Wheat stone bridge or a poterntiometer.

metric system

refers to a system of units using multiples and submultiples of 10 and essentially based on metre and kilogram as units of length and mass respectively.

metric ton

a unit of mass equal to 1000 kg or 2204.61 1b. 1 tonne = 0.9842 tor.

metrology

the branch of science dealing with the accurate measurement of the three fundamental quantities: mass, length, and time. It is generally extended to mean the systematic study of weights and measurements.

metronome

it is an instrument that is used to mark time. It is used as an aid in practising music by making clicking sounds at regular predetermined intervals.

mho

the reciprocal ohm, previously used as a unit of conductance. This unit is now replaced by the siemens.

mica

a family of silicate minerals with sheet like structures crystallizing in monoclinic forms having a highly perfect basal cleavage.

michelson interferometer

a device for calibrating finely divided scales, strain gauses, precision dial indicators, and other length-measuring equipment, using the wavelength of light as the unit of measurement.

michelson–morlery experiment

an experiment conducted by Michelson–Morley in 1881 to show that the velocity of light is not influenced by motion of medium through which it passes.

micro

symbol: μ A prefix which denotes 10^{-6}. For example, 1 mictrometre (μ m) = 10^{-6} metre (m).

micro radio meter

an instrument for the detection of radiant power which uses a thermopile connected to the moving coil if a galvanometer by very short leads.

micro voltmeter

a voltmeter calibrated in microvolts.

micro-circuitry

electronic circuits of extremely small size.

microammeter

minute

a unit of time. 1 minute=60 seconds.

mirror galvanometer

a galvanometer with a small mirror mounted on the moving coil, so that the deflection is optically magnified and measured by a ray of light reflected from the mirror to a scale.

mirror image

a shape that is identical to another except that its structure is reversed as if viewed in a mirror, so that the two cannot be super imposed. For example a left hand is the mirror image of a right hand.

misch metal

an alloy of cerium (50%), and other rare earths. It is used alloyed with iron (up to 30%) in lighter flints, and in small quantities to improve the malleability of iron. It is also added to copper alloys to make them harder, to aluminium alloys to make them stronger, to magnesium alloys to reduce creap, and to nickel alloys to reduce oxidation.

m.k.s. system

system of units having the fundamental units metre, kilogram and second for the length mass and time respectively.

mmhg

a former unit of pressure defined as the pressure that will support a column of mercury one millimetre high under speechified conditions. It is equal to 133.3234 pa. It is equivalent to the torr.

mode

one of several wave frequencies which an oscillator can generate or to which a resonator can be tuned. The value of the abscissa corresponding to the maximum ordinate of a frequency distribution curve.

model

a simplified description of a physical system intended to capture the essential aspects of the system in a sufficiently simple form to enable the mathematics to be solved. In practice some models require approximation techniques to be used, rather than being exactly soluble. When exact solutions are available they can be used to examine the validity of the approximation techniques.

modem

a device which converts the signals from one particular type of equipment into a form suitable for use in another.

moderator

a substance used in a nuclear reactor to slow down or thermalise fast moving neutrons which is essential to produce nuclear fission. They are substances of low atomic weight like carbon, paraffin wax, heavy water, etc.

modulation

refers to the process, or the result of the process, by which the amplitude or another characteristic of wave is varied as a function of the instantaneous value of another wave.

modulus

the absolute value of a number. For example, the absolute value of -8 is 8. The magnitude of a vector quantity. The modulus of the velocity of a particle, for example, is equal to its speed.

mohs hardness scale

a scale of hardness of materials based on a scratching test wherein any material can be scratched by the material which follows it in the scale.

mohs' scale

a method, for determining comparative hardness, by testing against ten standard minerals: (1) talc, (2) gypsum. (3) calcite, (4) fluorite, (5) apatite, (6) orthoclase, (7) quartz, (8) topaz, (9) corundum, (10) diamond. Thus a mineral with hardness 5 will scratch or abrade fluorite, but will be scratched by otherclase.

moire fringes

the pattern obtained when two regular sets of lines or points overlap.

molar conductivity

symbol A. The conductivity of that volume of an electrolyte that contains one of solution between electrodes placed one metre apart.

molar heat capacity

this is the amount of heat required to raise the temperature of 1 mol of substance through 1k.

molar thermal capacity

symbol: C. May be defined as the thermal capacity per unit amount of substance; i.e., the energy required to raise unit amount of substance (1 mol) by unit temperature (1 K). It is measured in J mole^{-1} K^{-1}.

mole

amount of a substance which contains as many atoms molecules, ions etc., as there are atoms in 0.012 kg of carbon-12 sl unit of amount of a substance.

molecular biology

the study of the structure of the molecules which are of importance in biology.

molecular dipole

an symmetrical distribution of charge in a molecule.

molecular flow

the flow of a gas through a pipe in which the mean free path of gas molecules is large compared to the dimensions of the pipe. This occurs at low pressures; because most collisions are with the walls of the pipe rather than other gas molecules, the flow characteristics depend on the relative molecular mass of the gas rather than its viscosity. The effect was studied by M. H. C. Knudsen (1871-1949).

molecule

one of the fundamental units forming a chemical compound; the smallest part of a chemical compound that can take part in a chemical atoms held together by covalent or coordinate bonds. Covalent substances that form macromolecules crystals have no discrete molecules (in a sense, the whole crystal is a molecule). Similarly, ionic compounds do not have single molecules, being collections of oppositely charged ions.

molecular orbital

when two atomic orbitals overlap they coalesce to produce a single 'molecular orbital'.

molecular spectrum

the spectrum emitted by molecules. Caused by transition between different states of molecular rotation, vibration etc.

molecule

the smallest unit of an element or chemical compound which can exist independently. A molecule of hydrogen, for example has two atoms of hydrogen; the molecule of neon on the other hands, has only one atom.

moment

a product of force and distance. The product obtained by multiplying a force by the perpendicular distance from a point to the line of action of the force, is called the moment of the force about the point.

moment of inertia

symbol I. The moment of inertia of a massive body about an axis is the sum of all the products formed by multiplying the magnitude of each element of mass (dm) by the square of its distance (r) from the line, i.e. $I_m = Sr^2dm$. It is the analogue in rotational dynamics of mass in linear dynamics. The basic equation is T = Ia, where T is the torque causing angular acceleration a about the specified axis.

moment of torsion

refers to the ratio of the magnitude of a torque to the angle of twist which that torque produces.

momentum linear

the product of mass and velocity of a body. When two bodies collide, the momentum is conserved. This is known as the law of conservation of momentum. Momentum is a vector quantity.

monatomic

refers to a molecule having only one atom of a substance.

monatomic molecule

a molecule of an element, consisting of a single atom of the element. Example, the molecules of inert gases.

monochromatic radiation

electromagnetic radiation, especially visible radiation, of only one frequency or wavelength. Completely monochromatic radiation cannot be produced, but lasers produce radiation within a very narrow frequency band. Compare polychromatic radiation.

monochromator

a device that gives monochromatic radiation when a radiation of many wave lengths is fed into it.

monoclinic

relating to crystals which have three unequal axes with one oblique intersection.

monoclinic crystal

three unequal axes, two of which are at right angles to each other.

monostable

a circuit is said to be monostable if it changes its operation from one stable state to another if supplied with an external trigger pulse.

monostable circuit

refers to an electronic circuit, usually a multivibrator, that is having one stable but can change to another state for a time after the application of a trigger pulse.

mony-body problem

the problem that it is very difficult to obtain exact solutions to systems involving interactions between more than two bodies – using either classical mechanics or quantum mechanics. To understand the physics of many-body systems it is necessary to make use of approximation techniques or model systems that capture the essential physics of the problem. For some problems, such as the three-body problem in classical mechanics, it is possible to obtain qualitative information about the system. Useful concepts in the quantum theory of many-body systems are quasiparticles and collective excitations. If there are a great many bodies interacting, such as the molecules in a gas, the problem can be analysed using the techniques of statistical mechanics.

moon

the earth's only natural satellite, which orbits the earth at a mean distance of 384 400 km. It has a diameter of 3476 km. It has no atmosphere or surface water. Its surface temperature varies between 80 K (night outside the earth to have been reached by man (1969).

moseley's law

the frequencies in the x-ray spectrum of elements, corresponding to similar transition are proportional to the square of the atomic numbers of the elements.

motion

a change in the position of a body or system with respect to time, as measured by a particular observer in a particular frame of reference. Only relative motion can be measured; absolute motion is meaningless. See also equation of motion; Newton's laws of motion.

motor

a machine that converts electrical energy into mechanical energy.

motor effect

the repulsive force between adjacent conductors carrying currents in opposite directions.

motor generator

an electric motor mechanically coupled to an electric generator. The motor is driven by a supply of specified voltage, frequency, or number of phases and the generator provides an output in which one or more of these parameters is different to suit a particular purpose.

mott scattering

coulombic-type scattering by nuclei in which transverse polarization of the scattered electrons is obtained.

moving-coil instrument

the term used for an electric measuring instrument that depends on the force on a small vertical rectangular coil carrying direct current in a magnetic field.

moving-coil microphone

a microphone whose electrical output results from a coil moving in a magnetic field.

moving-iron instrument

the term used for an electrical measuring instrument in which the current is passed through a fixed coil.

multimeter

an instrument that can be used to measure various electrical quantities like resistance, voltage currents etc.

multiplex

to send several messages simultaneously.

multiplication factor

symbol: k. I a nuclear chain reaction. This term refers to the ratio of the rate of production of neutrons to the rate of 'loss' of neutron (by absorption and leakage).

For subcritical reactions $k<1$
For supercritical reactions $k>1$
For critical reactions $k = 1$

multistable circuit

an electronic circuit that has more than one stable state.

multivibrator

a basic electronic circuit which consista of two transistors and other components, such as resistor and capacitors. Its main property has been that it can switch its output instantaneously from one voltage level to another.

mu-metal

the original trade name for a ferromagnetic alloy, containing 78% nickel, 17% iron, and 5% copper, that had a high permeability and a low coercive force. More modern versions also contain chromium and molybdenum. These alloys are used in some transformer cores and for shielding various devices from external magnetic fields.

muntz metal

a form of brass containing 60% copper, 39% zinc, and small amounts of lead and iron. Stronger than alpha-brass, it is used for hot forgins, brazing rods, and large nuts and bolts. It is named after G.F. Muntz (1794-1857).

muon

an elementary particle having a mass nearly 207 times the mass of an electron. There are two types of muons, one having a positive charge and the other a negative charge.

muonic atom

an atom in which an electron is replaced by a negatively charged muon orbiting either within or close to the nucleus.

music

the art of combining and regulating sounds of varying pitch to produce compositions expensive of various ideas and emotions.

musical scale

a series of note audible sensation arranged from low to high by a system of intervals, suitable for musical purposes.

mutual capacitance

the extent to which two capacitors can effect each other, expressed in terms of the ratio of the amount of charge transferred to one, to the corresponding potential difference of the other.

mutual conductance

the ratio of the change of anode current to the change in control grid voltage, when a small change is made in the anode voltage in a thermionic valve. Used as a measure of the valve's performance.

mutual induction

refers to the creation of the existence of mutual inductance when the relative position of two indictors cause the magnetic lines of force from one to link with the turns of the other.

mutual inductance, coeffidence of m

the e.m.f. induced in one circuit when the current in the second varies at the rate of 1 ampere/ second. It is measured in henry h.

mutual induction

when the current or magnetic field associated with a circuit is changed, an e.m.f. Is produced in a neighbouring circuit. This is called as the phenomenon of mutual induction.

myopia

inability of the eye to clearly see distant objects. The image of a distant object is formed in front of the retina, the defect can be a corrected by using a concave lens of appropriate negative power.

nadir

the point opposite the zenith on the celestial sphere.

nano

prefix meaning one-thousand-millionth.

nanosecond

one milli-microsecond.

natural frequency

that frequency at which a system vibrates in the absence of any external force.

natural gas

it is a mixture of hydrocabons and is found in deposits under the earth's surface. It contains upto 90% methane. It is used as a fuel both in industry and home.

natural radioactivity

the phenomena of radioactivity exhibited by naturally occurring radionuclides.

natural units

a system of units, used principally in particle physics, in which all quantities that have dimensions involving length, mass, and time are given dimensions of a power of energy (usually expressed in electronvolts). This is equivalent to setting the rationalized Planck constant and the speed of light both equal to unity.

natural wavelength

the wavelength corresponding to the natural frequency of a circuit is called its natural wavelength.

nautical

pertaining to ship, navigation etc.

nautical chain

a unit of length 1 nautical cnain=4.572 m.

nautical mile

a unit of distance being equal to 6082.66 feet.

navigation

it is the process of actually directing the course of a ship.

near field

the term is used in acoustics and represents the acoustic radiation field or domain lying close to an acoustic source.

near point

the point nearest the eye at which an object can be clearly seen. Normally, the average near point distance is taken to be 25 cm.

near sight

short sight. Myopia.

nebula

a cloudy, luminous patch which consists of a galaxy of stars, or of materials from which such galaxies are being formed.

neel point

the temperature at which ferrimagnetic and antiferromagnetic materials become paramagnetic.

neel temperature

the temperature at which the spins of the neighbouring ions in an antiferromagnetic material cease to be ordered antiparallel as the temperature of the material is increased, see antiferromagnetism.

negative bias

refers to the potential that is applied to an electronic device and is negative with respect to some fixed reference potential.

negative crystal

a uniaxial crystal, such as calcite, in which the extraordinary wave travels faster than the ordinary wave.

negative electricity

the kind of electricity predominating in a piece of resin which has been electrified by rubbing it with wool. It consists of an excess of electrons.

negative electron

syn. Negatron. An electron having a negative charge as opposed to the positively charged electron or positron.

negative glow

the luminous glow in a discharge tube between the cathode dark-space and faraday dark-space.

negative lens

a lens whose focal length or power is negative. A concave lens. A diverging lens.

negative mirror

a mirror with a negative power.

negative pole

the south pole of magnetic dipole.

negative pressure

it is another method of representing vacuum. Any pressure less than an atmospheric pressure 760 mm of mercury column is known as negative pressure.

negative resistance

the point at which the voltage-current characteristic has a negative slope, e.g. silicon-controlled rectifier, the magnetron, and the tunnel diode.

negative temperature coefficient

it represents a condition in physics wherein some characteristic of a material, such as volume, resistance etc., decreases with increase in temperature.

negative vector

a vector having the same magnitude as that of vector $\vec{a}$ but has the opposite direction is called a negative vectror of $\vec{a}$ and denoted by $(-\vec{a})$

negatron

it is a term used for electron to distinguish between negative electron and positron. Also, it is the name of four element vacuum tube which displays a negative resistance characteristics.

neon lamp

a small lamp made up of a pair of electrodes, treated to emit electrons freely, sealed in a glass bulb containing neon gas at low pressure. When a minimum voltage of between 60 and 90 volts is applied across the electrodes, the kinetic energy of the electrons is sufficient to ionize the neon atoms around the cathode, causing the emission of a reddish light. With d.c. the glow is restricted to the cathode; with a.c. both electroces act alternately as cathodes and a glow appears to emanate from both electrodes. The device consumes a very low power and is widely used as an indicator light showing that a circuit is live.

neon tube

a gas discharge tube filled with neon at low pressure, the colour of the glow being red.

neper

a unit used to express a ratio of powers, currents, etc., used especially in telecommunications to denote the attenuation of an amplitude A_1 to an amplitude A_2 as N nepers, where

$N = \ln(A_2/A_1)$.

1 neper = 8.686 decibels. The unit is named after John Napier (1550-1617), the inventor of natural logarithms.

neptunium series

one of the radioactive series.

nephoscope

a grid-like instrument for determining the speed of celestial objects inclusive of clouds by observation of time of transit.

nernst bridge

an electric circuit, like the whetstone bridge circuit, in which resistors are replaced by capacitor, at high frequencies.

nernst calorimeter

an apparatus which is used for determining the specific thermal capacity of a metal.

nerst effect

when het flows through a strip of metal placed in a magnetic field, the direction of flow being across the lines of force, an e.m.f. is developed perpendicular to both the flow and the lines. The direction of the current and e.m.f. produced depends on the nature of the metal.

nernst heat theorem

the entropy change for chemical reactions involving crystalline solids, is zero at the absolute zero of temperature. See also the third law of thermodynamics.

nernst calorimeter

an apparatus for determining the specific thermal capacity of a metal.

nernst zero of potential

an arbitrary zero of electrode potential, defined as that potential corresponding to the reversible equilibrium between hydrogen gas at 1 standard atmosphere pressure and hydrogen ions at unit activity.

network

refers to a group of transmitting stations linked by wire or micro–wave relay so that the same programme can be broadcast or telecast by all of them.

network, active

a network containing a source of energy.

network, passive

a network which does not contain a source of energy.

neumann's law

the magnitude of an electromagnetically induced e.m.f. (E) is given by E = dF/dt, where F is the magnetic flux. This is a quantitative statement of Faraday's second law of electromagnetic induction and is sometimes known as the Faraday–Neumann law.

neumann's principle

the symmetry elements of any physical property of a crystal must include the symmetry elements of the point group of the crystal.

neutral

particle which has neither positive nor negative net charge.

neutral beam

a narrow beam of uncharged particles is referred to as a neutral beam.

neutral equilibrium

equilibrium such that if the system is disturbed a little, there is no tendency for it to move further nor to return.

neutral filter

a light filter which absorbs equally all wavelengths, it reduces light intensity without any change of relative spectral distribution.

neutral point

refers to a point where two fields in a region have been equal and opposite, so that there is no resultant force.

neutral point magnetism

a point in a magnetic region where the net magnetic field is zero. The magnetic neutral points will exist, for example, near a permanent dipole magnet placed in the earth's magnetic field.

neutral temperature

the temperature of the hot junction of a thermocouple at which the thermo e.m.f. Around the circuit is maximum and the rate of change of e.m.f. with temperature is minimum.

neutretto

a meson with zero electric charge.

neutrino

refers to an elementary particle of zero charge and zero rest mass.

neutron

an elementary particle that is a constituent of nuclei of all atoms. Its charge is zero and mass slightly higher than the mass of proton, discovered by Tames Chadwick in 1932.

neutron age

refers to one sixth of the mean square displacement of a neutron as it shown, through a specified energy range, in an infinite homogeneous medium.

neutron bomb

it is a nuclear bomb. It releases a shower of life destroying neutrons but has practically little blast and contamination. Thus it is possible to occupy and use a very large area shortly after the deterioration of the bomb.

neutron bottle

the term is used in nuclear physics and refers to a vessel employed for storing ultracold neutrons in vacuum.

neutron counter

a device which counts the number of neutrons passing through any detecting medium.

neutron diffraction

the scattering of neutrons by atmos in solids, liquids, or gases. This techniw\ques, uses a flux of thermal neutrons from an nuclear reactor to study solid–state phenomena. Thermal neutrons have an average kinketic energy of about 0.025 eV (4×10^{-21} J) giving them an equivalent wave length of 0.1 nanometre, which is suitable for the study of interatomic interference. Interaction with the atomic nucleus gives diffraction patterns that complement those from X–rays.

neutron flux or neutron flux density

the intensity of neutron radiation also expressed as number of neutrons passing through a unit area in a unit time.

neutron number

the number of neutrons in the nucleus of an atom is known as its neutron number.

neutron scattering

the phenomenon by virtue of which there occurs a change in the direction of incident neutrons as they collide with the nuclei of atoms of a material.

neutron temperature

a concept used to express the

energies of neutrons that are in thermal equilibrium with their surroundings, assuming that they behave like a monatomic gas. The neutron temperature T, on the Kelvin scale, is given by T = 2E/3K, where E is average neutron energy and k the Boltazmann constant.

newton

si unit force. A force of 1 newton is that force which produces an acceleration of one m/s^2 in a mass of 1 kg.

newtonian fluid

a fluid wherein the amount of strain is proportional both to the stress and to the time. The constant of proportionality is known as the coefficeint of viscosity.

newtonian force

syn coulomb force. A force between points that falls off as the inverse square of distance between them.

newtonian mechanics

the system of mechanics that relies on Newton's laws of motion. Newtonian mechanics is applicable to bodies moving at speeds relative to the observer that are small compared to the speed of light. Bodies moving at speeds comparable to the speed of light require an approach based on relativistic mechanics, in which the mass of a body changes with its speed.

newtonian telescope

refers to the earliest type of reflecting telescope. Light from the converging mirror gets reflected back onto an angled plane mirror, and from there into the eyepiece.

newtonian mechanics

the classical mechanics, based on Newton's laws of motion.

newton's law of cooling

the rate of loss heat from a hot body is directly proportional to the difference of temperature over that of its surroundings, if the excess of temperature is not very large.

newton's law of gravitation

there is a force of attraction between any two massive particles in the universe. For any two point masses m_1 and m_2, separated by a distance d, the force of attraction F is given by $F = m_1m_2G/d^2$, where G is the gravitational constant. Real bodies having spherical symmetry act as point masses positioned at their centres of mass.

newton's laws of motion

(1) every body continues in its state of rest, or of motion with a constant velocity in a straight line, unless acted upon by some extrernal force. (2) Change of momentum is proportional to the force and to the time during which it acts, and is in the same direction as the force. (3) To every action there is an equal and opposite reaction.

newton's law of resistance

at moderate velocities the resistance of a medium is proportional to the square of the velocity.

newtonian fluid

a fluid with a flow rate proportional to applied stress.

nichrome

an alloy of nickel, chromium and iron, having a high melting point and large resistivity. Used for making electric resistors and heating elements.

nickel-iron accumulator

(edison cell, Nife or NIFE cell). It is a type of secondary cell in which the electrodes have been constructed of steel grids. The positive electrode gets impregnated with a nickelnickel hydride mixture. The negative electfode gets impregnated with iron oxide. Potassium hydroxide solution forms the electrolyte. The niclkel-iron cell has been lighter and more durable than the lead accumulator, and it can work with higher current. It e.m.f. is approximately 1.3 volts.

nickel plating

depositing a thin layer of metallic nickel by an electrolysis process.

nicol prism

a device made from crystals of Iceland spar used to produce place-polarized light.

nit

symbol: nt. a unit of luminance, defined as one candela per meter squared. The unit is identical with the si unit of luminance.

nitriding

introduction of nitrogen to the surface of steel to change the surface properties.

nmr spectroscopy

nuclear magnetic resonance spectroscopy.

no-load current

the magnitude of current flowing through a circuit when the output is open-circuit is called no-load current.

noble

non-reactive.

nodal line

line joining the positions of minimum disturbance nodes in an interference pattern.

nodal points

a pair of points on the principle axis for which there is unit positive angular magnification. An incident ray directed towards one nodal point emerges parallel to itself through the other nodal point.

node

a point in a stationary wave pattern where the vibration is minimum.

noise

in electricity the term refers to the unwanted or interfering currents and voltages in an electrical device.

noise factor

a measure of the noise. It is defined as the ratio of the signal-to-noise power ratio at the source to the corresponding ratio at the output.

noise pollution

the term is associated with acoustics and refers to the excessive noise in human environment.

no-load

refers to operation with no output but under rated conditions of voltage, speed etc.

nomogram

a graph consisting of three lines, each with its own scales, each line representing the values of a variable over a specified range. A ruler laid between two points on two of the lines enables the value of the third variable to be read off the third line.

non condensable gas

a gas whose temperature is above its critical temperature, so that it cannot be liquefied by increase of pressure alone.

non-euclidean geometry

a type of geometry that does not comply with the basic postulates of Euclidean geometry, particularly a form of geometry that does not accept Euclid's postulate that only one straight line can be drawn through a point in space parallel to a given straight line. Several types of non-Euclidean geometry exist.

non-inductive

the term used for a circuit component that is having a low inductance. Non-inductive coils could be made by doubling back the wire on itself before making the coil.

non-inductive capacitor

a capacitor constructed so that it's incidental inductance has been reduced to a minimum.

non-inductive circuit

a circuit with negligible inductance.

non-inductice resistor

a resistor designed to have the minimum amount of inductance.

non-ohmic

a circuit component, the current passing through it does not obey ohm's law.

normal

perpendicular drawn on a reflecting or refracting surface at the point of incidence.

normal adjustment

an image formed by an optical system is in normal adjustment if it is in a similar viewing position to the object. The term really refers to the adjustment of the system.

normal spectrum

spectrum having the spectral lines separated by angles which are proportional to the difference in their wavelength.

n.t.p.

normal temperature and pressure. Their values are respectively 237^0 k and 76 cm of mercury.

n-type semiconductor

an extrinsic semiconductor whose density of conduction of electrons exceeds that of mobile holes.

nuclear barrier

potential barrier. The region of high potential energy through which a charged particle must pass on entering or leaving an atomic nucleus.

nuclear battery

a device for converting nuclear energy into electrical energy.

nuclear capture

the phenomenon in which a particle say a neutron, proton, electron etc., combines with a nucleus is commonly known as nuclear capture.

nuclear cloud

the term is used in nuclear reactors and refers to the cloud of dust and gas which results from the debris of any nuclear explosion.

nuclear energy

energy obtained using nuclear fission or nuclear fusion.

nuclear fission

a nuclear reaction in which an atomic nucleus disintegrates into two nearly equal fragments with the release of a large amount of energy. The process may be spontaneous or may be caused by the impact of a particle.

nuclear force

a strong attractive force between nucleons in the atomic nucleus that holds the nucleus together. At close range (up to about 2×10^{-15} metre) these forces are some 100 times stronger than electromagnetic forces. See fundamental interactions.

nuclear fuel

a substance which undergoes nuclear fission or nuclear fusion in a nuclear reactor, a nuclear weapon or a star.

nuclear fusion

a nuclear reaction in which two light nuclei fuse together to form a heavy nucleus with the release of large amount of energy.

nuclear isomers

atoms of an element of the same mass but possessing different rates of radioactive decay.

neclear-physics

branch of physics that deals with the structure and properties of nuclei, nuclear reactions and nucleon-collisions.

nuclear power

the use of nuclear reactions for power generation (usually by generation of electricity but nuclear powered ships use the heat generated to raise steam to power the turbines directly without conversion to electricity).

nuclear reaction

a reaction in which there is a change in the nucleus of an atom; it generally involves nuclei, nucleons, gamma rays and sometimes lighter elementary particles.

neclear reactor

refers to a device in which

nuclear reactions occur on a large scale. A reactor may be built for the purpose of providing useful energy, producing new nuclides, or research. Present desings have been fission reactors in thermal reactors a moderator has been used to slow the neutrons so that a chin reaction can get sustained. Fast reactors are not having a moderator, and use fast neutrons. In this case the fuel has to be enriched (so that it contains more ^{235}U isotope). Fussion reactors have been reactors for producing energy by nuclear fusion.

nuclear transmutations

the changing of atoms of one element into those of another by suitable nuclear reactions.

neclear weapon

the term used for an explosice device in which the reduction in mass that provides the thermal energy is resulted from the fission of heavy nuclei.

nucleation

the start of the growth of a new phase from which crystallization begins.

nucleon

the common name for protons and neutrons which are constituents of all nuclei.

nucleon number

also called mass number a : the number of nucleons in an atomic nucleus.

nucleonics

the practical application of nuclear physics, and techniques associated with these applications.

nucleon

the common name for protons and neutrons that are constituents of all neclei.

nucleon number

the number of nucleous present in an atomic nucleus.

nucleor

the postulated core of a nucleon, supposed to be surrounded by a cloud pions.

nucleus, atomic

refers to the compact, comparatively massive which is positively charged centre of an atom and made up of one or more nucleons (protons and neutrons) around which is a cloud of electrons. The density of nuclei has been about 10^{15} kg m^{-3}.

nuclide

any species of atom that exists for measurable length of time and has a nuclear structure distinct from that of any other species of atom. Thus, isotopes of the same element are distinct nuclides.

numerical aperture

it is sine of half the angular aperture, used as a measure of the optical power of an objective.

nutation

an oscillation of the earth's poles about the mean position.

nyquist rule

if a response-vector locus be plotted for a servo system for positive and negative frequncies and if the point (-1, jo) is not enclosed, the system is unstable.

o.a.s.m. system

a system of units based on the ohm, ampere, second and metre.

o electron

an electron which is present in the fifth shell of electrons surrounding the atomic nucleus.

object

natural point objects self-luminous or otherwise, deliver diverging rays of light.

object plane

the plane perpendicular to the axis centred on the object.

objective

a lens or a system of lenses near the object in microscope or a telescope. Also called the object lens.

observable quantity

any measureable physical quantity in physics is known as observable quantity.

occlusion

1. the trapping of small packets of liquid in a crystal during crystallization. 2. The absorption of a gas by a solid such that atoms or molecules of the gas occupy interstitial positions in the solid lattice. Palladium, can occlude hydrogen.

occultation

the cutting off of the light from a celestial body when another body comes between the observer and it.

octal base

the standard eight-pin valve base.

octave

the interval between two musical notes whose frequencies are in the ratio 2 : 1.

octet

group of eight electrons that constitute the outer electron shell of an inert gas except helium or an atom.

odd-even nucleus

nucleus containing an odd number of proton and even number of nucleons.

odograph

an automatic electronic map tracer, which plots the exact course taken by a vehicle in which it is fitted.

oersted

symbol: Oe a unit of magnetic field strength in the c.g.s. system. It is equal to $10^3/4p$ A m^{-1}.

ohm

unit of electrical resistance. It was defined as the resistance of a column of mercury 106.3 cm long, having a mass 14,452 gram and a uniform cross-sectional area at 0 degree c.

ohm's law

the current (I) in a conductor is proportional to the potential difference (V) between its ends. This leads to V=IR, where R is the conductor's resistance. R is constant procvided the physical conditions in the conductors are unaltered. If V is in volts and I in amperes, R is in ohms. Components that conduct in accordance with ohm's law are said to be obmic.

ohmic

the term used for describing a substance or circuit component that has been obeying ohm's law.

ohmic contact

if the potential difference across a contact is proportional to the current passing through it, the contact is called ohmic.

ohmic loss

refers to power dissipation in an electrical circuit arising from its resistance rather than from other causes like back e.m.f.

ohmic substance

refers to a substance, the current flowing through which is in accordance with ohm's law.

ohmmeter

an instrument for measuring resistance in ohms.

ohmic

describing a substance or circuit component that obeys ohms law.

oil break

a term used in electricity which refers to the property of an electrical switch whose contacts are separated in an oil.

oil-drop experment

an experiment carried out by Millikan in 1913 to determine the charge on an electron. He deduced the charge by measuring the rate of descent of a charged oil drop in an electric field. See electron charge.

ondograph

an instrument which draws the waveform of an alternating voltage in a series of steps.

ondoscope

a glow-discharge tube use to detect the presence of high frequency radiation.

opacity

the term is used in optics and is defined as the ratio of amount of light flux incident upon a medium to the amount of light flux transmitted by it.

opaque

any substance that does not allow light to pass through it is called an opaque substance.

opaque projector (episcope)

refers to an optical instrument which is used for projecting an image of an opaque object (e.g., a diagram or picture) onto a screean.

open-circuit

refers to an electric circuit through which no current is passing.

opeque projector

an optical instrument for projecting an image of an opaque object onto a screen. High intensity illumination is used and the image is projected by a combination of mirrors and lenses.

opetrating point

the point on the family of I–V characteristic curves of an active electronic device, such as a transistor that represents the magnitude of voltage and current under specified operating conditions.

operating street

the stress to which any structure is subjected while use in service.

optar

a portable device for guidance of the blind, which uses techniques along with visible light.

optic axis

a direction in a doubly refracting crystal in which light propagates without double refraction.

optical

constructed to assist singt.

optical acitivity

the ability possessed certain chemicals to rotate the plane of polarized light when the latter is passed through the substance.

optical axis

in a lens, the straight line passing through the centres of curvature of the surfaces; light ray passing along this direction are neither refracted nor reflected.

optical centre

refers to the geometrical centre of lens through which an incident ray passes undeviated.

optical flat

a surface that is so flat that irregularities of surface flatness are not greater than a fraction of the wavelength of light. The surface can be tested by observing interference fringes when a known flat is placed in contact.

optical glass

a type of glass with properties suitable for making lenses, prisms, etc. There are two major groups : the crown glasses and the flint glasses, differing in their density and refractive constants.

optical illusion

an error to the average eye in the perception of certain lines, angles and spaces.

optical lever

refers to a device which is used for measuring angular displacement. The device has been commonly used in torsion balances, as in the mirror galvanometer.

optical maser

a maser in which the pumping frequency is in the optical region.

optical path

refers to the product of the refractive index of the medium and the distance traversed by the light in the medium.

optical pathlength

the total phase change between the source and a given position in the energy beam as measured along the direction of travel of the beam or wave-fronts.

optical pyrometer

a pyrometer whereing the luminous radiation from the hot body is compared with that from a known source. The instrument measures the temperature of a luminous source without thermal contact.

optical rotary dispersion

the phenomenon in which the amount of rotation of plane-polarized light of an optically active substance depends on the wavelength.

optical scanning

it refers to a process used for recording pulses on a magnetic tape. For this purpose photoelectric devices capable of reading characters and converting the information to electric impulses are used.

optical telescope

an astronomical telescope which is used to observe celestial bodies by the light they emit, in contrast to a radio telescope which is used to observe their radio frequency emissions.

optical temperature

the temperature of a celestial body as calculated from its light radiation.

optical thickness

the product of an optical material and its refractive index is called is optical thickness.

optical train

a series of lenses, mirrors and prisms of an optical system, through which light rays pass.

optic axis

the direction in a birefringent crystal along which the ordinary and extraordinary rays travel at the same speed. Uniaxial crystals have one such axis; biaxial crystals have two. See also birefringent crystal.

optics

branch of physics that deals with the study of light.

optimatic pyrometer

an instrumental for measuring the temperature of hot moving bodies, using two vacuum photocells illuminate by the surface of the body under investigation and by the filament of a comparison lamp; the current in the filament when a perfect match in brightness is obtained is a measure of the temperature of the body.

optoelectronics

a branch of electronics based on light beams rather than electric currents.

orbit

the closed path of a moving object used particularly for the path of planets around the sun or the path of moon around the earth. The path of an electron moving around the nucleus of an atom is also known as an orbit.

oribital

one which moves in an orbit. An orbital electron, for example, is one that moves around the necleus of an atom in an orbit.

order

an integer associated with a given interference fringe or diffraction pattern.

orthicon

a camera tube in which a low-velocity electron beam scan a photo-mosaic I capable of electrical storage.

orthochromatic film

photographic film which is sensitive to green as well as to the blue end of the spectrum.

orthogonal

mutually perpendicular. Having a set of mutually perpendicular axes.

orthorhombic

a crystal with three unequal but perpendicular axes.

oscillating magnetic field

a magnetic field which varies periodically with time.

oscillation

a regularly repeated to-and from motion about a point.

oscillator

a device for producing a.c. Signals of given frequency from a.d.c. input. It usually consists of thermionic values or transistors coupled with a suitable lc-r resonance circuit.

oscillatory circuit

a circuit containing a capacitance and inductance. The frequency of electrical oscillation produced by such a circuit is given by

$$f = \frac{1}{2\pi\sqrt{L.C}}$$

where L is the inductance and L is the capacitance in the circuit.

oscillogram

refers to the record produced by a recording oscillograph, or the reading from an oscilloscope.

oscilloscope

a device used to produce a visual image of one or more rapidly changing electrical quantities. The cathode-ray oscilloscope is the most common type.

osmium

a transition metal that is found associated with platinum. Osmium is the most dense of all metals. The metal is used in catalysts and in alloys for pen nibs, pivots, and electrical contacts.

Symbol: Os; m.p. 3054°C; b.p. 5027°C; r.d. 22.59 (20°C); p.n. 76; r.a.m. 190.23.

osmometer

an instrument for measuring osmotic pressure.

osmosis

the process of interdifusion of two liquids through a membrane is called osmosis.

osmotic pressure

the pressure developed due to the process of osmosis.

otto cycle

refers to the idealised reversible cycle of four operations which is occurring in a perfect four-stroke (spark ignition) petrol engine. These have been the constant-volume temperature rise, constant-pressure expansion, constant-volume temperature fall, and constant-pressure volume decrease of a gas. The cycle returns the gas to its initial state; the efficiency with which the engine transfers chemical energy into mechanical work has been the maximum attainable for this type of engine.

outage

the process of failure in an electric power system is known as outage.

output

it is the power, voltage or current delivered by any circuit, device, or plant. The terminals or other place where the signal is delivered.

output impedance

the impedance offered to the load by a circuit or device.

output transformer

refers to transformer that is used

to couple an output circuit to a load.

overcurrent release

syn. overload release. A tripping device which operates when the current exceeds a predetermined value.

overhead projector

a type of projector able to project on a screen large bright images of slides or transparent objects placed on a horizontal table. See also projectors.

overtones

the tones or frequencies emitted by a system in addition to its fundamental frequency are known as overtones. The intensity of overtones, is generally lower than that of the fundamental.

overvoltage

the difference between the potential at which a gas, especially hydrogen is evolved from a silution and the potential of a reversible electrode of the same gas in the same solution.

owen bridge

an ac bridge used to measure self-inductance in terms of capacitance and resistance.

oxygen point

refers to the temperature of equilibrium between liquid and gaseous oxygen at a pressure of one standard atmosphere, taken as a fixed point the international temperature scale at 90.188 kelvin.

ozone layer

syn. ozonosphere. See atmospheric layers.

p m r spectroscopy

proton magnetic resonance spectroscopy.

pachimeter

a device for measuring the elastic shear limit of solid material.

packing density

it refers to the number of devices or integrated circuits per unit of a sillicon clip.

packing fraction

the difference between the actual mass of a nuclide and the nearest whole number (i.e., the mass defect) divided by the mass number. See also binding energy.

pair production

it refers to the simultaneous production of an electron and its anti–particle from a gamma ray photon. The minimum energy that such a photon must have in 1022 Mev.

palaeomagnetism

the study of magnetism in rocks, which provides information on variations in the direction and intensity of the earth's magnetic field with time.

palladium

a silvery white ductile transition metal occurring in platinum ores. It is used in electrical relays and as a catalyst in hydrogenation processes. Hydrogen will diffuse through a hot palladium barrier.

Symbol: Pd; m.p. 1552°C; b.p. 3140°C; r.d. 12.02 (20°C); p.n. 46; r.a.m. 106.42.

panel

a switch board or control board containing a set of related cards, relays, jacks. etc.

paper capacitor

a capacitor in which the dielectric is made of paper.

parabaloon

a specially designed air-inflated radar antenna.

parabolic mirror

a concave mirror which has the form of a paraboloid of revolution. All light rays emanating from a source located at the focal point are reflected as parallel rays.

paradox

any statement or proposition that seems self contradictory or absurd but actually expressing a possible truth.

parallax

the change in the apparent relative orientations of objects when they are viewed from different positions.

parallel

elements in an electrical circuit are in parallel if connected so that the current divides between them and rejoins at the other side. The word 'shunt' is sometimes used. For resistors in parallel, the resulting resistance r is given by:

$$\frac{1}{r} = \frac{1}{r_1} + \frac{1}{r_2} + \frac{1}{r_3} + \ldots$$

for capacitors in parallel, the capacitance of the combination is given by:

$$c = c_1 + c_2 + c_3 + \ldots$$

parallel forces

if the forces on an object are passing through one point, their resultant can be obtained by using the parallelogram of vectors. It the forces have been parallel the resultant can be obtained by addition, taking sign into account. There may also be a turning effect in such cases, which can be obtained by the principle of moments.

parallelogram of forces

if two forces act on a point but their lines of action are not identical the following procedure must be applied. Each force is represented by a line, the direction of the line being the line along which the force acts. The length of the line represents the magnitude of the force on some scale previously decided on. An arrowhead is always placed on the line to indicate the direction in which the force acts.

parallelogram of vectors

refers to a method which is used for finding the resultant of two vectors acting at a point. The two vectors would be shown as two sides of a parallelogram: the resultant would be the diagonal through the starting point.

$$F = \sqrt{(F_1^2 + F_2^2 + 2 F_1 F_2 \cos\theta)}$$

$$a = \sin^{-1}[(F_1/F) \sin\theta]$$

parallel-tuned circuit

an electric circuit that has two parallel branches. One branch of the circuit has a capacitance and a resistance in series and the other branch has a resistance and an inductance in series.

paramagnet

substances that get weakly magnetised on being placed in a magnetic field. When placed in non-uniform magnetic field, they move from weaker parts to the stronger parts of the field.

paramagnetism

the property exhibited by a paramagnetic substance, of having magnetic properties greater than unity (that of air) and being attracted to magnet.

parametric amplifier

a low noise microwave amplifier wherein gain is obtained by periodically changing a circuit parameter, e.g. capacitance.

parasite

the term is associated with current in an electric circuit due to some unintentional cause. Such a current is quite troublesome in electrical measurements and is often undesirable.

parasitic capture

the absorption of a neutron by a

nuclide, which does not result in a nuclear fission or the production of a useful artificial element.

parastate

a state of a diatomic in which the spins of the two nuclei are anti-parallel.

paraxial

describing rays incident on a surface close and parallel to the axis. Only paraxial rays pass or appear to pass through the focal point of a spherical reflecting or refracting surface. See also mirror, parabolic mirror.

paraxial rays

incident rays parallel and close to the axis of a lense.

parent element

generally an element which produces another element or isotope, whether by spontaneous radioactive decay or as target element in a nuclear bombardment, is called the parent of the newly produced element or isotope (which is called its daughter element). Specifically, with reference to a radioactive series or family of elements, the element or isotope starting the series is called its parent.

parent necleus

a nucleous which undergoes radioactive deacy to another nucleus, the resulting nucleus is known as the daughter nucleus.

parity

a property of the wave functions that describe physical system in quantum mechanics.

parsec

symbol: pc a unit of distance used in astronomy. A star that is one parsec away from the earth has a parallax (apparent shift), due to the Earth's movement around the Sun, of one second of arc. One parsec is approximately $3.085\ 61 \times 10^{16}$ meters.

partial pressure

the partial pressure of a gas in a mixture of gases occupying a fixed volume is the pressure that the gas would exert if it alone is present in the total volume.

partials

components of a sound wave with frequencies above the fundamental frequency. The partials include the overtones together with non-harmonic components.

particle

an abstract simplification of real object the mass is concentrated at the object's centre of mass; its volume is zero. Thus, relational aspects can be ignored.

particle, physics

the branch of physics that deals with elementary particles, their properties and interactions.

particulate matter

matter which is composed of small liquid or solid particles.

partition coefficient

the ratio of the equilibrium concentrations of a solute dissolved in two specified immiscible solvents. It is independent of the actual concentrations.

pascal

symbol: Pa the SI unit of pressure, equal to a pressure of one newton per square meter 1 Pa = 1 N m^{-2}).

pascal's law

pressure applied anywhere to an enclosed body of fluid is transmitted equally in all directions. This pressure acts at right angles to every portion of the surface of the container, force per unit area being uniform throughout.

pascal's principle

pressure applied at any point of a fluid at rest is transmitted without loss to all other parts of the fluid.

paschen series

a series of lines in the infrared region of the spectrum of hydrogen that arise when the electrons in 4th, 5th,... orbit jump to the 3rd permitted orbit.

paschen's law

at a constant temperature, the breakdown voltage of a gas is a function only of the product of the gas pressure and the distance between parallel plane electrodes

passive junction

a wave guide junction that has no source of energy.

pauil's exclusion principle

no two electrons in an atom can have the same quantum numbers n,i,m, and s. The principle is very important in the theoretical building up of the periodic table.

peak value

refers to the maximum value of an alternating physical quantity.

peclet's number

a dimensionless number for a fluid flowing past a body and equal to parndtl's number x reynolds number.

peirels stress

the minimum energy required to remove a dislocation from its rest position of minimum energy.

peltier effect

the change in temperature produced at a junction between two different metals or semiconductors when electric charge is passed through it. If the current direction is reversed then a heating effect becomes a cooling one or vice versa. The temperature change is directly proportional to the current.

pencil

a narrow beam of rays from a single point.

pendulum

a pendulum consists of a small mass oscillating to and fro with simple harmonic motion, at the end of a very light string.

penetration factor

the probability that an incident particle, in a nuclear reaction, will pass through the nuclear barrier.

penning effect

the ionization of one species c gas molecule by collision wit another species in a mixture c gases, when the former specie is in a metastable excitatio level which is above th ionization potential of the othe

pentode

a thermionic valve with fiv electrodes-cathode, three grid and an anode. The addition of suppressor grid to the tetorec kept at the cathode potentia helps suppress the loss c secondary electrons ejected b the anode. See also tetored.

penumbra

region of partial shadow obtained when an object in th path of light from a source cut off a part of light.

perfect gas

an ideal gas which would obe the gas laws exactly. It woul consist of perfectly elasti molecules, their volume and th intermolecular forces betwee them being zero.

perfectly inelastic collision

momentum of particles afte such a collision is complete determined by the knowledge c their motion prior to collisior

The principle of conservation of total momentum holds good. After such a collision the two colliding bodes stick together e.g. a collision between a bullet and a target.

$$m_1\vec{V}_1 + m_2\vec{V}_2 = (m_1 + m_2)\vec{V}$$

$$\Delta K_v = \frac{1}{2}\frac{m_1 m_2}{m_1 + m_2}(\vec{V}_1 - \vec{V}_2)^2$$

pericynthion

refers to the time or the point at which a satellite launched from the earth into lunar orbit is nearest to the surface of the moon.

perigee

the shortest distance of a satellite from the earth.

perihelion

the point in a solar orbit which is nearest to the sun.

perilune

the time or the point at which a satellite launched from the moon into lunar orbit is closet to the surface of moon.

period

the time taken for one complete cycle of a periodic motion. It is equal to the reciprocal of the frequency of the motion.

periodic motion

motion in which the body returns to the same condition of motion after regular intervals of time. e.g. simple harmonic motion.

periodic system

arrangement of the chemical elements in the periodic table.

periodic table

a table of the chemical elements in increasing order of atomic number, arranged to show the chemical similarities between groups of elements.

periscope

an instrument for seeing objects, that are above the eye-level of the observer, or for which direct vision is obstructed. It consists of two mirrors at 45 degree to the direction being viewed.

permalloy

an alloy having a high permeability at low magnetic flux density and a low hysteresis loss.

permanent echo

a signal which is reflected from an object that is fixed with respect to a radar site.

permanent gas

a gas that cannot be liquefied by increasing its pressure at room temperature, but must also be cooled. Such a gas has a critical temperature below room temperature. See critical state.

permanent magnet

a substance that possesses magnetic properties without the influence of any external magnetic field.

permanent set

the increment of plastic deformation following the exceeding of the elastic limit.

permeability

the absolute permeability of a substance is the ratio of the magnetic flux density, b, in the substance to the applied magnetic field h.

permeance

the reciprocal of reluctance.

permeaseter

an instrument for measuring the magnetic characteristics, in particular the permeability, of a ferromagnetic material.

permissible dose

the amount of radiation which may be safely received by an individual within a specified time. Also known as telerance dose.

permittivity

symbol: e. The mutual force between two charge Q_1 and Q_2 a distance r apart may be given by the equation:

$F = Q_1Q_2 / 4\pi er^2$.

The constant e is termed the permittivity of the medium. The unit is the coulomb^2 newton^{-1} metre^{-2} ($C^2\ N^{-1}\ m^{-2}$), or farad metre^{-1} (Fm^{-1}).

perpetual motion

motion of a machine, which once set in motion goes on moving without receiving energy from any external source.

pertology

the study of the origin, structure, and composition of rocks.

perturbations

deviations in the motions of the planets from their true elliptical orbits, as a result of their gravitational attraction for each other.

perversion (lateral inversion)

refers to the effect which is produced by a mirror in reversing images apparently left to right. For example, writing appears backwards when reflected; the image of a person raising the right hand appears to raise the left hand.

phase

a stage in a cycle which a repetitive motion or wave has reached at a given time. Two waves are said to be in phase is their correcponding points coincide.

phase angle

the time difference expressed in electrical degrees, between the occurrence of the positive peaks of two fine waves of the same frequency.

phase constant

the space rate of decrease of the phase of a wave.

phase contrast microscope

a microscope which uses the difference in phase of the light transmitted or reflected by an object to form an image by relative differences in intensity.

phase delay

refers to the ratio of the phase shift of a periodic quantity to its frequency.

phase diagram

a graph combining two conditional parameters of a substance drawn so that a particular curve shows the boundary between two phases of the substance.

phase difference

refers to the difference in phase of a wave at two points. Also the difference in phase between two waves arriving simultaneously at a point in space.

phase modulation

refers to a type of modulation in which a carrier wave has ben made to carry the information in a signal (audio or visual) by fluctuations in the phase of the carrier. The difference in phase between the modulated and the unmodulated carrier has been proportional to the amplitude of the signal.

phase rule

(Gibbs phase rule) for any equilibirium system, the expression.

$P + F = C + 2$

which relates the number of degress of freedom, F, to the number of phases, P and the number of components, C. See degrees of freedom, phase.

phase shift

any change that takes place in

the phase of one quantity or in the phase difference between two or more quantities.

phase splitter

a circuit wherein a single input waveform produces two output waves having a given phase difference, e.g. the driving circuit for a push-poll amplifier.

phase velocity

the velocity with which the phase in a travelling wave is propagated. It is equal to I/T, where T is the period. Compare group velocity.

phasor

a rotating vector that is used for representing an alternating current or some other sinusoidally changing quantity. The projection of the phasor on a fixed line gives its amplitude at any time.

phlogiston theory

a theory of combustion, that all combustible materials were supposed to contain phologiston, that was released during combustion to leave calx.

phon

the unit of loudness level.

phonometer

an instrument for measuring sound intensity.

phonon

the phoning is a quantum of thermal energy. It is given by hf, where h is the plank constant and f the vibrational frequency. It refers to lattice vibration of crystals.

phosphor

a substance which emits light at temperatures below the temperature at which they would exhibit incandescence. Fluorescent substances are used on the screens of cathode-ray tubes or in fluorescent lamps.

phosphorescence

the absorption of energy by atoms followed by emission of electro-magnetic radiation. In general usage the term is applied to the emission of cold light produced without a high temperature.

phot

a photometric unit of illuminance or illumination equal to 1 lumen per square centimetre. Foot candle, lux.

photocathode

refers to a cathode that emits

electrons by the photoelectric effect.

photocell

refers to any device which is used for producing an electric signal fromelectromagnetic radiation. Originally, photocells had been photoelectric cells, i.e. devices in which a current got produced between two electrodes by the photoelectric effect. The present common type depends on photoconductivity. Other types of photocell have been photodiodes or depend on the phototovoltaic effect.

photo conductive effect

the increase in the electrical conductivity of some substances when the amount of light falling on the substance is increased e.g. selenium.

photoconductivity

may be defined as the increase of electrical conductivity in certain materials, produced by incident electromagnetic radiation. The photons absorbed by the solid give up energy to electrons, freeing them and there by increasing the number o electrons in the conduction band.

photo-disintegration

the disintegration of a nucleus when a photon is incident on it. The nucleus usually emits neutrons or small charged fragments.

photo-fission

nuclear fission caused by photons.

photocathode

a substance which emits electrons when light is incident on it due to photo-electric effect, and which acts as a cathode.

photodiode

a semi-conductor diode that is sensitive to electro-magnetic radiation.

photodisintegration

the ejection of particles from atomic nuclei on absorption of electromagnetic radiation. Most commonly a neutron is ejected.

photoelasticity

the double refraction observed in certain materials only when stressed. A number of synthetic materials are photocells examples being perspex and cellophone.

photoelectric alarm

an electronic alarm circuit which includes a photo-electric relay.

photoelectric cell

a generally term for any cell the electrical properties of which are effected by illunination. An electromagnetic radiation i the form of visible light; it transforms light energy into electrical energy. It is an instrument for detecting and measuring light electrically.

photoelectric constant

a constant associated with photoemission equal to the ratio h/e, where h is plank's constant and e is electronic charge.

photoelectric effect

may be defined as the emission of electrons from a solid surface when it gets irradiated with electromagnetic radiation. In the photoelectric effect, the number of electrons emitted depends on the intensity of the radiation and not on its frequency.

photoelectricity

a group of phenomena in which electric effects are produced by electromagnetic radiation.

photoelectrons

electrons ejected from a solid, liquid, or gas by the photoelectric effect or by photoionization.

photoemission

the emission of photo-electrons by the photoelectric effect or by photoionization.

photoemitter

an emitter which emits a good yield of electrons when illuminated sufficiently.

photography

the term used for the production of a permanent record of an image on suitable paper or film. Normally the image has been produced by the optical system.

photoionization

refers to the ionization of atoms or molecules by electromagnetic radiation. Photons absorbed by an atom may be possessing sufficient photon energy to free an electron from its attraction b the nucleus. The process is $M + hv \rightarrow M^+ + e$.

photomeson

a meson produced by the interaction between a photon and an atomic nucleus.

photometer

an instrument used to measure the relative brightness of objects. The brightness of the object is matched with that of a screen illuminated by a lamp of known power.

photometry

the branch of physics that deals with the measurement of the amount of light energy emitted or absorbed by a body.

photomicrograph

a photograph obtained with the aid of a microscope.

photomultiplier

a device in which electrons originally emitted from a photocathode initiate a cascade of electrons by secondary emission in an electron multiplier. It is much more sensitive as a radiation detector than a single photoelectric cell. See also photoelectric cell.

photon

the term used for a 'particle' of electromagnetic radiation. The energy (W) carried by a photon has been related to the frequency (v) by the Planck constant (h): W = hv. Its momentum p has been given by $p = h/\lambda$ (where λ is the wavelength) and by p = W/c. The speed of photons has been that of the speed of light (c); the rest mass has been zero.

photon flux

the number of photons in a light beam reaching any surface in a unit time is known as photon flux.

photoneutron

a neutron released from a nucleus in photonuclear reaction.

photopic vision

vision at normal levels of light intensity. Under such conditions the cones in the retina are the main receptors.

photoproton

a proton released from a nucleus in a photonuclear reaction.

photosphere

refers to the intensity luminous and visible portion of the sun. Its temperature is estimated to be around 6000 degree k.

phototransistors

semi-conductor devices which are sensitive to light.

photovolatic effect

an effect in which an e.m.f. develops between two layers of materials when an electromagnetic radiation is incident on them.

physical change

any change in body or substance which does not involve an alteration in its chemical composition.

physics

the study of the properties of matter and energy.

pi-missions

exchange particles responsible for strong nuclear forces. Their charge can be positive, negative or zero. The mass of meson is nearly 270 times the mass of an electron.

piezoelectric crystal

a crystalline dielectric which exhibits the piezoelectric effect. Examples are rochelle salt and quartz.

piezo-electric effect

the production of a small e.m.f. across certain substances on being subjected to external pressure. Such substances are known piezo-electric substances.

pinch effect

when an electric current, either direct or alternating, passes through a liquid conductor, the conductor tends to contract in cross-section, due to electromagnetic forces.

pin-hole camera

it is a box into which light can enter only through a very small hole. As light rays travels in straight lines in a given medium (air in this case), an inverted image gets formed on the wall of the box opposite the pin-hole.

pion (pi-meson)

a type of meson. There are three types of pion, having positive negative, or zero charge. The charged points have rest energy 139.6 MeV and mean life 2.6×10^{-8} s. Each decays to give a muon and a neutrino. The neutral pion has a rest energy 135 MeV and has mean life 8×10^{-17}s. It decays by emitting electromagnetic radiation. Pions are strongly interacting bosons with zero spin. See also meson, elementary particle.

pirani gauge

a hot-wire vacuum gauge for measuring very low gas pressures as a function of the resistance of the hot filament.

pitch

the characteristic of sound that depends on its frequency. A shrill sound is of a high pitch and corresponds to a larger frequency. Low pitch notes have low frequency.

pitch of a screw

the distance between successive crests of the thread in a screw, measured parallel to the axis of the screw.

pitot tube

a double rube placed with one end in a stream of fluid, parallel to the flow, to measure fluid pressure. It has two openings. One is usually at the side, in the outer section of a double-walled tube, and measures static pressure, p. The other, in the inner section, faces the fluid flow and registers he total pressure. The other ends are connected to pressure-measuring devices. Pitot tubes can be used to measure fluid velocity. See Bernoulli effect.

planck

an old-fashioned unit of action equal to the product of energy of one joule and a time of one second.

planck's consant

symbol: h. It is a fundamental constant. It is the ratio of the energy (W) carried by a photon to its frequency (v). A basic relationship in the quantum theory of radiation has been W = hv. The value of h is 6.626 196 $\times 10^{-34}$ Js.

planck's radiation formula

an equation which expresses the variation of the intensity of black-body radiation with wavelength at a given temperature. It may be written as

$$J\lambda = \frac{c_1\lambda^{-5}}{e^{c2/\lambda T} - 1},$$

where Jλ is the energy per unit area per unit time at a certain wevelength λ, T is the absolute temperature, e is the base of natural logarithms, and c_1 and c_2 are constants.

planck's radiation law

the energy radiated per unit area per unit time per unit wavelength range at wavelength I from a black body at kelvin temperature T is given by

$El = 2pbc^2l^{-5}/[\exp(bc/lkT)-1]$

where b is the Planck constant, k the Boltzmann constant and c the speed of light in a vacuum.

plane of polarization

a plane perpendicular to the plane of vibration and containing the direction of propagation of light. It is also the plane containing the direction of progagation and the magnetic vector of the electromagnetic light wave.

plane polarization

a type of polarization of electromagnetic radiation, normally described with reference to a ray. In planepolarized radiation, the magnetic oscillations are all parallel and occur in one plane containing the ray. The electric oscillations are all parallel and occur in a plane containing the ray and at right angles to the plane containing the magnetic oscillations.

plane wave

a wave in which the wave fronts are everywhere parallel planes normal to the direction of propagation.

plane-concave lens

a lens having one face plane and the other concave.

plano-concave lens

a diverging lens wit one plane face and once concave face. See also lens.

plano-convex lens

a converging lens with one plane face and one convex face. See also lens.

plant factor

It is also known as capacity factor and is defined as the ratio of average power load of an electric power plant to its rated capacity.

plante cell

a primitive accumelator, consisting of rolled lead sheets dipping into dilute sulphuric acid.

plasma

a mixture of free electrons and ions or atomic nuclei. Plasmas occur in thermonuclear reactions, as in the Sun. The glowing region of ions and electrons in a discharge rube is also a plasma. Sometimes plasmas are referred to as a fourth state of matter.

plasma accelerator

an accelerator which produces a high-velocity collimated beam of plasma.

plasma gun

a device used to create and accelarate bursts of plasma.

plasmatron

a gas discharge tube in which the conducting path is provided by a plasma perviously generated, in the tube.

plasticity

the property of a substance not to return to its original shape and size when a deforming force has been removed.

platinum

a silvery-white malleable ductile transition metal. It occurs naturally either free or in association with other platinum metals. Platinum is used as a catalyst for ammonia oxidation (to make nitric acid) and in catalytic converters. It is also used in jewellery.

symbol: Pt; m.p. 1772^{0}C; b.p. 3830 $\pm$ 100^{0}C; r.d. 21.45 (20^{0}C); p.n. 78; r.a.m. 195.08.

plasticity

that property of a body by virtue of which it tends to retain its deformation without ruputure after removal of the applied deforming stress. The term defines the ease of deformation.

platinum black

a finely divided black form of platinum produced as a coating by evaporating platinum onto a surface in an intert atomosphere.

pneumatics

the branch of physics that deal with the dynamic properties of gases.

point contract transistor

a transistor having a base electrode and two or more point contact electrodes.

point source

a source of exactly spherical wave fronts. All sources can be considered to be point like if viewed from a large enough distance. The stars provide an obvious example.

poise

symbol: P a unit of dynamic viscosity in the c.g.s. system. It is equal to 0.1 n s m^{-2}.

poiseuille's formula

(Hagen's formula) an equation that describes the laminar flow of liquid through a pipe. The volume flow per second in a circular pipe of radius r and length l is given by:

$\pi r^4 \Delta p/8\eta l$

where Δp is the fluid pressure difference and n is its viscosity.

poisson ratio

symbol: v a measure of how a material changes shape when it is stretched. It is equal to minus the fractional change in cross-sectional area ($\Delta\alpha/\alpha$) divided by the fractional change in length ($\Delta l/l$). For many solids, including many metals, the value is about 0.3. It cannot exceed 0.5 for any material.

polar molecule

a molecule, the configuration of electric charge in which, constitutes a permanent dipole.

polarimeter (saccharimeter)

refers to a device which is used for measuring the angle of rotation of a plane-polarized beam caused by an optically active sample.

polarization

the term used for the restriction of the vibrations in a transverse wave so that the vibration takes place in a single plane.

polarization, angle of

the angle of reflection from a medium like glass, at which the reflected ray is completely polarized; the plane of vibration is at right angles to the plane of incidence.

polarization, electrolytic

changes in the characteristics of a voltaic cell when it produces large currents.

polarization, electric

the separation of the charges in the molecules of an insulator as an effect of an electric field. One face of an insulator in a field gains a net positive charge with the other becoming negative.

polarized light

light in which the transverse vibrations occur in a specific plane circularly or elliptically.

polarizer

an arrangement or instrument that produces plane polarized light from unpolarized light.

polaron

an exciton in a solid consisting of polar molecules resulting from the interaction between an electron and its strain field. The presence of a polaron can be detected by irregularities in the shape of the conduction band.

pole

refers to the geometric centre of a spherical reflecting or refracting surface. All distances from such reflecting or refracting surfaces are measured from the pole.

pole unit

a pole that when placed at a distance of one metre from a similar pole in vacuum, exerts a force of one newton on it.

polyatomic

describing a molecule that consists of several atoms. Examples are benzene and methane.

polychromatic radiation

electromagnetic radiation that has a mixture of different wavelengths.

polymorphism

the capability to exist in two or more crystalline forms.

positive column

a luminous region in an electric discharge in a gas near the positive electrode.

positive crystals

doubly refracting crystals in which the ordinary ray travels faster than extra-ordinary ray. Quartz is an example.

positive lens

a lens having positive focal length and power e.g. a convex lens.

positive mirror

a curved mirror with a positive power.

positive pole

a magnetic n-pole.

positive rays

refers to a stream of ions that are positively charged.

positron

the term used for the antiparticle of the electron; a paticle has been same mass as the electrons but with a positive charge. Positrons are found in cosmic-ray showers, where they result from pair production.

positronium

refers to an stable assembly of a positron and an electron. It decays into photons.

post office box

a box containing resistances that can be switched into the circuit, suitable for use as a whetstones bridge or potentiometer.

potassium-argon dating

a method of radioactive dating used for estimating the age of certain rocks. It is based on the decay of ^{40}K to ^{40}Ar (half-life 1.28×10^9 years). The technique is useful for time periods from 10^5 years ago back to the age of the Earth (4.6×10^9 years).

potential energy

energy possessed by a body by virtue of its position. The potential energy of a body of mass m raised through a height h is given by mgh.

potential induced

the potential acquired by a body due to the presence of another charged body in its neighbourhood. There is no transfer of charge to, or from, the body in question.

potentiometer

refers to an instrument which is used for measuring electrical potential differences by balancing two opposing potentials so that no current would be blowing through a galvanometer.

pound

a unit of mass, the pound is defined as 0.453 592 37 kilogrammes.

poundal

the f.p.s. unit of force. It is the force required to give a mass of one pound an acceleration of 1 foot per second 1 poundal = 0.138255 newton.

powder

symbol: P. The term used for a measure of the ability of a lens or mirror to converge a parallel beam, given by the reciprocal of the focal distance f.

$P = 1/f$

Generally, f has been in metres in which case P has been in dioptres (D).

powder metallurgy

the science or practice of manufacturing small metal articles by sintering powered metals under heat and pressure.

powder photography

a crystal diffraction method wherein the specimen is a randomly oriented crystalline power.

power

refers to work done per unit time. It is measured in watts. One watt is equal to 1 joule per sec.

power factor

it is the ratio of the total power, in watts, dissipated in an electric circuit to the volt amperes applied to the circuit.

power of lens

reciprocal of the focal length of a lens, expressed in metres.

power reactor

a nuclear reactor designed to produce useful quantities of electric power.

power transistor

a transistor designed to handle relatively high power, up to 100 watts, or to give a relatively high undistorted power gain,. Such transistor usually require cooling.

poynting vector

symbol: S the vector product of the electric field vector E and the magnetic field vector H (=B_0/m_0) in an electromagnetic wave. The poynting vector gives, in magnitude and direction, the power radiated through unit area at any instant. The unit is the watt per square meter. In a simple harmonic wave, the average value is ½E_0H_0, where E_0 and H_0 are the amplitudes.

practical units

ampere, volt and ohm are known as the practical units of current, potential difference and resistance respectively.

precession

when a body is rotating about an axis, it is said to preces if the axis of rotation moves around another axis at an angle to it.

presbyopia

a defect of vision wherein the person is unable to see near objects, generally occurs in older people. It can be corrected by using convex lenses. Also known as long sightedness.

pressure

sumbol: p. The pressure on a surface due to forces from another surface or from a fluid has been referred to as the force acting at 90^0 to unit area of the surface: pressure = force/area. The unit has been the pascal (Pa).

pressure broadening

the increase in the width of a spectral line resulting from collisions between atoms or molecules. It relates to pressure as there are more collisions at high pressure.

pressurre gauge

an instrument for measuring fliud pressure, such as a barometer or manometer. See barometer, Bourdon gauge, manometer.

pressure melting

the process of melting of ice due to applied pressure is called pressure melting.

pressure of the atmosphere

may be defined as pressure at a point near the Earth's surface due to the weight of air above that point. It value varies around about 100 kPa (100 000 newtons per square metre).

pressurized water reactor

a neclear reactor in which water,

used as moderator, coolant, and reflector, is kept under pressure to prevent it from boiling at the operating temperature.

preston's rule

in the anomalous zeeman effect, lines of the same series show the same pattern.

prevost's theory of exchanges

this theory states that all bodies emit and absorb radiation continuously. The rate of emission is dependant on the body's surface and its temperature.

primary cell

it converts chemical energy into electrical energy. The chemical reactions that take place in the cell are irreversible e.g. daniel cell.

primary colours

refers to a set of three coloured lights that when mixed together in the right proportions, yield the sensation of white. Normally the hues have been selected from the red, green, and blue regions.

primary fuel cell

a specially designed fuel cell in which the fuel and oxidant are continuously consumed.

principal axis

the line joining the centres of curvature of the faces of a lens, or the line normal to a reflector at the pole.

principle focus

principle focus of a lens or spherical mirror is the point of convergence of light coming from a source situated at an infinite distance.

principle of cathode ray oscilloscope

the path of a charged particle in transverse electric field is a parabola.

principle of moments

for any system in equilibrium, the sum of the clockwise moments is equal to the sum of the anti-clockwise moments.

principle of superposition

when two identical waves pass through a given region, the amplitude at any point in the region is equal to the algebraic sum of the amplitudes due to each wave.

principle points

the points on the principle axis of a lens system where the principle planes cut the axis.

principle of moments

if an object or system has been in equilibrium, the sum of the moments in any direction would be equal to the sum of the moments in the opposite direction.

principle of superposition

when two (or more) waves of the same type pass through the same region, the amplitude of vibration at any point is the algebraic sum of the individual amplitudes. Sign crest or trough, i.e. positive or negative) must be taken into account. The waves emerge from the region of superposition unaffected. See also interference.

printed circuit

refers to a circuit that has been constructed as an entity on an insulating board without the need for connecting wires, conducting film.

prismatic optical instruments

instruments in which a right angled prism is used to invert the inverted image produced by the objective.

prisms, optical

a tringular block of glass made of a material transparent to light. It forms an important component of a number of optical systems. It is generally used to disperse light into its constituent colours and produce a spectrum.

probability distribution of electrons

the probability that an electron within an atom will be at a certain point in space at a given time. Determined by the magnitude of the square of the wave function.

projectile

refers to an objects which is falling freely in a gravitational field, having been projected at a speed case that $\theta = 90^0$, the motion has been linear in the vertical direction.

projectors

optical arrangements able to produce a large real image on a screen.

promethium

a radioacgtive element of the lanthanoid series of metals. It is not found naturally on Earth but can be prodeced artificially by the fission of uranium. It is used i some miniature batteries.

Symbol: Pm; m.p. 1168°C; b.p. 2730°C (approx.); r.d. 7.22 (20°C); p.n. 61; stablest isotope ^{145}Pm (half-life 18 years).

prompt neutron

a neutron produced in a reactor by primary fission and not by decay of a fission product.

proof plane

a small shaped piece of foil with an insulating handle, used to investigate the distribution of change on the surface of an object.

propagation

the transmission of energy in the form of waves, such as light, radio waves, and other forms of electromagnetic radiation, and sound,.

propagation loss

the transmission loss suffered by radiant energy.

proportinal counter

a device in which the number of ions produced by an ionizing radiation is counted by measuring the height of the electric pulse produced by it.

proportional counter

a counter for ionizing radiation in which the potential difference applied is high enough for multiplication of ions, so that the height of the pulse is proportional to the number of ions produced by the particle, and thus to its energy loss. A counter used in this way is said to be i the proportional region.

proton

an elementary particle with a positive charge (+1.602 192 $\times$ 10^{-19} C) and rest mass 1.672 614 $\times$ 10^{-27} kg. Protons are nucleons, found in all nuclides. They are fermions with spin ½showing strong interactions. See also elementary particles.

proton number

the number of protons present in the nucelus of an atom. It is equal to the number of electrons in an atom.

proton-proton chain reaction

a series of nuclear fusion reactions by which hydrogen is converted into helium. It is thought that the reactions are responsible for energy production in the Sun and similar stars. There are in fact three possible sequences. The main one is:

$$^{1}H + {}^{1}H \rightarrow {}^{2}H + v + e^{+}$$

$$^{2}H + {}^{1}H \rightarrow {}^{3}He + g$$

$$^{3}He + {}^{3}He \rightarrow {}^{4}He + 2{}^{1}H$$

The two other sequences lead to ^{4}He also, through ^{7}Li and ^{8}Be.

proton storm

the storm of protons sent into space by a solar flare.

protostar

a developing star consisting of condensing interstellar gas and dust.

psychrometer

a hygrometer wherein strong draught is obtained past the wet and dry bulbs either by whirling on a sling or by a fan.

p-type conductivity

conductivity in a semi-conductor due to flow of holes.

p-type semi-conductor

an extrinsic semiconductor wherein the density of mobile holes is more than that of conduction electrons.

pulley

a class of machine. In any pulley system power is transferred through the tension in a string wound over one or more wheels. The force ratio and distance ratio depend on the relative arrangement of strings and wheels. Efficiency is not usually very high as work must be done to overcome friction in the strings and the wheel bearings, and to lift and moving wheels. There are two types of single pulley system. In the diagram, T is string tension; in each case it is assumed that efficiency is 100%. See illustration, p. 175.

pupil

refers to aperture of the eye. It is adjustable in size and generally appears black.

pyrheliometer

it is an instrument for measuring the intensity of direct solar radiation.

pyro-electricity

the characteristics of certain crystals, e.g., tourmaline, of acquiring electric charges on opposite faces when the crystals are heated.

pyroelectric effect

certain crystals develop electric charges when they are heated or cooled.

pyrolysis

chemical decomposition by the action of heat.

pyrometer

an instrument for measuring very high temperatures, by measuring the radiation emitted by the body.

pyrometry

the branch of physics which deals with the measurement of high temperatures.

pyrotechincs

fire-works.

q band

a radio-frequency range verying from 36 gigahertz to 46 gigahertz is known as q band.

quadrant

an instrument which can accurately measure angles upto 90 degree or more.

quadrant electrometer

it is a type of electrometer wherein a light foil covered vane, supported by a quartz fibre, moves within a hollow quadarntal segment of a cylindrical metal box. The opposite quadrants are connected together, but insulated from the case of the instrument. A mirror is carried to reflect a of light and measures deflecting of the vane

quadrature

periodic quantities having the same frequency and waveform are said to be in quadrature if they differ in phase by 90 degree, i.e. one wave reaches its maximum value when the other passes through zero.

quadripole

an electrical network that has only four terminals and a impedances presented at the terminals at specified frequency.

qualitative

pertains to quality or qualities.

quality

of a sound depends on the coexistence with the fundamental or other vibrations of various frequencies and amplitudes.

quality control

it is a system for verifying and maintaining a desired level of quality in a product or process by careful planning continued inspection and corrective action when required.

quality of sound

the characteristic of a musical note that is determined by the frequencies present. It enables a listermined by the frequencies present. It enables a listener to the difference between two notes of the same fundamental frequency played on different musical instruments. A pure tone has no overtones present and its waveforms, and it can be shown that these are formed by mixing a pure tone (the fundamental) with different higher frequencies. These frequencies are simple multiples of the fundamental frequency (f); i.e. 2f, 3f, and so on. The fundamental together with the 'overtones' are harmonics of the note; the different contributions characterize its quality.

quantifier

it refers to an expression which indicates the quantity of a proposition.

quantity

a particular, indefinite amount.

quantized

a physical quantity is said to be quantized if it can have only certain discrete value and cannot change continuously. The difference between successive discrete values are often known as quantum jumps.

quantum

a definite amount of energy released or absorbed in a process. Energy often behaves as if it were 'quantized' in this way. The quantum of electromagnetic radiation is the photon. See also photoelectric effect.

quantum electrodynamics

the use of quantum to describe how particles and electromagnetic radiation interact.

quantum electronics

the study of the amplification or generation of microwave power in solid crystals, on the basis of the laws of quantum mechanics.

quantum jump

a sudden change in the energy level of an atom or molecule, accompained by the emission or absorption of a quantum or quanta of radiant energy.

quantum mechanics

a physical theory dealing with atomic structure and phenomena subject to quantum conditions. It is based largely on Heisenberg's uncertainty principle, embraces also his matrix mechanics, Schrodinger's wave mechanics and also the transformation theory of Dirac and Jordan.

quantum number

these are integral or half integral numbers used to specify the state of a system in quantum mechanics. A set of these numbers describes an energy level of a particle or system of particles.

quantum state

a state of a physical system, such as a crystal or an atom, specifying the condition of its constituent particles and defined by a unique set of quantum numbers.

quantum statistics

a statistical description of a system of particles that obeys the rules of quantum mechanics rather than classical mechanics. In quantum statistics, energy states are considered to be quantized; if the particles are treated as indistinguishable, Bose–Einstein statistics apply and the particles are called bosons. All known bosons have an angular momentum nh, where n is zero or an integer and h is the Planck constant.

quantum theory

a mathematical theory originally inroduced by Max Planck (1900) to explain the black-body radiation from hot bodies. Quantum theory is based on the idea that energy (or certain other physical quantities) can be changed only in certain discrete amounts for a given system. Other early applications were the explanations of the photoelectric effect and the Compton effect, and the Bohr theory of the atom.

quark

hypothetical fundamental particle(s) which are postulated to be building blocks of elementary particles.

quarter-wave

the term is used in electromagnetism and is associated with an electrical length of one quarter wavelength.

quarter-wave plate

a plate of mica or some other birefringent crystal material of such thickness as to introduce a phase difference of one-quarter cycle between the ordinary and extraordinary rays resulting from the double refraction of light.

quartz

it is a double refracting crystal, optical uniaxial and positive and rotating the plane of polarization to the left or right according to the variety, and to different extents for different colours. It transmits wavelengths between 180-4000 nm.

quartz clock

a clock based on a piezoelectric crystal of quartz. Each quartz crystal has natural frequency of vibration, which depends on its size and shape. If such a crystal is introduced into an oscillating electronic circuit that resonated at a frequency very close to that of the natural frequency of the crystal, the whole circuit (including the crystal) will oscillate at the crystal's natural frequency and the frequency will remain constant over considerable periods (a good crystal will maintain oscillation for a year with an accumulated error of less than 0.1 second). In a quartz clock or watch the alternating current from the oscillating circuit containing such a crystal is amplified and the frequency subdivided until it is suitable to drive a synchronous motor, which in turn drives a gear train to operate hands. Alternatively it is used to activate a digital display.

quasar

the strange objects in the sky which look like stars but are not stars, have come to be known as "quasi-stellar sources" or "qss". This name is shortened to quasar.

quench frequency

the number of times per second a circuit is made to start and stop oscillatiors.

quenching

the process of stopping the discharge in a Geiger counter by preventing re-ignition.

quenching of metal

rapid cooling by immersion into water or oil to harden the metal

quick effect

a substance of high magnetic susceptibility tends to move into the strong region of a magnetic field. Similarly, a substance of high dielectric constant tends to move into a strong electric field.

quiescent current

the current flowing in the circuit under conditions of zero applied signal.

q.value

amount of the energy given out in a nuclear reactor. It is generally expressed as me v/ reaction.

r.f. heating

a general term which includes industrial induction or dielectric heating, particularly when the frequency of the alternating field is above about 25 kilo hertz.

racemic mixture

a mixture that contains equal amounts of the dextrorotatory and leverotatory forms of an optically active substance; the mixture is not optically active. See optical activity.

rack

it is a bar that is provided with teeth on one of its sides, adapted to engage with the teeth of a pinion or the like, s for converting circular into rectilinear motion or vice–versa.

rad

it is a unit of absorbed dose of ionizing. It may be defined as being equivalent to an absorption of 10^{-2} joule of energy in one kilogram of material.

radar

an acronym for radio direction and ranging. A system for the precise location of distant object (especially ships and aircraft) by means of radio. A microwave radio beam is transmitted, reflected by the distant object, and received on return to the transmitted, reflected by the distant object, and received on return to the transmitter. The directional antenna points in the direction of the object, the distance of wich is calculated from the time of travel of the wave at the speed of electromagnetic waves, 3×10^8 m s-1. Alternative the beam can be made to scan in continuous circles, and so locate all objects in any direction, the locations being plotted on a plan position indicator (PPI), a cathode-ray tube with a rotating time base. See also radio.

radar beacon

it is a radio device that is fixed at a location. It is used as a navigational aid.

radar camera

also known as radarscope. It is a specially designed camera which is used to photograph images on a radar-scope.

radar mile

the term is associated with the time, for a radar pulse to travel from the radar to a target 1.61 km distant and return, and equals 10.75 micro seconds.

radar range

the maximum distance upto which any radar is generally effective in detecting objects.

radialucent

the term is associated with a material which is transparently to x-rays and radiowaves.

radian

si unit of angle 1 radian = 57.296 degree.

radian efficiency

of an aerial; the ratio of the power radiated to the total power supplied to the aerial at a given frequency.

radiance

symbol le. In a given direction, the radiant intensity of a source of radiation per unit area projected at right angles to the direction. The unit is the watt per steradian per square metre.

radiant energy

energy that is transmitted in the form of radiation, particularly electromagnetic radiation. Radiant energy is the only form in which energy can exist in the absence of matter.

radiant flux

the time rate of flow of radiant energy is called radiant flux.

radiant hazard

the potential danger to health resulting from exposure to ionizing radiation or the consumption of radioactive substance.

radiant heat

heat emitted from a body in the form of electromagnetic radiation. At low temperatures it is nearly all in the infrared region but at a few thousand degrees the amount visible light becomes important, and at the radiating temperature of the Sun (6000K) ultraviolet is becoming significant. The fact that sunlight was part of the heat radiation of the Sun was discovered by Herschel (1800). See also black body.

radiant intensity

symbole i. the radiant flux from a point source per unit solid angle. The unit is the watt per steradian.

radiant potential

resonance potential. The energy necessary to transfer an electron from its normal position in an atom to some other possible position; i.e. to an energy level of greater energy.

radiant power

the raduant flux, i.e., the amount of radiant energy emitted, per second.

radiation

transmission of energy either as a wave or as a stream of moving particles, like x-rays or B-particles etc. The term generally refers to electromagnetic radiation.

radiation cerenkov

the visible light produced when charged particles e.g., a beam of electrons, travel through a transparent medium with velocity exceeding that of light in the medium.

radiation cloud

the term is associated with a given mass of vapours in the atmosphere carrying radioactive debris from a nuclear explosion.

radiation collision

a collision between charged particles in which part of the kinetic energy is converted into electromagnetic radiation.

radiation cooling

the process of cooling of gases to very low temperature by means of the resonant radiation pressure of intense laser light is called radiation cooling.

radiation damage

structural defectors arising from exposure to radiation.

radiation laws

refer to the physical laws expressing certain general basic principles obeyed by phenomena or radiation. The most important of these laws are Kirchhoffs law, Stefan-Boltzmann law. Planck's radiation formula and Wein's law.

radiation loss

that part of the transmission loss, due to radiation, of radio-frequency power supplied to aerial at a given frequency.

radiation monitoring

the process of continuous determination of the amount of radiation present in given area.

radiation physics

the branch of physics which deals which the study of ionizing radiation and its effects on matter.

radiation pressure

refers to pressure exerted on a surface when an electromagnetic radiation falls on it.

radiation pyrometer

an instrument which makes use of the heating effect of radiant power impinging on a detector such as a thermopile, bolometer, or thermocouple, to measure the temperature of the radiant source. For visible radiation a photo-electric device may be used.

radiation sicknes

illness caused by exposure to intoxing radiation. Initial system symptom are vomiting and diarrhoea, following in some cases by leukaemia.

radiation survey meters

instuments for the detection measurement of radiation, operating principally on the ionization-chamber or electroscope principle.

radiation therapy

treatment of a disease with any type of radiation.

radiative collision

a collision which takes place between two charged particles and from which electromagnetic radiation is emitted.

radio

the science, technique and process of communication by means of radio waves.

radio astronomy

the study of astronomical bodies and events by the rediowaves which they emit.

radio element

the term is associated with a radioactive isotope of an element.

radio emission

the phenomenon of emission of radio-frequency electromagnetic radiations by oscillating charges or currents.

radio energy

the amount of energy associated with a radio-frequency electromagnetic radiation.

radio frequency

refers to the frequency of electromagnetic radiation in the range 10 kilohertz to 1,00,000 megahertz.

radioactive

one which shows radioactivity.

radioactive age

the age of a geological or an archeological specimen as calculated by radioactive dating.

radioactive dating

a method of measuring the age of a specimen using the principles of radioactivity. See carbon dating.

radioactive debris

any radioactive substances carried through the air from the site of nuclear explosion.

radioactive series

a series of isotopes each of which after the first is the decay product of the previous one. The last member of the series, is stable.

radioactive tracer

a small quantity of radioactive isotope in a form suitable for following biological, chemical, or other process.

radiobalance

an instrument wherein the heating due to the absorption of radiation is neutralized by the cooling due to the peltier effect at one in junction of a thermocouple.

radiograph

a photographic image formed as a result of differential absorption of penetrating radiation.

radioisotope

refers to radioactive isotope of an element.

radioisotope

the radioactive isotopes of an element. Tritiume, for instance is a radioisotope of hydrogen.

radiology

the science and applications of radiation applied to radiotheraphy.

radioluminescence

the process of the emission of visible electromegnetic radiation from a radioactive substance.

radiolysis

the process of the chemical decomposition of material into ions, excited atoms and molecules, etc. by ionizing radiation.

radiometer

an instrument for measuring radiation in energy or power units. The term is generally used for instrument that detect and measure infrared radiation.

radiosonde

a balloon-borne instrument for the simultaneous measurement and transmission of meteorological data.

radium

a highly radioactive element discovered by curies in 1898. It is about a million times as radioactive as uranium. Radium salts are used to cure cancer by killing diseased tissues at a fast rate.

radius of curvature

of a mirrors or lens. The radius of the sphere of which the mirror or lens surface is part.

rainbow

means the splitting of sunlight into a spectrum of colours by droplets of water suspended in the air due to refraction and internal reflection of sunlight by them.

raman effect

the scattering of monochromatic light as it passed through a transparent medium. Interaction with the molecules of the medium case the light to be scattered, with some at wavelengths above and below that of the incident light.

randio luminescence

emission of light due to radiation from radioactive substances.

random cycle

a steam engine cycle, characterized by the introduction of water at boiler pressure by a pump, evaporation, adiabatic expansion to condenser pressure and condensation the initial point.

random sample

a sample taken in such a way that every individual object, or component comprising the group, set, or mass to be sampled, has an equal probability of forming part of the sample.

random walk

a concept applied to Brownian movement and diffusion based on the idea of finding the distance a walker is from a starting point if he or she can walk forward or backward, making the choices entirely randomly. After taking N steps, the average distance from the starting point is $\sqrt{N}$.

rankine efficiency

the efficiency of an ideal engine working under a rankine cycle.

rankine temperature scale

a scale of temperature with the freezing point of water as 491.7 degree and the boiling point of water as 671.7 degree at normal pressure.

raoult's law

at a particular temperature, the relative lowering in vapor pressure of a solution is proportional to the mole fraction of the solute dissolved in it. The law is true only for ideal solutions.

rarefaction

low pressure and low density regions in a medium obtained during the propagation of logitudinal waves, the distance between two successive rarefactions gives the wavelength of the wave.

raster

in television, a predetermined pattern of scanning lines which provides substantially unifor coverage of the area to be televised.

rationalized units

a system of units in which the equations have a logical form related to the shape of the system. Si units form a rationalised system of units.

ray

the rectilinear path adopted by a narrow beam of light to any other type of radiation.

ray diagrams

accurate or approximate diagrams showing how selected rays pass through an optical system. The rays are selected on the basis of known behaviour.

rayleigh criterion

two patterns of equal intensity may be resolved when the central maximum of one pattern falls over the first minimum of the other.

rayleigh's law

in magnetic materials subjected to magnetic forces low in comparison with the maximum coercive force, the hysteresis loss in a cycle changes directly as the cube of the eduction.

reactance

symbol: X a measure of the opposition of inductance or capacitance to alternating current. Reactance is the ratio of the peak voltage to the peak current. Like resistance it is measured in ohms; it causes the current to become out of phase with the voltage. Reactance depends on the frequency of the supply.

reacting force

according to Newton's third law of motion, when a body exerts a force on a second body, the second body exerts an equal and opposite force on the first the force exerted by the first body on the second is the acting force, and that exerted by the second one on the first is the reacting force.

reaction

if an abject a exerts a force on an object b, b exerts an equal and opposite force on s, this force being called the reaction.

reactive load

the load wherein the current and the voltage at the terminals are out of phase with each other.

reactor

an electrical apparatus possessing reactance used because of that property.

rearrangement reaction

a nuclear reaction in which nucleons are exchanged between nuclei.

recoil electron

an electron that has been set into motion by a collision.

rectifier

a device which lets the current flow through it in one direction only. It can thus be used to convert a.c. into d.c. A diode valve, a p-n junction, are common devices used as a rectifier.

rectilinear propagation

passage of radiation in straight lines in a constant medium.

rectillinear scanning

in television, a process of scanning an area in a predetermined sequence of narrow, straight, parallel strips.

red gaint

a type of cool gaint star that emits light in the red region of the spectrum. A star expands to a red gaint when it exhausts its nuclear fuel.

red shift

due to doppler effect, refers to the shift spectrum lines in the spectra of some celestial objects towards the red one of the visible spectrum is an increase in wave length of the lines.

reduced pressure

the ratio of the pressure of a substance to its critical pressure.

reflectance

a measure of the extent to which a surface is capable of reflecting radiation; defio of the intensity of the reflected radiation to the intensity of the incident radiation.

reflecting angle of

angle of a reflection.

reflecting, laws of

the angle of incidence and the angle of reflection are equal. The incident ray, the reflected ray and the normal all lie in the same plane.

reflecting microscope

a microscope in which a pair of concave and convex mirrors replaces the objective lines system.

reflecting power

the ratio of the amount of energy reflected to the among of energy falling on a body per unit time is known as its reflecting power.

reflecting telescope

it is a telscope using a concave mirror as an object glass. These telescopes are free from may a defects such as chromatic abberation etc. which are quite Common in refracting telescope generally used by astronomers.

reflection

the phenomena in which the light falling on a boundary separating two media is sent back into the first medium.

refraction, law of

two law that apply whenever any radiation is refracted, whatever the circumstances. In order to state the laws, the normal is defined — the perpendicular to the surface at the point of refraction. All angles named are measured from the normal.

(1) The refracted ray is in the same plane as the incident ray and the normal.
(2) the sine of the angle of incidence divided by the sine of the angle of refraction is constant for a given wavelength and a given pair of media; the angles lie on opposite sides of the normal.

reflection total internal

total internal reflection.

reflectivity

symbol; a p. The reflectance of a layer of material sufficiently thick that no change of reflectance would take place with increase in thickness.

reflectometer

an instrument which measures the ratio of the reflected electromagnetic energy to the incident energy at a reflecting surface or discontinuity.

reflector

relative density

the density of a substance as compared to the density of water at 4 degree c. Ratio of these two densities.

relative density bottle

a small glass bottle provided with a perforated stopper. It is used for determination of relative density of liquids.

The weight of the empty bottle is found = m_1
The weight of bottle + liquid upto the graduated mark is found =m_2
The weight of bottle + water up to the graduated mark is found =m_3

Then relative density = $\frac{m_2 - m_1}{m_3 - m_1}$

$= \frac{\text{Weight of certain volume of liquid}}{\text{Weight of same volume of water}}$

relative frequency

it is the ratio of the number of times any event occurs as compared to the number of occasions on which it might occur in the same period.

relative humidity

it is ratio of the amount of water vapour present in the air to the amount of maximum amount of water vapour the air could hold at that temperature.

relative molecular mass

symbol: M_r the ratio of average mass per molecule of the naturally occurring from of an element or compound to 1/12 of the mass of an atom of nuclide ^{12}C. This was formerly called molecular weight. It does not have to be used only for compounds that have discrete molecules; for ionic compounds and giant-molecular structures the formula in it is used.

relativistic mass

the mass of an object moving with a velocity v is given by:

where m_o is the rest mass of the same object.

relativistic velocity

any velocity that is sufficiently high to make the mass of an object significantly greater than its rest mass.

relativistic, particle

a travelling with a velocity close to the velocity of light say greater than 0.1 c, c, being the velocity of light.

relaxation time

time required to reduce stresses to 1/e of their original values.

relay

it is as device that is used to produce a change in the electric condition of another circuit by change of current or voltage in one circuit. Generally a relay consista of an electromagnet and an armature.

reluctance

the ratio of magnetomotive force to magnetic flux in a magnetic circuit. Its si unit is henry/metre.

reluctivity

the reciprocal of permeability.

rem

a unit of ionizing radiation. It is defined as that amount of radiation which will produce the same damage to human beings as 1 roentgen of high voltage x-rays.

rep

a unit of ionizing radiation. It is equal to the amount of ionizing radiation which causes absorption of 93 ergs/gm of some soft tissue.

report

the term is used in acoustics and refers to a sharp explosive sound.

resistance box

a device for providing variable known resistances. One type has a thick brass bar with gaps at intervals across which are connected fixed resistance. Combinations of these resistances can be chosen by inserting brass plugs in the gaps, thus shorting out selected resistors. Other types of resistance box have multi-switches to give the selection.

resistance, electrical

symbol: R the ratio of the potential difference across an electrical element to the current in it. Resistance measures the opposition of the component to the flow of charge. In an alternating-current circuit resistance is only one factor in the response of the component. See impedance. See also effective resistance, Ohm's law.

resistance furnace

a furnace in which the heat is generated by the internal ohmic resistance of the furnace.

resistance thermometer

a thermometer that measures temperature by the change in electrical resistance of a conductor. Usually a small coil of pure fine platinum wire is used, wound on a mica former. It is incorporated into one arm of a Whetstone bridge; the other arm has a variable resistor and a pair of 'dummy' leads, to compensate for temperature effects in the leads of the measuring coil.

The resistance varies with temperature according to an approximate equation of the form:

$$R = R_0(1 + aq)$$

where R is the resistance at q^0C, R_0 the resistance at 0^0C, and a is a constant.

More strictly:

$$R = R_0(1 + aq + bq^2)$$

where b is a second constant.

resistance wire

wire used to introduce a resistance into an electrical circuit. Resistance wire is made from alloys.

resistance, electrical

refers to the ratio of the potential difference across the ends of a conductor to the current flowing through it. For a conductor, it has been found to be directly proportional to the length and inversely to the area of the conductor.

resistive unbalance

the term is associated with the unequal resistance in the two wires of a transmission line.

resistivity

the resistance of a material of unit length and of unit area of cross section p is called the resistivity of material. It is measured in ohm-metre.

resistor

a component included in an electric circuit because of its resistance. Resistors may be variable or have a fixed value; they are made of resistance wire or carbon.

resistor core

the term is associated with an insulating support upon which a resistor element is wound.

resolution

the ability to distinguish two close objects separately, rather than as one single object.

resolution of vectors

the division of vector into components, usually at right angles to each other.

resolving power

a measure of the ability of an optical system to form detectable separate images of close objects or to separate close wavelengths of radiation.

resonance

a large amplitude vibration of an

oscillating object on being subjected to impulses at its natural frequency.

resonance bridge

an ac bridge in which the balance is a function of resonance of a circuit.

resonant resistance

the resistance value to which a resonant circuit is equivalent.

resonator

a system or device in .vhich some physical quantity can be made to oscillate by the oscillations in another system e.g., cavity resonator.

rest energy

the energy equivalent of the rest mass of a body generally expressed in electron volts.

rest mass

the mass of an object a measured by an object at rest with respect to the observer.

restitution, coefficient of

the ratio of the relative velocity of two colliding bodies immediately after collision to their relative velocity before collision.

resultant

a vector which has the same effect as number of vectors, is called resultant of all these vectors.

retardation

an alternative name of negative acceleration.

retardation plate

a thin transparent plate cut from a piece of birefringent material parallel to the optic axis.

retentivity

of a magnetic material; the property measured by the residual induction corresponding to the saturation induction for the material.

retina

it is inner surface of the eye where normal eye-lens forms an inverted image of the object.

reverberatio

persistence of sound even after the source is not emitting any sound.

reverberation time

it is the time required, from the moment of cessation of a sound for the intensity to drop by 60 db; viz, to on millionth of its original value.

reynold's number

a dimensionless quantity which determines whether the flow of a liquid through a cylindrical tube will be streamline or turbulent flow.

rhenium

a rare silvery transition metal that usually occurs naturally with molybdenum. The metal is chemiscally similar to manganese and is used in alloys and catalysts. Sumbol: Re; m.p. 3180°C; b.p. 5630°C; r.d. 21.02 (20°C); p.n. 75; r.a.m. 186.207.

rheology

the study of the deformation and flow of matter.

rheometer

an instrument used to measure the flow properties of solid materials by investigating the relationship between stress, strain and time.

rheostat

a variable resistor generally a coil wound over a cylindrical block. The resistance is changed by sliding a contact on the coil.

rhombhedral

crystals with three equal axes which are not at right angles.

rhs value

root mean square value.

ribbo microphone

a microphone in which the moving conductor is in the form of a ribbon directly driven by sound waves.

rigid body

a body in which the distance between every pair of particles remains constant under the action of force.

ripple tank

a device for producing waves on the surface of water and viewing these under stroboscopes light. It is used to demonstrate interference effects and other wave properties.

ritz formula

it is used in atomic physics in studying the spectra of atoms and involves the expansion of spectra equation

rochon prism

a birefrigent electro-optical crystal which divides incident unpolarized optical beam into two polarized components.

rods

the more sensitive cells of the retina of the eye. They are of most importance in vision in poor light, but cannot provide colour information.

roengten rays

x-rays.

rontgen

a measure of the ionizing effect of r or x-rays in air. A rontgen is the quantity of radiation which produces, in 0.001293 gramme of air ions carrying 1 e.s.u. of positive or negative charges.

root-mean square value

r.m.s. value of an alternating current is the value of the direct current that would produce the same heating effect as that produced by the given a.c.

root-mean-square velocity

the square root of the mean square velocity.

rotameter

a device that measures the rate of flow of fluids.

rotator

a rigid rotator is a particle of mass m, rotating in space at a constant distance from a fixed centre.

rotor

refers to the rotating part of an electric motor, dynamo or generator. Also known as armature.

rowland circle

a circle having the radius of curvature of a concave diffraction grating as diameter. If a slit is placed any where on the circumference of the circle, spectra are formed in exact focus also on the circumference.

rubidium-strontium dating

refers to a method of radioactive dating which is used for esimating the age of certain rocks. It has been based on the decay of ^{87}Rb to ^{87}Sr (half-life 5 $\times 10^{10}$ years).

rutherford

the quantity of any radioactive substance which has decay rate of 10 distiegrations per second.

rydbridge-schuster law

the difference of the wave-numbers of the limit of the principle series and the common limit of the diffuse and sharp series in alkali spectra is equal to the wave-number of the first line of the principle series.

rydbridge spectrum

refers to an absorption spectrum of a gas taken with ultraviolet radiation and used for determining ionization potential.

saccharimeter

an apparatus for determining the concentration of sugar solution by measuring the angle of rotation of the plane of vibration of polarized light passing through a tube containing the solution.

saccharometer

a fermentation tube used for the determination of the concentration of sugar solutions by ascertaining their density.

safety lamp

it is a lamp used by miner's to prevent immediate ignition of explosive gases.

safety value

it refers to the valve which opens to free confined gases or vapours exceeding a safe pressure.

salinometer

a kind of hydrometer used for estimation of concentration of salt solutions by measuring their density.

samarium

a silvdry element of thelanthanoid series of metls. It occurs in association with other lanthanoids. Samarium is used in the metallurgical, glass, and a nuclear industries.

sampling

a method of measuring only some portions of a signal, the resultant values are taken as representative of the whole. The rate of a sampling of a periodic quantity must be at least double the frequency.

sand paper

a strong paper coated on its surface wit a layer of sand such a paper is used for smoothing or polishing.

satellites

bodies which rotate in orbits around other bodies of greater mass under the influence of their mutual gravitational field. Particularly bodies, or moons, which rotate around planets, e.g. the moon is satellite of earth.

saturated vapour pressure

the pressure exerted by a saturated vapour.

saturation

the freedom from white of a colour. A pure spectral colour is a hue, and is said to be unsaturated. Unsaturated colours are tints; i.e., hues mixed with white.

saturation, magnetic

a magnetic material is saturated if it can be magnetized no more strongly. This can easily be explained using the domain theory.

sawtooth wave

a waveform generated electronically (such as the variation of voltage with time), having a uniform increase that regularly and rapidly drops to the initial value. A sawtooth wave is used as the time base for scanning circuits in a cathode-ray tube.

scalar

a quantity that can be defined by magnitude only e.g. volume, mass, density etc.

scalar function

a function of position and time which has a scalar value at each point.

scalar product

a multiplication of two vectros to give a scalar. The scalar product of A and B is defined by A.B = AB cosq, where A and B are the magnitudes of A and B and q is the angle between the vectors. An example is a force F displaced s. Here the scalar product is energy transferred (or work done):

W = F.s

W = Fscosq

where q is the angle between the line of action of the force and the displacement. A scalar product is sometimes called a dot product. See also vector product.

scanning

the process of exploring an area in a methodical manner so as to produce a electrical output that varies in time and is proportinal to the magnitude of the information scanned. The technique is used in television and radar.

scatter

to refract or diffract light or other electromagnetic radiation, irregularly so as to diffuse it in different directions.

scattering

refers to the 'spreading out' of a beam of radiation as it passes through matter, decreasing the energy moving in the original direction.

scattering coefficient

a measure of attenuation due to scattering of radiation as it traverses a medium containing scattering parties. This is also called total scattering coefficient.

scattering loss

part of the electromagnetic transmission power loss due to scattering in the medium or to roughness in the reflecting surface.

schlieren technique

the term used for a method of studying turbulent flow by high-speed photography.

schmidt optics

it refers to the optical system that is used in wide-field cameras and are reduced to a minimum by means of a spherical miror that is provided wit a corrective plate near its focus.

schottky noise

in the thermionic tubes; the variation of the output current resulting from the random emissio from the cathode in the spacecharge limited current state.

schrodinger's cat

a though experiment first put forward by Erwin Schrodinger. In quantum mechanics, a particle is described by a wave function, which expresses the probability of finding it in a particular region of space and time. He suggested a closed box containing a sample of radioactive material, a tube of cyanide, and a cat. The apparatus was to be constructed so that decay of a nucleus ejected a particle, which activated a mechanism to break the tube of cyanide. After a certain time, if a nucleus had decayed the would have died; if not the cat would still be alive.

schrodinger's wave equation

$$\frac{\partial^2 \varphi}{\partial x^2} + \frac{\partial^2 \varphi}{\partial y^2} + \frac{\partial^2 \varphi}{\partial z^2} + \frac{8\pi^2 m}{h}(E - V) = 0$$

Where φ is wave function, E is total energy and V is potential energy associated with wave.

schuler pendulum

a useful apparatus in navigation. It is an apparatus, which swings because of gravity, with a natural period of 84.4 minutes.

schwartzchild radius

a critical radius of a body of given as that must be exceeded if light is to escape from that body. It is equal to 2 GM/C^2, where G is the gravitational constant, c is the speed of light, and M is the mass of the body. If the body collapses to such an extent that its radius is less than the Schwartzchild radius the escape velocity becomes equal to the speed of light and the object becomes a black hole. The Schwartzchild radius is then the radius of the hole's event horizon.

science

it is the branch of knowledge that is concerned with the study of facts or truths systematically arranged.

scientific method

a research method where in a problem is identified, data collected, a hypothesis formulated and it is then experimentally verified.

scintillated

to twinkle like stars.

scintillation

refers to the twinkling effect of the light of stars.

scintillation counter

the term used for a detector of radiation in which radiation gives rise to the scintillations (flashes of light) in a phosphor. These are used for producing an electric pulse by means of a photomultiplier.

scintillation crystals

materials, e.g., anthracene, used to produce the scintillations in scintillation counters.

scintilloscope

a radiation survey instrument, built on the principle of visual counting of the scintillations produced by a bombardment by alpha particles.

scintillometer

an instrument which detectors radiation by emitting flashes of light.

sclerometer

an instrument used for measuring the hardness of substances according to the pressure that has to be applied to a diamond-pointed tool to produce a scratch.

scotopic vision

the term used for the vision at low levels of light intensity (night-time vision). Under such conditions other rods in the retina have been the main receptors and no colour could be distinguished. Compare photopic vision.

screen grid

a grid placed between the anode control grid of a thermionic valve, usually held at a fixed positive potential.

screw

a simple machine when given a completed circular turn of radius r, it advances linearly by a distance h, known as its pitch. Due to friction, the efficiency of such a machine is low. The force ratio however can be quite high.

search coil

a small coil of several turns of wire which is used to measure strength of a magnetic field. The coil is suddenly withdrawn from the magnetic field, the current induced in the coil being proportional to the magnetic field strength.

search light

a device that is used for throwing a strong beam of light in any direction. It generally consists of a light and a reflector

searle's bar

an apparatus for measuring the thermal conductivity of a good conductor. The specimen is a long narrow lagged bar heated at one end by a temperature bath or electric coil. It is cooled at the other end by a coil of copper tubing through which a steady steam of water is passed. The temperatures of the input and output water are measured (q_3 and q_4 respectively). In this way a temperature gradient is produced along the bar, which is found by measuring the temperatures (q_2 and q_3) at two intermediate points a distance l apart. These temperatures are measured by thermocouples or by thermometers placed in holes in the bar. Under steady-state conditions, thermal conductivity is calculated from the equation:

$$kA(q_2 - q_1)/l = mc(q_4 - q_3)$$

m being the mass of water passed in unit time, *c* the specific thermal capacity of the water, and A the bar's cross-sectional area.

second

unit of time in all systems of units.

second's pendulum

a simple pendulum whose period is two seconds.

secondary

it refers to the current induced by a primary winding where in current is inducted is an induction coil, transformer etc.

secondary cell

a voltaic cell in which the chemical reaction producing the e.m.f. is reversible and the cell can therefore be charged by passing a current through it. See accumulator.

secondary colour

a colour obtained by mixing two primary colours, e.g., green and blue.

secondary electron

an election emitted from an atom, molecule or surface as a result of collision with a charged particle or photon.

secondary emission

the term used for the emission of electrons from a surface as a result of the impact of high-energy to eject the 'free' electrons in the solid; i.e., to overcome the work function.

secondary emission of electrons

electrons given out from a surface due to the impact of high energy electrons or ions. Such an emission takes place, in a photomultiplier tube.

secondary standard

such a copy of a primary standard that the difference between the copy and the primary standard is known.

secondary winding

refers to the winding on the load side of a transformer irrespective of the transformer type.

seconds pendulum

a simple pendulum having a time period of two seconds.

seebeck effect

if the junctions of two metallic conductors are maintained at different temperatures, an e.m.f. Is produced across these junctions. The production of such an e.m.f. is called seebeck effect.

seed crystal

a small crystal that can initiate the process of crystallization in a supersaturated solution or a supercooled liquid. It is used in the manufacture of semiconductor devices.

segre chart

a graph wherein the number of protons in nuclides is plotted against the number of neutrons.

seger cones (pyrometric cones)

a serires of cones used to indicate the temperature inside a furnace or kiln. The cones are made from different mixtures of clay, limestones, feldspars etc.

seignette electricity

now known as ferroelectricity. The phenomenon was first observed on signette or rochelle salt, which was first made as a laxative by the pharmacist Seignette living in la rochelle.

seismograph

an instrument for recording earthquake shocks.

seismology

the scientific study of earthquakes and the phenomena as associated with them.

selectivity

refers to the property of a circuit, instrument etc. by virtue of which it can distinguish oscillations of a specified frequency.

selenium cell

a photo conducting cell consisting of a piece of light-sensitive selenium semi-conductor, which decreases its electrical resistance when light falls on it. It is powered by a battery.

selenium rectifier

a rectifier which consists of alternate layers of iron and selenium in contact.

self-diffusion

the process by virtue of which an arbitrary atom spontaneously moves to a new site in a crystal of its own species.

self inductance

may be defined as the property of an electric circuit which causes it to oppose any change of current in it, and which determines for a given rate of change in it the electromotive force induced in the same circuit.

self-induction

the production of a counter electromotive force in a conductor when its own magnetic field collapses or expands with a change in current in the conductor.

self induction, coefficient of

it is the magnetic flux linked with the coil when a unit current flows through it. It is also equal to the e.m.f. induced in the coil when the current changes through the coil at the rate of 1 ampere sec. Its unit is henry.

semiconductor

referst to a material such as silicon or germanium, that is having a resistivity midway (on a logarithmic scale) between that of conductors and that of insulators.

semi-conductor counter

a device for detecting ionizing radiation, consisting of a semi-conductor crystal with a potential difference across it.

semi-conductor diode

a single p-n junction through which the current increases exponential wit voltage in the forward direction. Very little current flows in the reverse direction. Its action thus resembles that of a diode valve.

semipermeable membrance

a membrane that allows certain molecules in a fluid to pass through while stopping others.

semitone

the smallest pitch interval between successive tones of the present western musical scales.

sensitivity

it is the response of a physical device to a unit change in the input.

sensitize

to make a thing sensitive.

sensitometer

it is an instrument which is used for testing the sensitivity of different types of films.

series

elements in a circuit are in series if connected so that each carries the same current in turn.

series wound motor

an electric motor in which the field winding is connected in series with the armature winding. Series wound motors are used for applications in which a high starting torque is required.

servomechanism

any electronic control system wherein a hydraulic, pneumatic or some other of controlling mechanism is actuated and controlled by a low energy signal.

servo motor

a motor forming part of a servo-mechanism.

sextant

refers to a navigational instrument which is used for the accurate measurement of the angle of a heavenly body above the horizon.

shade

refers to a comparative darkness that is caused by interception of rays of light.

shadow

a region where light from a source is obstructed to reach by an opaque obstacle. The region of complete darkness is known as umbra and the region of partial darkness is known as penumbra.

shaft

a ray or beam that is oscillating or rotating round straight bar for transmitting motion or torque. The shaft is generally supported on bearings and carrying genres, wheels or the like.

shank

a narrow shaft like part that connects two objects or two separated parts of the same object.

shaper

a machine tool having a cutting part for forming flat surfaces.

shear

to become fractured along a plane as a result of forces acting parallel to the plane.

shear strain

the angular displacement produced in a body.

shenstone effect

when an electric current has passed through some metals like bismuth a considerable increase in photoelectric emission is produced.

shield

a mass of material that surround a nuclear reactor core, or other source of radiation. It absorbs neutrons or other dangerous radiations.

shielding

it is the process of removal of the influence of an external energy field by surrounding a region with a wall of suitable material.

shift register

refers to a digital circuit used to displace a set of information in the form of pulsed either to the right or left.

shim

a thin strip or wedge of metal, wood etc. for driving into cervices, as between machine parts to compensate for wear.

shimmer

means to shine with or reflect a subdued tremulous light.

shock

to create strong internal stresses in a piece of metal as by unerven heating. It also refers to the physiological effect produced when an electric current passes through the body.

shock absorber

it is a device that is used for damping sudden and rapid motion.

shock proof

protencting against damage from shocks.

shock wave

a very narrow region of high pressure and temperature in which air flow changes from subsonic to supersonic.

short-circuit

if the teminals of a cell are connected externally by a wire of negligible resistance, the cell is said to be short-circuited.

short sightedness

a defect of vision. A person suffering with this defect fails to see distinctly the far objects.

short wave

refers to an electromagnetic wave of 60 meters or less.

shower

refers to a group of elementary particles and photons arising from the impact of a single particle of a high energy.

shunt

an element, generally of a low resistance, connected across component. If a shunt is connected across an mmeter then it increases the range of ammeter.

shunt wound motor

an electric motor in which the field winding is connected in parallel with the armature winding. It is used for maintaining a fairly steady speed.

sideband

range of frequencies lying on either side of a modulated carrier wave. The width of the sideband both above and below the modulated wave is equal to the highest modulating frequency.

sidereal

based on the stars, used especially of measurements.

sight

it is the power or facully of vision.

sigma circuit

an electric circuit used in nuclear reactor control systems for the rapid shout-down of the reactor.

sigma pile

an assembly consisting of a neutron source and a moderator, without any fusible material, which is used to study the properties of moderators.

sign convention

the term used for a set of rules which are used for determining the signs of distances related by various formulae in optics. In the most common real has been positive, virtual has been negative system, distances to real objects, images, and focal points have been positive, distances to virtual points have been negative.

The other main sign convention, the New Cartestian convention, is related directly to the sign convention in the mathematical treatment of Cartesian coordinates, it regards distances right of the pole as positive, those points to the left of it are negative.

signal

in an electronic circuit or system. The changing parameter by means of which information is conveyed through the system.

signal generator

any circuit or device which produces an electrical parameter that is adjustable and controllable. Most generally, a voltage source with variable amplitude, frequency, ad wave-form is used. The term is generally applied to sinewave generators; those generating pulse waveforms are known as pulse generators.

signal-to-noise ratio

refers to the ratio of one parameter of a wanted signal to the same parameter of the noise at any point in an electronic circuit, device, or transmission system.

silicon carbide

a crystalline compound. It is used as an abrasive and as an electrical resistor.

silicon ship

a single crystal of a semiconducting sillicon material, typically having mjircometer dime sions fabricated in such a way that it can perform a large number of independent electronic functions.

silicon solar cell

an element of a solar battery, consisting of alternate layer of p and n silicon which form the p-n junction at which radiant energy is converted into electricity.

simple harmonic motion

any motion that can be drawn as a sine wave. Examples are the simple oscillatior of a pendulum r a sound source and the variation involved in a simple wave motion. Simple harmonic motion is observed when the system, moved away from the central position, experiences a restoring force proportional to the displacement from this position. Theequation of motion for such a system can be written in the form:

$md^2x/dt^2 = lx$

l being a constant. During the motion there is a exchange of kinetic and potential energy, the sum of the two being constant (in the absence of damping). The period (T) is given by:

$$T = l/f$$

or

$$T = 2p/w$$

where f is frequency and w pulsatance. Other relationships are:

$$x = x_0 \sin wt$$

$$dx/dt = \pm w\sqrt{\ }(x_0{}^2 - x^2)$$

$$d^2x/dt^2 = q^2x$$

Here x_0 is the maximum displacement; i.e. the amplitude of the vibration. In the case of angular motion, as for a pendulum, q is used rather than x.

simple pendulum

idealy a simple pendulum consists of a heavy particle suspended by a perfectly flexible, weightless, string suspended from a perfectly rigid support. The length of suspension is called the length of simple pendulum. The motion of simple pendulum is S.H.M. and

its (T) time period is given by T

$$= 2\pi\sqrt{\frac{\ell}{g}}$$

where ℓ is the length of pendulum and g is acceleration due to gravity.

simulator

a device that copies behaviour of an actual system but is made from components which are easier, cheaper, or more convernient to manufacture. Simulators are frequently used for solving complex problems.

simultaneity

two events that occur not only at the same time but also at the same place.

sine wave

a wave form which resembles the plot of sine of an angle versus angle. The equation of such a wave has one variale proportional to the sine of another.

single phase

refers to a circuit that has an alternating current with one phase or phases differing by 180^0.

sinsoidal wave

refers to a wave the displacement of which varies as the sine (or cosine) of an angle that is proportional to time or distance, or both.

sinusoidal

having the characteristics of a sine wave.

siphon

a U-shaped tube, the two legs or which have been unequal in length; used to transfer liquid from one level to a lower.

skin effect

the phenomenon of non-uniform current distribution over the cross-section of a conductor, caused by the variation of the current in the conductor itself, resulting in a tendency of alternating currents to flow near the surface of the conductor. This effect increases the resistance and becomes more marked as the frequency rises.

skip distance

the minimum distance at which a sky wave can be received. This arises due to a minimum angle of incidence at the ionosphere below which a sky wave is not reflected. This minimum angle is a function of the frequency.

sky wave

a radiowave which reaches a point after reflection from the ionosphere and not directly from the transmitter.

slide wire bridge

it consista of a thin uniform wire of eureka (or maganin) generally one meter long which is stretched over a wooden board along a metre scale. The two ends of the wire are soldered to copper strips A & B. Another copper strip C is fixed on the board as shown in diagram. It is based on the principle of wheat stone bridge.

sliding friction

the force that slides - a body along a surface to overcome the force of friction.

slow neutron

a neutron with a kinetic energy of less than 10^2 eV (10^{-17} joule).

snell's law

the experimental law of the refraction of light, stating that the ratio of the sine of the angle of incidence to the sine of the angle of refraction is a constant which is independent of the magnitude of the angle incidence. This constant ratio is called the index of refraction.

$$\mu = \frac{\sin i}{\sin r}$$

snoek's law

alloys with an integral number of bohr magnetons per atom show very little, if any, magnetostriction.

soddy fajans displacement law

the emission of an aplha particle by a substance produces a displacement to the left by two places in the periodic table, i.e., a reduction of the atomic number of the substance by 2, whereas the emission of a beta particle produces a displacement to the right by one place in theperiodic table, i.e., an increase of the atomic number by one.

sodium vapour lamp

it is anverted U shaped glass tube which after being exhausted is filled with an inert gas (neon) at a pressure of about 10 mm. Specks of sodium metal are deposited inside in a scattered manner. Two tungsten spirals are sealed inside the two ends of the U–tube. One becoming hot it emits yellow light characteristic of sodium.

soft iron

iron containing a small amount of carbon. It is magnetized easily by placing it in a magnet but is demagnetized when the magnetic field is removed. Widely used in transformers, electric, bells, electromagnets as core material.

soft radiation

ionizing radiation of relatively long wavelength and low penetrating power as opposed to hard radiation which is of shorter wavelength and high penetrating power.

solar

pertaining to sun

solar battery

it is a device for converting solar energy into electricity by means of photo voltaic cells.

solar cell

any instrument that converts solar energy into electrical energy e.g., semiconductor devices operating by the photovoltaic effect an thermopiles. A solar battery is made up of several solar cells.

solar constant

it is the flux of solar energy passing normally through unit area at the earth's mean orbital distance. The value is 1390 w/ m^2 .

solar day

the time interval between two successive appearance of the sun at the meridian.

solar energy

the electromagnetic energy radiated from the sun. The tiny proportion (about 5×10^{-10} of the total) that falls on the earth is indicated by the solar constant. The total quantity of solar energy falling on the earth in one year is about 4×10^{18} J, whereas the total annual energy consumption of the earth's inhahitants is only some 3×10^{14} J. The sun, therefore, could provide all the energy needed. The direct ways of making use of solar energy can be divided into thermal methods and nonthermal methods.

solar heating

a form of domestic or industrial heating that relies on the direct use of solar energy. The basic form of solar heater is a thermal device in which a fluid is heated by the sun's rays in a collector and pumped or allowed to flow round a circuit that provides some form of heat storage and some form of auxiliary heat source for use when the sun is not shining. More complicated systems are combined heating-and-cooling devices, providing heat in the winter and air-conditioning in the summer. The simplest form of solar collector is the flat-plate collector in which a blackened receiving surface is covered by one or more glass plates that acts like a greenhouse and traps the maximum amount of solar energy. Tubes attached to the receiving surface carry air, water, or some other fluid to which the absorbed heat is transferred. The whole panel is insulated at the back and can thus form part of the roof or a building. More sophisticated sollectors focus the sun's rays using reflectors.

solar parallex

the angle subtended by the earth's equational radius at the centre of the sun at the mean distance between the earth and the sun (i.e. at 1 astronomical unit). It has the value 8.794 148 arc seconds.

solar prominece

a cloud of gas that forms temporarily in the upper chromosphere or inner corona of the sun. It has a lower temperature but higher density than its surroundings and is a bright projection.

solarize

to reverse an image partially from negative to positive, by exposure to light during development.

solar system

the sun, the nine major planets (Mercury, Venus, Earth, Mars, Jupiter, Saturn, Uranus, Neptune, and Pluto) and their natural satellies, the aserroids, the comments and meteoroids. Over 99% of the mass of the system is concentrated in the sun. The solar system as a whole moves in an approximately circular orbit about the centre of the Galaxy, taking about 2.2×10^8 years to complete its orbit.

solar wind

streams of plasma flowing approximately radially outward from the sun.

solder

an alloy used for soldering.

soldering

joining metals below 800 degree F. The joined metals are not melted.

soldering iron

an instrument for melting and applying solder.

solenoid

an electromagnet having an energizing coil approximately cylinedricalin form, wound as a helix with a small pitch or as two or more coaxial helices, and operating on a movable core or plunger.

solid

physically, a mass or body that exists in all three dimensions, i.e., has length, breath and thickness. Chemically a substance in a state of aggregation in which it has a definte shape and volumenand a higher degree of cohesion among its molecules than in any other state of aggregation.

solid angle

the solid angle subtended by a surface at a point.

solidify

to become solid.

solidifying point

the temperature at which a liquid solidifies.

solid–state

it refers to those electronic devices that can control current without use of moving parts.

solid–state physics

the study of the physical properties of solids, with special emphasis on the electrical properties of semiconducting materials in relation to their electronic structure. Solid–state devices are electronic components consisting entirely of solids (e.g. semiconductors, transistors, etc.) without heating elements, as in thermionic valves.

sonar

a method of measuring the thickness of deep-ocean sediments by exploding depth-charges thousands of feet below the sea surface and recording the echoes as reflected from boundary layers deep in the ocean floor.

sonic

refers to a speed equal to or more than the speed of sound in air the same height above see level.

sonic boom

refers to a loud noise.

sonic frequencies

sound frequencies, i.e., frequencies between 20 and 20,000 cycles.

sonic speed

the speed of an object moving an Mach 1 relative to the surounding fluid.

sonics

it is the branch of science that deals with the partical applications of sound.

sonometer

it is an instrument that is used for studying the vibrations of a fixed wire or string. It consists of a hollow wooden box with a wire stretched across its top. The wire is fixedat one end while the other end passes over a pulley and a load can be suspended from it. Any length of wire can be set into vibration b placing two inverted v–shaped bridges at the ends, by placing vibraing tuning fork on the sonometer. Resonance is produced when the natural frequency of the vibrating wire

(given by $f = \frac{1}{2\ell}\sqrt{\left(\frac{T}{m}\right)}$ is equal

to the frequency of the tuning fork. T is the tension in the wire and m is its mass per units length.

sorption

absorption of gases by solids.

sorption pump

a type of vacuum pump in which gas is removed from the system by absorption onto a porous solid cooled in liquid nitrogen.

sound

vibrations transmitted by air, or some other material medium, in the form of alternate compressions and rarefactional of the medium. Sound is often called a pressure wave. Sound is a longitudinal waveform, ad is characterized by its pitch (frequency), loudness (intensity), and quality. The speed of sound depends on the medium transmitting it. In air at 0°C it is 331.3 meter second^{-1}, and water at 25°C it is 1498 meter second^{-1}, and in glass at 20°C it is 5000 meter second^{-1}. The speed of sound in a medium is given by:

$$V = \sqrt{(E/p)}$$

where p is the density of the medium and E a modulus of elasticity. For a solid rod, E is the Young modulus; for a broad solid specimen it is the axial modulus; for liquids and gases, it is the adiabatic bulk modulus. Except t high pressures, this gives for gases:

$$V = \sqrt{(gp/p)}$$

where p is the pressure and g the ratio of the principal specific heat capacities. This is equivalent to

$$V = \sqrt{(gRT/M)}$$

where R is the molar gas constant, T the thermodynamic temperature, and M the mass of one mole of the gas. V is independent of pressure and is proportional to the square root of the temperature.

Solids also transmit transverse and torsional vibrations at a speed given by

$$V = \sqrt{(G/p)}$$

where G is the shear modulus.

sound barrier

a hypothetical barrier to flight beyond the speed of sound.

round ranging

it is a method for determining the distance between a point and the position of a sound source by measuring the tie lapse between the origin of the sound and its arrival at that point.

sound spectrogram

a gaphic representation produced by a sound spectrograph, of the frequency, intensity, duration and variation with time of the resonance of a sound or series of sound.

sound spectrograph

it is an electronic device that is used for recording sound spectrograms.

sound, velocity of

the velocity with which sound waves propagate in a medium. In air, its value is 332 m/s at 0^{0}C and increases with temperature. It is independent of changes in pressure. Its value is more in liquids and maximum in solids.

sound wave

a travelling wave produced by vibrations in an elastic medium at a rate that can be heard.

sounder

it is an instrument for receiving telegraphic impulses and converting them into sounds.

source

any thing or place from which something arises or is obtained.

space

it is unlimited or indefinetely great three dimensional expanse in which all material objects are located and all events take place.

space charge

a region in a vacuum tube or semiconductor having some net electric charge on account of excess or deficiency of electrons.

space craft

a vehicle capable of travelling in space.

space group

a set of operations (rotation about an axis) that when carried out on a periodic arrangement of points in space brings the system of points to self coincidence.

space probe

an unmanned spacecraft that investigates feathures within the solar system. A planetary probe examines the conditions on or in the vicinity of one or more planets and a lunar probe is designed to obtain information about the moon. Probes are propelled by rocket motors and once out of the earth's gravitational field use their propulsion systems for course changes. Many are powered by panels of solar cells, for both internal operation and radio communications.

space-ship

it refers to a rocket that is propelled vehicle. It is designed to carry man and cargo to the moon or plantes.

space-time

a concept originated by Minkowski and developed by Einstein as a fundamental principle of the theory of relativity. The apace-time continuum is a four-dimensional continuum, with four co-ordinate.

spacistor

a class of semiconductor devices using a single n-p junction which is biased oppositely to a normal transistor junction to avoid the frequency limitations due to carrier transit time imposed by conventional transistors.

spallation

a vigorous unclear decay due to bombardment of a target by high energy particles, resulting in the emission of a number of alpha- and beta-particles.

spark

a visible disruptive discharge of electricity between two places at opposite high potential.

spark chamber

an apparatus for detecting ionizing particles and making their tracks visible. A stack of up to 100 plates are connected alternately to a source of positive and negative high-voltage electricity and the chamber is filled with helium and neon. An incoming particle creates ion pairs along its track, the gas becomes conducting, and sparks jumps between the plates (and can be photographed).

spark counter

a type of delector for counting alpha particles. It consists of a wire or mesh held a close distance above the earthed plate.

spark gap

refers to an arrangement of electrodes specially designed so that a disruptive discharge takes place between them when the applied voltage exceeds a predetermined value.

spark transmitter

a transmitting set that produces electromagnetic waves by the oscillatory discharge from a capacitor through an inductor and a spark gap.

sparking plug

an instrument that provides an electric spark for exploding the air-petrol vapour mixture in the cylinder of an internal combustion engine.

sparking voltage

the minimum voltage across a spark gap which causes a spark.

specific

denoting a physical quantity per unit mass. For example, volume per unit mass is called specific volume.

specific charge

the ratio of the electric charge to mass ratio of an elementary particle.

specific conductance

it is the reciprocal of specific resistance

$$K = \frac{1}{\rho}$$

it is also known as conductivity (k).

specific gravity

means relative density.

specific heat

the amount of heat required to raise the temperature of unit mass of the substance through 1 degree C.

specific humidity

in meteorology, the mass of waver vapour in a unit mass of moist air, usually expressed in grams per gram or kilogram of moist air.

specific impulse

refers to the ratio of the thrust produced to the rate of fuel consumption in a rocket.

specific inductive capacity

another term for the dielectric constant of a substance. See dielectric constant.

specific inductive capacity

dielectric constant of a substance.

specific resistance

it is defined as the resistance

offered by 1 m length of the conductor having an area of cross–section 1 sq. cm.

$$\rho = \frac{R.a}{\ell}$$

Specific resistance (ρ) is expressed in ohm–cm or ohm–meter.

specific rotation

of an optically active solution is equal to the rotation of the plane of polarisation produced per decimetre length of the solution per unit concentration of the solution.

specific rotatory power

symbol: αm. May be defined as the rotation of plane-polarized light in degrees produced by a 10 cm length of solution has been 1 g of a given substance per millilitre of stated solvent. The specific rotatory power has been a measure of the optical activity of substances in solution. It could be measured at 20°C using the D-line of sodium.

specific surface

surface per unit mass.

specific thermal capacity

symbol: c. The energy which is needed to raise the temperature of unit mass of a given substance by unit temperature. Generally, it is expressed as the energy in joules that raises the temperature of one kilogram by one kelvin; the units have been then joules per kilogram per kelvin.

specific volume

the volume of a sustance per unit mass. The reciprocal of density, it has the units $m^3\ kg^{-1}$.

specific viscosity

ratio of viscosity of a material to the viscosity of water.

spectral line

a particular wavelength of light emitted or absorbed by an atom, ion or molecule.

spectral series

refers to a group of related lines in the absorptions or emission spectrum of a substance. The lines in a spectral series take place when the transitions have been all between the same energy level and a set of different levels.

spectrograph

an instrument wherein a photograph of a spectrum can be obtained.

spectrographic analysis

the qualitative and quantitative analysis of a substance, its composition and properties on the basis of its study with the spectrograph.

spectroheligraph

an instrument used to photograph the sun with light of a particular wavelength.

spectrometer

a scintillation counter adapted to the study of energy distribution.

spectrophotometer

a photometer for comparing two light radiations wavelength by wavelength.

spectroscopy

the study of matter and energy by the use of spectroscope.

spectrum

a type of graph which shows how different types of radistions relate to wave length (and energy). e.g. electromagnetic waves appear in electromagnetic spectrum visible light is a part of this spectrum. Spectrum of Electromagnetic waves :

Frequency

$$\frac{10^4 10^6 10^8 10^{10} 10^{12} 10^{14} 10^{16}}{10^{+4} 10^{+2} 10^{+0} 10^{-2} 10^{-4} 10^{-6}}$$

$$\frac{10^{18} 10^{20} 10^{22} (\text{Hz})}{10^{-8} 10^{-10} 10^{-12} 10^{-14}}$$

visible range is comprised of radiations with frequency wave length range as under

$$\frac{\text{Frequency} 3.84 \times 10^{14}}{\text{Wave length} 7.80 \times 10^{-7}}$$

$$\frac{\text{Hz} < f < 7.69 \times 10^{14}}{m > \lambda 3.90 \times 10^{-7}}$$

(Red) (violet)

spectrum analyser

a device which scans the spectrums to determine the frequency and amplitude of electromagnetic waves.

specular reflection

mirror scattering at one angle from the point of reflection.

speculum

a cu-tin alloy used for metal mirrors and reflection greetings.

speech

it refers to the power of speaking.

speed

the distance covered by a moving body in unit time. It is measured in m/sec and is a scalar quantity.

speed light

an electronic flash lamp.

speedometer

a device provided on an automobile or other vehicle for recording the rate of travel.

spherical

having a shape like a sphere.

spherical aberration

a defect of image due to the paraxial and marginal rays which are coming to focus at different points on the axis of the lens. It can be corrected by using parabolic surfaces as reflectors and refractors.

spherical wave

for a spherical wave

$$I = \frac{p}{4\pi r^r} . A = \frac{A_0}{r}$$

where A = constant→ Amplitude emitted by the source
r = distance from source
I = Power emitted by source.
equation for a spherical wave

$$S = \frac{A_0}{r} \cos 2\pi \left(\frac{I}{T} - \frac{r}{\lambda} \right)$$

spherometer

an instrument for measuring curvature of spherical surfaces and small thicknesses.

spike

a current or voltage of extremely short duration.

spill

the phenomenon of an accidental release of radioactive material.

spin

a quantum number assigned to electrons and other elementary particles. It can have only two values either + 1/2 or - 1/2.

spin quantum number

a quantum number assigned to electrons and other elementary particles. The spin of an electron can be with + 1/2 or - 1/2.

spiral scanning

of a cathode-ray tube, a type of scanning in which are electron beam executes a spiral trace.

spirit level

it is a device that is used for the determination of true horizontal or vertical direction by the centering of a bubble in a slightly curved glass tube or tubes filled with alcohol or ether.

spontaneous fission

nuclear fission that occurs independently of external circumstances and is not initiated by the impact of a neutron, an energetic particle, or a photon.

spool

it refers to any cylindrical object on which some thing is wound.

spoot light

refers to a strong focused light that is thrown upon a particular spot so as to make some object, person particularly conspicuous.

spout

to discharge forcibly in a jet.

spray angle

the magnitude of the angle formed by the cone of a liquid leaving a narrow orifice is called spray angle.

spreading resistance

the component of resistance on account of the bulk of the semiconductor away from the junctions and contacts.

spring balance

any instrument with which a force is measured by the extension produced in a helical spring. It is used in weighing. The extension produced is directly proportional to the force.

spurt

a gush suddenly in a jet.

sputtering

refers to the evaporation of particles of a cathode during the discharge of electricity through a gas. It can be used to coat a nonconductor with a thin metallic film.

square wave

a pulse train made up of rectangular pulses with mark-space ratio equal to unity.

square wave generator

a signal generator which supplies output voltage of square wave form.

stability

means firmness in position.

stability of balance

the tendencies of an oscillating balance to come to rest. The stability of a balance is opposed to its sensitiveness i.e. if stability of a balance is increased, its sensitivity decreases.

stable equilibrium

a body is said to be in stable equilibrium when it tends to return to its original state on being slightly disturbed from its state.

stalagmometry

the measurement of surface tension by determining the weight of a drop of the liquid hanging from the end of a tube.

standard calorie

the amount of heat required for raising the temperature of one gram of water from 3.5^{0}C to 4.5^{0}C. Also called 4^0 calorie.

standard cell

a cell whose e.m.f. remains constant over a large length of time. It changes very little with change in temperature.

standard conditions

when used in connection with experiments or measurements, especially those concerning or involving gases, this term means the temperature of 0^{0}C. and the pressure of 760 millimetres of mercury.

standard pressure

an internationally agreed value; a barometric height of 760 mm hg at θ degree c; 101 325 pa.

standard temperature

273.15 degree k, 0 degree c, melting point of water.

standing wave

(1) a periodic wave which at all points in space is having simultaneous proportionate variations with time. (2) The resultant of the encounter of two waves identical in wavelength and amplitude, and travelling through a medium at identical velocity, but in directly opposite directions.

stanhope lens

a thick biconvex lens having front surface of radius two-thirds the thickness and a concentric back surface with radius one-third the thickness.

star

a heavenly body which is a huge source of energy. Energy production in stars is thought to be due to thermonuclear reactions. Sun is example of a star.

strak effect

the wavelength of light emitted by atoms is changed by the application of a strong transverse electric field to the source, the spectrum lines are split up into a number of sharp defined components. The displacements are symmetrical about the position of the undisplaced line, and are proportional to the field strength up to about 1000,000 volts per cm.

stark-einstein law

each molecule taking part in a chemical reaction induced by exposure to light absorbs one quantum or radiation causing the reaction

startopause

the boundary between the stratosphere and the mesosphere.

star

a prefix used with a practical electrical unit to name the corresponding electrostatic unit. e.g., the electrostatic unit of charge is called the star coulomb.

star coulomb

the unit of electric charge in the metric system.

states of matter

the three states in which matter usually exists, viz. solid, liquid and gas. Plasma, an assembly of ions and electrons is called the fourth state of matter.

static electricity

electricity characteristic of charges are at rest, as opposed to current electricity.

static pressure

pressure on a surface on account of a fluid at rest or due to another surface.

static tube

it is a tube that is used for measuring the static pressure of a fluid in motion. It is so placed in the fluid that it is not affected by pressure changes caused due to the motion of the fluid.

statics

branch of mechanics which deals with the behaviour of bodies under the action of forces, the bodies involved being at rest and not in motion.

stationary

means having fixed position.

stationary state

a state of a system when it has an energy level permitted b quantum mechanics. A transition from one stationary state to another can only occur by the emission or absorption of an appropriate quanta of energy in the form of photons.

stationary wave

when two sets of waves of same type (longitudinal or transverse) having equal amplitudes and equal frequencies, travel with same speed, along the same straight line but in opposite directions, their superposition upon each other gives a set of resultant waves which do not move either way with time. These waves are known as stationary waves or standing waves.

$$S_1 = A \sin 2\pi\left(\frac{t}{T} - \frac{x}{\lambda}\right)$$

$$S_2 = A \cos 2\pi\left(\frac{t}{T} + \frac{x}{\lambda}\right)$$

$$S = S_1 + S_2 = \left(2A \cot\frac{2\pi}{\lambda}\right)\cos 2\pi.\frac{t}{T}.$$

The point where the resultant amplitude has a maximum value $\left(\text{i.e } 2A \text{ for } x = \frac{k.\lambda}{2}\right)$ is known as antinode.

The point where the resultant amplitude has a value of zero (i.e. $(2k + 1)\ \frac{\lambda}{2}\ k = 0, 1, 2...$) is called node.

The distance between two consecutive nodes or antinodes i. $\frac{\lambda}{2}$.

statistics

it is a branch of science that deals with the collection, classification, analysis, interpretation etc. of numerical facts or data. It makes use of the mathematical theories of probability.

stator

the fixed part of an electric motor or dynamo, or some similar device.

statoscope

a type of Aneroid barometer. It is used to register small changes in atmospheric pressure.

stauroscope

it is an optical instrument and is used for the determination of the position of plane of light variations in sections of crystals.

steam

water in the gaseous state. Water when heated to its boiling point is converted into waver vapour, called steam.

steam calorimeter

a calorimeter wherein the amount of heat supplied is calculated from the mass of steam condensed on the body under test.

steam engine

a machine which takes heat from a steam boiler performs external work, and reducts a portion of heat to a condecser.

steam line

the curve showing the change of the boiling point of water with pressure.

steam point

boiling point of water at atmosphere pressure.

steelyard

an ancient weighing device, still widely used.

stefan-boltzmann's law

it states that the energy emitted per unit area, E_b, of a black per second is proportional to the fourth power of the absolute temperature T of the body thud

E_b a T^4 or $E_b = \sigma . T_o^4$

where E_b = Heat energy radiated σ = Stefan's constant (5.67 × 10^8 watt merer^2 ok^{-4}) for bodies which are not perfectly black it is modified as $E = \varepsilon . \sigma .(T^4 - T_0^4)$

where T and T_0 are the temperatures of the body and the surroundings respectively.

ε is emissivity of the body.

For a perfectly black body we have $E_b = \sigma\ (T^4 - T_0^4)$

step-down transformer

a transformer that is used for increasing an available voltage

step-up transformer

a transformer that is used for increasing an available a.c. voltage.

steredian

si unit of solid angle. The solid angle subtended by a cone at its vertex is the area enclosed by the cone from the surface of a sphere of unit radius with vertex as the centre.

stereo

an equipment that reproduces stereophonic sound.

Stereography

it refers to the art of delineating the form of solid bodies on a plane.

stereoscope

an instrument that shows different views of the same scene to the two eyes giving the impression of depth.

stereoscopic

possessing the property or conveying the effect of depth, perspective or three-dimensionality.

stereoscopic image

an image which appears a three dimensional object local in space.

stereoscopic vision

vision in depth or in three dimensions owing to the spacing of the eyes which permits them to see objects from slightlyu different angles.

stimulated emission

when an atom or molecule has been in an excited state it may make a transition to a lower-energy state spontaneously, with emission of a photon.

stokes

units of kinematic viscosity. When the dynamic viscosity is measured in poise and the density is measured in grams per cubic centimetre, the kinematic viscosity is in stokes.

stokes law of radiation

it was supposed by G. Stockes that in fluorescence only radiations of wavelength longer than that of the exciting light could be emitted. In line spectra these are known as stokes lines.

stokes' law

the velocity necessary to propel a spherical body of given radius at uniform speed, through a viscous medium:

$$V = \frac{2ga^2(d_1 - d_2)}{9\eta}$$

where a is the radius of the sphere, d_1 and d_2 the densities of the sphere and the medium, respectively, and η the coefficient of viscosity. V will be in cm per sec if g i cm per sec^2, a in cm, d_1 and d_2 in g per cm^3 and η in dyne-sec per cm^2 or poises.

storage battery

it is a voltaic battery made up of two or more storage cells.

storage cell

a cell whose energy can be renewed by passing a current through it in opposite direction to that of flow of current generated by the cell e.g. lead storage cell (battery).

straggling

the process of random variations in some property associated with mobility of ions through matter is called straggling.

stp

standard temperature and pressure.

strain

$$\text{Strain} = \frac{\text{change in shape}}{\text{original shape}}$$

strain has no unit, it is a simple number
longitudinal strain

$$= \frac{\text{change in length}}{\text{original length}} = \frac{\Delta \ell}{\ell}$$

volumetric strain

$$= \frac{\text{change in value}}{\text{original value}} = \frac{\Delta v}{v}$$

shearing strain = tan θ

strain energy

the magnitude of potential energy stored in a body by virtue of its elastic deformation is known as strain energy.

strain guage

a device for measuring the strain or distortion on a surface.

strain grandient

that variation in strain set up in a structure which has been stressed beyond its yeld point and thus suffered varying degrees of deformation.

strain hardening (work hardening)

an increase in the resistance to the further plastic deformation of a body as a result of a rearrangement of its internal structure when it is strained, particularly by repeated stress.

strangeness

symbol s. A property of certain elementary particles called hadrons (K–mesons and pyperons) that decay more slowly than would have been expected from the large amount of energy released in the process. These particles where assigned the quantum number s to account for this behaviour. For nucleons and other nonstrange particles s = 0; for strange particles s does not equalizer but has an integral value. In quirk theory hadrons with the property of strangeness contain a strange quark or its antiquark.

stratosphere

the region of the atmosphere above troposphere. In this region, the temperature remains nearly constant and the atmosphere is calm and undisturbed.

stray capacitance

the capacitance introduced into a circuitry by the leads and wires used to connect circuit components.

stray current

any undesirable current generated by the discharge of static electricity.

stream line

it refers to a line in the fluid such that the tangent to it at any point is in the direction of the fluid at that point.

stress

force per unit applied to a body. If the force stretches the body, it is called tensile stress.

stress modulus

the stress divided by the strain of any elastic deformation.

stripe

a relatively long, narrow band of different colours.

stroboscope

an instrument which can be used to make objects moving with a periodic motion look stationary and viewed as if they are at rest.

stylus

it is the needle that is used to cut a phonograph record.

subatomic

consisting of particles smaller than, or forming a part of, the atom.

subatomic particles

this term is applied to all particles of less than atomic mass, i.e., the elementary partilces (proton, neutron, electron, positron, neutrino, meson and γ-rays or photons), as well as the α-particles and deuterons, the charge and mass of which indicates them to be composite particles.

sub carrier

a carrier wave used to under take another carrier wave.

subcritical

a nuclear reactor in which the nuclear chain reaction is not self-sustaining.

sublimation

change of state from solid to vapours, without that solid first changing to liquid.

sub-shell

in bohr's atomic theory, each electron shell is considered to be made up of various sub-shell. Each of these has the same orbital quantum number. The shells are known as s-shell, p-shell, etc.

subsonic

objects having speed less than the speed of sound i.e., for which the speed is less than mach. 1.

substance

the substance of a body is expressed in terms of the number of constituent particles.

subtractive process

a process of colour mixing by subtraction.

suction

it is the force that, due to a difference in pressure, attracts a substance to a region of lower pressure.

suction pump

it is type of pump. It is used for raising a liquid by suction. It is made up of a piston that moves up and down in a cylinderical vessel.

summetry

the correspondence of parts of a figure with reference to a plane line or point of summetry. Thus a circle is symmertical about any diameter; a sphere is symmetrical about a plane of any great circle.

sun

the star at the centre of the solar system. It is the source of the most of the energy that is available on earth either directly as light, heat etc. or indirectly as the source of energy for plant growth.

sun beam

a beam or ray of light.

sun glow

a diffused light seen around sun.

sunspots

dark patches observed on the sun's surface that are regions of cool gas. Their presence is connected with local changes in the sun's magnetic field. They appear in cycles having a period of about 11 years.

super critical

a nucklear reactor in which a nuclear chain reaction is self-sustained.

superconductivity

with reference to electricity, the extremely high conductivities possessed by certain substances at temperatures very close to absolute zero.

super cooling

the cooling of liquid below its freezing point at that pressure.

The effect can be achieved with pure liquids. Solidification occurs if a small impurity is added to the super cooled liquid.

supercritical

the term used for an arrangement of fissile material that has been sustaining a branching a branching chain reaction; i.e., more neutrons are being produces than are wasted and escape.

superheated steam

steam produce by heating water under increased pressure. Its temperature is more than 100 degree c.

super heating

heating a liquid about its boiling point when the liquid is in a metastable state.

super high frequency

radio frequencies in the range 3000 to 30,000 omega hertz.

super position principle

principle of super position.

super sonic

speeds greater than mach 1 or greater than the speed of sound.

superficial expansion

it is directly proportional to the original area and rise in temp.

$A_2 - A_1 \alpha A \sigma (T_2 - T_1)$

$\Delta A \alpha A_0 \Delta t$

$\Delta A = \beta . A_0$.

where β = coefficient of superficial expansion.

superelastic collision

a collision for which the restitution coefficient is greater than one.

superfluid

a fluid which flows without friction and which has an abnormally high thermal conductivity, e.g. helium below 2.186 k.

superfluidity

a property of liquid helium at very low temperatures.

superheated steam

steam obtained by heating water under increased pressure. Its temperature is more than 100 degree c.

superheating

the term used for raising of a liquid's temperature at a given pressure above its boiling temperature at that pressure without change of state.

superposition principle

if two or more waves reach a point, the resulting displacement at the point is the algebraic sum of the displaement of individual waves at that point. This principle explains the phenomenon of interference.

supersonic flow

in aerodynamics, flow of fluid over a body at speeds greater than the acoustic velocity and in which the shock waves start at the surface of the body.

supersonics

it is a branch of science that deals with the study of supersonic phenomenon.

supervoltage

any voltage between 500 to 2000 kilo volts.

supplementary units

in S. I. system we have two supplementary units in addition to seven basic units. These radin (rad) and steradian (Sr)

Radian θ (in radians) $\frac{\text{length of arc}}{\text{radius}}\, \theta = \frac{\ell}{r}$

Steradian (Sr), q (in steradians)

$$= \frac{\text{surface area cutout of sphere}}{(\text{Radiud})^2}$$

$$\theta = \frac{S}{r^2}$$

surface charge density

it indicated the amount of charge per unit surface area.

surface colour

this term is used for light reflected by a surface distinct from the common body colour. This reflection occurs due to penetration into the medium. Transmitted light is complementary to the reflected light.

surface colouric

coloured light reflected by a surface as distinct from the more common body colour which arises from reflection after some penetration into the medium. Transmitted light by bodies showing surface colour is complementary to the reflected colour.

surface contamination

it is the deposition and attachment of radioactive materials to a surface.

surface density (σ)

when a conductor is charged the charge is distributed all over its surface and the amount of charge per unit area surrounding a point is called surface density of charge at that point.

At pointed ends of a surface, the surface density is maximum.

$$s = \frac{Q}{4\pi r^2}$$

surface energy

the energy per unit area of exposed surface.

surface tension

the force acting across the surface of a liquid per unit surface length perpendicular to an imaginary line drawn on to surface. It is measured in N/m.

surface wave

the component of ground wave which travels along the surface of the earth.

surfascope

an instrument used for the optical measurement of roughness of plane and cylindrical metal surfaces.

sucseptibility

symbol: X. May be defined as the ratio, for a given substance, of the magnetization of a sample to the magnetic field strength applied. In SI it has been equal to $(\mu_r - 1)$, where μ_r is the relative permeability. The value of X ascertains whether a substance shows paramagnetism, diamagnetism or ferromagnetism.

susceptibility

if a bar of iron is placed in a magnetic field, it gets magnetised and the pole strength or magnetisation depends upon the strength of magnetic field. Thus if H is the magnetic field and O is the resulting intensity of magnetisation then $\frac{\sigma}{H}$ =K is the susceptibility of the specimen. The value of k (susceptibility) and μ (permeability) are high for ferromagnetic substances.

sweep circuit

an oscillator circuit that generates a saw tooth waveform ideal for producing a linear vertical and horizontally beam sweep in a cathode ray tube.

swing

it indicates the variation in voltage or current or any other electrical quantity.

switch

this term is used for manual, or mechanically actuated device to connect or disconnect the electrical circuit.

synchrocyclotron

a particle accelerator in which charged particles can be accelerated to relativistic speed by modulation of frequency of the accelerating electric field.

synchrometer

a device which counts the number of cycles in a given signal during a given time.

synchronous motor

an a.c. motor which has a rotation speed proportional to the frequency of the power supply.

synchronous orbit

an orbit of the earth made by an artificial satellite with a period exactly equal to the earth's period of rotation on its axis, i.e. 23 hours 56 minutes 4.1 seconds. If the ortbit is inclined to the equatorial plane the satellite will appear from the earth to trace out a figure–of–eight track once every 24 hours. If the orbit lies in the equatorial plane and is circular, the satellite will appear to be stationary. This is called a sationaty orbit (or geostationary orbit) and it stationary orbits, with three or more spaced round the orbit to give worldwide coverage.

synchronous rotation

the rotation of a natural satellite in which the period of rotation is equal to its orbital period. The moon, for example, is in synchronous rotation about the earth.

synchrotron

a particle accelerator in which the electric field is kept at a constant frequency while the magnetic field is moedulated.

synchrotron process

the phenomena of emission of E.M. radiation by relativisic electrons orbiting in a mag. field.

synchrotron radiation

high energy electrons within a synchrotron emit light as a consequence of their acceleration in a strong magnetic field; this emission is known as synchrotron radiation.

syntony

the condition in which two oscillating circuits have the same resonant frequency.

system internationale d'Unites

is a rationalised M.K.S. system of units.

t

stands for tesia, tritium.

tablot

a unit of luminous energy. It equals the luminous energy carried by a luminous flux of 1 lumen in one second.

tacho

refers to speed.

tachometer

instrument used to measure angular speeds.

tachyons

a class of particles which travel with a velocity greater than the velocity of light are known as tachyons.

tackle

it is a system of leverage that makes use of pulleys, as a combination of ropes and blocks. It is used for. Hoisting, lowering and shifting objects or materials.

tail

refers to the luminous stream that is seen extending from the head of a comet.

tandem generator

refers to an arrangement of two linear accelerators end to end.

tangent galvanometer

refers to a galvanometer in which a magnetized needle has been pivoted to rotate in a horizontal plane at the centre of a large fixed vertical coil. Current flowing through the coil moves the needle.

tandem generator

an arrangement of two linear accelerators end to end.

tangential acceleration

the component of linear acceleration which is tangential to the path of particle moving in a circular path.

tangent law

when a freely suspended magnet is acted upon B two uniform magnetic fields of strength F and H at right angles to each other, the magnet comes to rest in a certain position making an angle with H. In this position the moment of couple due to the field H is equal and opposite to the moment of couple due to field F.

$F = H \tan \theta$.

tape

a magnetic tape on which sound has been recorded.

technic

it refers to the study of science

as an art.

tektite

a small black, greenish, or yellowish glassy object found in groups on the earth's surface and consisting of a silicaceous material unrelated to the geological formations in which it is found.

telecommunications

the telegraphic or telephonic communication of signals, images, or sounds by line or radio transmission.

telegraph

transmission of messages using electrical impulses sent through wires. Messages are sent using a universally accepted code of dots and dashes which are identified by the length of time for which the current passes through a circuit.

telemeter

a device for recording a physical event at a distance. Telemeter is used in an artificial satellite which transmits measurements made in space back to earth by radiowaves.

telephone

it is an apparatus with the help of which sound is transmitted to distant points with the help of electrical impulses. Sound waves are converted into electrical impulses, by the carbon microphone, which flow to the receiver and are converted into sound waves, by making an iron diaphragm vibrate.

telephoto lens

a lens construction used to produce a relatively large image. It is a combination of convex and concave lens.

telescope

refers to an optical system which is used for collecting radiation from a distant object and producing an enlarged image. Optical telescopes use visible radiation. There are two types: refractors (or refracting telescopes) in which the light could be collected by a converging lens; and reflectors (or reflecting telescopes) in which a converging mirror has been used. The light collected by the objective forms an image, which is magnified by a eyepiece. The largest astronomical telescopes are all reflectors. Telescopes for non-astronomical use are refractors that produce an upright image (know as terrestrial telescopes).

telethon

a television broadcast that lasts several hours.

television

refers to the broadcasting of a still or moving picture with the help of radio waves to a receiver that projects it on a picture tube for viewing at a distance from the point of origin.

telestar

it refers to one of a series of low altitude, active communication satellites for broad band microwave communication and satellite tracking in space.

temperature

means a measure of the degree of hotness of a body. According to kinetic theory of gases, the kinetic energy of the molecules of a gas is proportional to its temperature.

temperature coefficient

a constant which determines how a physical quantity varies with temperature. For example, the temperature coefficient of linear expansion tells by how much the length of a substance change, due to change of 1 degree in the temperature.

temperature coefficient of resistance

the ratio of the change of resistance in a wire due to a change of temperature of 1 degree c to its resistance at 0 degree c.

temperature colour scale

a thermodynamical relation which correlates the temperature of an incandescent substance with the colour of light it emit.

temperature gradient

rate of change of temperature with distance.

temperature humidity index

it is a number representing an estimate of the effect of temperature and moisture on human computed by multiplying the sum of dry bulb and wet bulb temperature readings by 0.4 and adding 15, with 65 considered as the highest comfortable index.

temperature of inversion

it refers to the temperature, of the hot junction is a thermocouple, at which the thermo e.m.f. changes sign.

temperature scale

any temperature scale consists of two fixed points which generally correspond to two easily reproducible systems.

These are assigned certain definite values and the interval between them is decided into an equal number of parts. The celcius scale is most commonly usedand the fixed points in it are the ice point (0°C). and steam point (100°C) interval between them is divided into 100 equal parts, each part being equal to 1°C, other scales used are, Fahrenheit, Romer and Kelvin. Thses are related to celcius scale as

$$\frac{C}{100}=\frac{F-32}{180}=\frac{R}{80}=\frac{K-273}{100}$$

tempering

it refers to the process used for increasing the toughness of an alloy by heating it to a perdutermined temperature, maintaining it at this temperature for pre determined time and then cooling it to room temperature at a predetermined rate.

temporary magnetism

magnetism induced by a magnetic field that disappears as soon as the magnetic field is removed.

tenacity

the maximum tensile stress which a material is capable of withstanding; tensile strength.

tensile strain

strain produced by tension; the ratio of the increase of withstanding; tensile strength.

tensile strength

the tensile force per unit area to be applied to a material to just break it.

tensile stress

stress produced by tension; the ratio of the force to the cross-sectional area.

tensimeter

an instrument for measuring differences in vapour pressure.

tensiometer

an apparatus for measuring the surface tension of liquid. An apparatus for measuring the tension in a wire, fibre or beam. An apparatus for measuring the moisture content of soil.

tera

symbol T. It is a prefix that is used in the metric system to denote one million times. For example, 10^{12} volts = 1 teravolt (TV).

terminal

a point of an electrical circuit to which a connecting lead can be connected.

terminal speed

the steady speed reached by a body when it falls freely through a viscous fluid.

terminal velocity

$$\frac{C}{100} = V_0 = \frac{2r^2(\rho - \rho')g}{9\eta}$$

where
ρ = density of spherical body
ρ' = density of fluid
if ρ>ρ' = body will move downward
if ρ <ρ' = the body will move upward.

terminator

the boundary, on the surface of the moon or a planet, between the sunlight area and the dark area.

ternary fission

a rare form of nuclear fission as a result of which a heavy nucleus breaks up into three fragments of comparable mass.

terrestial magnetism

earth's magnetism.

terrestial telescope

telecope.

tertiary colour

a colour obtained by mixing two secondary colours.

tesla

symbol: T. It is the SI unit of magnetic flux density. It is equal to a flux density of one weber of magnetic flux per square metre. 1 T = 1 wb m^{-2}.

tesla coil

an air-roer transformer having a few turns of heavy wire as primary and many turns of fine wire as secondary; it is capable of producing electromagnetic radiation at a very high frequency or potential.

tetrode

a thermionic valve that contains four electrodes. It has a screen grid between the control grid and anode of a triode valve. This improves the performance on a triode valve as an amplifier and oscillator at high frequencies.

texture

microscopic structures.

theodolite

an optical instrument for measuring horizontal and vertical angles with greater accuracy. It is an essential tool in surveying.

theorem

a rule that is generally expressed by an equation or a formula.

theorem of parallel axis

if I_0 is the moment of inertia of an object about an axis, the moment of inertia about an axis parallel to the given axis and at a given distance d, from it is given by

$I = I_0 + md^2$

where m = mass of the object.

theorem of perpendicular axis

if Ix, ly denote the moment of inertia of a body about x – axis and y – axis respectively, the moment of inertia about an axis perpendicular to x–y plane and passing through the point of intersection of x–and y–axis is given by

$I_f = Ix + Iy$

therm

a unit of heat.

1 therm = 10^5 B. Th. U = 1.055 Joules.

thermal agitation

refers to the random movement of the molecules of a substance.

thermal barrier

the limit to the speed with which an aircraft or rocket can travel in the earth's atmosphere due to overheating caused by friction with the atmospheric molecules.

thermal capacitance

the ratio of the entropy added to a system to the resulting rise in temperature.

thermal conductivity

coefficient of thermal conductivity.

thermal diffusion

a method of separating heavier gas molecules from lighter ones by maintaining a temperature gradient over a volume of a gas containing particles of different masses. It is also used for separating the isotopes of an element.

thermal equilibrium

state of a system where in no heat flow takes place between its components. If two bodies are in thermal equilibrium, they have the same temperature.

thermal expansion

refers to the increase in the dimension of a body on heating.

thermal fatigue

failure resulting frun rapid cycles of alternate heating and cooling.

thermal gradient

the term is associated with the rate of fall of temperature along the surface with respect to distance.

thermal growth

expansion arising from thermal cycling.

thermal inductance

it is defined as the product of temperature difference and time divided by its entropy flow.

thermal inertia

another name for specific heat.

thermal neutrons

neutrons having slow speed and energy; such neutrons are of importance in nuclear fission reactions in nuclear reactors. They have energy 0.1 ev.

thermal reactor

a nuclear reactor in which the nuclear fission reactrions are caused by thermal neutrons.

thermal unit

it is a unit of heat energy.

thermal x-ray

the term is associated with electromagnetic radiation of low energy.

thermionic current

it refers to the electric current that is produced due to flow of thermions.

thermionic emission

refers to the emission of electrons or ions due directly to the temperature of the emiter, the rate of emission increasing rapidly with the increase in temperature.

thermionic tube

a vacuum tube in which the cathode is heated in order to emit electrons all or some of these electrons are collected by an anode. Additional electrodes are usually provide, to control the passage of the electrons from the cathode to the anode. Also called thermionic vacuum tube.

thermionic value

an evacuated glass envelope containing a system of electrodes and in which thermionic emission of electrons is made use of and that acts as a value i.e. allows the current to flow in one direction only. Depending on the number of electrodes a value is classified as a diode, triod, pentode etc.

thermionics

study of emission of electrons

when substances are heated.

thermistor

an electrical component, usually a semiconductor, whose electrical resistance varies rapidly with temperature. Used as a sensitive temperature measuring device.

thermo

refers to any device which consists of a thermograph and a barograph. Such a device is used to simultaneously record temperature and pressure of a gas.

thermobarograph

an instrument for measuring and recording atmospheric temperature and pressure, consisting of a thermograph and a barograph.

thermobarometer

an instrument used to measure atmospheric pressure. It is sometimes also used to find out altitude and it can also be used as a thermometer.

thermocouple

a device for measuring temperature in which a pair of electric conductors are so joined as to produce a thermolectric effect. When the ends of two dissimilar metals or any pair of electrical conductors, are joined, a thermoelectric effect is produced which causes an electric current to flow around the circuit formed by the two wires, the magnitude of the current being proportional to the difference in temperature between the hot and cold junctions.

thermodynamics

the study of general laws which govern processes involving heat and other forms of energy.

thermodynamic temperature

symbol: T. A temperature which is measured in kelvins. The size of the kelvine has been the same as that of the degree Celsius, and temperatures on the Celsiuse scale can be converted to thermodynamic temperatures by adding 273.15. The thermodynamic temperatures scale has been independent of the working substance. It based on the principles of a reversible heat engine.

thermoelectric effect

seebeck effect, peltier effect, thomson effect.

thermoelectric power

refers to the rate of change of the thermo e.m.f. of a thermocouple with the change of temperature of the hot junction.

thermoelectric thermometer

thermocouple.

thermo-electricity

electricity produced by the direct conversion of heat energy into electrical energy.

thermograph

a self-registering thermometer/ an apparatus which records temperature variations during a period of time on a graph.

thermoluminescent-dating

a method for dating the firing of samples of pottery.

thermo–motor

anengine which operates by heat.

thermo–nuclear reaction

a reaction involving a thermonuclear change

thermopile

it is an arrangement of thermocouple in series. Such detecting and measuring radiant energy.

thermosphere

the region of the upper atmosphere in which the temperature increases with height.

thermostat

a device which is used to keep the temperature in a place within in a particular range. Thermostats are present in a number of common household devices such as cookers, refrigerators, irons, freezers and heating boilers. Many thermostats are bimetallic strips.

thermostatics

it is a branc of physics. It deals with the study of thermal equilibrium.

thick lens

a real lens, as distinct from a hypothetical lens. In a thick lens the separation between the two surfaces cannot be ignored.

thomson effect

the existence of an electric potential gradient along a conductor due to the temperature difference at different points of the conductor.

thomson scattering

the scattering of photons of electromagnetic radiation by electrons according to j.j.

thomson's formula named after Sir Joeseph John Thomson.

thoron

the conventional name for radon-220.

three phase

having three equal alternating voltage between which there are relative phase differences of 120 degree.

three pin plug

the standard method of joining a cable to a mains socket. A main's cable has three wires. These are colour coded, each wire goes to a particular pin in the plug.

threshold

the lowest value of any stimulus, signal or agency which will produce a specific effect. Example, threshold frequency.

threshold frequency

light falling on a metal surface will give rise to the emission of photo-electrons, only if the frequency of the light is greater than certain threshold value which is characteristics of the metal used.

threshold of hearing

that minimum intensity level of a sound wave which is audible. It occurs at a loudness of about 4 phons.

threshold voltage

the voltage where particular characteristic of an electronic device first occurs.

throttle

refers to a lever, pedal, handle etc. used to control or obstruct or check the flow of a fluid.

thrust

it is a pushing force or pressure that is exerted by a thing or a part against a contiguous one.

thyratron

a gas-filled thermionic valve in which a voltage applied to the control grid initiates, but does not limit, the anode current. It is used as an electronic switch.

thyristor

it is a silicon controlled rectifier. Its anode—cathode current is controlled by a signal applied to a third electrode, the gate.

tides

the alternate rise and fall of the sea which occurs about every twelve hours. Tides are due to gravitational pull of the moon and to a lesser extent, the gravitational pull of sun

timbre

the characteristic quality of sound. It is independent of pitch and loudness but depends upon the relative strenance. It depends on the number and intensity of the overtones present.

timbre of sound

the property of a note that enables us to assign it to its sources is known as the quality or timbre. It depends on the number and intensity of the overtones present.

time

measurement of duration between events. The si unit the second is based on vibration of radiation absorbed by ceasing atoms.

time bomb

a bomb than can be set to explode at a specific time.

time clock

a clock with an attachment that records the exact time or arrival and departure on a time clock.

time dilation (time dilatation)

the principle predicted by Einstein's special theory of ralativity, that intervals of time are not absolute but are relative to the motion of the observers. If two identical clocks are synchronized and placed side by side by side in inertial frame of reference they will read the same time for as long as they both remain side by side. However, if one of the clocks has a velocity relative to the other, which remains beside a stationary observer, the travelling clock will show, to the observer, that less time has elapsed than the stationary clock.

time lag

syn. time delay. The time that passes between the closing of one circuit in a circuit-breaker and the closing of the main current circuit.

time lapse photography

a form of sinephotography used to record a slow process, such as plant growth. A series of single exposures of the object is made on cine film at predetermined regular intervals. The film produced is then projected at normal speeds and the process appears to be taking place at an extremel high rate.

timer

a device used for controlling machinery in a specified way at a predetermined time.

time signal

a signal sent electrically or by radio to indicate precise moment of time.

time switch

a switch which incorporates a type of clock mechanism for making and/or breaking a electric circuit at times that are predetermined by the setting of the mechanism.

tint

the colour sensation of mixing a hue with white. This reduces the saturation of the hue.

tip

a slender and or extremity.

tokamak

it is an axially symmetric torodial system in which the plasma and suppresses the instability.

tomography

a technique for using x-rays for photographing one specific plane of the body, for diagnostic purposes.

ton

an imperial unit of mass equal to 2240 lbs. Sometimes it is called the long ton to distinguish it from the U.S. short ton.

tondal

a unit of force. It equals 309.6911 n.

tone

it refers to a sound considered with refers to its quality, strength, source etc.

tone control

device for adjusting the frequency response of an audio-frequency amplifier so as to compensate for deficiencies in the audible output and therefore achieve a more pleasing result.

tonne

symbol : t. a metric unit of mass. 1 t = 1000 kg. Generally called a metric ton, it differs in size from an imperial ton by about 1½%.

tonometer

an instrument for measuring the pitch of the sound. An instrument for measuring vapour pressure. Instrument for measuring blood pressure or the pressure within an eye-ball.

topology

the branch of geometry concerned with the properties of solids that are unchanged by continued deformations, such as twisting or stretching. It is useful in the analysis of complicated electrical networks.

toroid

it is a surface that is generated by the revolution of any closed plane curve about an axis lying in its plane.

toroidal

having the shape of a toroid or torus.

torque

a twisting or wrenching effort. It is the produced of a force and its moment arm, i.e., it equals the force multiplied by the centre of rotation at which it is exerted.

torque in a coil placed in a magnetic field

if a rectangular coil PQRS suspended in a magnetic field or uniform field strength B, the length of the loop PQ = RS = l and its breadth QR = SP = b. When a current I is passed through the loop, the torque developed by it is given by

$\tau = B.I.\, l.b.\, \sin\theta$
$= I.A.B.\sin\theta$
Where A = Area of the coil, and θ = angle between the area of loop and magnetic field If there are N turns in the coil, then

$\tau = N.I.A.B.\ \sin\theta$
N.I.A = electric dipole moment or magnetic dipole moment (M), hence $\tau = M.B.\ \sin\theta$ if $\theta = 90^0$, t = M.B. (it is maximum)

$$\text{Or } m = \frac{\tau max}{B}$$

torr

a pressure equal to the pressure of 1 mm hg.

torricell's vacuum

it refers to the space in which mercury vapours are present, at the top of a column of mercury when a long tube which is sealed at one end is filled with mercury and inverted in a trough containing mercury.

torsion

the angular strain produced in a body on being subjected to a torque.

torsion balance

a device for measuring very small forces by the torsion they cause in a write or fibre.

torsion bar

a metal bar having elasticity when subjected to torsion. It is used as a spring.

torsion wave

a wave motion in which the vibrations in the medium are rotatory single harmonic motions around the direction of energy.

torus

a solid generated by rotating a circle about an external line in its plane, also called an anchor ring. It has the shape of the inner tube of a tyre. If r is the radius of the rotating circle and R the distance between the centre of the circle and the axis of rotation, the volume of the torus is $2\pi^2Rr^2$ and the surface area is $4\pi^2$ Rr.

total internal reflection

reflection which takes place within a substance because the angle of incidence of light striking the boundary surface is in excess of the critical angle.

total luminous flux

the total light emitted by a light source in all directions.

total radiation pyrometer

an instrument used for measuring high temperatures.

tourmaline

a mineral crystal which bits dichroic properties, i.e., doubly refracting with selective absorption of the ordinary ray while transmitting the extraordinary ray.

tours

a 'doughnut' or anchor-ring shaped solid of circular or elliptical cross-section.

townsend coefficient

the number of ionizing collisions per centimetre of path of a charged particle in the direction of the applied electric field.

townsend discharge

a discharge in which additional ionization is solely due to ionization of the gas by electron collisions.

tracer

see radioactive tracing.

track

refers to an illuminated track of an ionizing particle created in a cloud chamber, bubble chamber, etc.

traction

adhesive fricition of a body on same surface as a wheel on a rail or tyre on road etc.

trajectory

the path traversed by a projectile.

trans

a prefix indicating "across".

transconductance

the mutual conductance between the control grid of a thermionic valve and its anode; it is expressed in mhos.

transducer

an instrument that receives energy in the form of waves from one transmission system and supplies waves energy to another system or media.

transinet

a term applied to phenomena, usually damped oscillatory motion, voltage, current etc., which takes place in a system due to a sudden change of conditions and which exist for a relatively short-time after the change has occurred.

transition temperature

the temperature at which one form of a substance changes into another; the temperature at which both forms can coexist.

transit time

the time taken by an electron to pass directly from one specified point to another under given operating conditions.

translation

the movement of a body or system such that all points are moved in parallel directions through equal distances.

translatory motion

a motion that involves a non-reciprocating movement of matter from one place to another.

translucent

any substance that permits the passage of light in such a way that an object cannot be seen clearly through the substance.

transmission

it refers to the process of transmitting.

transmission coefficient

it refers to transmittance.

transmission factor

the ratio of the flux of a physical quantity transmitted through a body to the incident flux. It has no units.

transmittance

the ratio of the radiant power transmitted through a material to the incident radiant power.

transmittancy

the ratio of the transmittance of the solution to the transmittance of the same path length of solvent.

transmitter

the device, apparatus, or circuits by means of which the signal is transmited to the receiving parts of the stem in any telecommunication system.

transmutation

the process whereby one nuclide is converted into another nuclide.

transmutation of elements

the process of converting one chemical element into another. Artificial transmutation can be done to some extent with the help of suitable nuclear reactions.

transparent

permitting the passage of light in such a way that objects can be seen clearly through them.

transponder

refers to a radio or radar receiver, that automatically transmits a replay prompt on reception of a certain signal.

transport number

the proportion of the total electric current passing through an electrolyte which is carried by a particular type of ion. The anion transport number plus the cation transport number equals unity.

transuranic elements

elements whose atomic number is greater than the atomic number of uranium. All of them are radioactive.

transverse

means in cross direction.

transverse wave

a wave motion in which the vibrations are perpendicular to the direction of propagation of the wave.

triangle law of vectors

it states, "if two vectors can be represented in magnitude and direction by two sides of triangle taken in order, then the resultant vector can be represented in magnitude and direction by the third side of the triangle taken in opposite order".

triatomic

a molecule consisting of three atoms.

tribo

means friction.

tribo electricity

static electricity produced by friction.

tribology

the study of friction and lubrication.

triboluminescence

the emission of light when certain crystals are crushed.

trichroism

it refers to plecchroism of a biaxial crystal such that it exhibits three different colours when viewed from three different directions under transmitted light.

trichromatisms

means to make use of three colours.

trickle charge

of a storage battery, a continuous charge at a low rate approximately equal to the internal losses and suitable to maintain the battery in a fully-charged condition.

triblinic crystal

a crystal with unequal axes, none of which are at right angles to each other.

trident

it is a three pronged instrument.

trigger

any stimulus which initiates a particular response from an electronic circuit or device.

trimmer

syn. trimming capacitor. An adjustable capacitor with a small maximum capacitance in parallel with a fixed capacitor to enable the capacitance of the combination to be adjusted.

trimophism

it is the property shown by certain substances. Substances showing this property crystallize in three structurally distinct forms.

triode

it consista of three electrodes (i.e. anode, cathode and grid). The grid is inserted between the filament and the ar,jode plate. The grid controls the flow of electrons from the filament to the plate and hence the plate current. The addition of grid makes the valve useful for magnifying oscillations. When the triode is used for magnifying a current it is called amplifier.

triple bond

three covalent bonds binding two atoms in a chemical compound e.g., acetylene, ch-ch.

triple point

it is the temperature at which the gas, liquid and solid phases of a substance can co-exist in equilibrium. The triple point of water is taken as 273.16 k.

triton

nucleus of tritium.

tritum

an isotope of hydrogen containing 1 proton and 2 neutrons in the nucleus. It is a radxioctive substance with a half life of 12.3 years.

tropopause

the layer of atmosphere that separates troposphere and stratosphere.

troposphere

region of atmosphere just above the earth's surface. It extends in height to about 10 miles at the equator and about 5 miles at the poles. The temperature in this region decreases with height.

trough

in transverse wave motion, the maximum distance below the line of mean position. Two successive troughs are separated by a wavelength of the wave.

tune

to bring into harmony.

tuned circuit

a resonant circuit consisting of a coil and a capactor producing resonance at a given frequency.

tuning fork

a metallic fork having two prongs which, when struck, produce a pure sound tone.

turbine

a motor in which impact of a current of waver, air or another fluid upon the blades of a wheel rotates the shaft of a motor.

turboelectricity

electricity produced with the help of a turbine.

turbo engine

it is a jet propulsion engine. In it air from the atmosphere is compressed for combustion by a turbine driven compressor.

turbogenerator

a stream turbine driving an electric generator. This is the normal method of generating electricity in power stations. In a conventional power station the steam is raised by burning a fossil fuel (coal, oil, or natural gas); in a nuclear power station the steam is raised by heat transfer from a nuclear reactor.

turbulence

the state of being turbulent.

turbulent flow

flow of liquid wherein the speed of the fluid changes rapidly in magnitude and direction. The motion of a fluid becomes turbulent when its speed increases beyond a certain typical speed.

turnnel diode

a semiconductor diode, based on the runnel effect. It consists of a highly doped p–n semiconductor junction, which short circuits wit negative bias and has negative resistance over part of its range when forward biased. Its fast speed or operation makes it a useful device in many electronic fields.

turnnel effect

an effect in which electrons are able to tunnel through a narrow potential barrier that would constitute a forbidden region if the electrons were treated as classical particles. That there is a finite probability of an electron tunnelling from one classically allowed region to another arises as a consequence of quantum mechanics. The effect is made use of in the tunnel diode.

turns ratio

refers to the radio of the number of turns in the primary coil of a transformer to the corresponding number in the secondary coil.

turns table

it refers to the rotating disc on which the record in a phonograph rests.

tweeter

a loudspeaker of small dimension designed to reproduce sounds of relatively high frequency.

twilight

the soft diffused light from the sky when the sun is below the horizon.

twilight zone

refers to the lowest level of ocean to which light can reach.

twin engine

having two engines of equal power.

twinkle

means to shine.

twinning

the union of crystals from a twin (a compound crystal consisting of two parts)

two-phase

having two equal alternating voltage between which there is relative phase difference of 90 degree.

tyndall effect

it refers to the scattering of light by particles in its path and the beam of light becomes visible.

udometer

it refers to rain gauge.

uhf

ultra high frequency.

ultimate strength

the value of limiting stress at which a material completely breaks down.

ultra sound camera

a camera that converts a sound pressure "acoustic image" into an electrical TV. Like image by means of piezo-electric effect.

ultra violet rays

electromagnetic radiations with wavelengths between that of visible light and that of x-rays.

ultracentrifuge

a high speed rotating machine for separating very small particles.

ultragravity waves

the gravity waves which have periods ranging from 0.1 to 1.0 second.

ultrahigh frequency

a radio frequency in the range between 3 GHz and 0.3 GHz (wavelength 10 cm–1m).

ultralight vacuum

a vacuum having pressure of the order of 10 power -10 mm of mercury column or less is called ultralight vacuum.

ultramicrobalance

a highly sensitive balance for precise weighing to 10^{-8} grammes.

ultramicrometer

a micrometer that is capable of measuring very small magnitudes.

ultramicroscope

a modified compound microscope able to view the submicroscopic particles in a colloidal suspension when this is suitably illuminated.

ultrasonic cleaning

a general method of separating dirt or any undesired particles from a substance by vibrating it at frequencies greater than sound in a suitable stationary medium or vice versa.

ultrasonic coagulation

the bonding of small particles into larger aggregates by the action of ultrasonic waves.

ultrasonic communication

communication through water using suitably modified sonar equipment.

ultrasonic frequency

a frequency above 20,000 hz.

ultrasonic frequency

refers to a frequency above 20,000 hz.

ultransonic generator

an instrument that produces waves of ultrasonic frequency.

ultrasonic machining

the use of an ultrasonic generator and transducer with certain types of machine tools to facilitate drilling and cutting operations on hard, brittle or crystalline materials.

ultrasonic stroboscope

a light interrupter whose action is based on the modulation of a light beam by an ultrasonic field.

ultrasonics

a study of waves whose frequency is about 20,000 hz. Such waves cannot be heard by human ear.

ultraviolet absorber

a substance which absorbs ultraviolet radiation and then dissipates the energy in a harmless form.

ultraviolet

a force of electromagnetics radiation shorter in wavelength than visible light. Ultraviolet wavelengths range between about 1 nm and 400 nm.

ultraviolet rays

electromagnetic radiation having wave length in the range 50 - 400 a degree.

umbra

the region of complete shadow.

umklapp process

a collision process between phonons, or between phonons and electrons. The process is responsible for thermal resistance in non-conducting materials.

uni-axial crystal

a double reflecting crystal with only one optic axis.

unified field theory

a single theory to account for the electromagnetic, gravitational, strong, and weak interactions by one set of equations. So far, attempts to find such a theory have been unsuccessful, although there has been some progress in unifying the weak and electromagnetic interactions.

uniform acceleration

acceleration that is constant in magnitude and direction.

uniform motion

motion at constant velocity.

uniform speed

constant speed.

uniform velocity

motion in straight line with constant speed.

uniform velocity

motion in a straight line in which the speed remains constant.

unipolar transistor

a transistor in which current flow is because of the movement of majority carries only.

unit

a quantity adopted as a standard of measurement in terms of which similar quantities can be measured. For example, the unit of length is 1 metre, the unit of mass is 1 kilogram and the unit of time is 1 second.

unit cell

the smallest repetitive volume that comprises that complete pattern of a crystal.

unit planes

conjugate planes of a system having a unit lateral magnification.

unit pole

a magnetic pole when placed 7 cm from an equal pole, in a vacuum, is repelled with the force of 1 dyne.

unit stress

the amount of load acting on a unit area.

unity power factor

an electric circuit having power factor as unity.

univariant system

a thermodynamical system

having only one degree of freedom, in accordance with the phase rule, is called univariant system.

universal motor

an electric motor that is suitable for use with direct current or alternating current.

unsaturated

describing a colour that is a tint, i.e., a hue mixed with white.

unsaturated vapour

a vapour at a certain temperature that does not contain the maximum amount of the substance in the gaseous phase.

unstable equilibrium

a body is said to be in unstable equilibrium if, on being slightly disturbed from its equilibrium position, it tends to move away from its original position.

upthrust

an upward force acting on an object immersed in a fluid. The magnitude of the force is equal to the weight of the fluid displaced by it.

uranium

a toxic radioactive silvery element of the actinoid series of metals. Its three naturally occurring radioisotopes, ^{238}U (99.283% in abundace), ^{235}U (0.711%), and ^{234}U (0.005%), are found in numerous minerals including the uranium oxides pitchblende, uraninite, and carnotite. The readily fissionable ^{235}U is a major nuclear fuel and nuclear explosive, while ^{238}U is a source of fissionable ^{239}Pu.

symbol: U; m.p. 1132.5°C; b.p. 3745°C; r.d. 18.95 (20°C); p.n. 92; r.a.m. 238.0289.

utilization factor

the term is commonly used in electric power distribution and is defined as the ratio of the maximum demand of a given system to its rated capacity.

vacancy

an unoccupied site in a crystal lattice which is normally occupied by an atom or ion.

vaccum

region of space in which there are no atoms or molecules. Generally the term refers to space containing air or some other gas at very low pressure. It is difficult to obtain perfect vaccum in the laboratory.

vacuum distillation

distillation carried out at reduced

pressure, which lowers the boilig point of the liquid.

vacuum evaporation

it is a technique used for producing a coating of one solid on another, usually a coating of metal or semiconductor, by evaporation an high temperature in a vacuum.

vaccum switch

an electric switch which has its contacts in an evacuated chamber so as to reduce sparking.

vacuum ultraviolet

part of the ultraviolet region of the spectrum, wherein radiation is absorbed by air. The wavelength is less than 200 nm.

valence electron

in an atom, an electron in an incompletely filled (usually outer) shell, available for chemical bonding to form a molecule. See electron shell.

valency band

range of energies in a semiconductor that corresponds to energy star that can be occupied by the valency electrons in the crystal.

valve reactor

a circuit having a valve that is arranged to operate as a reactor. It is employed in radio transmitters for frequency modulation and in circuits for automatic frequency control.

valve voltmeter

refers to an amplifier that uses therminonic valves with a measuring instrument in the output circuit. Such instruments are used to measure both d.c. and a.c. voltage.

vapourization

change of start of a liquid to vapour.

vapour

a substance in the gaseous state at a particular temperature so that it can be liquefied by the application of a pressure alone i.e. a gas below its critical temperature.

var

a unit of power similar to watt, used for the reactive power of an alternating current. One var is one volt time one ampere.

varely effect

in an ionic solid an energetic charged particle or photon can ionize a negative ion to give it a positive charge and induce it to take up an interstitial position.

variable capacitor

a specially designed capacitor whose capacitance can be continuously altered by moving one set of metal plates with respect to another.

variable force

a force for which the direction or magnitude or both change with time.

varindor

an inductor whose inductance varies sharply with the amount of current flowing through its winding.

variometer

a variable inductance consisting of two coils in series, arranged so that one coil can rotate within the other. Also used as device for measuring inductance.

vector

a physical quantity which requires both a magnitude and a direction for its complete description. Velocity, acceleration, force are examples or vector quantities.

vectors, triangle law of

the resultant of two vector quantities completely represented by two sides of a triangle taken in order is given by the third side of triangle taken in the reverse order.

velocity

the distance covered by a body per unit time in a given direction. It is a vector quantity and its units are m/s.

velocity microphone

a microphone whose electrical output corresponds to the particle velocity of the impressed sound waves.

velocity modulation

a type of emulation in which the velocity of a beam of electrons is made to fluctuate at the frequency of a superimposed electric field, usually a radio-frequency.

velocity ratio

the ratio of the distances through which the points of application of the applied force and the resistance move in a machine. For an ideal machine it is equal to the mechanical advantage.

velocity, relative

the rate at which a body, a, changes its position with respect to a second body, b, is called the relative velocity of a with respect to b.

venturimeter

a guage used to measure the speed of flow of a liquid. It is based on the bernoulli's equation.

verneuil method

a method of single crystal growth, originally intended for the preparation of artificial gemstones, on which powder is dropped through an oxyhydrogen flame so that it falls molten on to a ctrystal seed.

vernier motor

a small rocket motor used to correct the flight path or velocity of a missile or spaceraft.

very low freqency

a radio frequency in the range between 30 k hz and 3 k hz.

vhf

very high frequency.

vibration

a regularly repeated to-and-fro motion abut a mean position.

vibration

a periodically repeated to-and-for motion about a mean position.

vibration magnetometer

see magnetometer.

video frequency

the frequency of the television video signal.

video signal

in a television system, the signal which conveys the whole of the intelligence present in the image, together with the necessary synchronizing and equalizing pulses.

vignetting

refers to the progressive reduction in the cross-sectional area of a beam of light passing through an optical system as the obliquity of the beam is increased.

villari effect

the susceptibility of an iron wire is increased by stretching when the magnetism is below a certain value, but diminished when above that value.

virgin neutrons

neutrons from any source which have not been involved in any collisions.

virial law

the mean kinetic energy of a system is equal to its virial that depends only on the forces acting on the atoms and not on their motions.

virtual image

an image that cannot be shown on a surface but is visible as in a mirror.

virtual mass

the actual mass of a body, plus its apparent additional mass.

virtual work

the work done on a system when it is assumed to be displaced by an infinitesimally small amount. If the system is in equilibrium, the virtual work is zero.

viscometer

instrument for measuring the viscosity of a fluid. They are based on the properties of fluids that are affected by viscosity.

visibility

visibility is measured by the ratio of the luminous flux in lumens to the total radiant energy in ergs per second or in watts.

visible radiation

light of wavelength in the range between 4000-7000 a which is visible to the human eye.

vitreous

glass like material.

vitreous humour

gelatinous substance found behind the lens in the human eye.

volta effect

the e.m.f. established when two dissimilar metals are brought into contact with each other.

voltage

the e.m.f. of a source of electricity or potential difference between two points. It is measured in volts.

voltage divider

number of resistors, indictors, or capacitors connected in series with several terminals at intermediate points. The total voltage across the chain can be split into known fractions by making connections at the various points.

voltage doubler

an electronic circuit which delivers a direct current voltage approximately twice the peak alternating current voltage it feeds on. Usually consists of two rectifiers whose outputs are connected in series.

voltage stabilizer

a device or circuit to maintain a voltage at its output terminals which is the substantially constant and independent of other changes in the input voltage or in the load current.

voltaic cell

syn. galvanic cell. A primary cell made up of plates of dissimilar metals dipped in an electrolytic solution.

voltameter

a electrolytic cell where in a metal is deposited on a cathode by electrolysis of a metallic salt.

volt amperes

symbol : va. the product of an effective voltage and effective amperage in an alternative current circuit.

volume

refers to the measure of space occupied by a body.

vtvm

abbreviation for vacuum-tube voltmeter.

wadsworth prism

an equilateral glass prism having a plane mirror at 45 degree with the base. A ray passing through the prism at minimum deviation is reflected by the mirror to 90 degree deviation from the incident ray.

wall effect

any significant effect of the inside wall of a container or reaction vessel on the behaviour of the enclosed system.

wall energy

refers to the energy per unit area of the boundary between the domains in a ferromegnetic material.

wanner optical pyrometer

polarizing pyrometer.

water expansion of

unlike most other substances, water expands on cooling below 4 degree C. The density of water is maximum at 4 degree C.

watt

the si unit of power. It is represented, piratically, by the work done at the rate of joule or 10 power 7 ergs per second. It is also equivalent to the product of volts and amperes.

watt-hour

a unit of work or energy, equal to one watt operation for one hour.

watt-meter

an instrument for measuring power consumed in an electrical circuit.

wave front

the locus of all the points in a wave motion which have the same phase.

wave function

a mathematical quantity, used is wave mechanics, analogous to the amplitude of ordinary waves. The square of the wave function of a particle at a particular point represents the probability of locating the particle in unit volume at that point.

wave guide

hollow metallic conductor through which microwaves can be propagated over short distances.

wave mechanics

system of mechanics developed from quantum theory based on de Brogue's hypothesis that every moving particle has a wave associated with it. Developed by Schrodinger.

wave motion

energy transfer by propagation of a periodic disturbance. The disturbance could be in the form of displacement of molecules of a gas, a displacement of elements of a string, etc.

wave number

reciprocal of wave length of a wave. It is equal to the number of wave lengths present per unit length.

wave train

a successive of waves, particularly a group of wave of limited duration.

wavetrap

a tuned circuit generally a rejector incorporated in a radio receiver that reduces interference at a particular radio frequency.

waves, audibile

waves that can be heard by a human ear. The frequency of such waves lies between 20 - 20,000 vibration per second.

wavicle

a less common name for a photon; used to imply that it has the character of both a wave and a particle.

weber

si unit of magnetic flux. 1 wb = 1 volt sec. One weber is equal to the magnetic flux linked with a circuit of one turn which when reduced to zero in one second produces an e.m.f. of one volt.

wedge

a piece of metal or wood thick at one end and sloping to thin edge at the other. It is used to separate one part of a body from another or to separate two bodies. Knife, nail, chisel are examples of wedge.

weight

the force with which the earth attracts a body. w = mg where m is the mass of the body and g, the acceleration due to gravity. Due to variation of g, it varies from place-to-place.

weight density

the weight of a body per unit volume, is called its weight density.

weight-factor

the number of microstates which correspond to a given macrostate.

weightlessness

the state of loss of weight experienced by a person in an orbiting space-craft.

weissenberg effect

the tendency of a fluid to creep up along a rotating shaft instead of being thrown out by centrifugal force.

wet cell

a primary cell which has a substantial amount of free electrolyte in the liquid form.

wet contact

a contact through which direct current flows.

wetting angle

the term is commonly used in fluid mechanics and is associated with the contact angle lying between 0 degree and 90 degree.

wien's displacement law

for black-body radiation the rate of energy radiation per unit area per unit wavelength range at constant kelvin temperature T_1 can be plotted against wavelength l_1. For temperature T_2 the peak cmesat l_2, such that $l_1T_1 = l_2T_2$ = constant
This rule was deduced by Wien (1893) by thermodynamics, but he could not evaluate the constant nor explain the shape if the graph. The problem was solved by Planck.

wien effect

the increase in the conductivity

of an electrolytic solution produced by high electrical fields.

wigner coefficients

alternatively called clebch-gordan coefficients.

wigner force

a force between nucleons where there is no space or spin exchange. The force is always attractive.

wilson cloud chamber

cloud chamber.

wimhurst machine

an apparatus for generating static electricity; an electrostatic generator.

wind tunnel

a hollow tube through which a uniform flow of air is passed.

wollaston prism

a polarizing prism used for obtaining plane polarized light. It is constructed of quartz and can be used for ultra violet radiation also.

wood effect

the process by virtue of which transparency is exhibited by alkali metals to ultra violet light.

wood's glass

glass with a high transmission factor in the ultraviolet range of the spectrum but relatively opaque to visible radiation.

woofer

a loudspeaker with dimension, used to reproduce sound of relatively low frequency.

woofer

a loudspeaker used for the low-frequency section of a high fidelity sound reproduction system.

word

a string of bits used to store information in a computer.

work function

the energy that must be supplied to the free electrons in a metal so as to enable them to escape the metal surface.

work function

the energy which must be supplied to the free electrons in a metal to enable them to escape from the metal.

working substance

refers to the substance that is subjected to temperature and pressure change in a heat engine.

working substance

the substance subjected to temperature and pressure changes in a heat engine.

w-particle

a hypothetical thought to be exchanged between elementary particles undergoing a weak interaction.

wrench

a force along with a couple whose axis is the line of action of the force.

x–axis

the axis along which the abscissa is measured.

xi-particle

refers to an elementary particle classified as a hyperon.

x-ray absorption

the taking up of energy from an x-ray beam by a medium through which the beam is passing.

x-ray analysis

the use of x-ray radiations to detect heavy elements in the presence of lighter ones, to give vertical edge absorption to identify elemental composition and to identify crystal structures by diffraction patterns.

x-ray astronomy

refers to the study of x-ray emission from stars. Since x-rays are absorbed by the earth's atmosphere instruments have to be mounted in space probes.

x-ray crystal spectrometer

an instrument designed to produce an x-ray spectrum and measure the wavelengths of its components by diffracting x-rays from a crystal with known lattice spacing.

x-ray crystallography

the study of crystalline substances by studying, the diffraction patterns formed by passing x-rays through a crystal.

x-ray diffraction

the scattering of x-rays by matter, especially crystals, with accompanying variation in intensity due to interference effects. Also known as x-ray micro-diffraction.

x-ray flourescence

emission by a substance of its characteristic x-ray line spectrum upon exposure to x-ray. Also known as x-ray emission.

x-ray hardness

the penetrating ability of x-rays; it is an inverse function of the wavelength.

x-ray irradiation

subjection of a material, object or patient to x-rays.

x-ray spectrograph

an x-ray spectrometer equipped with photographic or other recording apparatus; one application is flourescence analysis.

x-ray spectrometer

an instrument for producing x-ray spectrum of a material and measuring the wavelengths of the various components.

x-ray spectrometry

the measure of wavelengths of x-rays by observing their diffraction by crystals of known iattice spacing. Also known as roentgen spectrometry; x-ray spectroscopy.

x-ray spectrum

spectrum of x-rays given out by an element when bombarded by cathode rays. The frequencies of the emitted x-rays are characteristic of the atomic number of the element.

x-ray stars

stars which emit x-rays, they have been discovered by instruments carried outside the earth's atmosphere by space probes.

x-rays

streams of x-radistion.

x-unit

see. x-ray unit a small unit of length equal to 1.002 x 1 metre, previously used to describe short ultraviolet and x-ray wavelengths.

xenon

a colorless orderless monatomic element of the rare-gas group. It occurs in trace amounts in air. Xenon is used in thermionic tubes and strobe lighting.

xenon ac lamp

an arc lamp filled with xenon giving a light intensity approaching that of the carbon arc; particularly valuable in projecting motion pictures.

xenon override

the process in which the excess reactivity is provided to do away the poisoning effect of xenon build up, is called xenon override of the nuclear reactor.

zero–gravity

it refers to a the condition wherein the apparent effect of gravity becomes zero as on a body in orbit.

zero point energy

refers to the energy possessed by the atoms or molecules of a substance at 0 degree k. It cannot be explained on the basis of classical physics but can be accounted for as a quantum effect.

zero potential

the electrical potential that exists across the interface of all aolids and liquids. Also known as electro-kinetic potential.

zero-branch

a spectral band whose fortrat parabola lies between two other fortrat parabolas, with its vertex almost on the wave number axis.

zero-phase sequence relay

relay which functions in conformance with the zero phase sequence component of the current voltage or power of the circuit.

zero-point entropy

when a substance is not in thermo-dynamic equilibrium, the entropy of the substance retained by the substance at absolute zero, is called its zero-point entropy.

zeroth law of thermodynamics

if two bodies a and b are in thermal equilibrium with a third body c, then a and b are in thermal equilibrium with each other as well.

zero vector or null vector

a vector whose magnitude is zero is known as a zero vector. The direction of zero vector is not defied. It is represented by

0 e.g. $(\vec{o}) = 0$

properties of zero vector

$\vec{a} + \vec{o} = \vec{a}$

$\vec{a} - \vec{o} = \vec{a}$

$x + \vec{o} = o$

zeta

zero energy thermonuclear apparatus. A torous-shaped apparatus used for studying controlled thermonuclear reactions at harwell.

zetta

symbol: Z a prefix denoting 10^{21}. For example, 1 zettamter (Zm) = 10^{21} meter (m).

zinc

a bluish-white transition metal,

applied as a coating (galvanizing) to protect steel from corrosion.

zinc-silver chloride primary cell

a reserve primary cell that is activated by adding water; it can have a high capacity, up to 40 watt-hours, per pound and long life after activation.

zirconium

a hard lustrous silvery transition element that occurs in a gemstone, zircon ($ZrSiO_4$). It is used in some strong alloy steels.

zodiac

zone of celestial sphere containing paths of sun, moon and planets, bounded by two circles, equidistant from the ecliptic and about 18 apart; divided into 12 signs of the zodiac named after 12 constellations.

zodiacal light

a faint luminous glow in the sky that can be observed on a moonless night on the western horizon after sunset or on eastern horizon before sunrise. It is caused by the scattering of sunlight by dust particles in interplanetary space.

zoming

the displacement of various portions of the lens or surface of a microwave reflector so the resulting phase front in the near field remains unchanged. Also known as stepping.

zone refining

a technique used to reduce the level of impurities in certain metals, alloys semiconductors, and other materials. It is based on the observation that the solubility of an impurity may be different in the liquid and solid phases of a material.

zone theory of solids

a treatment of crystalline solids accounting for the electronic properties.

zoom

to change the magnification of an image while maintaining the subject in focus.

zoom lens

a cinematic or television camera lens whose focal length can be adjusted continuously to vary the magnification without loss of focus.

zwitterion (ampholyte ion)

an ion that has a positive and

negative charge on the same group of atoms. Zwitterions can be formed from compounds that contain both acid groups and basic groups in their molecules. For example, aminiethanoic acid (the amino acid glycine) has the formula $H_2N.CH_2.$ COOH. However , under neutral conditions, it exists in the different form of the Zwitterion $^{+}H_3N,CH_2.COO^{-}$.